Using & Managing uucp

Using & Managing uucp

Ed Ravin
with Tim O'Reilly, Dale Dougherty,
and Grace Todino

O'REILLY™

Bonn · Cambridge · Paris · Sebastopol · Tokyo

Using & Managing uucp

by Ed Ravin, with Tim O'Reilly, Dale Dougherty, and Grace Todino

Update Editor: Gigi Estabrook

Production Editor: John Files

Printing History:

September 1996: Second Edition.

ISBN: 1-56592-153-4

Table of Contents

Preface

What Is UUCP?

UUCP is the network primeval for UNIX systems. First designed in 1976 as part of a research project at AT&T Bell Laboratories, UUCP—which stands for Unix-to-Unix CoPy—gave UNIX systems the ability to transfer files and execute programs remotely via a telephone line or serial connection. Although 20 years have passed since the first version of UUCP appeared, it is still very much in use, doing the same basic things.

Before Internet connectivity was easily available, UUCP was the main method for relaying electronic mail from one UNIX system to another. Although UUCP by itself can only communicate with one other computer at a time, with the help of a few clever add-ons, UUCP became the basis for Usenet: a sprawling, world-wide network of computers exchanging electronic mail and news postings. Usenet traffic also found its way onto the ARPAnet, the high-speed, government-sponsored research network that evolved into today's Internet.

In spite of its age and limitations, UUCP is still widely used. It's a relatively simple and inexpensive way to get two computers talking to each other. The only special hardware it needs are a modem and a phone line. And it's not just UNIX systems in the act—DOS, Windows, Macintosh, and many other platforms have implementations of UUCP.

How UUCP Fits In (and Under)

UUCP knows how to do only two things: transfer files and execute commands. But these are the very building blocks of computer communications, and as any kindergarten child can tell you, with enough blocks (and enough floor space) there's no limit to the things you can make. In computer networking terminology, UUCP is a *transport*, a way to carry data from one place to another. Applications such as electronic mail or a Usenet news system use UUCP to bring their data from one computer to another. UUCP doesn't know whether it is transferring electronic mail, news postings, or digitized chopped liver—or whether the data is going to be transferred again after it arrives at the remote system. All of that is managed by the applications.

Why Use UUCP on the Internet?

If you have a high-speed connection to the Internet, or even a high-speed modem to a local Internet Service Provider (ISP), UUCP may at first seem antiquated or even irrelevant. Why do people with up-to-date network connectivity still use this non-interactive, limited, and old-fashioned protocol to transfer data? Surprisingly, UUCP has many uses in a modern networked environment. It can be more efficient (transfer more data in less time) than some interactive applications, especially on a network with long response times. It can also be scheduled to run within specific time slots, a feature that is good for dial-up Internet links that are on the network for only brief periods, or for a business environment that needs to restrict peak hour usage. And though UUCP isn't much good for using the World Wide Web or other highly interactive applications, it's perfect for unattended fetching of mail or for downloading large files in the middle of the night.

What's in This Book

This book explains how the individual UUCP commands work and how to use them for transferring files, executing remote programs, or sending electronic mail. It also explains how to set up, administer, and troubleshoot a UUCP connection, whether it runs on serial links, dialup modems, or a TCP/IP network. We describe both the UUCP software packages supplied with all major commercial UNIX systems and the "freeware" Taylor UUCP distributed with Linux and FreeBSD/NetBSD.

The book is divided into two main parts, using UUCP and managing UUCP, plus appendixes.

Using UUCP

The first part of the book describes the UUCP commands and how to use them for transferring files and sending mail in a UUCP-networked environment. Here's a brief explanation of what you'll find in each chapter:

Chapter 1, *Introduction to Using UUCP*, explains the basic concepts of UUCP networking and gives an overview of the user programs provided with UUCP. We also mention a few "things to watch out for," and explain the syntax for specifying remote systems and files.

Chapter 2, *File Transfer*, teaches you how to send files from one system to another using UUCP commands. We describe the *public directory* for staging UUCP file transfers and why you'll want (or not want) to use it.

Chapter 3, *Executing Remote Commands*, describes how to execute programs on another system.

Chapter 4, *Checking on UUCP Requests*, covers how to find out the status of your UUCP jobs. It explains the commands that browse the UUCP logs for you, and tells you where to find the logs yourself (if you're so inclined).

Chapter 5, *Logging In on a Remote System*, describes the **cu** and **tip** commands that let you dial out to a remote system using the modems or serial links configured for UUCP.

Chapter 6, *Using Electronic Mail*, explains the basics of electronic mail in a UUCP environment, and how to use electronic mail instead of the regular UUCP commands for file transfers.

These chapters assume that your UUCP links to other computer systems are already up and running. They also assume that you are reasonably familiar with using a UNIX system—signing on, copying files, and other basic tasks.

Managing UUCP

The second part of the book describes the nuts and bolts of UUCP for system administrators who want to install and manage a UUCP network. Here's a breakdown of what you'll find in these chapters:

Chapter 7, *Introduction to UUCP Administration*, outlines the different kinds of UUCP software on UNIX systems: the elderly and fading Version 2, the ubiquitous and solid BNU (a.k.a. HoneyDanBer), the maverick BSD/OS (UUNET) version, and the young and rambunctious Taylor UUCP.

Chapter 8, *How UUCP Works*, explains UUCP's innards by chronicling the life of a UUCP job, from a gleam in the user's eye to its transfer to the remote system.

Chapter 9, *The Physical Connection*, tells you about how RS-232 serial connections and modems work, and how they connect to UNIX systems.

Chapter 10, *Setting Up a UUCP Link*, details how to use UUCP to get your system talking to another system.

Chapter 11, *Making Sure the Link Works*, explains how to test and verify that your UUCP link is set up properly.

Chapter 12, *Access and Security Considerations*, explains the security exposures for a system that provides UUCP services and the features in UUCP that let you control how it is used.

Chapter 13, *UUCP Administration*, shows you how to keep your UUCP system working properly, and the various (mostly automated) tasks that make this possible.

Chapter 14, *Troubleshooting UUCP*, presents a one-stop reference guide for diagnosing and fixing whatever's wrong with a UUCP link.

Appendixes

The appendixes cover ancillary topics such as setting up a modem for UUCP or configuring mail and news applications to work with UUCP. Here's what you'll find in the appendixes:

Appendix A, *Useful Shell Scripts and Programs*, lists a few scripts and programs that heavy users of the UUCP commands might find of interest.

Appendix B, *The Spool Directory/Working Files*, explains the innards of the UUCP spool directory and how UUCP stores its pending jobs.

Appendix C, *Status and Error Messages*, lists the numerous UUCP messages you might encounter and explains what problems might be causing them.

Appendix D, *UUCP for non-UNIX platforms*, provides pointers to UUCP software that runs on Mac, PC, Amiga, and other non-UNIX platforms.

Appendix E, *Sendmail and UUCP*, gives a brief overview of how to configure the **sendmail** mail system to work with UUCP.

Appendix F, *News and UUCP*, explains how Usenet News software such as C/News and **inn** work with UUCP.

Appendix G, *The UUCP Mapping Project*, describes the world-wide UUCP nodename registry and how it is used for mail routing.

Appendix H, *UUCP Management Tools*, lists scripts and programs that you may find useful to help manage your UUCP site.

Appendix I, *Setting Up a Modem*, explains how to set up a typical Hayes-compatible modem for use with UUCP, including bidirectional configuration.

Appendix J, *UUCP Protocol Internals*, goes into more detail about the different UUCP protocols that are available, and how to choose between them.

Appendix K, *The UUCP g Protocol*, gives a complete description of the standard **g** protocol used over telephone and serial lines. This will help you to understand better how UUCP works, and why it sometimes doesn't.

Appendix L, *Other Resources*, lists other sources of information regarding UUCP, including related books, Web sites, and a few handy software packages.

Obtaining the Example Programs

The example programs in this book are available electronically in a number of ways: by *ftp*, *ftpmail*, and *bitftp*. The cheapest, fastest, and easiest ways are listed first. If you read from the top down, the first one that works for you is probably the best. Use *ftp* if you are directly on the Internet. Use *ftpmail* if you are not on the Internet but can send and receive electronic mail to Internet sites (this includes CompuServe users). Use BITFTP if you send electronic mail via BITNET.

FTP

To use FTP, you need a machine with direct access to the Internet. A sample session is shown, with what you should type in boldface.

```
% ftp ftp.uu.net.
Connected to ftp.uu.net.
220 FTP server (Version 6.21 Tue Mar 10 22:09:55 EST 1992) ready.
Name (ftp.uu.net:yourname): anonymous
331 Guest login ok, send domain style e-mail address as password.
Password: yourname@domain.name (use your user name and host here)
230 Guest login ok, access restrictions apply.
ftp> cd /publised/oreilly/nutshell/uucp
250 CWD command successful.
ftp> binary (Very important! You must specify binary
             transfer for compressed files.)
200 Type set to I.
```

```
ftp> get uucp.tar.gz
200 PORT command successful.
150 Opening BINARY mode data connection for uucp.tar.gz.
226 Transfer complete.
ftp> quit
221 Goodbye.
%
```

The file is a compressed *tar* archive; extract the files from the archive by typing:

```
% gzcat uucp.tar.gz | tar xvf -
```

System V systems require the following *tar* command instead:

```
% gzcat uucp.tar.gz | tar xof -
```

If *gzcat* is not available on your system, you can use the separate *gunzip* and *tar* commands:

```
% gunzip uucp.tar.gz
% tar xvf uucp.tar
```

FTPMAIL

FTPMAIL is a mail server available to anyone who can send electronic mail to and receive it from Internet sites. This includes any company or service provider that allows email connections to the Internet. Here's how you do it.

You send mail to *ftpmail@online.ora.com*. In the message body, give the FTP commands you want to run. The server will run anonymous FTP for you and mail the files back to you. To get a complete help file, send a message with no subject and the single word "help" in the body. The following is an example mail session that should get you the examples. This command sends you a listing of the files in the selected directory, and the requested example files. The listing is useful if there's a later version of the examples you're interested in.

```
% mail ftpmail@online.ora.com
Subject:
reply-to yourname@domain.name        (where you want files mailed)
open
cd /published/oreilly/nutshell/uucp
dir
mode binary
uuencode
get uucp.tar.gz
quit
.
```

A signature at the end of the message is acceptable as long as it appears after "quit."

All retrieved files will be split into 60KB chunks and mailed to you. You then remove the mail headers and concatenate them into one file, and then *uudecode* or *atob* it. Once you've got the desired file, follow the directions under FTP to extract the files from the archive.

BITFTP

BITFTP is a mail server for BITNET users. You send it electronic mail messages requesting files, and it sends you back the files by electronic mail. BITFTP currently serves only users who send it mail from nodes that are directly on BITNET, EARN, or NetNorth. BITFTP is a public service of Princeton University. Here's how it works.

To use BITFTP, send mail containing your *ftp* commands to **BITFTP@PUCC**. For a complete help file, send HELP as the message body.

The following is the message body you should send to BITFTP:

```
FTP  ftp.uu.net  NETDATA
USER  anonymous
PASS your Internet email address (not your bitnet address)
CD  /published/oreilly/nutshell/uucp
DIR
BINARY
GET  uucp.tar.gz
QUIT
```

Once you've got the desired file, follow the directions under FTP to extract the files from the archive.

Questions about BITFTP can be directed to Melinda Varian, **MAINT@PUCC** on BITNET.

The Nutshell Format

Commands

The commands are described according to the tasks they perform. When the syntax of a command is given, as in the following example:

> **uucp** [*option*] *source dest*

the items that you, the user, would type in as shown are printed in **boldface**. Those items that you supply are shown in *italics*, and those that are in brackets [] are optional. For example, the proper way to use the **uucp** command is to enter the word "uucp" followed by an option (if desired), the name of the *source* file and the *dest*ination file.

Examples

We have included several examples to show the results that you can expect when you type in a command. Of course, when you run these commands, things will look a little bit different on your computer.

Examples are set off from the main text in smaller type. Items that a user following the example would enter are shown in **boldface**. System messages and responses are shown in normal type.

An example would appear as follows:

```
$ uuname
fatcat
slowboat
$
```

The local system prompt is "$". The user would enter "uuname" and then press the RETURN key. The system responds by printing "fatcat" and "slowboat," and then giving another prompt.

Note to Our Readers

We see each Nutshell Handbook as reflecting the experience of a group of users. They're not written by "experts," but by people who have gone through a similar learning process as you. Our goal is to share what we know from experience so that you can become more productive in less time.

As publishers, this goal is reflected in the way we maintain the series by updating each title periodically. This allows us to incorporate changes suggested to us by our readers. We'd like new users to benefit from *your* experience as well as ours.

If you have a suggestion or solve a significant problem that our handbook does not cover, please write to us and let us know about it. Include information about the UNIX environment in which you work and the particular machine you use. Please also let us know about any errors you find, as well as your suggestions for future editions, by writing to:

O'Reilly & Associates, Inc.
101 Morris Street
Sebastopol, CA 95472
1-800-998-9938 (in the US or Canada)
1-707-829-0515 (international/local)
1-707-829-0104 (FAX)

info@ora.com (to get on our mailing list or request a catalog)
bookquestions@ora.com (to ask technical questions or to send comments)

If we are able to use your suggestion in the next edition of the book, we will send you a copy of the new edition. You'll have our thanks, along with the thanks of future readers of this handbook.

Acknowledgments

This book is based on two previous O'Reilly & Associates books: *Managing UUCP and Usenet*, by Tim O'Reilly and Grace Todino, and *Using UUCP and Usenet*, by Grace Todino and Dale Dougherty. The UUCP portions of both books have been extracted, combined, updated, and expanded to produce the edition before you.

Acknowledgments from Previous Editions

Many small corrections were submitted by Akio Kido and by Jeremy Epstein, and their suggestions triggered a thorough review of other out-of-date aspects of the book. Other improvements were suggested by Vern Hoxie, Philip Meese, Thad Floryan, and Greg Woods. In addition, Mark Taub provided a copy of the latest SCO UNIX documentation for our reference. Everyone's help in keeping this book up to date is gratefully acknowledged. Jerry Peek and Mike Loukides also made useful suggestions. Thanks also to Rosanne Wagger and Ellie Cutler who produced the tenth edition.

The eighth edition was prepared by Jean Marie Diaz. She also made minor corrections for the ninth edition.

Guy Harris of Auspex suggested the corrections and additions made in the seventh edition. For the sixth edition, Rick Adams (then at the Center for Seismic Studies) and Carl S. Gutekunst of Pyramid Technology Corporation provided a large number of minor corrections. Carl also provided additional details on UUCP history, and largely rewrote the section on the *USERFILE*.

Clem Cole (then at Stellar Computer), Andy Tannenbaum of Interactive System Corp., Lyndon Nerenberg of Nexus Computing Corporation, and John Gilmore of Nebula Consultants reviewed drafts of the fourth edition.

Not to be forgotten is Mark Horton, who reviewed the original edition, which provided the base for the current work. In addition, at the time the original edition was being prepared, Masscomp kindly provided us with copies of the UUCP manual that they were developing and again provided us with review copies of their manual as it was being revised for BNU by Steve Talbott. Their help and support was greatly appreciated.

Thanks for help with the first edition are also due to Greg Chesson of Silicon Graphics, Steve Howard of the College of Business Administration at the University of Cincinnati, Barry Shein of Boston University, and Ross Alexander of Athabasca University, each of whom answered questions or provided missing information.

Of course, the standard disclaimer applies: errors that remain are our own.

Acknowledgments, Using and Managing UUCP

Many, many thanks to our technical reviewers: Stan Olan Barber, Don Desrosiers, Steven Dick, Kyle Jones, Giles Lean, Rick Morrow, Lyndon Nerenberg, John Pezzano, Ian Lance Taylor, Tom Watson, and Mitch Wright. Any errors that remain are our fault, not theirs.

Additional thanks to Simson Garfinkel, for reviewing the chapter on UUCP security, Brad Schoening, who reviewed the "Using UUCP" section, Jamie Hanrahan of Kernel Mode Consulting, whose paper on the UUCP *g* protocol was adapted for Appendix K, and Stan Olan Barber, who contributed Appendix G on the UUCP Mapping Project.

Although they didn't know it at the time, we were assisted by IBM's AIX Customer Support team in Austin, Texas, who supplied us with a few enlightening tidbits about the internals of BNU UUCP, and the "frequent posters" on the Taylor UUCP mailing list and the comp.mail.uucp newsgroup, whose sage advice on solving UUCP problems and explaining UUCP internals was a welcome source of inspiration. Also, Peter Honeyman was kind enough to supply a few obscure historical details about BNU UUCP.

Ed Ravin adds:

I am obliged to thank Ian Lance Taylor, a second time, for his authorship of Taylor UUCP: a free software package of sterling quality, with excellent documentation. The existence of Taylor UUCP, along with so many other high-quality free software packages, has helped energize the new wave of "free UNIX" systems such as Linux; it has also rejuvenated the aging UUCP functions for modern times and modern computers. I'm especially impressed with the technical innovations in Taylor UUCP, in which nearly all the remaining problems with traditional versions of UUCP were quietly and effectively fixed.

And last, my thanks to the O'Reilly staff: Gigi Estabrook, Update Editor for this new edition; John Files, Production Editor; Kismet McDonough-Chan, quality checks; Seth Maislin, index; Lenny Muellner, tools; Chris Reilley, graphics; and Eden Reiner and Mary Jane Walsh, interior design. I am also grateful to Tim O'Reilly and Frank Willison of O'Reilly & Associates, who blithely ignored my misgivings about whether someone who was more of a programmer than an author would be right for this project. They obviously knew what they were doing, although I had my doubts at first.

For Deborah, who had no doubts at all.

New York, NY
Summer, 1996

1

Introduction to
Using UUCP

Basic Networking

Networking consists of computers talking to each other. The things that we humans find useful on a computer network, such as the ability to share files with another computer, to exchange electronic mail or news postings, or to remotely log in and use the other computer's resources, are all done via *network applications.*

UUCP is a method of networking that lets one computer transfer files to and execute programs on another computer. Upon this simple framework, network applications like electronic mail or Usenet news weave their tapestries of application functionality.

Most users never use UUCP directly—on a properly administered system, mail and news will circulate back and forth without any hint as to the underlying network transport. For example, when using UUCP to connect to an Internet Service Provider (ISP), users on the UUCP-connected system can use electronic mail as if their system was directly on the Internet.

Batch Processing

UUCP is a *batch processing* system—all requests are stored until UUCP is ready to handle them. UUCP calls these requests *jobs.*

Before a user's job can be executed, UUCP must first make a connection to the remote system—usually by making a phone call. Even when UUCP connects to the other system, it may not process your job right away—other requests might be ahead of yours in the queue. UUCP can send only one file at a time to another remote system, causing all other jobs destined for that system to wait in line behind it.

Although patience is always a virtue when dealing with computers, it's a necessity with UUCP—it's not unusual for a job to take several hours to complete, especially if there is trouble reaching the remote system. If you're anxious about your UUCP requests, be sure to use the command-line option that requests notification via electronic mail when your job completes. Even if you don't use that option, UUCP will still notify you if the job fails or gets excessively delayed.

Limitations of UUCP

Although this book describes what UUCP can be told to do, on most systems UUCP will be set up to do as little as possible. Access to remote files and commands is almost always heavily restricted, to keep malicious or inquisitive users from damaging files. If you are trying to transfer files or execute remote commands, you will usually find that only one or two directories or commands are permitted.[*] If you want to retrieve files from another system, a user on that system may have to assist you by placing the files in a public directory that can be reached via UUCP. Except for large binaries, it's often simpler to use electronic mail to send your files (see Chapter 6, *Using Electronic Mail*).

Even a working UUCP network has its outages—telephone lines are busy, modems break down, someone accidentally unplugs a serial cable. When you are stuck in traffic in a growing backlog of UUCP requests, you may not always be able to resolve the problem yourself. If you're not the administrator of your machine, sometimes you'll need to ask the system administrator (or the administrator on the remote system or service provider) to fix things for you. Chapter 4, *Checking on UUCP Requests*, explains how you can distinguish a temporary problem from a serious network blockade, and what the system administrator might have to do to fix it.

---

[*] Of course, it doesn't have to be this way—you can use UUCP as a transport for your own applications, as long as you are able to control the UUCP permissions on all the machines with which you'll be talking.

Overview of UUCP User Programs

Once UUCP communications are in place on a system, there are several programs you can use to make UUCP requests or to check system status:

- The **uucp** command is used to request a file transfer to or from a remote machine. It is similiar to the **cp** command for copying files, with added syntax to specify which system the file resides on.

- The **uux** command requests execution of a command on a remote machine. The commands that can be executed are usually limited to prevent unauthorized use of the remote computer. Most sites use **uux** only for transferring mail and news. But among cooperating systems, such as those owned by the same organization, **uux** can be used for anything—like remote printing or software distribution.

- The **uulog** and **uustat** commands show information on the status of **uucp** or **uux** requests.

- The **uuname** command lists the names of computers that your system can connect to via UUCP, or optionally lists the UUCP name of your local system.

- The **cu** command is part of the UUCP installation, but it has little to do with UUCP. Its job is to let a user make a connection to a remote system using the modems or serial links that are otherwise used for UUCP exchanges. BSD and BSD-derived systems come with a command called **tip**, which also provides dialout functions.[*]

- The **ct** command (on some System V machines) uses the above-mentioned modems to call up a user and present a login prompt on his or her terminal, effectively "reversing the charges" for a toll call.

Every System Has a Name

Every computer on any network must have a name that distinguishes it from other computers on the same network; a UUCP network is no exception.

---

[*] If any of the numerous full featured, user-friendly telecommunications programs such as Kermit, Seyon, or Minicom are installed on your system, you will find these programs much easier (and more functional) than **cu** or **tip**.

The **uuname** command lists out the names of other systems that your computer is linked to via UUCP. For example:

```
$ uuname
topcat
skimbles
koshka
```

This example shows that there are three systems known to this computer: *topcat*, *skimbles*, and *koshka*. These systems, who are all "one hop" away from the local system, are known in UUCP parlance as neighbors.

The local system has a name too—to see it, use **uuname** with the –l option:

```
$ uuname -l  # that's lower case "ell", as in "local"
tabby
```

When using UUCP commands, you rarely need to specify the name of your local system, but others will need it if they are using UUCP to send files to your system.

UUCP Names Versus Internet Hostnames

Systems that are connected to the Internet also use names to tell each other apart. Alas, a system's Internet hostname is rarely the same as its UUCP name. UUCP names are usually limited to 14 characters,[*] while Internet hostnames can be as long as 256 characters. Internet hostnames also include a domain name, which is a name associated with the company or institution that owns the computer. For example, if the systems mentioned above (*topcat*, *skimbles*, *koshka*, and *tabby*) were all located at the offices of Fee Lines, Inc. (a shipping company) whose domain name is `feelines.com`, their Internet hostnames might look like the following:

```
topcat.feelines.com
skimbleshanks.feelines.com
koshka.feelines.com
tabby.feelines.com
```

In some environments, you will use one system name for UUCP requests, and another (though usually similiar) system name for electronic mail addressing. This will be covered in more detail in Chapter 6, *Using Electronic Mail*.

---

[*] Older UUCP versions limited names to six or seven characters. Taylor UUCP allows names of any length.

UUCP Syntax

When you need to specify a file or user on a remote system, UUCP commands use arguments like this:

system!resource

system is the UUCP name of the remote system, ! is the exclamation point (SHIFT 1 on most keyboards), and *resource* is the file, command, or user you are interested in on the remote system. For example:

```
uucp koshka!/this/file topcat!/that/file
```

references the file */this/file* on the system *koshka*, and the file */that/file* on the system *topcat*. Anything following the exclamation point (the ! character)[*] is interpreted by the remote system named to the left of the exclamation point. If you don't specify a system to the left of the exclamation point, UUCP assumes you mean the local system. Sometimes, as with a local filename, you can just specify the filename and leave off the ! entirely.

To ! or \! ?

Some of the command interpreters found in the UNIX world, notably the C-shell (**csh** or **tcsh**) and the GNU Bourne-Again Shell (**bash**), treat the exclamation point in a special way—they use it for re-executing previously typed commands. Anyone trying to use UUCP commands can easily run into problems with this feature:

```
% uucp thisfile koshka!/usr/spool/uucpppublic
csh: /usr/spool/uucppublic: event not found
```

In order to prevent these shells from misinterpreting the exclamation points in your UUCP commands, you need to prefix the exclamation point character with the backslash character \. This tells the shell to "quote" the exclamation point; that is, use it literally instead of as an expansion command. For example:

```
% uucp thisfile koshka\!/usr/spool/uucppublic
%
```

Fortunately, these shells let you turn exclamation point substitution off (and on again) via user commands. Table 1-1 shows the commands needed.

---

[*] Many UNIX users pronounce the ! character as "bang," which simplifies verbal descriptions of UUCP commands.

Most of the shells have other ways of repeating commands: all but **csh** support the arrow keys or other control characters for command line recall and editing, and **bash** also supports the powerful **fc** built-in command for flexible editing and repeating of commands.

Table 1–1: Disabling and Enabling ! Expansion in UNIX Shells

Shell	Disable ! Expansion	Enable ! Expansion
bash	`set +o histexpand`	`set -o histexpand`
csh	`set histchars`	`unset histchars`
tcsh	`set histchars`	`unset histchars`
zsh	`set -K`	`set +K`

Another option is to switch to a shell that does not intercept exclamation points. The Korn shell (**ksh**) and Bourne shell (**sh**) come to mind. However, on a Linux system, **sh** is usually a link to **bash.**[*]

If you you decide to keep ! expansion in your shell, you will have to use the \ character repeatedly when typing UUCP commands.

---

[*] Also, on Linux **csh** is usually a link to **tcsh**.

2

File Transfer

Getting files to and from a remote system is the first thing the average person wants to do on a computer network. The commands for transferring files in a UUCP network are easy to learn, but UUCP's draconian limitations on file access and somewhat perverse interpretations of filenames often send back error messages instead of successful transfers. This chapter is your guide to getting your files from here to there (and from there to here) with minimum hassle.

NOTE   You can also use electronic mail to transfer files. See Chapter 6, *Using Electronic Mail.*

Copying Files

When you want to copy a file on a UNIX system you usually use the **cp** command. For example:

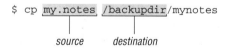

```
$ cp my.notes /backupdir/mynotes
       |           |
     source     destination
```

cp, in this example, copies the file *my.notes* to the directory */backupdir*, with the same name.

The **uucp** command for copying files from one system to another has a similar syntax, except that instead of specifying file names as in the **cp** command, you specify system names and file names, joined by the exclamation point:

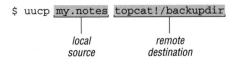

$ uucp my.notes topcat!/backupdir

      local   *remote*
     source   *destination*

This requests the UUCP system to copy the file *my.notes* in the current directory to the system *topcat*, directory */backupdir*. If *topcat*'s UUCP system is willing to let the originating system write files in *topcat*'s */backupdir*, the transfer will succeed.

As with the **cp** command, you can specify a directory as your destination, and **uucp** will copy the source file into that directory with the same filename. You can also specify more than one source file to be copied:

```
$ uucp file1 file2 file3 file4 robocat!/backupdir
```

This copies the four files *file1*, *file2*, etc. to the remote host *robocat*, into the directory */backupdir*.

Using the Public Directory

One directory on each UNIX system is designated the "public directory," where any local or remote user can read or write files. It is usually called */var/spool/uucppublic*, a bit of a mouthful (or fingerful) for the average typist. (On some systems, it will be */usr/spool/uucppublic*, and on others, either name will work.) For the rest of this section, we'll refer to the UUCP public directory as PUBDIR.

CAUTION   The public directory is called "public" for a reason—any user on that system can read or write to it. This means that files sent via the public directory can never be confidential—and worse yet, could be altered or deleted by another user. This may not matter on a small system with only a few (presumably friendly) users, but it is clearly a cause for concern if you are sending files through an ISP or a public UNIX system. Unless you trust *all* of the users on both your local system and the remote system, use electronic mail instead of the public directory.

A PUBDIR by Any Other Name

uucp tries to save you the trouble of typing the name of the public directory by letting you use the ~ (tilde) character by itself as a shorthand equivalent for the name of the public directory on the remote system:

```
$ uucp some.stuff copycat!~
```

Anything to the right of the exclamation point is always interpreted by the system named to the left of the exclamation point. This means you can use the ~ character by itself as shorthand for the *local* system's public directory. For example:

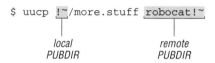

```
$ uucp !~/more.stuff robocat!~
```
          | |
        local   remote
        PUBDIR   PUBDIR

By using the ~ character to specify PUBDIR on the remote system, not only do you no longer need to type out the long name of the public directory, but you don't even need to know what it is.

The ~ character is also interpreted by many shells (including **ksh**, **bash**, and **csh**) as a shorthand character for user home directories on the local system. However, the command shells only expand the ~ character if it appears at the *beginning* of a word, while proper usage of ~ in a **uucp** command will always be in the *middle* or at the *end* of a word. It's generally not a problem, unless you make a typing mistake and put a space in front of the ~.

UUCP will also interpret "*~user*" the same way the shells do—*koshka!~user* will be expanded into the home directory of the named user on the system *koshka*. This feature dates back to the days when it wasn't considered a security problem to allow UUCP access to users' home directories. Nowadays, most sites prevent UUCP from accessing any files outside the public directory.

Retrieving Files From a Remote System

The **uucp** command can also be used to fetch a file from another system. For example, if you know that the file *hotstuff* is cooling its heels over in the public directory on system *fatcat*, you can retrieve that file with this command:

```
$ uucp fatcat!~/hotstuff !~
```

Note that when you don't specify a system name before the exclamation point, **uucp** assumes you're talking about the local system. If the local system was named *tabby*, this would be the same as specifying:

```
$ uucp fatcat!~/hotstuff tabby!~
```

Although it would be more convenient to retrieve a file into your home directory, you generally can't. UUCP is almost always configured to keep out of users' home directories.

NOTE   Be sure to retrieve your files from the public directory within a
          reasonable amount of time; many systems automatically delete
          files in the public directory tree after several days.

Notifying Users When a Job Finishes

As we said before, UUCP jobs take time to complete. The **uucp** command doesn't actually perform any file transfers—it only submits a request to do a file transfer to the UUCP daemons, which perform the operation in the background. You can ask UUCP to send email when the transfer has completed, either to you, to a user on the remote system, or to both:

```
$ uucp -m -nboris contraband topcat!~/boris/contraband
```

The **−m** option asks UUCP to send email to you when the job has completed, and **−nboris** asks UUCP to send email to the remote user *boris*.

Spool Now, Transfer Later

One of the quirks of file transfer using UUCP is that due to spooling (UUCP storing the information about your request for later execution), the reading or writing of files on your local system may not take place until hours after you make your request. When reading or writing does occur, it will be done by the UUCP pseudo-user, not by you.

As the name implies, a pseudo-user is not a real person, but rather a user-ID on a UNIX system usually named *uucp* that owns the directories where spooled jobs are kept. For all practical purposes, you can consider the UUCP pseudo-user another user on your local system, with the same

problems that you ordinarily have when trying to read or write files belong-
ing to a different user. For example, if you are transferring a file out of your
home directory that is ordinarily only readable by you, the job will fail
because the UUCP pseudo-user, like all other users on your system, is
unable to copy the file out of your directory.

One way to avoid this problem is to tell UUCP to make a copy of the file
when you submit your job. The −C option to **uucp** causes UUCP to copy the
source file for the transfer into a temporary directory owned by UUCP (usually */var/spool/uucp*).* Taylor UUCP assumes the −C option unless you turn
off file copying with the −c or −**nocopy** option.†

You may also want to doublecheck your file and directory permissions to
make sure UUCP can read the files that you want to send. Remember, if you
choose this method, not only the UUCP pseudo-user can see your files, but
every other user on the local system can also.

Using uuto and uupick

Since it's fairly common to send a file to a user on another system, UUCP
provides a command to simplify this type of file transfer. The **uuto** command is like the **uucp** command, except that the destination is "system!user"
instead of "system!filename." The **uuto** command sends the file into a special
subdirectory of the remote system's public directory; the directory is *PUB-
DIR/receive/username/source_system*, when *username* is the user the file is
destined for, and *source_system* is the system that is sending the file.

uupick is for the receiving user to run. It lists any files that have arrived in
the *PUBDIR/receive* subdirectory for the user, and provides a simple menu
for moving files into the user's home directory.

uuto and **uupick** should be supplied with most modern UNIX systems, but if
they're not on your system, they're simple enough that they can be implemented in shell scripts. Appendix A, *Useful Shell Scripts and Programs*,

---

* In BNU UUCP, even the −C option will not work if you want to transfer a file out of a directory that does not permit outsiders to list its contents.

† Using the −C option also prevents mishaps if you delete a file that is part of a pending UUCP
request—without −C, the job fails because UUCP will be unable to find the file after it contacts
the remote system.

includes a script similar in functionality to **uupick**. Here's a sample use of
uuto and **uupick**:

```
tabby$ uuto thisfile thatfile copycat!furryguy
```

This use of **uuto** causes the two files *thisfile* and *thatfile* to be spooled for
delivery to a subdirectory of the public directory on *copycat*, with email to
be sent to user *furryguy* on copycat if the transfer succeeds. If these files
were sent from the system *tabby*, they will be placed in the directory *PUB-
DIR/receive/furryguy/tabby* on copycat. (UUCP is allowed to create subdirectories upon request in PUBDIR, which is about as laissez-faire as UUCP ever
gets.)

User *furryguy* on the remote system *copycat* can retrieve this file (and any
other files sent to him via **uuto**) with the **uupick** command:

```
copycat$ uupick
from tabby: file thisfile ?
m
copycat$
```

Here, the user used the **m** subcommand to **uupick** to move the received file
into his local directory. **uupick** will give you a complete list of its subcommands if you type a **?** (question mark).

NOTE   Since **uuto** and **uupick** use the public directory to transfer files,
              the cautions stated previously about the lack of privacy and
              security apply here as well.

Finding Out the Status of a Job

The UUCP system lets you use the **uustat** command to check up on the status of your jobs.[*] Without any arguments, the **uustat** command shows you
any jobs queued by your userid:

```
$ uustat
koshkaN5aa1   10/08-23:23  R  koshka  boris   ~/hotstuff
copycatN7f8e  10/08-23:25  S  copycat S  copycat  boris   ????
```

The exact output of the **uustat** command varies from system to system, so
your system may look a little different. But all versions of **uustat** list the job

---

[*] Older BSD versions of UNIX only have the **uulog** command. See Chapter 4, *Checking on
UUCP Requests*, for more information on uulog. BSD/OS supplies the **uusnap** command, which
provides a "snapshot" of current UUCP status.

ID, the remote system name, the user who submitted the request, and a (usually cryptic) summary of the request. If **uustat** with no arguments does not print anything, it means you do not have any jobs waiting in the queue. You can also try running **uustat −a**, which shows you all pending UUCP jobs, regardless of which user submitted them.

Job IDs

The first column in **uustat**'s output above is the *job ID* of the UUCP request. UUCP assigns a unique identifier to each request, usually composed of the name of the remote system with a few numbers and/or letters appended to it[*]. You can use the job ID of your request to track its progress through the UUCP system, or to tell UUCP to cancel it if you change your mind.

Most UUCP commands can be given the **−j** option, which tells them to print the job ID onto standard output:

```
$ uucp -j munitions.txt fatcat!~
fatcatN0034
```

Using the **−j** option, you can find out the job ID of your request immediately, instead of subsequently issuing a **uustat** query.

Killing a Pending Request

The **uustat** command can also be used to kill a job that is still in the queue.

```
$ uustat -k fatcatN0034
```

The **−k** option to **uustat** is used to specify the job number that you want to kill. Unless you are the root user, **uustat** lets you kill a job only if you were the one who requested it in the first place.

For more information on using **uustat** and other commands to see the status of a UUCP job, see Chapter 4, *Checking on UUCP Requests*.

---

[*] Older versions of UUCP ("Version 2") used numeric-only job IDs.

Automatic Error Notification

UUCP always sends you email if it encounters a problem trying to fulfill your requests. For example, let's suppose that user *mary* on the system *tabby* issued the command:

```
$ uucp !~/thing copycat!/staging/data
```

If this command fails, *mary* might receive this error message in email from the Taylor version of UUCP:

```
From uucp@tabby.feelines.com Thu Oct  5 04:13:43 1995
Return-Path: uucp
Received: (from uucp@localhost) by tabby.feelines.com (8.6.12/8.6.9)
          id EAA01826; Thu, 5 Oct 1995 04:13:41 -0400
Date: Thu, 5 Oct 1995 04:13:41 -0400
From: uucp <uucp@tabby.feelines.com>
Message-Id: <199510050813.EAA01826@tabby.feelines.com>
To: mary@tabby.feelines.com
Subject: UUCP failed

Message from UUCP on tabby Thu Oct  5 04:13:41 1995

The file
        /var/spool/uucppublic/thing
could not be transferred to
        copycat!/staging/data
as requested by
        tabby!mary
for the following reason:
        permission denied by remote
```

The UUCP daemon is usually a bit circumspect about the exact reason your request failed. For example, "permission denied by remote" could mean that the permissions for the directory */staging/data* on *copycat* do not permit UUCP to write files into that directory. It could also mean that UUCP on *copycat* has been configured to prohibit writing files anywhere outside PUB-DIR, no matter what the directory permissions on */staging/data* are.

Here's a sample error from the BNU version of UUCP:

```
From uucp Tue Oct 10 01:08:25 1995
Date: Tue, 10 Oct 1995 01:08:24 -0400
From: uucp
Message-Id: <9510100508.AA22867@robocat.feelines.com>
To: boris@robocat.feelines.com

REQUEST: robocat!/home/boris/somedata.txt --> tabby!~/storage/ (boris)
(SYSTEM: tabby)  remote access to path/file denied
```

This error message is essentially the same as the previous example, but expressed in a more cryptic fashion. Again, see Chapter 4 for more information on diagnosing UUCP problems.

Public Exposure

A drawback of using the **uucp** command to transfer files is that once the files arrive on a system, they are placed in publicly accessible directories with access permissions that allow any user to read, write, or delete them.

This is an obvious liability on a large system with many users—inquisitive folks on the local system (or any of its UUCP neighbors) can browse the public directory on your system and read any file within it. Users who are more than curious can change or delete files before you have a chance to retrieve them.

Even in environments where users sharing a group of computers can trust each other, there's still the potential for accidents: UUCP will happily overwrite existing files when doing a file transfer. If two users both try to copy a file with the same name to the public directory on the same system, UUCP will copy over the first user's file, and replace it with the second user's file—all without any error messages. The same thing can happen when using the **uuto** command to send files: if two users on system A both send a file with the same name to the same user on system B, one file will overwrite the other.

In spite of these problems, you can still safely transfer files via UUCP—as described in the next chapter, the **uux** command for running programs on a remote system keeps all files that it transfers protected from other users. Since this route is taken when electronic mail is sent between systems, email is reasonably secure from the problems described here.

Command Summary

To close this chapter, here's a summary of the usage and most frequently used options of the UUCP file transfer commands. See your system documentation for the complete description of what options are supported by your version of UUCP.

The uucp Command

The **uucp** command copies files from one system to another:

> **uucp** [options] *source-file destination-file*

or

> **uucp** [options] *source-file* [...] *destination-directory*

source-file and *destination* are filenames or directory names, either a normal pathname for files on the local system, or:

> system!pathname

for files on a remote system. If the destination ends in /, it is assumed to be a directory, and UUCP will attempt to create that directory if it does not already exist. If the pathname begins with ~/, then it is expanded to the name of the UUCP public directory on the appropriate system.

Options

−C	Copy the local source file(s) to the spool directory before attempting the transfer. This is the default in Taylor UUCP.
−c	Do not copy the local source file(s), they must be readable by the UUCP user in order to be successfully transferred. This is the default in BNU UUCP.
−f	Do not make new parent directories in order to copy a file. The default is to attempt to create parent directories where required.
−j	Display the UUCP job ID after accepting the request.
−m	Notify the sender by email when the job is finished.
−n *user*	Send email to *user* on the remote system when the file arrives.

The uuto Command

The **uuto** command copies files from the local system to a remote system, and deposits the file in a subdirectory of the public directory under the name of the remote *user*. It also sends email to the remote *user* announcing the arrival of the file.

> **uuto** [options] source-file ... *system!user*

Options

−m   Notify the sender by email when the job is finished.

−p   Copy file(s) to spool directory before attempting the transfer.

The uupick Command

The **uupick** command displays an interactive menu listing files that have been sent to the user from a remote system via UUCP. **uupick** looks for files in the public UUCP directory, in the subdirectories *PUB-DIR/receive/user/system/* for the *user* invoking the command. The user will be prompted with each file, one by one, and offered the choice of moving, deleting, or ignoring the incoming files.

```
uupick [-s system]
```

Options

−s *system*   Process only files that have arrived from the specified remote *system*.

3

Executing Remote Commands

With the **uux** command, the UUCP networking facility can be used to execute commands on a remote system. **uux** can use local files as input to the remote command, write the output of the command to a file (either local or remote), and even pipe the output into another remote command. However, there are broad restrictions on the commands that can be executed remotely. (The administrator on the remote system must give specific permission for remote users to access each command.) These restrictions prevent **uux** from being very useful for the average user.[*] If you need access to commands on a remote system, you should obtain an account on that system and use a communications program such as **cu** or **tip** to call into the remote system and execute commands (see Chapter 5, *Logging In on a Remote System*).

The **uux** command is most often used to transfer mail and Usenet news articles. Electronic mail processed by a UUCP-connected system will usually use **uux** to invoke the **rmail** command on the neighboring system. Likewise, a system sending Usenet news to a UUCP-connected system calls **uux** to invoke the **rnews** command, which forwards Usenet news articles.

For the purposes of this chapter, we assume that the system administrator has set up **uux** to allow access to a printer on a neighboring system.[†] This

---

[*] Remote execution was more widely used back in the days when UUCP was often the only local area networking method within a company. It has fallen into disfavor now that UUCP is almost exclusively a wide-area networking technology.

[†] Actually, a smart system administrator sets up a system's print queues so they invoke **uux** automatically without user intervention, the same way electronic mail works on most UUCP-connected systems. But then we'd have nothing with which to demonstrate **uux** commands.

means that the system with the printer (let's call it *princecat*) must allow your local system to execute commands that send files to the desired printer.* The system administrator on *princecat* might write a script that would let your system access only a specific printer, or he might be a more trusting soul and allow your system to execute any of the standard printer commands. To keep the examples in this chapter interesting, we will assume the latter.

The uux Command

When you invoke **uux** on the local system, you supply the name of the remote system and the command that you to want to execute there. It causes a UUCP request to be queued up for the remote system. As with all **uucp** requests, if something goes wrong, the UUCP system will send you email with the error. Some versions of UUCP software on the remote system will also send you mail announcing the completion of your request even if nothing goes wrong.

For security reasons, **uux** is restricted to executing the commands that the remote system administrator has determined are safe for execution on that system. A typical installation might allow only the **rmail** and **rnews** commands for sending mail and news. You'll need to ask your system administrator what commands can be executed in your environment.

For our atypical system in this chapter, the administrator of *princecat* has kindly allowed users on our local system to run the commands **enable** (to make sure a printer is online), **lpr** (to send files to the printer), and **lpstat** (to list out the status of print jobs). Here's how a user on the local system would run **enable** via **uux**:

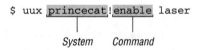

```
$ uux princecat!enable laser
```
        System   Command

As with UUCP file transfer requests, **uux** only queues commands for later execution. The actual execution of the command does not take place until the remote system is contacted, the request is transferred, and the remote system gets around to executing the job.

---

* We describe how to do this in Chapter 12, *Access and Security Considerations*.

> ### *uux*
>
> Execute a command on a remote UNIX system.
>
>   uux [options] command-string
>
> ## Options
>
> **–**   Take the standard input supplied to the **uux** command and feed it to the remote command. You may also use **–p**—the two options are interchangeable.
>
> **–a** *user*   Notify *user* upon completion.
>
> **–b**   Print the standard input when the exit status indicates an error.
>
> **–c**   Do not copy files to the spool directory.
>
> **–C**   Copy files to the spool directory.
>
> **–j**   Print the **uucp** job ID.
>
> **–n**   Suppress mail notification when the job completes (including errors).
>
> **–p**   Same as the **–** option (described above).
>
> **–z**   In BNU, sends mail notification, even if the job runs without any errors. In Taylor and BSD versions, notifies the user only if the command fails.

uux Errors

If something goes wrong, the UUCP daemon lets you know via an email message (unless you've specifically asked to suppress email with **uux –n**). Here's a message we might receive if the remote system doesn't permit us to use the **enable** command:

```
From: uucp@princecat.feelines.com
Received: (from uucp@localhost) by princecat.feelines.com (8.6.12) id
        BAA03604 for tabby!boris; Mon, 23 Oct 1995 01:12:12 -0400
Date: Mon, 23 Oct 1995 01:12:12 -0400
Message-Id: <199510230512.BAA03604@princecat.feelines.com>
To: boris@tabby.feelines.com
Subject: Execution failed
To: tabby!boris
```

```
Message from UUCP on princecat Mon Oct 23 01:12:11 1995

Your execution request failed because you are not permitted to execute
        enable
on this system.
Execution requested was:
        enable laser
```

Local and Remote Files

To make use of the printer on *princecat*, we need some way of getting the data files on the local system that we want to send over to *princecat* to be printed there. One way to do that is to use the **uucp** command to copy the file that we want to print to the public directory on *princecat*; then, use the **uux** command to run the **lpr** command on the remote system, supplying the name of the file that we just transferred there. For example:

```
$ uucp schedule.ps princecat!/var/spool/uucppublic/schedule.ps
$ uux princecat!lpr -Plaser /var/spool/uucppublic/schedule.ps
```

Of course, running commands this way is clumsy. If another user is printing a file with the same name and also storing it in the public directory, you might accidentally print their file instead of yours. And, if something goes wrong with the first **uucp** command to transfer the file, the **uux** command will run anyway, with either no file to print or worse yet, an older version of the file. If you want to delete the file after it is successfully printed, you can't—unless you have an account on the remote system and can log in and do it manually.

To take care of all this housekeeping, **uux** lets you specify filenames on its command line, and it automatically copies those files to the remote system before running the command. The files are copied to a "workspace" direc- tory on the remote system, and given unique names that won't conflict with anyone else's UUCP requests. And, after running the command, the remote system automatically deletes the files that were copied into the workspace. Unlike file transfers via the **uucp** command, all **uux** processes and working files are kept private so that the remote command invocation and its associ- ated data files are reasonably protected against interference from other users.

The syntax for specifying files to **uux** is the same as specifying files to **uucp**: *system!filename*. Here's how to run the same sequence of commands above with only one **uux** command:

```
$ uux princecat!lpr -Plaser !schedule.ps
```

Note that without the ! to flag the file as being on the local system, **uux** would not copy anything, and your remote command will look for *schedule.ps* on the remote system (and probably won't find it).

uux can also copy files from other systems in order to complete your request:

```
$ uux princecat!lpr -Plaser billcat!~/invoice.ps copycat!~/order.ps
```

Assuming that all of those files are in the public directories on their respective machines, **uux** will create UUCP file transfer requests for each file, drag them over to *princecat*, and run the **lpr** command.

Redirecting Input/Output

You can also pipe files to **uux** via standard input. The – option (a bare hyphen) or **–p** option tells **uux** to read from standard input and feed it to the standard input of the command to be executed on the remote system. For example:

```
$ psroff -t -man /usr/man/man1/uucp.1 | uux - princecat!lpr -Plaser
```

This entry tells **uux** to take input from the **psroff** command, and supply it as standard input to the **lpr** command when it is executed on *princecat*. (In this case, it's used to format the local online documentation for the **uucp** command.)

Using Special Characters

uux accepts a few special shell characters and lets you redirect input and output as if you were running a shell command on both the local and remote systems simultaneously. It will also let you quote arguments so that you can supply arguments with the ! character to the remote system. Table 3–1 shows the special characters and operators that are accepted by the **uux** command.

Table 3–1: Special Characters for uux

Symbol	Purpose
<	Input from file
>	Output to file
|	Pipe output to another command (not supported in Taylor UUCP)[a]
;	Delimit multiple commands (not supported in Taylor UUCP)
( )	Quote arguments on remote system

a. If the remote system is running Taylor UUCP, it will not properly interpret the | or ; characters. It does not matter what version of UUCP is running on your local system.

Since you don't want your local shell to interpret any of the special characters, you must always quote **uux** arguments that use those characters. For example:

```
$ uux "copycat!lpstat > !~/lpstat.copycat"
```

This would run the **lpstat** command on *copycat* to list the status of its printer queues, write the output to a temporary file, and then initiate a UUCP transfer of that temporary file to your local system's public directory.

When using special shell characters in a **uux** command, you can either put the entire list of command arguments in quotes (as shown in the example), or escape just the special characters themselves with quotes or the \ character. You might choose the latter method if you had other characters in your command that you wanted to have expanded by your local shell, such as filename wild cards or shell variables.

Using Pipes

You can also run commands in a pipeline on a remote (non-Taylor) system, feeding the output of one command into another just as you would at your local shell prompt. To specify a pipeline, use the pipe symbol after the first command, and drop the *system!* part from the subsequent commands. Here's an example that runs **lpstat** and emails the results to a specific user:

```
$ uux "copycat!lpstat | rmail (koshka!olga)"
```

The parentheses around *koshka!olga* tell **uux** to treat the strings literally, and not as a file specification. The **uux** command executes **lpstat** on system *copycat* and pipes the output to **rmail**. (**rmail** is a restricted form of the **mail** command.)

Limitations of uux

The number and complexity of operations you can perform on a remote system are limited by the commands allowed by the remote system administrator. And unless you're in an environment where your computers and users can trust each other, only one or two commands will be available to you. The **rmail** program is the only command usually enabled by default. Without **rmail**, the UUCP system wouldn't be able to send you any error messages.

Apart from security restrictions, there are some other intrinsic limits on what can be run via **uux**:

- You can't run a command interactively. As a rule, only a program that can run in the background, without user intervention, can be executed remotely.

- Standard output is discarded unless you explicitly redirect it to a file, or pipe it to another command.

- When redirecting output to a file, the file should be located in the public directory.

- A remote command is executed by the UUCP pseudo-user. Processes created to run remote commands belong to the user-ID *uucp* and any files created by the UUCP job will be owned by *uucp*, and have global read/write permissions. To keep a job's data from being accessed by other users, the remote command must pipe it to a program that has the authority to store the data in a safe place (like **rmail** and **rnews**).

In this chapter:
- *Using the uustat Command*
- *Using the uulog Command*
- *Checking the Logfiles Directly*

4

Checking on UUCP Requests

No sooner do you execute a UUCP command than you start worrying if your request will succeed. This chapter is about tracking your request through the innards of the UUCP spooling system and determining if it has succeeded or failed. Although it isn't necessary to know what goes on behind the scenes to use the UUCP commands, the more you know about UUCP, the easier it will be to determine what went wrong with a UUCP request. (And things do go wrong.)

Remember that UUCP itself generally sends you an electronic mail notice if your job fails or is unduly delayed. Of course, UUCP's idea of delay may not be the same as yours—it might be 24 hours or more before UUCP lets you know that things are amiss.

It's important to understand that the status messages reported by UUCP are not necessarily error messages. Do not repeat a UUCP command unless you are sure that the job has been deleted because of an error. If you repeat a request, you will probably end up submitting a duplicate copy of the transfer, and tying up the line for more time.

This chapter tells you how to use the two main UUCP commands for following the progress of UUCP requests: **uustat** and **uulog**. These commands will help you determine how far along a job is, and ultimately, whether it has succeeded or failed.

If you want to learn more about how UUCP transfers files, see chapter 8, *How UUCP Works*. Also Appendix B, *The Spool Directory/Working Files*, is a guide to the temporary workspaces that UUCP uses during a file transfer. We will refer to it several times in this chapter.

Using the uustat Command

The **uustat** command shows you the status of pending UUCP jobs.[*] It tells you if a job is still waiting in the queue. If **uustat**, when invoked with the appropriate options, does not list your job, then it has been completed and cleared from the queue. **uustat** can also be used to kill a UUCP job (remove the request from the queue). Here is a summary of common ways of invoking the **uustat** command; for the full list of options to **uustat**, see your system documentation.

---

uustat

Provide information about pending **uucp** or **uux** requests, cancel a pending request, or rejuvenate a pending request.

Options

```
uustat [-a | -m | -p | -q | -k job ID | -r job ID ]
       [ -s system ] [ -u user ]
```

With no options, **uustat** shows all UUCP requests that are pending for the current user.

−a	Report all queued jobs.
−k *job ID*	Kill request *job ID*.
−m	Report accessibility of other systems.
−p	Show any active UUCP processes.
−q	Report the number of jobs queued for all systems.
−r *job ID*	"Rejuvenate" the job associated with *job ID*. The UUCP system will act as if the job has just been submitted, which will extend the amount of time the job can remain queued before being deleted.
−s *system*	Report the status of jobs for *system*.
−u *user*	Report the status of jobs for *user*.

---

[*] BSD 4.3 and BSD/OS do not support **uustat**; instead, they supply the command **uusnap**, which is similar to **uustat −q**.

The typical way to use **uustat** is to invoke it without any options: it will give you a list of your jobs that are still in the queue, with the most recent job at the top of the list. Since the output of **uustat** differs between BNU and Taylor versions of UUCP, we'll look at both.

BNU uustat

Here is some sample output from the BNU UUCP **uustat**:

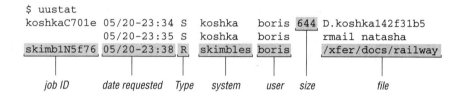

```
$ uustat
koshkaC701e 05/20-23:34 S   koshka    boris 644 D.koshka142f31b5
            05/20-23:35 S   koshka    boris     rmail natasha
skimb1N5f76 05/20-23:38 R   skimbles  boris     /xfer/docs/railway
```

| job ID | date requested | Type | system | user | size | file |

uustat shows the following information about each job:

- *job ID* is the tracking name assigned by UUCP to the request.

- *date requested* is the date and time when the command is submitted.

- *Type* is a type of request; "S" is for sending and "R" is for receiving.

- *system* is the remote system name.

- *user* is the userid of the person (boris in this listing) who initiated the transfer.

- *size* is the size of the file (in bytes) to be sent.

- *file* is the path where the file can be found. If the file begins with the letter "D.", it has been copied into the spool directory. For remote command execution requests, this field lists the command and any arguments or files.

Taylor uustat

The Taylor UUCP **uustat** presents essentially the same information as the BNU version of the command, but it uses English to describe the pending requests:

```
$ uustat
koshkaN0002 koshka  boris 10-08 23:05 Sending /usr/spool/uucppublic/junk (297
bytes) to ~
fatcatN0001 fatcat  boris 10-08 23:17 Requesting ~/junk to /var/spool/uucppubl
ic/morejunk
bigcatC0QBl bigcat  boris 10-29 13:37 Executing rmail president@whitehouse.gov
```

```
(sending 32768 bytes)
princecatC000J meow boris 04-07 17:09 Executing rmail lpr -Plaser (sending 453
bytes)
```

Seeing System Status

Although the above examples show how a user can find out which of their
jobs are still in the UUCP queue, they don't give us any hints as to *why* the
jobs haven't completed yet. For that, we will use the −q option to **uustat**.
This option gives a summary of the status of all systems that have UUCP
requests outstanding, and shows for each system the status of the last connection attempt. Here's a BNU example of **uustat** with the −q option:

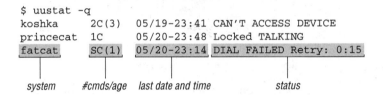

In this listing, the local system is currently communicating (or trying to communicate) with *princecat*, while the other two systems *koshka* and *fatcat*
have not been reachable (the number of commands queued is shown, with
how long the commands have been in the queue in parentheses).

Taylor **uustat** −q is similar, except that it breaks down the number of queued
commands by type:

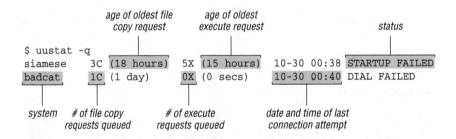

Here, C means UUCP (file copy) requests and X means uux (command execution requests).

uustat −q answers many questions about pending UUCP jobs—in particular,
when the system last tried to contact the remote system (the date and time
are listed for each system) and what happened when the conversation was

attempted (the status message is listed). A rundown of the UUCP status messages reported by **uustat** is in Appendix C, *Status and Error Messages*.

Seeing Past Successes

If **uustat −q** doesn't list the system you were looking for, then there are no jobs waiting for that system. You could assume that they completed successfully, but if you'd rather see it with your own eyes, the **−m** option will show you the last communications status of all systems known to UUCP. The output is the same as **uustat −q**, except that it also includes systems with no jobs queued for them. Usually, they look like this:

```
princecat       10-29 15:36 SUCCESSFUL
koshka          10-23 02:59 SUCCESSFUL
```

Jobs By User or By System Name

If you are a user on a large system, such as a public UNIX system or ISP with many UUCP connections, **uustat** may show you far more output than you're interested in seeing. You can narrow down the scope of what **uustat** displays either by username or by system. To report on jobs sent by a specific user (**uustat** without any options reports your jobs), use the **−u** *userid* option. And to list only those jobs for a particular system, use the **−s** *system* option:

```
$ uustat -q -s koshka
koshka      2C(3)   05/19-23:41 CAN'T ACCESS DEVICE
```

uustat is finicky about what options you can use with **−u** and **−s**. For example, you can't combine the **−m** option with **−s** *system*. Of course, this being UNIX, you can always pipe the output of **uustat** to **grep**:

```
$ uustat -m | grep princecat
princecat       10-29 15:36 SUCCESSFUL
```

Dear Job Letters

If the UUCP daemons cannot reach a particular remote system for more than a day, you will receive an email message that looks like this:

```
Subject: Warning from UUCP

We have been unable to contact machine
'deadcat' since you queued your job.

Job: tabby!/u1/fred/testfile --> deadcat!~/fred (5/20)
```

```
The job will be deleted in several days if the
problem is not corrected.  If you care to kill
the job, execute the following command:

    uustat -k deadcat2N5f76

Sincerely,
tabby!uucp
```

You might want to take a closer look if you receive one of these messages—a modem may be broken at the local or the remote system (and will need to be fixed), or there may be a serious problem somewhere that will soon cause email and UUCP requests to be lost.

If UUCP gives up and deletes your job, it will send you a similar email notice announcing your job's unfortunate demise. As the helpful suggestion in the above example indicates, you can cause your job to prematurely expire with the **uustat −k** command (should you decide it is no longer worth sending). On the other hand, you can prevent the UUCP daemons from killing your request by using the **uustat −r** command to "rejuvenate" the job. This command changes the timestamps on the queued files to the current date and time so that the job appears to be freshly submitted, and the expiration clock that triggered the above email message starts all over again.

Using the uulog Command

If you want a blow-by-blow description of what is happening to your UUCP request, use the **uulog** command. **uulog** displays the status messages logged by UUCP programs for each job request. The messages are listed in the sequence in which they occur with the most recent at the bottom of the report. As with **uustat**, you can use command-line options to focus on particular systems or types of jobs.

BNU uulog

The BNU **uulog** command without any options lists the status messages for all systems. Unless you want to see every last detail of UUCP activity on your system, you will want to use the command-line options to pick out only the status information you're interested in seeing. For recent events, you can ask **uulog** to just show you recent messages (−*nn*: *nn* is the number of lines you want to see). For things that are happening now, you can use **uulog −f** to get a real-time display of the logfile as new messages are added to it.

uulog

```
uulog [options]
```

Options

−s *system*
> Print status messages for file transfers to remote *system*. (If this option is not specified, print messages from all remote systems.)

−f *system*
> Perform **tail −f** of log messages for system.

−*nn* Display last *nn* lines of log messages for each system specified, or from all systems if no −s options also appear.

−x Show the *uuxqt* log (**uux** requests from remote systems) for the given system or user.

Additional Taylor UUCP options

−u *userid*
> Display log messages only for the jobs of a particular user. Depending on the configuration of Taylor UUCP, may need to be used with the −s *system* option.

−F Like −f, but "follows" the logfile for all systems. Only available on systems configured for Taylor-style logfiles.

−S Show statistics logfile.

Here's a sample inspection of the five most recent UUCP log messages:

```
$ uulog | tail -5
uucp skimbles (9/2-0:14:46,31567,0) CONN FAILED (WRONG TIME TO CALL)
uucp fatcat  (9/2-0:21:28,31570,0) OK (startup)
uucp fatcat  (9/2-0:21:32,31570,0) Remote requested. (tabby!/home/bo
ris/thing --> fatcat!~ (boris))
uucp princecat  (9/2-0:21:41,18186,0) CONN FAILED (NO DEVICES AVAILA
BLE)
uucp fatcat   (9/2-0:21:48,31570,1) OK (conversation complete)
         |          |         |                  |
       host     date/time    pid              message
```

Although some of these messages may look ominous, like "CONN FAILED,"
they are a normal part of UUCP's business—if there's only one modem
attached to the local system, UUCP can't call two systems at once. You can
tell which log message refers to which job via the *pid* (process ID), which
identifies the process that is writing each log message. In this example, one
process (pid 31570) is happily copying a file while another process is turned
away because there are no modems available.

Taylor uulog

Since Taylor UUCP can be told to use different styles of logging, the behavior of **uulog** will vary somewhat depending on your local system configuration. Some system administrators (and Linux distributions) set up Taylor to
mimic BNU for familiarity's sake, while others prefer Taylor UUCP's "native"
logging format. Just to make things more confusing, some Linux distributions don't install the Taylor **uulog** command—you may need to find the
Taylor UUCP source distribution and install it yourself.

Just about all of the BNU features of **uulog** are supported by the Taylor
uulog, with a few additions. The most useful one is the −F option, which
will follow the logfile for all UUCP activity, letting you monitor more than
one system at a time. Another option, −S, will show you the file transfer
statistics, which will give you an idea of how fast UUCP is able to transfer
data:

```
$ uulog -S -5
koshka!nobody S (10/29-11:29:50) (C,80,2) [cua2] <- 2067 / 0.585 secs,
3533 bytes/sec
koshka!boris S (10/29-15:36:15) (C,641,1) [TCP] <- 93013 / 29.027 secs
, 3204 bytes/sec
koshka!boris S (10/29-15:36:21) (C,641,3) [TCP] <- 2593 / 1.605 secs,
```

```
1615 bytes/sec
koshka!fred M (11/3-22:10:55) (C,3755,1) [TCP] -> 18412 / 0.147 secs,
125251 bytes/sec
princecat!root S (11/4-11:31:07) (C,129,1) [stdin] <- 24 / 0.037 secs,
 648 bytes/sec
```

The -> and <- symbols indicate the direction of data transfer (think of them as little arrows). <- is a transfer to the system named in the left hand column, -> a transfer from it. If your system is configured for Taylor-style logfiles, the statistics will be less cryptic:

```
$ uulog -S -2
boris koshka (1995-11-04 12:22:52.35) received 2593 bytes in 1.605 sec
onds (1615 bytes/sec) on port stdin
root·princecat (1995-11-04 13:19:52.81) sent 24 bytes in 0.280 seconds
 (85 bytes/sec) on port TCP
```

Seeing Local uux Requests

The **uulog** command can also show you the logs from execution requests made by other systems. For example, suppose a friend of yours on *fatcat* claims that he sent you electronic mail last week, but you never received it. Assuming that mail between your local system and *fatcat* was relayed via UUCP, in order for *fatcat* to send mail it has to run **uux** to request that your system run the **rmail** command on its behalf. So by scanning the execution log on your local system (with the **uulog −x** command), you should be able to tell if the letter made it to your system:

```
$ uulog -x fatcat
nobody fatcat (10/10-01:31:26,1542,0) ERROR: /bin/rmail: No such file or
directory
uucp fatcat (10/15-00:01:04,382,0) Executing X.fatcatC000T (rmail boris@t
abby.feelines.com)
uucp fatcat (10/15-01:14:04,832,0) Executing X.fatcatC000Z (rmail natasha
@tabby.feelines.com)
```

As we can see here, an execution request was denied because UUCP couldn't find the **rmail** command to submit email on the local system; it did work properly a few days later, probably because the system administrator fixed it.

Checking the Logfiles Directly

Under most circumstances, **uustat** and **uulog** will give you sufficient information about the status of your UUCP jobs, or of the neighboring UUCP hosts.

But there are some bits of logfile, or status information, that you might find only by digging into the actual logfiles UUCP keeps in its spool directory.

On most systems, you can find the UUCP logfiles in the directory */var/spool/uucp* and its subdirectories. The BNU and BSD/OS versions of UUCP (and Taylor systems configured to keep their logfiles in BNU format) keep their logfiles across several different directories—by UUCP request type and by system name. Taylor UUCP systems can optionally be configured to keep just one logfile for all activity, but in a format that can be easily parsed by shell scripts, or other programs, to extract the desired information. Version 2 and BSD 4.3 UUCP also keep most log messages in a single file in the spool directory.

Appendix B, *The Spool Directory/Working Files*, describes the spool directory, the files within, and which ones might be worth perusing when looking for status information.

5

Logging In on a Remote System

Although it's not directly related to the UUCP protocol, one of the components of a UUCP installation is the **cu** program.[*] **cu** allows a regular user to use a computer's modems or serial ports to connect to a remote system and use it interactively. System administrators are fond of using **cu** to test modems and UUCP configuration files.

You can use **cu** to connect to your UUCP neighbors, or give it a phone number so that you can call any other system that has a modem and is willing to let you sign on.

NOTE   UNIX communications software has advanced substantially since **cu** was written. Programs like **kermit**, **seyon**, or **minicom**[†] provide much more functionality, are easier to use, and deliver reliable, efficient file transfer. We recommend that you upgrade to one of these programs instead of relying on **cu**.

BSD 4.3 and BSD/OS systems do not support **cu**: instead, they supply a program called **tip** for remote login.[‡] If you find **cu** on a BSD 4.3 or BSD/OS system, it is probably just a link to **tip**. Other UNIX systems, such as SunOS and Solaris, supply both **tip** and **cu**. And Taylor UUCP **cu** includes most of

---

[*] **cu** stands for "call UNIX." Of course, you can also call non-UNIX systems with **cu**.

[†] **seyon** and **minicom** are included in many Linux distributions, and are also available from public software archives on the Net. **kermit** is available in both source and binary for common platforms from *ftp://kermit.columbia.edu/kermit*.

[‡] **tip** stands for "terminal interface program."

the features of **tip** not already found in **cu**. **tip** is very similar to **cu**, and we provide a summary of **tip** in this chapter. Consult your system documentation to see if **tip** is supported on your system.

Remote Login with cu

cu can be used to contact systems that are members of your UUCP network, or any other system, including non-UNIX systems. Like UUCP, **cu** can communicate over dial-up and hardwired connections.* We explain how to set up these connections in Chapter 9, *The Physical Connection*, and Chapter 10, *Setting Up a UUCP Link*.

With **cu**, you can use a remote system from your terminal on the local system. During this session, the local system acts transparently, transmitting input from your terminal to the remote system and receiving output from the remote system and displaying it on your terminal screen. It is just as though your terminal were directly connected to the remote system.

One difference you may notice is that the speed of transmission is typically slower, especially over phone lines, and thus system response could be delayed. You might also get occasional pauses while your error-correcting modems struggle with line noise or random "garbage" characters on the screen (or mysteriously appearing on the remote system as if you typed them yourself) if you are using older, non-error-correcting modems. Sometimes it helps to disconnect and dial in again to see if you get a better line.

Contacting a Remote System by Name

You can use the name of the remote system to establish a connection with another system on the UUCP network.†

For example, to dial in to system *fatcat*, you would enter:

```
$ cu fatcat

Connected
login: daphne
Password:

daphne@fatcat:~$
```

---

* The **cu** supplied with Taylor UUCP and some varieties of System V Release 4 UUCP can make connections over a TCP/IP network, but this is useful only for testing the UUCP link.

† The **uuname** command will list the names of remote systems that you can contact this way.

---

cu in a Nutshell

Call up another host system via a direct line or a modem. When a *system* is known to UUCP, the command "cu *system*" will connect to that system using the contact information in the UUCP configuration. 8 bits and no parity will be used on the call, unless the −o or −e options (see below) are specified.

```
cu [options] telno | system
```

Options

−d	Print diagnostics of session.
−e	Use even parity.
−l *line*	*line* is the name of the communications line device.
−h	Emulates local echo and supports calls to other computer systems which expect terminals to be in half duplex mode.
−o	Use odd parity.
−s *speed*	Set the baud rate to *speed*.
−t	Perform carriage return/linefeed mappings for calling dumb ASCII terminals.
−m	Ignore carrier detect while connecting (AIX systems only).
telno	The telephone number. Use = to wait for a secondary dial tone; − to get a brief pause.
system	Call the *system* known to UUCP.

---

cu will print **Connected** after it has successfully reached the remote system—this happens fairly quickly if the system you are calling is linked via a serial cable, but takes 30 seconds or more if **cu** needs to first dial out using one of the local system's modems.

Once connected, you should see the login prompt for the remote system. If you don't, tap the RETURN key a few times, or whatever key sequence is appropriate for the system you are calling. Once you've signed on, you can type commands and see their results just as though you were sitting at a local terminal of the remote system.

When you're ready to sign off, use whatever commands you usually use to exit the remote system (i.e., the **exit**, **logout**, or $\boxed{\text{CTRL-D}}$ commands on a UNIX host). The other side should be kind enough to hang up the connection when you sign off, and **cu** should detect this and exit automatically. You can also force a logout via **cu** subcommands (see the section below, "Disconnecting from **cu**," for more details).

Call by Name

If you want to log into a system that is already one of your UUCP neighbors, you can do so with "**cu** *system*." Since **cu** shares the UUCP configuration database with the other UUCP commands, it can find the modems and phone numbers needed to contact that system.

Some system administrators place systems into the UUCP configuration that are not UUCP hosts, but are common dial-up destinations. Depending on how UUCP is set up (see Chapter 10, *Setting Up a UUCP Link*), these entries may show up when you run the **uuname** command. You would be able to **cu** to them, but you would not be able to perform any other UUCP operations with them.

Specifying a Phone Number

If you want to call a system that is not one of your UUCP neighbors, you must specify the phone number of the remote system. On most systems, this should be as simple as:

```
$ cu 17185554737
Connected
```

If your system has **tip**, you can also invoke it with just the phone number:

```
$ tip 17185554737
```

Some systems have more than one call-out device and you might want to specify a particular line or device with the *–l device* option:

```
$ cu -l tty006 17185554737
```

This instructs **cu** to dial out over the modem attached to serial line *tty006*. If you like, you can spell out the entire device name */dev/tty006*, but **cu** accepts it either way.

If you want a particular serial port that is directly connected to another system, you would only specify the line, and no phone number:

```
$ cu -l tty006
```

Using the Modem

In some cases, you may find that you need to "dial by hand" rather than use the built-in dialing capabilities of **cu**. In most cases, **cu** will allow you to connect to the modem directly, as if the modem was a directly connected system:

```
$ cu -l tty006 -s 19200
```

This will give you a connection to the modem at 19200 bits per second (*bps*)—you can now enter modem commands (such as **AT** commands for Hayes-compatible modems) to change modem settings or dial your desired number.

Some versions of **cu** fail when you try to connect to the modem, because they expect a signal on the serial port to indicate that the remote side is connected. You'll know this is happening if **cu** hangs up as soon as you connect:

```
$ cu -l tty0 -s 19200
Connected

Lost Carrier
User defined signal 1
$
```

If your **cu** behaves this way, try using the **−m** option to tell it to ignore the Carrier Detect signal from the modem, or check the system documentation. Chapter 9, *The Physical Connection*, explains the mechanics of connecting to serial ports.

Most modern modems can automatically convert between different baud rates—the user generally connects to the modem at the highest possible speed, and if the modem makes a connection that is slower than that speed, the modem converts the data to the faster speed and performs flow control to make sure no data is lost. Your modems should be set up to use flow control and baud rate conversion (Chapter 9 and Appendix I, *Setting Up a Modem*, explain how to do this).

If your system uses older, non-adjusting modems (such as all 1200-bps modems and most 2400-bps modems), you need to match the speed of your connection to the modem with the speed at which the modem will be communicating. For example, if your system runs an old 2400-bps modem that will not perform speed conversion, and you want to dial a BBS running an even older 1200-bps modem, you need to invoke **cu** with the **−s 1200** option. Otherwise, when you call in at 2400 bps, the modem will automatically downshift to 1200 bps after making the connection, turning your session into gobbledygook.[*]

Dialing Commands

UUCP supports a generic set of dialing commands for dialing pauses that, when used in a phone number given to **cu**, are translated into commands that the modem recognizes. For example, to dial a number from an office telephone system that requires users to press 9 and then wait for an outside dial tone. you might invoke **cu** with:

```
$ cu 9=12128759901
```

The equal sign (=) is translated by **cu** into a command that asks the modem to wait for a dial tone after dialing the 9, and before dialing the rest of the digits. Another generic modem command is a dash (−), which causes a one-second pause.

For more information on using and setting up modems, see Chapter 9, *The Physical Connection*, and Appendix I, *Setting Up a Modem*.

Problems Making the Connection

There are a variety of problems that might occur when you try to connect to a remote system. If you don't see the **Connected** message when you run **cu**, then you've encountered one of them. For example, you might see:

```
Connect failed: Requested device/system name not known.
```

In this case, either the system name or the device name that you supplied on the command line is not known to the UUCP system. Check the system name against the list printed by the **uuname** command, or check the device name against the entries in the */dev* directory. Even if the device file exists, it may have the wrong permissions or ownerships. Chapter 10, *Setting Up a UUCP Link*, and Chapter 11, *Making Sure the Link Works*, explain how to deal with this problem.

---

* cu is one of the few telecommunications programs on UNIX systems that does not permit you to change the baud rate during the connection.

Before accessing the specified line or device, **cu** checks to make sure that UUCP is not currently using it. If the modem or the serial line is busy, you might get the following message:

```
Connect failed: No Device Available
```

Either there are no modems or serial lines available because they are all in use, or the system is misconfigured and there are no modems or serial lines available at all. Use the **uustat −p** command (see Chapter 4, *Checking on UUCP Requests*) to see what UUCP-related processes are running. It will list out any processes that are using UUCP-owned ports.

If you get the **Connected** message but no login prompt, press RETURN a few times. You can also try sending a BREAK signal, via the ~%**break** subcommand to **cu** (see below).

If no login prompt appears, it may be that the remote system is having problems answering the line, or perhaps the line is busy. You might see an error message from the modem, but often modem messages are turned off to simplify dialing. If you can try again from a terminal near the modem, do so; if the modem has a speaker, you may hear the busy signal or other telephonic errors. Another way to test the number you're calling is to dial it from a regular telephone and see if a computer modem answers. When you think you've waited enough, you can disconnect from **cu** with the ~. subcommand (see below).

If you see the **Connected** message indicating that you are getting through to the other modem, but you do not get a login prompt on your screen, there may be a problem on the remote system. Check with the administrators at the remote system to make sure their side is working properly.

If you get through, but see garbage on your screen, either you have a horrible connection, or the communications settings on the two systems are mismatched. Try typing a few keystrokes, slowly, and see what happens. If you get one character printed on your screen for every keystroke, and if some of the characters printed look right while others don't, it is probably a parity problem—try calling in again with either the −e or −o options (for even and odd parity respectively). If you see multiple garbage characters printed with each key you press, then you are probably calling at the wrong baud rate, or the modem switched rates on you while you weren't looking. See if you can reprogram the modem to do baud rate conversion, or call in at the correct baud rate (again, see Appendix I, *Setting Up a Modem*).

There is also a debugging option, **−d**, that an inquisitive user or administrator can use to track down problems in establishing communications with another system. We show how to use this option in Chapter 11, *Making Sure the Link Works*.

Using tip

tip does not use the UUCP configuration files to find its devices or system names. Instead, it looks in files named */etc/remote* and */etc/phones*. Therefore, just because you can contact the remote system through UUCP doesn't necessarily mean you can use the system name for remote login with **tip**.

---

tip in a Nutshell

Establish connection to another machine. Remote machine may be identified by a recognizable *name* (defined in the */etc/remote* file, or by a telephone number.

    tip [*option*] [*name/telno*]

Options

−*speed*   Set the baud rate to *speed*.

−v   Display commands from the *.tiprc* file as they are executed

---

Tilde Escape Sequences

cu and **tip** run as two processes: transmit and receive. The transmit process reads from standard input and passes whatever the user types to the remote system. The receive process reads data from the remote system and displays it on the user's terminal on the local system. Both processes filter out lines beginning with a tilde (˜), which are interpreted as commands.

These commands, or *tilde escape sequences*, perform a variety of tasks. On most systems, when you enter the tilde, it will prompt you with the local system name in brackets:

    fatcat$ ˜[tabby]

Enter the command letter or word and press RETURN . The command you'll use most often is the one needed to end a remote login session and exit **cu**

(˜. or tilde-dot). Note the sidebar with the complete list of **cu**'s other "escapes."

The **tip** command has its own set of tilde escapes, which are conveniently supported as additional escapes in Taylor **cu**.

Disconnecting from cu

To disconnect a **cu** link, first log out from the remote machine. Under most circumstances, the remote side will hang up their modem or close their serial port, and **cu** will detect this and exit. If you instead see another login prompt, you'll need to use **cu**'s disconnect command: enter the tilde-dot (˜.) sequence on a new line and press the RETURN key. For example:

```
fatcat$ logout


Welcome to Fee Lines, Inc.

fatcat login: ˜.
Disconnected
$
```

After entering this exit sequence, **cu** tells you it has disconnected from the remote system. Then it exits, returning you to your local system prompt (*$*).

Depending on how the dial-in line on the remote system is set up, disconnecting **cu** may or may not also log you out. Unless you know for sure that the remote system will log you out when you disconnect, you should first log out of the remote system before disconnecting.

Tilde-Tilde

Sometimes, you'll want to send a line beginning with the tilde character to the remote system. The usual reason is that you're using **cu** or **rlogin** on the remote system and need to send the remote system a tilde command. But if you type a line beginning with tilde, the **cu** process running on your local system will interpret it instead. Fortunately, there's a way to tell your local **cu** that you want to send a line beginning with tilde to the remote system: begin your command with tilde-tilde. The local **cu** will strip off the first tilde and send the rest to your session with the remote system. For example, if you are using **cu** to connect to a remote system, and also running **cu** on the remote system, and want to close the latter **cu**, you would enter tilde-tilde-dot (˜˜.) on a new line.

cu Tilde Escapes

~.   Close the serial port on the local system and exit **cu**.

~!   Escape to an interactive shell on the local system.

~!*cmd*...   Run the command on the local system (via **sh −c**).

~$*cmd*...   Run the command locally and send output to the remote system.

~%cd [*dir*] Change the current directory on the local system to *dir*.

~%take *file* [*target*]
            Copy *file* from the remote UNIX system to *target* on the local system.

~%put *file* [*target*]
            Copy *file* from the local system to *target* on the remote UNIX system. If *target* is omitted, *file* is used in both places.

~~ ...   Send a line beginning with a ~ to the remote system. For example, if you were connected to remote C through remote B, use ~~. to logoff C and return to B.

~%break   Send the BREAK sequence to remote system.

~%debug   Turn debug mode on (not in Taylor UUCP).

~%nostop   Toggle between XON/XOFF flow control and no flow control. In Taylor **cu**, ~%nostop turns off XON/XOFF flow control, and ~%stop turns it back on.

~+ *command*
            Run *command* on local system, with standard output/input redirected to the remote system (Taylor UUCP only).

~>:*file*
~>>:*file*   Redirect subsequent output from the remote system to the named *file* on the local system (not in Taylor UUCP). With ~>>:, output is appended to any existing file, otherwise *file* will be overwritten if it exists.

~>   End an output diversion started with ~>: or ~>>: (except for Taylor UUCP).

---

tip/Taylor cu Tilde Escapes

~^D or ~.   Close the connection.

~c [*dir*]   Change directory to *dir* on local system.

~!   Escape to a shell on the local system.

~>   Copy a file from the local to remote system. The file is dumped onto the communications line—the remote system must be expecting it for a transfer to work.

~<   Copy output from the remote system to a file on the local system. The transfer ends when the **eofread** string (see below) is matched in the remote system's output.

~p *file* [*target*]
   Send *file* to the remote UNIX host.

~t *file* [*target*]
   Take *file* from the remote UNIX host.

~| Pipe output from a remote command to a local process.

~$ Pipe output from a local command to a remote process.

~#   Send a BREAK to the remote system.

~s   Set a variable. To list variables, use ~s all (~v with Taylor cu).

~^Z   Stop **tip** (only on systems with job control enabled). The session can be resumed with the **fg** command.

~^Y   Stop only the "local input" **tip** process (only on systems with job control enabled). Output from the remote system will continue to be displayed. Input to the remote session can be resumed with the **fg** command.

~?   Print a summary of tilde escapes.

Transferring Files with cu

cu provides a method for transferring small text files over a login session between two UNIX systems. You might use this capability if you didn't want to wait for a UUCP transfer to occur, or if you are using **cu** to talk to a remote system that does not have UUCP connectivity to your system.

However, **cu**'s file transfer capability lacks error checking and is limited to text files.* If you need interactive file transfer as part of your remote login session, you will be much better off using **kermit** or other modern communications packages that have file transfer capabilities far beyond those of **cu**.

If you must use the file transfer capability in **cu**, be aware of its limitations: you can transfer only text files, and they may arrive garbled or with pieces missing. Your chances of success are better with shorter files and over serial links where flow control is working properly.

The **cu** commands for transferring files between UNIX systems are ˜**%take** and ˜**%put**. There's usually some degree of confusion about the direction of file transfer when you use these commands. It will perhaps help to remember that the local system is your point of reference in file transfers. Thus, you *take* a file from the remote system and, in reverse, you *put* a file to the remote system.

Take from remote system

To copy a file from a remote UNIX system, you would *take* the file and copy it over to your system. The syntax is:

    ˜**%take** *from* [*to*]

˜**%take** is a tilde escape that you enter once you are logged on to the remote system. *from* is the name of the remote system file and *to* is the name you want to give the file on your system. The new filename (*to*) is optional; **cu** uses the original name of the file if it is not given.

For example, here we copy the file *thing* from system *fatcat* and assign it the same filename on the local system:

```
fatcat$ stty tabs
fatcat$ ˜%take thing
stty -echo;mesg n;echo '˜>':thing;cat thing;echo '˜>';mesg y;
stty echo
˜>:thing
2 lines/85 characters
fatcat$
```

The **stty tabs** commands may need to be invoked before you use ˜**%take** so that any tabs present in the file will not be expanded into spaces when the file is transferred.

---

* Although with the right software, you can invoke a reliable file transfer program from within **cu** (see "Zmodem Under cu" later in this chapter).

Inside the %take command

Except for Taylor UUCP systems, the **%take** command uses a special feature of **cu**'s Receive process: any received lines beginning with ˜>: are interpreted as commands to redirect output. All output received from that point on is written to the file named in the ˜>: line, until another line beginning with ˜>: is received. **cu**'s Receive process also supports ˜>>:, which works the same way, except that the redirected output is appended to the file named instead of creating a new file.

CAUTION Since **cu**'s Receive process does not know or care whether the ˜>: or ˜>>: commands are typed by you or via some program running on the remote system, you can use shell scripts or programs to initiate ˜%take file transfers. But this leaves open a serious risk, the ˜>: or ˜>>: characters can trigger a file transfer without your permission if they are sent to your session at the right moment. For this reason, you should not routinely use any version of **cu** that supports the ˜>: escape, unless your UNIX vendor has rectified this problem. This is not a problem in Taylor UUCP or **tip**, which do not write to local files unless you specifically ask them to.

Let's see what the commands in the ˜%take script mean. (Note that you don't need to type this dialog. It is described in detail so you can understand what is happening.)

Command	Description
stty −echo	Do not echo back every character typed.
mesg n	Turn off messages to the user's terminal so they do not pollute the file transfer.
echo '˜>':*thing*	Send the string "˜>:*thing*" to the standard output of the remote system, where *thing* is the name of the file to be copied. The notation "˜>:*file*" echoed on the remote system diverts the output to a file on the local system.
cat *thing*	Send the file called *thing* to standard output.
echo '˜>'	Send the string "˜>" to the standard output of the remote system. This ends the output diversion.
mesg y	Allow messages to be sent to the user's terminal.

The **stty** and **mesg** commands perform "housekeeping" tasks. The crucial commands that perform the file transfer are **echo** and **cat**. (These two commands should exist on every UNIX system.) Thus, you can write a shell script using the same syntax to perform additional tasks. For example, you could create the following script that allows you to copy multiple files from the remote system to your local system:

```
for x
do
    echo "~>:$x"
    cat $x
    echo "~>"
done
```

Assuming that you have saved this script on the remote system in a file called **takeit**, the command:

```
$ takeit file1 file2
```

would "take" *file1* and then *file2*. The command:

```
$ takeit *
```

would "take" all of the files in the current directory on the remote system.

~%take does not work when you copy files from a non-UNIX system. However, since you already know what each command in the ~%take script does, you can sometimes still write a script containing commands on the non-UNIX system that perform the same functions as **cat** and **echo**.

Put on remote system

When you want to copy a file from the local system to another UNIX system, you are essentially *put*ting it on the other system. You would enter the command ~%put while logged in to the remote system:

~%put *from* [*to*]

~%put is a tilde escape that you enter once you are logged on to the remote system. (Using **tip**, enter ~%p.) *from* is the name of the local file and *to* is an optional name for the file on the remote system. For example, to copy a file called *plans* in your working directory on the local system to a file called *plans.new* on another system, you would enter:

```
fatcat$ ~%put plans plans.new
stty -echo; cat - > plans.new; stty echo
12 lines; 184 characters
$
```

cu sends a control line for the file transfer and prints the number of lines and characters sent when the transfer is complete.

You can specify a full pathname as the *from* filename, but you should be sure to specify a *to* filename as well, since the ˜%**put** will fail if the *from* filename includes the name of a directory that is not present on the other side.

For example, the command:

```
˜%put /usr/tim/thing
```

fails if the directory */usr/tim* does not exist on the remote system. However:

```
˜%put /usr/tim/thing thing
```

will work, since the *to* file will be created in the current directory on the remote system.

Executing Commands Locally

When you are logged into a remote system using **cu**, your keystrokes are generally used as input to commands on the remote system. But you may also want to run a few commands on your local system without first closing your **cu** session. **cu** provides several tilde escapes for doing so.

To run a command on the local system while logged in to the other system, enter the command as:

```
˜!command
```

For example, if you are calling *fatcat* from *tabby*, you might want to list out your local directory on *tabby* to make sure a file you want to send is really there.

```
fatcat$ ˜!ls
R46         list1       ratings
R68         macguffin   thing
R110A       miles       trains
!
fatcat$
```

Typing ˜! followed by a RETURN lets you escape to an interactive shell on the local system. When you exit that shell, you will be returned to your **cu** session.

You can also send the output of a command to the remote system while running it on the local system by using:

```
~$command
```

One possible use of this escape sequence is to copy a file from a local UNIX system to a remote non-UNIX system. For example, let's suppose you are logged in to a VAX/VMS system (called *mars*) using **cu**, and you would like to copy a text file called *thing.UNIX* from your UNIX directory. While on *mars*, you would enter:

```
mars$ create thing.vms
 ~$cat thing.UNIX
```

The **create** command on the VAX is similar to the UNIX **cat >** for creating text files. The second line invokes the **cat** command on the local (UNIX) system, but the output of the command is sent to the remote system, where it is presumably captured in the file that was just created (*thing.vms*). Typing CTRL-Z would close the file on the VAX.

Zmodem under cu

Taylor UUCP supports bidirectional piping with the ~+ escape. This lets you run a reliable file transfer program such as the Omen Technology-derived **sz** and **rz** Zmodem file transfer programs that are included on many Linux systems. **sz** sends files via the Zmodem protocol, **rz** receives files via Zmodem, and both programs are smart enough to work properly when run under Taylor **cu**.

Assuming you have **sz** and **rz** installed on both the local and remote systems,* you would first invoke either **sz** or **rz** on the remote system (depending whether you wanted to send from or receive to the remote system), then escape to the local system and invoke the opposite Zmodem program via the ~+ escape. For example:

```
fatcat$ sz my.file
**B00000000000000
~+rz
rz waiting to receive.
Receiving: my.file
Bytes received:   15292/ 15292:    1603 Bytes per sec
Transfer complete.
cu: shell: Exit status 128
fatcat$
```

---

* The public-domain versions of **sz** and **rz** can be found on any Slackware archive or Sunsite mirror, under the name *lrzsz-0.12a.tar*. The commercial versions of these programs are available at *http://www.omen.com*.

Changing directories

If you try to change directories on the local system using the tilde shell escape (˜!), your command is submitted to a sub-shell and has no lasting effect. Use the sequence ˜%cd instead. Look at the following example:

```
fatcat$˜!pwd
˜[tabby]!pwd
/home/nutshell/uucp
!
˜!cd /home/boris
˜[tabby]!cd /home/boris
!
˜!pwd
˜[tabby]!pwd
/home/nutshell/uucp
!
˜%cd /home/boris
˜[tabby]%cd /home/boris

fatcat$˜!pwd
˜[tabby]!pwd
/home/boris
!
```

The sequence **%cd** allows you to change the working directory on the local system; this persists for your remote login session. Note that when you disconnect from the remote system, you will return to the local directory that you were in when you began **cu**.

tip Environment Variables

tip differs from **cu** in that it allows variables that control its operation to be set within its environment. Variables may be set during the **tip** session with the ˜s escape sequence, or may be set automatically, upon entering **tip**, by specifying options and their values in *.tiprc* in the user's */home* directory. In *.tiprc*, the ˜s prefix should be omitted.

tip variables have Boolean, numeric, string, or single character values. An assignment should not have blanks in it. Numeric, string, and character values can be set by combining the variable with = and a value (e.g., ˜s ba=1200), while Boolean values are set just by naming them and unset by naming them with the "!" prefix (e.g., ˜s !verb). See Table 5–1 for a list of **tip** variables and their descriptions.

Current option settings can be displayed with the escape sequence ˜s all.

Table 5–1: tip Environment Variables

tip Variable	Type	Description
beautify (be)	*Boolean*	Discard unprintable characters in session script.
baudrate (ba)	*number*	Baud rate for connection.
dialtimeout (dial)	*number*	Number of seconds to wait for a connection after dialing.
echocheck	*Boolean*	Wait for echo of last character transmitted during file transfer. Default is *off*.
eofread (eofr)	*string*	String signifying end of transfer during ˜< file transfer. Should match a shell prompt.
eofwrite (eofw)	*string*	String signifying end of transfer during ˜> file transfer.
eol	*string*	String signifying an end-of-line.
escape (es)	*character*	Escape character. Default is ˜ (tilde).
exceptions (ex)	*string*	Characters which should not be discarded by beautification. Default is \t\n\f\b.
force (fo)	*character*	Character to force literal data transmission. Default is ^P.
framesize (fr)	*number*	Amount (in bytes) of data to be written to buffer between writes in receiving files.
host (ho)	*string*	Name of host.
prompt (pr)	*character*	Character signifying end-of-line on remote host. Default is \n.
raise (ra)	*Boolean*	Map lower case letters to upper case on remote machine. Default is *off*.
raisechar (rc)	*character*	Character used to toggle upper case mapping mode. Default is ^A.
record (rec)	*string*	Name of file in which session script is recorded. Default is *tip.record*.
script (sc)	*Boolean*	Record everything transmitted by remote system in script record file, except those affected by the **beautify** switch. Default is *off*.
tabexpand (tab)	*Boolean*	Expand tabs to spaces in file transfer (8 spaces each). Default is *off*.
verbose (verb)	*Boolean*	Print messages while dialing and during file transfer. Default is *on*.

Table 5–1: tip Environment Variables (continued)

tip Variable	Type	Description
SHELL	*string*	Name of shell for use by ˜! escape. Default is taken from the environment (usually **/bin/sh**).
HOME	*string*	Home directory for use by ˜c escape. Default is taken from the environment.

Taylor cu Environment Variables

Taylor **cu** also supports environment variables similar to **tip**. You can list out their current values with the ˜v command, set them with the ˜s command, or set a variable to false with "˜s! *variable*."

Table 5–2 lists the Taylor **cu** environment variables (with descriptions).

Table 5–2: Taylor cu Environment Variables

Variable	Type	Description
binary-prefix	*string*	A string used to quote binary characters during a file transfer (default ^V, character value 22).
binary	*Boolean*	If false, newlines (character value 10) in files being sent are converted to carriage returns (character value 13).
delay	*Boolean*	Wait one second before printing the local system name during a tilde escape.
echo-check	*Boolean*	If true, **cu** tries to check file transfers by comparing what the remote system echoes back.
echonl	*character*	Character to look for after sending each line of a file.
eofread	*string*	The string to look for when receiving a file with ˜<. Should match a shell prompt.
eofwrite	*string*	End-of-file indicator for the ˜> command. Default is ^D.
eol	*character list*	List of characters used for end of line (and therefore, to recognize tilde escapes).
escape	*character*	The escape character. The default is ˜ (tilde).
kill	*character*	Line delete character to use if echo check fails.
resend	*number*	The number of times to resend a line if echo check fails.

Table 5-2: Taylor cu Environment Variables (continued)

Variable	Type	Description
timeout	*number*	Number of seconds to wait when doing echo checking, or waiting for the **echonl** character.
verbose	*Boolean*	If true (the default), prints information during file transfers.

Capturing Output of a Session

Sometimes (for example, when calling up an on-line database) you may want to capture the output of your remote session. This is also a brute force way of copying files from a non-UNIX system, since the files of interest could be displayed on the screen, then extracted from the capture log afterwards with a text editor.

tip supports capturing output via the **script** and **record** environment variables. **cu** does not support capturing output, but the UNIX **script** or **tee** commands can be used to save the output from an entire **cu** session.

Using script

The **script** command starts a new shell for you in which all output from commands you type are logged to a file (named **typescript** by default). For example:

```
$ script
Script started, file is typescript
$ cu ...
```

After terminating **cu**, type ^D or **exit** to end the subshell and output capturing started by **script**.

Using tee

The **tee** command is a "pipe splitting" utility. Output piped through **tee** is copied—one copy goes, as usual, to standard output, the other can be piped on to other programs or put into a file. If the file already exists, it will be overwritten.

tee is not a generalized scripting utility since it will only work with the output of a single command. However, in the case of **cu**, the entire dialogue with the remote system can be thought of as the standard output of a single **cu** command. The result is nearly the same as with **script**.

To make a transcript of a **cu** session with **tee**, type:

```
$ cu ... | tee scriptname
```

Other communications programs, such as **kermit**, also support capturing output, and unlike the **script** or **tee** commands, allow it to be turned on and off during the session.

You will find that capturing output this way captures *everything*, including things you'd rather not see, such as your typing errors, extra carriage return or linefeed characters, or control characters from running screen-oriented programs like the **emacs** or **vi** editors. If you're careful with what commands you run when using **cu** under a capture command, you should be able to filter out the unwanted characters without too much difficulty.

Call Me Modem

One little-known feature of the UUCP suite on some UNIX System V systems is the **ct** command.* **ct** is the reverse of the **cu** command: while **cu** is meant for calling a remote computer that will present a login prompt and let you sign on, when **ct** calls, it supplies the login prompt and waits for someone sitting at the remote modem to sign on. **ct** is most often used when a user wants to "reverse the charges" for a toll call to the remote system, or when a site's security policy mandates that remote connections should be set up via dial-out calls rather than dial-in.

To use **ct**, the user dials in the usual way and logs on. Then he invokes **ct**, supplying the telephone number where he is calling from. Finally, he logs out, hangs up, sets his modem for auto-answer, and waits for **ct** to call back.

When the phone rings, the user's modem answers the line, and if all is working properly, a login prompt from the remote system appears on the screen. The user can now sign in to the remote system, without worrying about the phone bill.

The catch with using **ct** is that both you and the remote system need to terminate the existing call before callback can take place. Unless you tell it otherwise, **ct** will try to hang up your current session before dialing out. But depending on the types of modems and the behavior of the local telephone exchange, the modem and phone line on the remote system may not be freed up in time when **ct** tries to dial out.

---

* ct stands for "call terminal."

Getting **ct** to work usually requires a few trial runs. The best method for trying out **ct** is in a place with an unused phone line nearby (with or without a
modem attached). From your terminal, use **ct −h** to call into the free line:

```
$ ct -h -s 9600 5554499
```

If the called phone rings, you know that **ct** is able to find a modem and dial
out. If you have a modem available, let it answer **ct**'s call, and see if you
can log in to the calling system.

The ct Command

ct hangs up the current session, calls a terminal at the specified telephone number (*telno*) using a UUCP dial-out device that supports the
specified *speed*, and starts a login process for that terminal.

```
ct [ -h ] [ -v ] [ -s speed ] [ -w num ] [ -x num ] telno
```

Options

−h   Don't hang up the current session.

−v   Verbose mode—issue descriptive messages as **ct** pro-
            gresses.

−w *num*   Wait up to *num* minutes for a modem to become available.

−x *num*   Set debugging level *num*. Higher values of *num* will cause
            more messages to be printed.

We've had the best success with **ct** when invoking it through a batch command, such as the UNIX **at** batch facility.[*] This way you can schedule the **ct**
command to run in the near future, giving yourself enough lead time to log
off and let the modem and phone line reset before **ct** makes its move.
Here's an example:

```
$ echo "ct -s 9600 -v 5551509" | at now + 1 minute
Job c00d10db9.00 will be executed using /bin/sh
$
```

---

[*] On some systems, the **at** facility is restricted to the users listed in a permissions file such as
/var/adm/cron/at.allow. You may need to add your username to this file before you can use **at**.

This schedules the quoted **ct** command to run one minute later, which should be enough time to log out gracefully and free up the modem. The output of **ct** will be emailed to you, so that you can diagnose any problems that occurred during the dialout. When you are satisfied with the reliability of your callback procedure, you can drop the **−v** option so that **ct** will run silently.

Another strategy is to use the **nohup** command to invoke a shell script with the desired **ct** command line:

```
#!/bin/sh

sleep 5
nohup ct -s9600 -w5 -h -x9 5559999 > $HOME/callme.log 2>&1 &
```

If the above script is saved to a file named *callme*, you could run it with:

```
$ nohup callme &
```

And immediately log out. **ct** will try for up to five minutes (the **−w5** option) to obtain a modem and dial the specified number.

A limitation of **ct** is that it does not let you specify which modem to use when dialing out. It always chooses the first available device that matches the specified speed.

6

Using
Electronic Mail

Overview

Electronic mail is one of the most useful things a computer can do—keeping you in touch with friends, relatives, and perfect strangers all around the world. Although you are probably familiar with sending short notes or even long letters via electronic mail, you might not have realized that you have been using a file transfer system the whole time. This chapter shows you how you can use electronic mail, instead of individual UUCP commands, to send files back and forth.

Why use electronic mail to transfer files? The reasons are legion:

- If you are concerned about privacy and the integrity of your data, it is much safer to use email than the UUCP public directory.

- If you are sending files to a single user, it is simple and convenient.

- You can send your data to anyone in the world (assuming your computer has access to the world-wide email network), not just the comparatively few systems with which you share UUCP connections.

- With the right mail-reading software on both sides, you can send text, graphics, audio files, or a file of any format as a binary attachment, and they will all be handled correctly when they arrive in the other user's mailbox.

Although the information in this chapter refers frequently to the Internet and Internet connections, if you're using a private network on a desert island somewhere, you can still use all these techniques to transfer files—there's no particular dependence on the Internet, just on the commands and software used to send and receive the email messages.

Email Addressing

The standard Internet format for an electronic mail address is:

    username@domainname

username is the name (or mail alias) of the user to which you want to send email, @ is the symbol used to separate the username from the rest of the address, and *domainname* is the computer name or institutional name for the computer system to which the email is destined. If you don't specify *@domainname*, your email is assumed to be addressed to a user on your local system.

An older form of addressing uses the exclamation point as a separator between "hops," which are different systems in a chain expected to relay a message from one system to the next. This kind of addressing dates back to the days when the only network links were UUCP links and you needed to explicitly specify the route that a message would take. An example would be:

    fatcat!raspi!moose!brad

This example sends email to the host *fatcat*, which relays it to the host *raspi*, which then relays it to *moose*, where the email is delivered to the local user *brad*. This type of addressing is more or less obsolete, although it still works in most places that have UUCP hookups.

If a system supports only this form of old-fashioned mail addresses, it can still receive mail from the Internet if one of its UUCP neighbors is willing to act as a relay. But the mail messages will need to be addressed along the lines of:

    brad%moose%raspi@fatcat.feelines.com

Assuming that *fatcat.feelines.com* is the Internet name of *fatcat*, this is the equivalent of the route shown in the previous example. The percent sign (%) is the modern way of specifying routes—each host in the chain, upon receiving the message, discards the domainname portion of the message, including the @, changes the rightmost % to an @, and then tries to resend the message.

It's generally not a good idea to mix the ! and @ on the same mail address:

```
raspi!moose!brad@fatcat.feelines.com
```

This kind of addressing often fails because there is no standard way to route it. It will usually be routed as in the previous example, first to *fat-cat.feelines.com*, who sends it to *raspi!moose!brad*, but some mail handling programs will try to send it to *raspi* first, and fail since *raspi* is not one of their local UUCP neighbors.

These kinds of gymnastics with mail routing were once very common, but are rarely necessary nowadays. You want to avoid them whenever possible, usually by connecting to an ISP that will help you get your own domain name.

Why Can't I ...

You may be asking at this point, "Why bother reading the rest of this chapter? Can't I just include any file I want to send out into my email message, and off it goes?"

It turns out that most text files of reasonable length can indeed be sent this way. But when you want to send binary files, or text files that are very large or have nonstandard characters, it just won't work anymore.

Transparency

When you send a message from point A to point B, you'd like the message to arrive exactly the way you sent it. That quality of transmission is called *data transparency*. Unfortunately, the standards that have evolved for electronic mail guarantee only that characters in the regular seven-bit ASCII character set (character values 32 through 126) will always be sent properly. Characters with the eighth bit set (characters whose values range from 128 to 255, often used in non-English texts) may be converted to seven-bit data. Control characters (characters in the range from 0 through 31, and sometimes also 128 through 159) may also get converted or deleted by electronic mail-handling programs.

Data Integrity

When a friend sends you an electronic mail letter, you don't necessarily know that you are reading the entire letter exactly as she sent it. But as long as the letter reads properly and there are no sentences suddenly unfinished or partial paragraphs floating about, you assume that the letter has arrived undamaged.

Now suppose that the electronic mail letter is your company's customer list and contains a thousand names, addresses, and phone numbers. How do you read through the entire message to see if any pieces are missing? If you are sending important data via electronic mail, you need some scheme whereby your correspondent can tell whether the entire file has arrived successfully.

Maximum Message Size

Every electronic mail system enforces some kind of maximum message size—usually by placing an upper limit on the size of a message in transit. This limit will vary from one computer to another depending on system capacity, the bandwidth of the system's communications links, or the particular software running on that system. On Internet links, these limits are usually one megabyte (1,000,000 bytes), so most users won't run into this problem. But many mail-handling programs default to a mere 100,000 bytes on a UUCP link. If your mail passes through one of those systems, you will probably need to chop your message into smaller chunks, put each chunk in a single message, and have your recipient piece them back together. Since this is a tedious, error-prone task, it's best to entrust it to a program, such as the ones described in this chapter.

Sending Files via Email

As you may suspect, there are various ways to get around these limitations on electronic mail. All of them involve converting binary files into ASCII characters that will not be molested by electronic mail handling software. The solutions differ only in how much burden they place upon the user to perform the conversion, and how difficult it is to restore the files to their original form.

MIME

The simplest solution is to use mail software that supports the newest standards for Internet mail, known as MIME (Multipurpose Internet Mail Extensions). MIME-capable mail software includes the ability to "attach" any file to your message. Although the regular part of your email message can be read with any standard mail program, your recipient will need MIME-capable software in order to properly decode the attachments. Any file you attach with MIME-capable mail software, even a text file, will be encoded into a stream of ASCII characters that looks like garbage to a human onlooker, but can be easily decoded back into the original file with a MIME-compatible mail reader.

One popular MIME-capable mail program is the **pine** mail client.[*] Take a look at the sample screen from **pine**, in which the user is sending a message and attaching a file to it. **pine** provides a user-friendly menu at the bottom of the screen that includes a Help option.

Sample pine Screen

```
PINE 3.91   COMPOSE MESSAGE                    Folder: INBOX   20 Messages

To      : editor@ora.com (Walter Editor)
Cc      :
Attchmnt: 1. /home/hildy/draft3.doc (131 KB) "News Story Draft"
Subject : Draft story attached
----- Message Text -----
You'll never.believe what happened to me today!  Read all about
it in the attached file...


        --- Hildy



^G Get Help   ^X Send      ^R Read File ^Y Prev Pg   ^K Cut Text  ^O Postpone
^C Cancel     ^J Justify   ^W Where is  ^V Next Pg   ^U UnCut Text^T To Spell
```

Because the MIME extensions support error checking and preserve the original name of the file, they are the simplest and most reliable way to transfer files. They also place little burden upon your correspondent, as long as they have a MIME-capable mail reader.[†]

---

[*] Actually, **pine** is a *mail user agent*, which is a program that presents mail to a human being. Programs that present mail to other computers are called *mail transfer agents*. Mail user agents you're likely to run into on a UNIX system include **pine**, **elm** and the ubiquitous **mail** or **mailx**.

[†] Numerous MIME-capable programs and conversion tools are available; for more information, visit the *comp.mail.mime* newsgroup.

uuencode and uudecode

The original UUCP solution for transferring binary files via email is a pair of programs called **uuencode** and **uudecode**. Although MIME, atob/btoa, or **shar** (described in the next section) are all better solutions at this point, it's still good to learn about **uuencode** and **uudecode** because you'll no doubt receive mail in this format one day.

The **uuencode** command, which can be obtained for both Unix and non-Unix systems, converts any file into ASCII characters that can be safely sent out via email. To decode the file, the recipient must break out the encoded portion of the message and feed it to **uudecode**. Here's how a user might send a binary file via **uudecode**:

```
$ uuencode < /home/tim/myfile.bin myfile.bin > myfile.uu
```

This creates a file *myfile.uu* which will contain something like this:

```
begin 644 myfile.bin
M66]U=&@Z(%1H92!F:65L9"!!<P!D:7-T:6YG=6ES:&5S(&YO="!O;FQY(&)F
M<F]M('1H92!S;WW5L+B'@5AE!F;0*5&AE(&9O<F4N!AF0=AE1E:6;E
M=R!A;F0@=&UI<W0'07)E(&%L;"!B=70?070@VYE+C!VE:&5T:&5R(&]D
M96Q@*W#8VE(87987N"N=I=F4@;71E(&%S(&9N921;EN=61E(%970$@964<VEN
M99RP*06YD('1H<F]U9V@@7D@<V]F("!L970@=65@;75S=6:6,F(=<FEN'A0
M<E<@,:@862869L(&]09'86YF(-O=#9R;"7D9R;VM=;XAVE@@9!5@9&5P
7=&@@;V8=&AE(&=O;G4;B!B;!B;W=L++@IO
'
end
```

Note that the first line of a **uuencoded** file contains the filename and a file protection mode that will be used for recreating the file. The next few lines are the ASCII encoding of the file data, and the "end" line finishes the **uuencoded** output.

Upon receiving this data as email, the recipient would save the message into a file, go into the file with a text editor, delete the mail headers and other lines up to the "begin" line, and save it into a new file (we'll call it "thing"). To decode the data, one would:

```
$ uudecode < thing
```

And *myfile.bin* would be recreated.

One disadvantage of using **uuencode** and **uudecode** is that they have hardly any error checking. If a line of email is lost or truncated, **uudecode** will probably still create a file for you, but it won't match the original anymore. Another problem is that files created with **uuencode** are as much as 40% larger than the originals.

You can address these problems by using a file compression utility like **compress**, **zip**, or **gzip** before encoding the file. Although this creates an extra uncompression step for the recipient (and you have to make sure they have the appropriate uncompression software available), it prevents a damaged file from going by unnoticed, and has the added advantage of making your email message substantially smaller. For example:

```
$ compress myfile.bin
$ uuencode < myfile.bin.Z myfile.bin.Z > myfile.uu
$ mailx -s "your file enclosed" boris@koshka.feelines.com < myfile.uu
```

Whether or not you need the extra error checking, compressing files is always a good idea if you are sending large amounts of data via email.

shar and unshar

shar stands for **sh**ell **ar**chive. It packs multiple files into a single shell script that, when executed, recreates the original files. Version 4.0 of **shar**, which should be included with the average Linux system, can be told to run **compress** (or **gzip**) and **uuencode** on the source files, which allows the resulting shell archive to be sent as email. **shar** will also split the file into chunks below a specified limit, which lets you send a large file, piece by piece, through an electronic mail system that refuses large messages.

unshar isn't strictly necessary—all it does is look through the files you give it for mail headers, removes them, and then pipes the resulting file into the UNIX shell */bin/sh*. However, **uudecode** and the right decompression program must be available to decode the individual files in the archive. The shell script created by **shar** also tests the received files to make sure they are the same size as the source files on the original system.

shar can be retrieved from any GNU mirror site. The primary location is *ftp://prep.ai.mit.edu/pub/gnu/sharutils-4.2.tar.gz*.

Tarmail, btoa, and atob

Another set of conversion programs that have been floating around for a few years are **btoa**, **atob**, and **tarmail**. **btoa** and **atob** perform the same function as **uuencode** and **uudecode** respectively, but they are more reliable, easier to use, and have a smaller file size penalty than **uuencode**.

When you encode a file with **btoa** (which stands for **b**inary **to** **A**SCII), it also outputs a checksum that will be used by **atob** to test the integrity of the received file. **atob** is also quite forgiving about its input—there's no need to strip mail headers—you just pipe an email message formatted by **btoa** into

atob, which then skips any extra headers or message until it finds the
encoded binary file. Here's how a user would send a binary file called
myfile.bin with **btoa**:

```
$ btoa < myfile.bin > myfile.tmp
$ mailx -s "Binary File Enclosed" arnold@ruby.ora.com < myfile.tmp
```

Usually included with **btoa** and **atob** are two companion shell scripts called
tarmail and **untarmail**. **tarmail** accepts a list of files (or directories) and first
uses the UNIX **tar** command to wrap the files up into a tar archive (a single
file that can be expanded back out into the original multiple files), then runs
the UNIX **compress** command to shrink the size of the archive file, runs **btoa**
to convert the file into an ASCII image that can be sent through email, and
then calls the UNIX **mail** program to send the data to its destination. The
untarmail script is called by the recipient to perform the reverse procedure.
For example:

```
$ tarmail walter@ora.com "latest news stories" page1 page2 page3
```

would send the files *page1*, *page2*, and *page3* after first piping them through
tar, **compress**, and **btoa**. The recipient can feed the entire message to **untarmail**, or save it to a file, run **atob**, **uncompress**, and **tar** by hand if desired.

btoa and the other programs listed in this section are available from many
sources; see Appendix A, *Useful Shell Scripts and Programs*, for more information.

tarmailchunky and untarmailchunky

A handy extension to **btoa** and **atob** is the **tarmailchunky** command and its
counterpart **untarmailchunky**. **tarmailchunky** is like **tarmail**, except that
before it mails the compressed and encoded archive, it splits it up into
chunks less than 64,000 bytes and sends each chunk as a separate email
message. This lets you bypass a mail link that has a maximum message size
smaller than the file you want to send. Your recipient should save the mail
messages as individual files, and then run **untarmailchunky** with the list of
files (in order). **untarmailchunky** will strip the mail headers on the individual
files, run them through **atob** and **uncompress**, and call **tar** to unpack the
original files.

tarmailchunky and **untarmailchunky** are short shell scripts, and easy to modify to your own needs. We list them in their entirety in Appendix A.

7

Introduction to UUCP Administration

> *Dealing with* uucp *... is an advanced topic best left to system administrators and those with iron stomachs.*
> *—Linux Configuration and Installation, by Patrick Volkerding, Kevin Reichard, and Eric F. Johnson*
>
> *The animal featured on the cover of Managing UUCP and Usenet is a grizzly bear ... the most aggressive of the bear family.*
> *—Colophon from Managing UUCP and Usenet*

Grin and Bear It

Despite rumors to the contrary, you don't need an iron stomach to administer a UUCP connection. What you do need is a basic understanding of computer communications and the patience to apply it when problems develop.

Each system on a UUCP network has files that describe the other systems to which it is linked, and what types of communications links are available. Setting up the communications links (i.e., modems and serial connections) and creating these description files is the primary task of the UUCP administrator. But once UUCP is up and running, it requires minimal supervision and maintenance.

Versions of UUCP

The first UUCP system was built in 1976 by Mike Lesk at AT&T Bell Laboratories as part of a research project. It became such a success that an improved version developed by Mike Lesk, David Nowitz and Greg Chesson was distributed with UNIX Version 7, and became known as **Version 2**

UUCP. Version 2 was updated in 1981, and additional updates were released by AT&T in System V Release 1 (SVR1) and System V Release 2 (SVR2).

Meanwhile, an independent set of updates was made at Duke University. While the Duke UUCP is no longer used, it became the basis for the versions shipped with the Berkeley Software Distribution from the University of California at Berkeley (BSD 4.*x*), as well as with DEC's Ultrix and older versions of Sun's SunOS. BSD 4.3 UUCP was a descendent of this version.

With System V release 3 of UNIX, AT&T began distributing a new version of UUCP that had been developed (in 1983) by Peter **Honey**man, David **A.** Nowitz, and **Brian** E. Redman. They rewrote UUCP to iron out some deficiencies in Version 2, make UUCP administration easier, and provide support for more advanced communications devices and networks. This version became popularly known as **HoneyDanBer** UUCP (derived from the author's names), but most vendor documentation today calls it "Basic Networking Utilities," or BNU, which was AT&T's official name for the product. We will refer to it as **BNU UUCP** throughout this book.

The latest version of BNU appeared in UNIX System V release 4 (SVR4). It included a few new features such as the ability to resume aborted file transfers and an improved implementation of UUCP's main file transfer protocol.

BNU UUCP is used by most major vendors, including Sun (both SunOS 4.1 and Solaris), IBM (AIX), SCO (SCO UNIX), SGI (IRIX), DEC (Digital UNIX), HP (HP-UX), AT&T GIS (NCR), and others. Some of these vendors based their UUCP on the SVR4 version, while others (notably IBM, SCO, and HP) appear to descend from earlier versions.

One commercial UNIX that does not use BNU is BSD/OS from Berkely Software Design, Inc. (BSDI). **BSD/OS UUCP** is an entirely different UUCP, derived from a version commissioned by Rick Adams and made available by UUNET Technologies. This version mimics the BSD 4.3 Version 2-based implementation, but was written entirely from scratch to avoid the copyright problems associated with software based on UNIX Version 7 source code. The BSD/OS UUCP includes some BNU-style features and a few bells and whistles not found in any other UUCP version.

The newest version of UUCP is called **Taylor UUCP**, after its author, Ian Lance Taylor. Frustrated by the inflexibility of the Version 2-based UUCP on his system (he wanted to change the UUCP nodename without changing the system's hostname), he ended up writing his own version and making it publicly available under the GNU Public License. Taylor UUCP soon became a standard part of the "free Unix" distributions (Linux, NetBSD, and

FreeBSD), and has matured to the point where it rivals (and often exceeds) vendor versions of UUCP in features and performance. The current version as of this writing is 1.06.1.

Taylor UUCP has many new features not found in vendor versions of UUCP, including:

- A new UUCP protocol that can transfer files faster and let UUCP send and receive files at the same time, potentially doubling your communications bandwidth.

- Another new UUCP protocol that can communicate over a link that uses XON/XOFF flow control.

- Support for some of the SVR4 extensions, such as restarting aborted file transfers.

- Significantly less use of CPU time than many other UUCP packages.

- Improved modem dialing and device handling abilities.

- The ability to use a new, easier to read configuration file format as well as configuration files from the other versions of UUCP.

- The ability to maintain a separate username and password database instead of using */etc/passwd*.

- Many, many new configuration parameters giving the system administrator more control over aspects of UUCP's behavior.

Fortunately, the UUCP standards are defined well enough so that the different varieties of UUCP generally have no problems communicating with each other.

Which Version Do I Have?

If you do not know the version of UUCP that is installed on your system, there are several ways to find out. First, try your system's documentation— the paper manuals included with your system or the commands **man uucico** or **man uucp** should give you a few hints. If you see the words "BNU," "Basic Networking Utilities," "HDB" or "HoneyDanBer" mentioned, or mention of the *Systems* or *Devices* files, you have BNU UUCP. If you see references to the files *L.sys* or *L-Devices*, your system has Version 2 or one of its variants.

Detecting Taylor UUCP is simple: running **uuname −v** (or any UUCP command with the −v option) on a Taylor system will print out a copyright notice and the version number.

Another test is to list out the directory */usr/lib/uucp* or */etc/uucp*. If it contains files named *Systems* or *Devices*, then you are using BNU UUCP. If you see *L.sys* or *L-devices*, it is Version 2 or BSD. However, remember that Taylor UUCP can be configured to use other configuration directories or told to use BNU or Version 2 configuration files. And some systems will not contain any configuration files until the system administrator creates them.

Which Version Do I Want?

If you don't like the version of UUCP that came with your commercial UNIX system, you can always install Taylor UUCP. Many sites have replaced their vendor UUCP with Taylor UUCP, especially ISPs or other environments with a large number of UUCP links. Many of Taylor UUCP's features, in particular the bidirectional protocols, are only available when both sides of the link are using Taylor UUCP.

UUCP Versions In This Book

This book tries to cover all modern versions of UUCP running on UNIX systems: BNU, Taylor, and BSD/OS. When space permits, we'll also mention some of the features found (or not found) in older Version 2 or BSD 4.3 implementations.

Scope of This Section

The second part of this book is for system administrators who want to install and manage a UUCP network. It is divided into the following chapters:

Chapter 8, *How UUCP Works*, gives a conceptual overview of how UUCP file transfers work, with an emphasis on how the UUCP programs make use of various configuration files that you, as the administrator, need to set up.

Chapter 9, *The Physical Connection*, describes RS-232 cabling, the theory of serial communications, the UNIX system files that control serial communications parameters, and the control of incoming logins on serial ports.

Chapter 10, *Setting Up a UUCP Link*, describes the UUCP configuration files and the procedure for establishing communication with other systems. This chapter assumes you have already set up a physical link, as described in Chapter 9.

Chapter 11, *Making Sure the Link Works*, describes how to test a UUCP link and details the part of setting up a link that is as much art as science: figuring out the "chat script" used to log in to another system.

Chapter 12, *Access and Security Considerations*, describes the mechanisms that you can use to increase or decrease the level of security for your system, and how to prevent your UUCP connections from being misused.

Chapter 13, *UUCP Administration*, describes the UUCP administrative shell scripts that perform routine maintenance. It also covers tasks that the system administrator must carry out periodically to keep the system running smoothly.

Chapter 14, *Troubleshooting UUCP*, outlines how to methodically track down problems with your UUCP links and provides pointers to other resources that can help you solve your problems.

Appendix A, *Useful Shell Scripts and Programs*, lists scripts and programs that heavy users of the UUCP commands might find of interest.

Appendix B, *The Spool Directory/Working Files*, explains the innards of the UUCP spool directory and how UUCP stores its pending jobs.

Appendix C, *Status and Error Messages*, lists the various messages you may see from UUCP and explains what problems might be causing them.

Appendix D, *UUCP for Non-UNIX Platforms*, provides pointers to UUCP software that runs on non-UNIX platforms such as the Apple Macintosh, IBM PC, or Amiga.

Appendix E, *Sendmail and UUCP*, gives a brief overview of how to set up the **sendmail** mail system to work with UUCP.

Appendix F, *News and UUCP*, explains how Usenet News software such as **C/News** and **inn** work with UUCP.

Appendix G, *The UUCP Mapping Project*, describes the world-wide UUCP nodename registry and how it is used for mail routing.

Appendix H, *UUCP Management Tools*, lists scripts and programs that you may find useful to help manage your UUCP site.

Appendix I, *Setting Up a Modem*, explains how to set up a typical Hayes-compatible modem for use with UUCP.

Appendix J, *UUCP Protocol Internals*, goes into more detail about the different UUCP protocols available, and how to choose between them.

Appendix K, *The UUCP g Protocol*, provides a detailed explanation of the standard **g** protocol used over telephone and serial lines. This will help you understand better how UUCP works, and why it sometimes doesn't.

Appendix L, *Other Resources*, lists other sources of information about UUCP and a few related topics.

We're Rooting for You...

This handbook assumes that you are at least superficially familiar with UNIX system administration and that you have superuser (root) privileges. Most of the examples that follow will show the system prompt "#" to indicate that the commands shown can be executed only as the user *root*, either because of file permissions or because the command itself is restricted. Commands that are shown preceded by the system prompt "$" can be executed by any user. All the command prompt and shell script examples in this section are for a Bourne-like shell, such as **sh**, **ksh**, or **bash**.

Please note that even though we have tried to cover all versions of UUCP in current use, there may be differences in syntax from system to system. Vendors often make minor enhancements or changes when implementing software on a particular system. Please refer to the online documentation, or reference manuals supplied with your system if the examples supplied here do not work as shown. Also, if a Taylor UUCP example in this book does not work for you, it may be that you have an older version—run **uuname** −**v** and see if you are at version 1.06.1 or above. If not, consider upgrading to the current release.

8

How UUCP Works

A UUCP configuration consists of a number of related programs. However, from the users' point of view—or from the point of view of a mail or news system that transfers data via UUCP—the interface to UUCP is composed of only two programs:

- **uucp** is used to request a file transfer to or from a remote machine. It works much like **cp**, with added syntax for addressing remote machines.

- **uux** is used to request execution of a command on a remote machine. The commands usually invoked this way are **rmail** for sending mail, and **rnews** for sending Usenet news articles.

From the system administrator's viewpoint, there are many more components of UUCP. A background program, or *daemon*, called **uucico** sets up the connections between two systems and transfers files or execution requests back and forth.[*] Another daemon, called **uuxqt**, is invoked to process execution requests from a remote system. In order for these daemons to do their jobs, there are a handful of configuration files that need to be in place; they give information on the systems to be called, and the mechanisms to be used to place the call. It is the job of the administrator to set up these files.

There are also a number of administrative programs and scripts that usually run automatically via the UNIX **cron** facility, which may need manual intervention on very busy networks or if problems occur.

---

[*] Most UUCP enthusiasts pronounce **uucico** as "you-you-cheek-oh," as in the name "Chico."

UUCP has a well-deserved reputation for being difficult to set up. However, the setup instructions will make a lot more sense if you first understand how the whole system works. When it comes time to administer a running network, this understanding will prove even more important. So let's take a moment to look behind the scenes.

Behind the Scenes

UUCP is a "store-and-forward" network. Requests for file transfers or remote execution of commands on another system are not executed immediately but are spooled for execution until communication is established between the two systems. Depending on how the configuration files are set up, communication may be established immediately or may wait until a later time. (For example, many systems wait for evening, when rates are lower, to establish a telephone connection with a distant system.)

The **uucp** program itself does not copy files from system to system, nor does **uux** actually execute commands on a remote system. When a user invokes **uucp** or **uux** or sends email to a user on a remote system, these two things happen:

- A workfile containing information such as the name of the source file and destination file, **uucp** or **uux** options, the type of request (send, receive, or execute), and priority or *grade* of the request is created in UUCP's workspace directory, usually named */var/spool/uucp*. Depending on the version of UUCP you're using and the command-line options specified on the UUCP request, a data file may be created that contains a copy of the file to be transferred. For remote execution requests (including electronic mail transfers), data files are always created.

- The **uucico** daemon is called upon to actually make the transfer. **uucico** is usually started by **uux** or **uucp** whenever a new UUCP request is queued. It should also be invoked on a regular basis (usually hourly) by the UNIX **cron** facility so that any jobs still in the queue will get serviced.[*]

When **uucico** starts up, it scans the spool directory for workfiles (jobs), attempts to contact other systems, and then executes the instructions in the workfiles.

---

[*] In BNU, **cron** invokes a program called **uusched**, which invokes **uucico** for each system that has work pending. The extra step allows UUCP to randomize the order of the calls to neighboring systems.

The workfiles contain a description of the files you'll transfer and the system to which you'll transfer them, but they do not tell **uucico** when or how to do the transfer. This information is contained in a set of configuration files, usually in the directory */etc/uucp*. Together, the various configuration files form a kind of database for the systems, phone numbers, modems, and serial ports that UUCP uses. The system administrator's job is to set up this database, a job that is harder than it needs to be because the format for BNU and Version 2 UUCP configuration files aren't all that easy to understand. Taylor UUCP lets you use a new style of configuration files that is more "human readable."

Configuration Files

Regardless of the version of UUCP running on your system, the same general information is needed in the configuration database. When **uucico** wants to reach a remote system, it needs to know these things:

- The name of each system that can be reached via UUCP

- The time of day **uucico** is allowed to call each system

- The physical link (i.e., a modem, serial connection, or network connection) used to reach each system

- The telephone numbers needed to dial each system—or for systems connected over a TCP/IP network, the appropriate network addresses and port numbers

- The login names and passwords to use to sign onto each system

In BNU UUCP, this information is stored in a configuration file called *Systems*. In Taylor UUCP, this file is named *sys*, and in BSD 4.3, BSD/OS, and Version 2, *L.sys*.

The system, on the other side, that receives the UUCP call also needs to know a few things before it lets a remote system use its resources. Here are a couple of things it needs to know:

- That the calling systems's user ID is allowed to use UUCP

- The commands that the calling system is allowed to execute, and the directories and files to which the calling system may read and write

Since UUCP uses a variety of devices to communicate with a remote system, it keeps the definitions of the devices it uses in a separate configuration file, known as *Devices* (BNU), *port* (Taylor), or *L-devices* (BSD and Version 2).

For example, for UUCP connections being made over a modem, a BNU *Systems* file contains the word **ACU**, which stands for Automatic Call Unit, or automatic dialer. The definition of **ACU**, namely how many modems there are and to which serial ports they are attached, is kept in the *Devices* file. This lets the system administrator change the types or number of modems on the system without interfering with the UUCP connection information.

For connections over a modem link, **uucico** must look up how to dial the modem. This information is stored in yet another configuration file, called *Dialers* in BNU and *dial* in Taylor.[*] The exact procedures for dialing a remote system may vary from one brand of modem to the next, and because the information is in a separate file, it can be changed without disturbing other UUCP definitions.

There are also files that control which parts of your filesystem UUCP will make accessible to a remote system, and which commands UUCP will let a remote system execute. BNU keeps this information in a file called *Permissions*. Taylor UUCP keeps the access control (and many other configuration features) in the *sys* file along with the systems connectivity entries, and Version 2 has two files called *USERFILE* and *L.cmds*.

The access control and security abilities of the different versions of UUCP vary widely; Chapter 12, *Access and Security Considerations*, tries to make sense of it all.

As you can see, a fair amount of information needs to be put in place before a simple file transfer can occur. And it all has to be correct, or UUCP will sullenly refuse to connect to other systems or transfer data. BNU and Taylor both provide an auxiliary command (**uucheck −v** in BNU, **uuchk** in Taylor) that parses the configuration files, points out any major problems, and interprets the configurations so that you can see if the UUCP system is being given the right instructions.

Figure 8−1 displays the sequence of events for a successful call from a BNU system to another system.

---

[*] BSD 4.3 has a few pre-defined dialing types, but no configurable scripts as in BNU. Version 2 has no configurable dialing, except for some very old (and obsolete) versions that had dialing database files called *acucap* or *modemcap*.

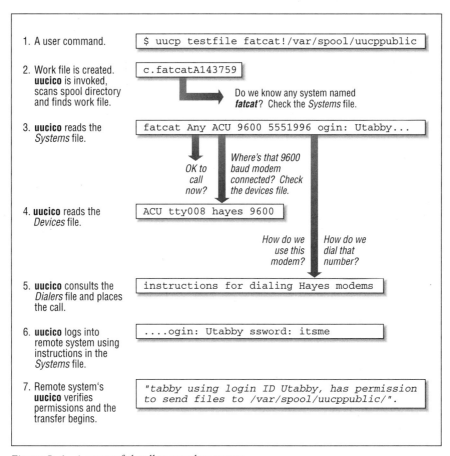

The figure content:

1. A user command.

```
$ uucp testfile fatcat!/var/spool/uucppublic
```

2. Work file is created. **uucico** is invoked, scans spool directory and finds work file.

```
c.fatcatA143759
```

Do we know any system named *fatcat*? Check the *Systems* file.

3. **uucico** reads the *Systems* file.

```
fatcat Any ACU 9600 5551996 ogin: Utabby...
```

OK to call now?

Where's that 9600 baud modem connected? Check the devices file.

4. **uucico** reads the *Devices* file.

```
ACU tty008 hayes 9600
```

How do we use this modem?

How do we dial that number?

5. **uucico** consults the *Dialers* file and places the call.

```
instructions for dialing Hayes modems
```

6. **uucico** logs into remote system using instructions in the *Systems* file.

```
....ogin: Utabby ssword: itsme
```

7. Remote system's **uucico** verifies permissions and the transfer begins.

```
"tabby using login ID Utabby, has permission
to send files to /var/spool/uucppublic/".
```

Figure 8–1: A successful call to another system

Possible Hitches

There are several reasons why the file transfer may not occur immediately. First of all, the systems file may explicitly restrict outgoing calls to a particular time. Second, either the outgoing telephone line from the local system or the incoming telephone line on the remote system may be busy.

If any of these things occurs, **uucico** is not able to make the connection. Instead, it will leave a status file in the spool directory that contains the time last called and a message describing the status of the request. The next time **uucico** is invoked, it will try again, as long as a minimum retry period has elapsed. This minimum period is designed to keep UUCP from tying up the telephone lines trying to call a remote system that is down. The minimum retry period usually starts at 55 minutes.

All UUCP versions except for Version 2 use an *exponential backoff* algorithm. The retry period is shorter at first and lengthens as the number of failures increases. Some versions allow you to specify an alternate retry period on a system-by-system basis.

Note that the retry period is the minimum period within which **uucico** can try this system again, once it has been invoked. The retry period does not by itself cause **uucico** to be invoked; this happens via a **cron** job (or a user command).

Figure 8-2 follows the life of a UUCP request as **uucico** tries to connect to the remote system and transfer the file. Routine status messages are listed on the left; possible problem messages are listed on the right. You can look up what the messages mean in Appendix C, *Status and Error Messages*.

Connection: The Chat Script

When **uucico** connects to the remote side, it needs to provide a username and password to the remote system. This part of the dialogue between the two systems is driven by a "chat script," which tells **uucico** what characters to expect from the remote side and what characters to send in response. Under control of the chat script, an automatic login can be performed.

The chat script consists of alternating "expect" and "send" fields. A sample (and simple) chat script might look like:[*]

```
ogin: Utabby word: meow
```

And **uucico** would interpret this script as follows:

- Wait for (expect) the character string "...ogin:" (a login prompt) to arrive from the remote host. All other received data is ignored until the expect string is matched.

- When "ogin:" is received, send the characters "Utabby" (the username UUCP will use on the remote system). By default, send strings are followed by a carriage return, unless you specify otherwise.

- Wait for (expect) the character string "...word:" to arrive from the remote host. This is the password prompt from the remote system.

---

[*] Chat scripts are explained in detail in Chapter 11, *Setting Up a UUCP Link*.

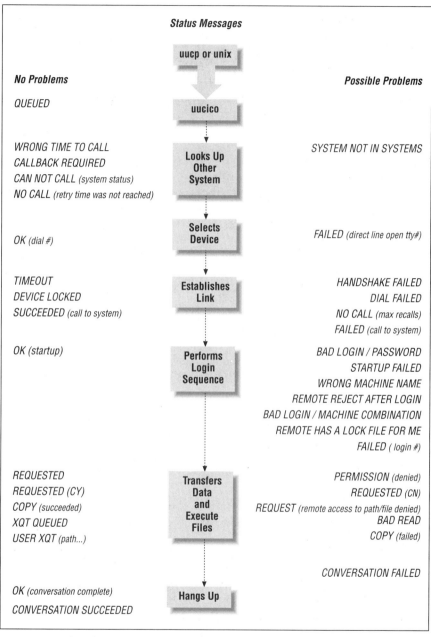

Figure 8-2: The life of a UUCP request

- When "word:" is received, send "meow" (and that default carriage return again). This sends the password, and presumably, once you've gotten past this point, the login is successful. If another **uucico** appears on the remote side, the UUCP link can proceed.

Unfortunately, most chat scripts are not this simple—sometimes it is difficult to write a reliable chat script because of the numerous things that can go wrong when dialing a remote system.

Once connected via the chat script, the two **uucico** programs—one on each system—work in tandem to make the transfer. First, they introduce themselves by exchanging their UUCP nodenames. Usually, both systems must have an entry in their systems files in order for each to permit a conversation, but a trusting site can be set up to allow an unknown site to transfer files (this is known as "anonymous UUCP," akin to the anonymous FTP servers found all over the Internet).

Next, the two systems must decide on the UUCP communications protocol to use. The choice of protocol usually depends on the type of physical communications link. For example, UUCP's default *g* protocol (named for its creator, Greg Chesson) does checksumming to produce a reliable transfer over an unreliable link, such as a telephone line. For a reliable link—like a network connection—UUCP can use a protocol that does not test for errors, such as the *t* or *e* protocols; error checking is performed by the operating system's networking software.

Connection: The Transfer

After the preliminaries are out of the way, the actual transfer occurs. The **uucico** on the calling system is run in "master role," which controls the link and specifies the request to be performed (send, receive, or execute). The receiving system's **uucico**, in "slave role," checks local permissions to see if the request can be performed, and if so, the transfer begins.

The sending system transmits packets of data; the receiving system sends back an acknowledgment for each packet received. (Depending on the protocol in use, each packet may be checksummed; packets that did not come through correctly are resent.) While the file is being received, it is stored in a temporary file in the target system's spool directory. Once the transfer is complete, the target system's **uucico** copies it to the requested destination.

If any of the requests processed are for remote command execution (that is, **uux** requests), an execute file is created in the spool directory of the target system. In most UUCP versions, the target system's **uucico** will fork off a

copy of the **uuxqt** daemon after receiving an execute request, so that the
command execution takes place as soon as possible.* The **uuxqt** daemon
reads the execute files in the spool directory, checks permissions to make
sure that the execution request is within the access controls set up by the
system administrator, and then executes the command requested. Depending on the execution request, **uuxqt** may need to create new UUCP jobs,
such as sending the output of a command back to the requesting user.

When the calling system's **uucico** is done with all of the requests it has
queued for the remote system, it sends a hang-up request. If the remote
uucico has any jobs waiting for the local system, it refuses the hangup and
the roles are reversed.†

One side or the other may hang up prematurely due to problems on the
link: bad line noise, lost carrier, perhaps even a system crash. You will usually see one of the following messages in the log:

```
ALARM 1
Timed out waiting for packet
```

This indicates that **uucico** stopped receiving valid packets from the remote
side, or perhaps stopped receiving any data at all. (If this problem happens
repeatedly, it may be caused by misconfigured modems, serial ports, or network connections that remove characters from the data stream. Bad flow
control settings are often the culprit.)

The next time the two sides successfully connect, they will either resend the
entire file that was in progress when the previous conversation broke off, or,
if both systems support SVR4 file restarts (newer BNU versions and Taylor
UUCP), resume sending the file midway, from the last byte that was successfully sent in the previous call. This feature saves a lot of time and communications bandwidth over the older UUCP versions.

Hanging Up

When nothing is left to be transferred in either direction, the two **uucicos**
agree to hang up.

---

* In older Version 2 systems, **uucico** did not invoke the **uuxqt** daemon until the UUCP link was
hung up, leading to backlogs and CPU overloads on systems that handled a large number of
uux requests.

† If the Taylor UUCP *i* protocol is in use, there is no need for role reversal, since both sides can
send files simultaneously.

Throughout this entire process, the **uucico** programs on both systems write a variety of progress messages into a logfile. Except for Taylor UUCP, any errors that occur are also written into a separate error logging file.

Dial "M" for Modem

BNU and Version 2 UUCP use the term ACU (Automatic Call Unit) to describe a modem, and also have separate files describing how to dial a modem. Modern modems all come with built in dialing capability and plug directly into a telephone jack; back in the prehistoric days of telecommunications, modems didn't dial by themselves.[*] Early modems were designed to be used in conjunction with an ordinary telephone. The call was dialed by hand, and then the telephone handset was placed into a device called an *acoustic coupler* so the modem could "talk" through the telephone.

As modems increased in speed, they needed to be wired directly to the telephone line instead of using the acoustic coupler. A telephone was attached to the modem along with a switch to toggle between voice and data. A person would dial the phone, make sure there was another modem on the other side, and throw the switch to data mode.

As technology marched on, a new device was created to replace the human. This was the automatic call unit, or programmable dialer, that let a computer control the dialing of a telephone line. It was connected to a computer by a special interface defined by the RS-366 standard. Some dialers could service an entire bank of modems.[†]

The separate interface for dialing complicated the dial-out process: a program would open one device for controlling the dialer, then another device for communicating via the modem. BNU and Version 2 UUCP still have placeholders in their configuration files for a second device name for the automatic call unit.

Modern modems use the same serial port for both communicating with the modem's built-in dialer and for transmitting data through the modem, and thus have no use for more than one device name.

---

[*] For that matter, they didn't plug into a telephone jack either—in the Bad Old Days telephones were usually wired directly into a nondetachable wall box, and telephone companies did not permit their customers to plug in user-supplied devices like answering machines and modems.

[†] Keep in mind that UNIX was originally designed by the telephone company! According to our sources, in the early days of UNIX, direct serial connections were rarely used even for individual terminals—everything was done by modem, even within the local office.

Modem Protocols

The rules and regulations that describe how computers talk to each other are called *protocols*. We've already mentioned the ones that UUCP uses so that two **uucico** programs can communicate with each other. Modems too, use specific protocols to transfer data.[*] If the modems on either end of the phone line do not speak the same protocol, then they will hang up the phone in disgust. When your modem calls a modem on another computer, the two modems must find a common protocol to use. This initial phase of a modem conversation is called *handshaking* or *negotiating*.

If you listen to a modem as it first connects, you'll first hear a steady tone when the called modem answers the phone. The pitch of this tone is one of the indicators as to what protocols the answering modem supports. When the calling modem detects the answer tone, it puts its own tone on the line. The answering modem hears the other modem's tone, and now that both modems know that they are no longer alone, they send out more tones and other funny noises that let them agree on a protocol to use. The protocol selected also defines the speed at which the connection will run.

A calling modem usually tries to make a connection at the highest possible speed. However, if it calls a modem of lesser capabilities, it will *fall back* to a lower speed that the remote modem understands. Even when the modems on both sides of a connection have the same capabilities, they might fall back when they encounter a noisy or otherwise impaired phone connection that cannot support a faster speed. For example, many users of 28800 bps modems find that they rarely connect at the highest possible speed due to line impairments.

Compression and Correction

Once the two modems agree on the protocol and speed, if either one has error correction and/or data compression capability, it will ask the other modem if it too supports those features. If so, the two modems will turn on whichever sets of features they have in common. To get the best bandwidth out of data compression, the two computers should be set to communicate

---

[*] Some modem protocols you may have heard of: V.34 (for 28800 bps communication), V.32 (14400 and 9600 bps), V.22*bis* (2400 bps), Bell 212A (1200 bps), and Bell 103 (300 bps and below).

with their respective modems at a *higher* data rate than the modems communicate with each other. This way, the modems' automatic compression of data will make the link appear to be faster than it really is.

For compression and error control to work, the computer-to-modem link must have *flow control*, a way for the modem to stop the computer from sending data when the modem is not ready to receive it (and vice versa). Otherwise, the modem or the computer will lose data when the data comes in too fast for the modem or computer to process it in time.

Most modems that are 9600 bps or higher have a bewildering array of protocols, communications modes, and settings. One of your first tasks in setting up a UUCP link with modems will be to make sure your modems are properly configured. Fortunately, most modems need no more than a few settings changed to work with UUCP; details are in Appendix I, *Setting Up a Modem*.

Setting Up a Link

Once you are armed with a basic understanding of what goes on in a transfer, you are ready to begin the steps for setting up a UUCP link. Here are the steps:

1. Establish a physical communications link between the two systems in question. For a dial-out link, you must first connect each system to a modem, and configure the modems and serial ports properly. (See Chapter 9, *The Physical Connection*.)

2. Give your system a name by which it will identify itself over the UUCP network. (See Chapter 10, *Setting Up a UUCP Link*.)

3. Create entries in the UUCP systems configuration file that describe when and how to reach the other systems with which you will communicate. Each of the other systems must do the same for you. (See Chapter 10.)

4. If other systems will be dialing in to your system, you must create the UUCP login IDs and passwords that they will use. For sites that you will dial into, you must obtain login IDs and passwords for UUCP access.

5. Create entries in the UUCP devices configuration file to let UUCP know the kind of device you are using (i.e., a modem, direct serial port connection, or a network link). For a modem, you may need to describe the modem to UUCP, because some modems require different commands. (See Chapter 10, *Setting Up a UUCP Link*.)

6. If you want to use a modem type that your system does not already know about, or if you need to fine-tune the way your system dials the modem, you must also write dialing instructions for that modem. (See Appendix I, *Setting Up a Modem.*)

7. Put in place security mechanisms to limit what other UUCP hosts can do on your system, and to make sure that the resources created for UUCP are used only for their intended purposes. You can control the files and directories on your system that remote systems have access to, and the commands they can execute with **uux**. You can also control permissions on a system-by-system basis, by creating separate user IDs for each UUCP neighbor. (See Chapter 12, *Access and Security Considerations.*)

The gory details of configuring UUCP will vary depending on whether you are using BNU, Taylor, or Version 2 UUCP. But the basic thrust of what you need to do is the same on all systems. Keep your mind on the basic objectives, and the details will fall into place.

Files and Directories

UUCP uses the following directories:

- The configuration directory, usually called */etc/uucp* or */var/lib/uucp*, holds all of UUCP's configuration files that describe what remote sites can be called and how to call them.

- The library directory, usually called */usr/lib/uucp*, contains the UUCP daemons and administrative shell scripts. Older UUCP implementations also kept the configuration files here, but in order to allow the */usr* filesystem to be shared over a network, the configuration files were moved to a nonshared filesystem. Out of deference to the hordes of system administrators who would not know where else to look for the configuration files, many systems install symbolic links in */usr/lib/uucp* that point to the files in the configuration directory.

- The spool directory, usually called */var/spool/uucp*, is used to store workfiles, data files, and execute files for spooled transfers. UUCP's logfiles are usually here as well. With all except the oldest Version 2 systems, the spool directory contains numerous subdirectories to organize the different kinds of files stored within. See Appendix B, *The Spool Directory/Working Files*, and Chapter 13, *UUCP Administration*, for details.

- The public directory, usually called */var/spool/uucppublic*, is used to make sure that there is at least one place on every system where remote systems can read and write files.* For security reasons, it is undesirable to give UUCP access to the entire filesystem.

User programs such as **uucp** and **uux** are usually found in */usr/bin*.

UUCP Login IDs

All UNIX systems that support UUCP need to have at least one username installed in */etc/passwd*: the **uucp** administrative user.† This is the user ID that owns several critical UUCP files, and programs such as **uucico** and **cu** are usually set to run under this user ID. On some systems, this user ID can be used for maintaining the UUCP configuration. This can be done by logging in directly to it, or using the **su** command from another login. The background jobs started by **cron** to retry jobs and perform routine UUCP maintenance should also run under the authority of this user ID.

Any errors encountered by UUCP programs or background jobs are usually emailed to the UUCP administrative user. If you don't check the email for *uucp* on a regular basis, make sure you set up the mail system so that email for *uucp* is redirected to someone who can act on any UUCP problems at your site.

On most UUCP links, **uucico** must log in to the remote system as if it is a regular user, by providing a login name and password (Taylor UUCP can optionally maintain a separate username/password database that is used only for validating UUCP connections. This is described in Chapter 12, *Access and Security Considerations*). These login IDs are usually created, one per UUCP neighbor, by the system administrator.‡ The difference between the UUCP administrative user ID and a UUCP neighbor's user ID is plain enough when looking at the */etc/passwd* file:

```
uucp:*:5:1:uucp:/usr/lib/uucp:/bin/sh
Utabby:*:6:1:uucp:/var/spool/uucppublic:/usr/lib/uucp/uucico
```

---

* Older AT&T UUCP documentation refers to the public directory with the name PUBDIR, without explanation; this name is still used in some BNU UUCP scripts and output messages.

† Most systems use **uucp** for this username, but a few might use **uucpadm** instead. There's nothing sacred about the exact username used, as long as ownerships and file permissions are set up properly.

‡ Some systems assign the same UUCP login ID to all their UUCP neighbors, but this practice allows one's UUCP neighbors to spoof each other, and is not recommended. (Again, see Chapter 12, *Access and Security Considerations*.)

The UUCP administrative user has a shell defined (*/bin/sh* in this example) and can actually log in or be accessed via the **su** command. A UUCP login ID (many system administrators use the convention of beginning a UUCP login ID with a capital U) always has its shell set to the path of the **uucico** command, so that when the remote **uucico** logs in, it is connected to the local **uucico** for a UUCP conversation. If you try to use **su** to access a UUCP login ID, you'll get something like this:

```
# su Utabby
Shere=koshka
```

The "Shere=" message is the start of a UUCP conversation. **su** usually invokes the user shell defined in */etc/passwd*, in this case **uucico**. When **uucico** starts up, it tries to open up a UUCP session on standard input. You can escape **uucico** by typing CTRL-P S CTRL-J . These three characters (that's a capital "S" in the middle) are a mortal insult to **uucico**, which causes it to quit. (Chapter 11, *Making Sure the Link Works*, helps explain why this works.) If this doesn't work, wait a minute or two for **uucico** to time out or kill it from another terminal.

9

The Physical Connection

To communicate with a modem or another computer, your system needs to be connected via a serial cable or a network connection. Until this link is working, nothing else matters.

To get a serial link working, you must first wire the right cable from the computer system to the modem (or to another computer or terminal server).[*] Then, you have to figure out what UNIX device name corresponds to the serial port that you've just hooked up. And if you want to support incoming calls, you'll need to make changes to your UNIX configuration to run the terminal-handling software that will let another computer open a UUCP session.

This chapter covers only how to set up a serial (computer-to-modem or computer-to-computer) link. For configuring UUCP to run over a TCP/IP network, see Chapter 10, *Setting Up a UUCP Link.* However, you may find this chapter of interest if you are using SLIP or PPP dial-up connections, since the same principles for serial connections apply regardless of the software using the modem.

---

* Many IBM PC-compatible systems use internal modems that plug directly into the PC's motherboard. From the computer's point of view, these modems (assuming the interrupts and I/O ports are configured correctly) are exactly the same as an external serial port, a properly wired cable, and a modem.

How Serial Links Work

Computers speak in the language of ones and zeroes, known as *bits* (an abbreviation for binary di**gits**). Inside the computer, the bits are passed back and forth in groups called *words*. A word can be 8, 16, 32, 64 bits or even larger sizes on high-end systems. All other things being equal, a bigger word size lets a computer process data faster.

But outside the computer, in order to simplify cabling and minimize electrical interference, most computer-to-computer communications links send only one bit at a time. These are known as *serial* links, because a word of data is sent as a stream of bits, one bit following the other in series.

The EIA RS-232 Standard

The Electronic Industries Association EIA-232D standard (commonly referred to as RS-232) describes the serial interfaces used to connect computers or terminals to modems. With a little bending and creative interpretation of the standard, RS-232 cables are also used to connect computers to other kinds of serial devices: dumb terminals, printers, terminal servers, and ports on other computers.

RS-232 cables consist of up to 25 wires, each with a specific function and each intended to carry a different signal. Only two of the wires are commonly used for data transmission; the rest are used for various kinds of control signals.

In RS-232, a computer sends data over a wire by changing electrical voltages on it. A voltage between +3 and +25 volts is considered a "0" bit and a voltage between -3 and -25 volts is considered a "1" bit. The voltages are measured with respect to a common ground wire, called the *signal ground*, since you need two wires to complete an electrical circuit.

Data is sent in eight-bit words (called *octets* by the standards committees, or *bytes* by everyone else), with extra bits at the beginning and the end of each word to show the receiving computer where the word boundaries are (this is called *framing*, and the extra bits are called the *start bit* and the *stop bit*).

The important thing to remember when hooking up an RS-232 cable is that each wire can send a signal in only one direction—either out of a device, or into it. It's like a telephone handset: the earphone is for sending dial tones and voices into your ear, and the mouthpiece is for receiving sounds from your mouth. A properly wired connection plugs every output signal on one side's RS-232 port into an input on the other side, and vice versa. Try holding the telephone handset upside-down, with the mouthpiece by your ear, and see how hard it is to hold a conversation—that's how a computer feels when its RS-232 cable is miswired.

Cables and Connectors

The RS-232 standard defines two different classes of device, each with different wiring on their serial connectors. Modems are called Data Communications Equipment (DCE), and computers, dumb terminals, or serial printers are called Data Terminal Equipment (DTE). In the standard, both modems and computers use the same kind of connector on their serial ports (DB-25, a trapezoid-shaped connector, with its 25 pins in two rows).[*] This connector comes in both male and female: male connectors have protruding pins, while female connectors have little sockets.

Although computer and modem manufacturers generally agree on the function of each signal on an RS-232 port, they don't agree on what kind of connectors to use on those ports.[†] Modem manufacturers almost always use the DB-25 female jack, but computer manufacturers keep coming up with new connectors. To be fair, they actually have a good reason: the DB-25 connector is bulky, clumsy, and most of the 25 pins go unused. Some of these non-standard connectors have become unofficial standards because so many systems use them, in particular the nine-pin (D-9 male[‡]) connector found on IBM PC-compatible systems. Some types of connectors may be used by multiple manufacturers, but have different wiring depending on the company that built the device. This is especially true of the RJ-45 eight-pin telco-style connectors used on many multiport serial boards. And every now and then you'll see a device with a standard-looking connector, but with nonstandard wiring that requires special cables.

Figure 9-1 shows what kind of connectors you're likely to find in back of your computer or modem, and what they mean. For example, a DB-25 female jack on the back of a modem is always wired as DCE, but a DB-25 female jack on the back of a Sun workstation is wired as DTE; a DB-25 female jack on the back an IBM PC compatible isn't a serial port at all, it's a parallel printer port. The DB-25 male or D-9 male jack on the back of an IBM PC is the (DTE-wired) serial port.

---

[*] This style of connector is called a "D-connector" by the more technical types. It comes in many sizes, including the D-9 (nine pins), D-15 (15 pins), D-50 (50 pins), and so on.

[†] The nice thing about standards is that there are so many of them to choose from.

[‡] The real name for this connector is D-9, but the name "DB-9" seems to have stuck in common usage.

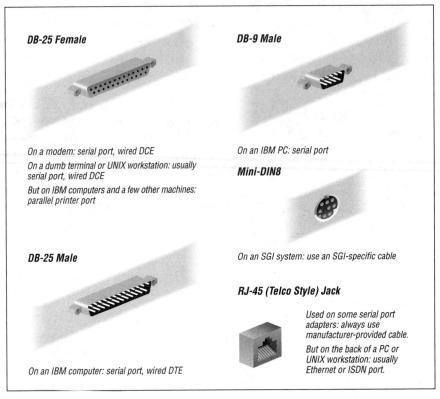

Figure 9–1: Common serial port connectors

This chapter is meant only as an introduction to RS-232 and to provide you with enough information to set up a working RS-232 link. For more authoritative treatments of RS-232 and serial communications in general, please consult an appropriate textbook or standards document.

RS-232 Signals

Many of the signals defined by the RS-232 standard are rarely used. Table 9–1 lists the signals that are needed for a working RS-232 link, and their pin numbers on the most common types of connectors (DB-25 and D-9).[*]

---

* Many of the "extra" pins are for another communications mode also defined by RS-232, called *synchronous communications*, where instead of start and stop bits, signals on pins 15, 17, and 24 are used to control the timing of the data stream. The mode of communication that we're talking about in this chapter is called *asynchronous*.

Table 9–1: RS-232 Signals and Their Functions

D-9 Pin Number	DB-25 Pin Number	Function	Direction DTE DCE
Not used	1	Frame Ground	
3	2	Transmitted Data (TxD)	→
2	3	Received Data (RxD)	←
7	4	Request to Send (RTS)	→
8	5	Clear to Send (CTS)	←
6	6	Data Set Ready (DSR)	←
5	7	Signal Ground (GND)	
1	8	Data Carrier Detect (DCD)	←
4	20	Data Terminal Ready (DTR)	→
9	22	Ring Indicator (RI)	←

The IBM PC-style nine-pin serial port does not use Frame Ground, which is for extra protection against electrical interference and isn't strictly necessary. Nine-pin to 25-pin adapters and cables are readily available, and often come in the box when you purchase a modem meant for an IBM PC compatible. If you have a Silicon Graphics computer with a mini-DIN8 connector, you'll need to purchase an SGI-specific adapter cable for it. Do not use a cable meant for an Apple Macintosh, since the pinouts are not exactly the same. Eight-pin connectors like those used on SGI, Apple Macintosh, and any system that uses RJ-45 connectors usually leave out one or more of the "important" signals, which may cause problems in some situations.

Although the pin numbers vary depending on what connectors you are using, they are usually the same at the modem, which almost always uses a DB-25 female DCE-wired connector. The pin numbers used in the rest of this chapter all refer to the DB-25 connector.

Data Transmission

Only two of the 25 pins are used for data transmission:[*]

  2   Transmitted Data
  3   Received Data

The words "Transmitted" and "Received" above are from the point of view of the computer or DTE, who receives data from the modem (DCE) on pin

---

* The RS-232 standard also calls for secondary transmit and receive lines, but they are rarely if ever implemented.

3, and sends data to the modem on pin 2. The modem's pins 2 and 3 are wired so that it receives data on pin 2, and sends data on pin 3. So to connect the data signals of a modem and computer's RS-232 ports, you want to make the connection *straight through*, as shown in Figure 9–2.

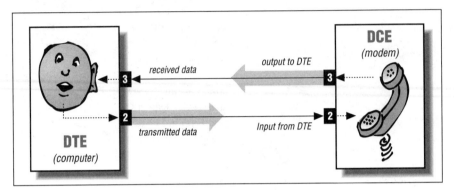

Figure 9–2: A straight-through connection

To make a connection between two computers (DTE←→DTE), you need a cable with lines 2 and 3 *crossed*, so that one computer's Transmitted Data ends up on the other computer's Received Data. This is often called a *null-modem* or *modem-eliminator* cable. Figure 9–3 shows this crossover connection between two computers.

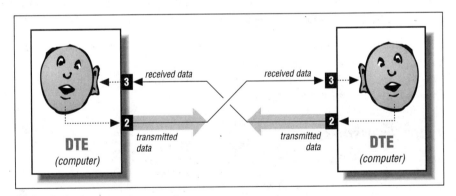

Figure 9–3: A crossover connection

A minimum cable must also have pin 7, the signal ground. Pin 7 provides the reference voltage against which all RS-232 signals are measured. It is always connected to pin 7 on the other side of the cable (assuming that both sides of the cable use DB-25 connectors). Without this connection, none of the other signals will work.

Pin 1 is a safety ground to prevent electrical interference. When used, pin 1 should be connected at one end of a cable only: the computer side of a computer-modem connection or one side only of a computer-computer connection. Most people can get along fine without it, but you may want to investigate the wiring of pin 1 if you have long cable runs or are experiencing excessive line noise.[*]

WARNING If you use a cable with Pin 1 wired on both ends (and many of them are), you may create a shock hazard or a dangerous grounding loop if the devices you connect are plugged into separate electrical supplies or different circuit breakers. Make sure any cables you run between rooms, or between devices plugged into different AC outlets do *not* have pin 1 wired straight through.

If you do not know whether a device with DB-25 connectors is DTE or DCE, you can always tell by measuring the voltage on pins 2 and 3.[†] The transmitter should always have a negative voltage, even when no data is being sent. If pin 2 is negative, the device is DTE. If pin 3 is negative, the device is DCE.

Control Signals

Some kinds of information can't be expressed in an RS-232 data stream—like whether or not the other RS-232 device is powered on, or whether or not a modem has successfully dialed in to a remote modem. Pins 4, 5, 6, 8, 20, and 22 are called *control signals* because they communicate control information from one side to the other.

A control signal has two states: on (asserted) and off (de-asserted). When a computer or modem asserts a control signal, it is telling the device on the

---

[*] As noted in the BSD 4.3 UUCP documentation, "Proper earth grounding can make RS-232C connections virtually immune to electrical noise and lightning; improper grounding can make the system much more vulnerable. Whether or not pin 1 should be used is a tricky problem in electrical engineering, and sites that are very concerned about noise and lighting protection should have their entire communications network analyzed by a professional. At the very least, Frame Ground must not be confused with or connected to the Signal Ground, pin 7."

[†] A volt-ohm meter (VOM) for measuring voltage and resistance is a standard piece of a system administrator's diagnostic toolbox. Although you won't need it too often, it will help you immensely if you need to test a cable or connector. Inexpensive VOMs can be purchased from any hobby electronics store or supply catalog.

other side of the wire that the condition associated with that particular signal is true.* Table 9–2 lists the RS-232 control signals, their names, and their associated meanings.

Table 9–2: RS-232 Control Signals

Pin Number	Name	Meaning When Asserted
4	Request To Send	DTE (computer) willing to accept data
5	Clear To Send	DCE (modem) willing to accept data
6	Data Set Ready	DCE (modem) is powered on
8	Data Carrier Detect	DCE (modem) has connected to another modem
20	Data Terminal Ready	DTE (computer) is powered on
22	Ring Indicator	DCE (modem) sees that the phone line is ringing

The control signals are used throughout an RS-232 connection. On an outgoing call, the first thing a computer does when opening a serial port is assert the DTR (Data Terminal Ready) signal. This tells the modem that the computer is ready. The modem responds by asserting the DSR (Data Set Ready) signal. If the computer is following the RS-232 standard properly, it will ignore all inputs on other pins of the RS-232 port until it sees DSR asserted. Likewise, the modem will not pay any attention to any other signals on the serial port until it sees DTR asserted.

Once both the modem and the computer are aware of each other's existence, the computer can send dialing commands to the modem. If the modem succeeds in connecting to another modem, it will assert DCD (Data Carrier Detect). The computer now starts exchanging data with the remote system presumably attached to the remote modem. Figure 9–4 shows how the modem control lines are wired in a straight-through serial connection.

If the computer feels like hanging up the line, it de-asserts DTR. The modem, duty-bound by the RS-232 standard, takes the loss of DTR as a command to disconnect the phone line. When the line is disconnected, the modem also de-asserts DCD, since it is no longer online with the other modem. On the other hand, if the remote modem drops the connection, the local modem will de-assert DCD to show the lost line. The computer could then react as needed to this condition. For example, if a UUCP conversation

---

* If you've still got the volt-ohm meter hooked up to your RS-232 port, you might be confused when you measure a control signal—a control signal is asserted with a positive voltage (space), and turned off with a negative voltage (mark). This is the opposite of the RS-232 data signals, where mark means binary 1 and space means binary 0.

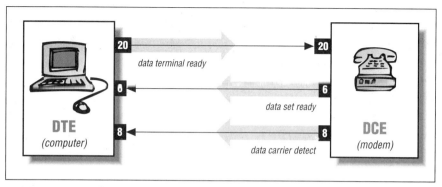

Figure 9-4: Modem control signals

is in progress when the carrier is lost, the daemon will print an error message and exit.

For incoming calls, modems are usually set up not to answer the line unless DTR is asserted at their serial interface. Some computers, however, do not assert DTR on their ports until they are notified via the RI (Ring Indicator) signal on pin 22 that an incoming call has arrived. This keeps the modem from picking up the line until the computer is ready for it. When the computer decides that it's time to answer, it asserts DTR and waits. In either case, once the modem has DTR and sees the phone ringing, it will answer, synchronize with the remote modem, and assert DCD. At this point, the computer can safely assume that both sides are connected and it can begin to send data.

Handshaking using the RS-232 control signals is sometimes referred to as *modem control*. As we will see later, on some UNIX systems you can choose whether or not to enable modem control on a serial line.

Another important function for control signals is keeping the two sides from overwhelming each other with data. Sometimes a modem or a computer is unable to keep up with the data stream, and needs to tell the other device to "hold off" and cease transmitting. This process is known as *flow control*. When the handshaking is done via RS-232 control signals, it is known as hardware flow control.*

---

* As opposed to *software flow control*, where special characters in the data (usually DC1 and DC3, decimal values 17 and 19) are used to tell each side to pause and resume sending data (DC1 and DC3 are also known as Control-Q and Control-S, or XON and XOFF). Although software flow control is adequate for terminals, it often fails with computer-to-computer communications, usually because the computers want to send binary data that includes the flow control characters.

In the RS-232 standard, flow control is defined only for *half-duplex* connections; that is, for connections in which data can be transmitted only in one direction at a time. Most RS-232 devices, including the modems and computers under discussion here, are *full-duplex*: they send data in both directions at the same time. The RS-232 standard has been adapted, *de facto*, for full-duplex communications as well.

In the half-duplex standard, the DTE asserts RTS when it wants to send data (hence the name of the signal, "Request To Send"). The DCE replies with CTS ("Clear To Send") when it is ready, and the DTE begins sending data. Unless RTS and CTS are both asserted, only the DCE can send data.

However, in the full-duplex variations, RTS and CTS both become flags indicating whether or not the device is willing to accept data. When a DTE is ready for data, it asserts RTS. When a DCE is ready to accept data, it asserts CTS. If either device is suddenly unable to keep up with the data it is receiving, it lowers the appropriate signal, and the other device must stop sending until the control signal is reasserted.

Table 9–3 shows what a conversation between a computer and modem might look like if both modem control and flow control are used. A plus sign signifies raising the voltage on the line and a minus sign signifies dropping the voltage.

Table 9–3: RS-232 Control Signals: an Example

Device	Signal	Meaning
Computer	DTR +	*I want to call another system. Are you ready?*
Computer	RTS +	*And by the way, you may send me data.*
Modem	DSR +	*I'm turned on . . .*
Modem	CTS +	*And I'm ready for action. Go ahead and dial.*
Computer	TxD . . .	*(Dialing commands sent out)*
Modem	. . . RxD	*(Dialing responses)*
Modem	DCD +	*I've got your party, sir.*
Computer	TxD . . .	*(Data sent out)*
Modem	. . . RxD	*(Data received)*
Modem	CTS -	*Hold on for a moment!*
Modem	CTS +	*I'm OK again. Shoot!*
	. . .	*Previous four steps may be repeated, with either device in the sending role, and either device using flow control.*
Computer	DTR -	*I'm done. Please hang up.*
Modem	DCD -	*Whatever you say.*

Nonstandard Behavior

As alluded to earlier, some computers don't completely adhere to the RS-232 standard. For example, some manufacturers don't include DSR in their RS-232 interfaces, which forces software on the computer to assume that DSR is always true, since it has no way of telling otherwise. And some features of the standard, such as modem control or DCD sensing, can be turned off by software configuration on the computer. For their part, most modems can be set up to lie about DCD or to ignore DTR, and are often set that way by the factory. And, not to be outdone, some serial cables do not have all the wires you would like them to have, so some control signals may not work at all until you buy, build, or steal the right cable.

When setting up an RS-232 link, keep all of the above in mind, and make sure that the modems, cables, and computers you are hooking up are all behaving as close as possible to the RS-232 standards.

Pulling the Wool Over Their Eyes

Connecting a computer to a modem is generally easy, since a DTE to DCE connection is what RS-232 was originally designed for. A straight-through cable connecting pins 2 through 8, 20, and 22 (or all 25 pins) will almost always do the trick. These cables are readily available at computer stores or via electronics supply catalogs.

Things are more complicated, however, for a direct connection between two computers. Both computers, wired as DTE, expect to be hooked up to modems.* If you connect two DTE devices with a straight-through cable, it doesn't work; the two devices can't even tell that they are plugged into anything. Like the upside-down telephone handset mentioned earlier in the chapter, the two computers can talk all they want into their earphones, and listen to their mouthpieces for signs of life, but they won't hear a thing.

To connect two computers wired as DTE, we need a cable that will cross connect each DTE's outputs to the other DTE's inputs. The most important wires to cross over are pins 2 and 3, the data lines. Each DTE sends data on pin 2 (TxD), and receives it on pin 3 (RxD)—a crossover cable must connect each DTE's pin 2 to the other DTE's pin 3. (As shown back in Figure 9–3.) This type of cable is also known as a *null-modem* cable.

---

* Unless one of your computers has an RS-232 port wired as DCE—in which case, things are simple again and you can use a straight-through cable from the DCE interface to the other computer's DTE port.

Just as the data pins must be crossed over, so must the control signals. A DTE asserts DTR when it wants to use the RS-232 port, and expects to see DSR and DCD asserted in response. A DTE using hardware flow control asserts RTS when it is ready to receive data, and expects to see CTS asserted before it will send any data. All of these signals can be cross-wired so that the two DTE's will communicate with each other, each one appearing to be a DCE to the other.

The wiring diagram for a typical null-modem cable is shown in Figure 9–5.

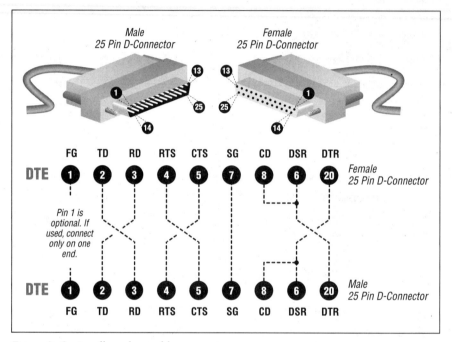

Figure 9–5: A null-modem cable

This crossover technique allows DTR (pin 20) on each DTE interface to drive both DSR (pin 6) and DCD (pin 8) on the other. Whenever either side asserts DTR, the other side thinks it is getting DSR and DCD. Pins 4 and 5 are also crossed over, so that the two sides can still use hardware flow control. Pin 22 (Ring Indicator) is not connected in a null modem cable, since without a modem, there's no phone line to ring.

CAUTION Some null-modem adapters tie together pins 4 and 5 (RTS and CTS) and/or 6, 8 and 20 (DSR, DCD and DTR) on the *same* side of the cable. This hard-wires the affected control signals so that each DTE thinks it is always asserted. Although these kinds of adapters will work most of the time, they cause problems on a UUCP link that needs hardware flow control. You need this kind of adapter only if one of your computers has a nonstandard RS-232 port that is missing some of the control signals—it should be avoided otherwise. Use a volt-ohm meter to test out your null-modem adapter if you're not sure of its pedigree.

The Breakout Box

An invaluable tool for troubleshooting RS-232 connections is a *breakout box*. The breakout box plugs into the middle of an RS-232 connection, and has LED indicators that display the states of the various control signals and whether there is data on the TxD or RxD pins. A good breakout box will also give you a miniature patch panel, and switches for rearranging the wiring of an RS-232 connection. If you don't trust the null modem adapters that you have at hand, or think you might have to build a custom cable, a breakout box will save you from hours of frustration.

Making Your Own Cables

If the only way you can get a serial connection working is with a breakout box crossing wires in some nonstandard manner, you probably need to make your own cable.

Parts for building cables (or building your own handheld adapters) are available from computer communications supply catalogs. Some supply houses will, for an extra fee, wire a cable to your specifications. What's best for you depends on how many cables you're making, and how much time or money you have to spend.

Before using a home-built (or custom-ordered) cable, test every pin with a volt-ohm meter to make sure it is wired correctly. This is much less painful then finding out later that the cable is miswired.

A few cabling tips:

- If you are stringing cables through walls or ceilings, you should use straight-through cables with all necessary lines, then use secondary cables to do any null modem tricks. This will give you more flexibility in the long run and is simpler to troubleshoot.

- Keep your cables away from sources of electrical noise, such as fluorescent lights, elevator motors, and air conditioning equipment.

- If your office is already wired for twisted pair (such as Category 5 wiring for Ethernet networks), you can purchase DB-25 to RJ-45 adapters and run serial connections through the existing wiring.

- Many descriptions of RS-232 claim that the maximum length of an RS-232 cable is 50 feet. In practice, RS-232 cables can be much longer. 500 feet is usually considered a "safe" upper limit, though some installations have runs as long as 800 or 1000 feet. The longer the run, the more trouble you're likely to have at higher baud rates. You'll get better results with long cable runs if you use low-capacitance cables.

- Extender devices are available from electronics supply houses that allow eight-wire RS-232 connections to work over long lengths of four-conductor telephone-style cable. These devices are also used to set up mini-networks that allow multiple computers to share the same modem.

Although we've tried our best to describe to you how RS-232 serial communications is supposed to work, some UNIX systems or modems have their unique quirks or nonstandard behavior. Always check the documentation for the devices you are trying to connect. Pay close attention to the manufacturer's cabling recommendations and to the pin-out diagrams for the serial ports. It may be difficult to translate the raw description given for each device into the information necessary to connect them to one another, but you will succeed if you persevere.

Configuring UNIX Serial Ports

Getting the serial port wired up is only half the battle. The other half is getting UNIX to communicate over the serial port. User programs in UNIX (such as the UUCP daemons) use serial ports by means of *special files*. A special file, at first glance, seems to be a regular filename in the UNIX filesystem, but it is really a "pointer" to a system device handler, or *driver*, that understands the serial port hardware and knows how to transfer data between the serial port and user programs.

Special files are just about always stored in the */dev* directory, or a subdirectory within. Special files that point to serial ports usually have names that begin with */dev/tty* or */dev/cua.** The device driver software in UNIX that is invoked via these special files is called the *tty driver*. To get UNIX to recognize your serial port, and thus allow you to run the UUCP daemons to communicate over the serial port, you need to do the following:

- Identify the special file that corresponds to the serial port in question.

- Tell the *tty* driver about hardware flow control or other special settings.

For a serial port that will be accepting incoming calls, do the following:

- Run the appropriate software (usually **getty**) to provide a login prompt on that port. This means changing system configuration files so that the right program is started up at boot time and restarted after each call.

- Provide **getty** with the special file name, speed, and other attributes of the serial port, so that it can properly accept incoming calls.

For serial ports that will be used for both incoming and outgoing calls, other steps may be necessary, depending on which variety of UNIX you are using. Some UNIX systems require you to use two device names for the same serial port: one for incoming (usually named */dev/tty*xx) and one for outgoing (usually named */dev/cua*xx).

Serial Diversity

Handling serial ports and incoming calls is, alas, one of the areas of UNIX that varies substantially from one vendor to another. Be sure to read through your system's documentation on how to hook up terminals and modems before trying to set up serial ports. If your system supports a menu-driven or graphic user interface, such as **smit** on AIX systems, **admintool** on Solaris 2.3 and up, **sam** on HP-UX, and the **toolchest** menus on IRIX, you should use it to perform these tasks if at all possible.

For more detailed information on configuring UNIX serial ports, you might want to read the Nutshell Handbook *Essential System Administration*, 2nd Edition, also published by O'Reilly & Associates, on which some of the information in this section is based. If you are using Linux on an IBM PC-compatible system, another good source of information is the *Linux Network Administrators Guide*, also published by O'Reilly & Associates (or available via public archives on the Internet).

---

* *tty* is an abbreviation for Teletype, a common type of printing terminal in the 1970s.

Identifying the tty Special File

Most UNIX systems keep their *tty* special files in the directory */dev*, under names like */dev/tty0* or */dev/tty12*. System V Release 4 keeps special files for terminal lines in the directory */dev/term*, with individual names corresponding to a *tty* line number (e.g., */dev/term/14*). Sometimes there are links to the older names in */dev*.

Usually, the lowest numbered special file (i.e., */dev/tty0* or */dev/tty00*) corresponds to the lowest numbered serial port on the system. But the name of the special device file does not have to relate in any way to the serial port it refers to; this is controlled by the *major* and *minor* numbers of the special file. To see those numbers, use the **ls −l** command:

```
$ ls -l /dev/tty2
crw--w--w-   1 root       users       4,   2 Dec 16 17:36 /dev/tty2
```

The device file's major number picks the device driver that will be run to handle any I/O requests made via the special file, and the minor number tells the device driver which of the different physical ports under its control should be used for the I/O. On a Linux system, for example, minor number 0 is the first serial port (known as COM1 when running DOS on the same system), minor number 1 is the second (COM2), and so on.

The correspondence between minor numbers and actual ports gets a bit confused when you add a serial port expansion board to your system. Be sure to read carefully through the expansion board, and driver software, documentation.

Allowing Incoming Calls

To handle an incoming call on a serial port, whether or not there is a modem attached to it, a program must be running and waiting for something to happen on the serial port.

The command **getty** is usually used to wait on serial ports. Nearly all UNIX systems start **getty** (and other programs) via the configuration file */etc/inittab*.

The **getty** program monitors the serial port, starting a login process when activity is detected on the line (e.g., when a modem signals its presence by asserting DCD).[*] **uugetty** is a variant of **getty** that is supplied on many systems; it performs the same functions as **getty** but it is designed for bidirectional lines.

Starting Up getty (most systems except SunOS)

Many varieties of UNIX—with the notable exception of SunOS 4—use the */etc/inittab* file to bring up **getty** on each serial port where incoming calls are desired. The */etc/inittab* file is read by **init**, which is the first process started on a UNIX system. Based on the command lines in */etc/inittab*, **init** will start up various different programs as the system boots. Most systems already have a **getty** or two started this way for logging in on the console, and any attached terminals. Some systems will have "placeholder" entries to make it easy to turn on logins on a particular port. Entries look like this:

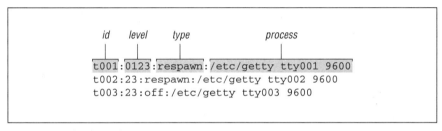

```
         id    level   type              process
          |      |      |                  |
        t001:0123:respawn:/etc/getty tty001 9600
        t002:23:respawn:/etc/getty tty002 9600
        t003:23:off:/etc/getty tty003 9600
```

Figure 9–7: /etc/inittab

Field	Function in */etc/inittab*
id	A one- to four-letter identifier that is used by **init** to label entries in its process table, generally (but not always) corresponding to the device name for the serial line. Port IDs vary from system to system. Consult your documentation for details.
level	A string of characters consisting of [0-6,a-c] the *run level* of the process. **init** will start the process associated with this line when the system run level matches one of the run levels listed here.
type	If set to "respawn," **init** will restart the process after it exits; if set to "off," the process is never started. This is useful for setting a

---

[*] A fine distinction: On BSD systems prior to BSD 4.3, it is */etc/init*, not *getty*, that sleeps on the line. When DCD is asserted, *getty* is executed and prints the login prompt. In other systems, *getty* sleeps directly on the line.

process   placeholder, or for temporarily disabling incoming calls on a serial line.

process   The program invoked when **init** activates an entry. For serial lines, the process is the **getty** (or **uugetty**) program that puts up the login prompt. Linux systems also use **agetty** or **mgetty**.

getty and **uugetty** can take a number of options. The options differ from system to system, but there is usually a way to specify a timeout that will cause **getty** to automatically hang up a line if a user takes too long to log in.

getty takes as an argument the device name of the serial port on which it is to run. (This is the name of the special file in the */dev* directory corresponding to this device.)

Another argument to **getty** is a label that is used to look up the appropriate entry in another file, */etc/gettydefs*, that contains serial communications parameters such as baud rate, parity, etc. The speed (baud rate) is conventionally used as the label, but other labels may be used as well, or instead of, the speed.

After editing */etc/inittab*, you will probably need to notify **init** of the changes by sending it the HUP signal (**kill –HUP 1**), or by issuing the command **init q** (**telinit q** on some systems).

/etc/ttytab (SunOS 4) and /etc/ttys (BSD)

In SunOS 4, the starting up of **getty** processes is controlled by the */etc/ttytab* file; BSD 4.3 and up also uses the */etc/ttys* file for the same purpose. To make your life more confusing, SunOS 4 systems also have a */etc/ttys* file, but it is there only for compatibility with older software and may be safely ignored.

Whenever you add a new device or change an existing one already connected to a serial port, you must modify */etc/ttytab* (or */etc/ttys*) to describe the correct device for that line. You'll notice that the file contains many, many entries, almost all of them turned off. You only need to change the devices you are interested in—leave the other entries alone.

Here are some sample entries for */etc/ttytab* and */etc/ttys*:

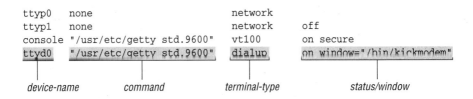

```
ttyp0   none                          network
ttyp1   none                          network      off
console "/usr/etc/getty std.9600"     vt100        on secure
ttyd0   "/usr/etc/getty std.9600"     dialup       on window="/bin/kickmodem"
```

    device-name   *command*   *terminal-type*   *status/window*

Here's a breakdown of the sample entries:

- *device-name* is the special file in the */dev* directory for the the *tty* port.

- *command* is the command and arguments that **init** should invoke to monitor this *tty*. (Whether this command is actually run or not depends on the *status* field.)

- *terminal-type* is the default terminal type for this line.

- *status/window* is zero or more keywords, separated by spaces. Use the keyword *on* to enable the line, to run the specified *command*, or *off* to disable incoming calls on the line. The keyword *secure* indicates that the *root* user may log in on this terminal. You can also specify *window*=**cmd** to have **init** run a particular command before invoking the command specified in field 2 (i.e., **getty**); this is useful if you have a cantankerous modem that needs to be reprogrammed after each call.

Bidirectional Ports and Dial-out Devices

UNIX systems have a minor dilemma to resolve when using the same serial port for both initiating connections and receiving incoming calls. To allow incoming calls, a **getty** must be running, and it must have opened the special file for the desired serial port. To make an outgoing call while this serial port is idle, another program such as **cu** or the UUCP daemon **uucico** must also open the special file for the serial port. Hence the conflict: both programs want exclusive use of the serial port, yet both programs must be running at the same time.

This problem is solved in different ways on different systems. IRIX, HP-UX,[*] SCO UNIX, Digital UNIX (DEC OSF/1), and most Linux configurations provide a special version of **getty**, called **uugetty**, that is willing to share the

---

[*] HP-UX offers both **uugetty** and multiple device files similar to the SunOS and SVR4 scheme, also described in this section. The latter is preferred by the HP-UX documentation; consult the peripherals manual for details.

serial line with any dial-out program that comes along, and uses UUCP's lockfile scheme to avoid conflicts. AIX combined the functions of **uugetty** into **getty**; invoking **getty** with **−u** or **−r** options make it behave in **uugetty** mode. Later SCO UNIX versions also combine **getty** and **uugetty**.

SunOS and SVR4 systems support bidirectional devices with two types of device files. The dial-in devices are conventionally named */dev/ttyd*n, where *n* is a number indicating which modem line it is (the lines are by convention numbered sequentially, beginning with 0, regardless of the terminal line they correspond to), and the corresponding dial-out device for the same line has a name of the form */dev/cua*n.[*] The dial-out special file is used for making outgoing calls with **cu** or **uucico** (and any other programs, like **kermit** or **seyon**, that can make outgoing calls), while the dial-in special file is supplied to **getty** for handling incoming calls. The dial-in and dial-out device files for the same serial line have different minor device numbers, offset by 128 in SunOS.

The difference between these two device files is how they react when opened by a program. A program opening the dial-in special file (usually **getty**) will be suspended until DCD is asserted on the serial port. A program opening a dial-out special file will be refused if a session on that port is already in progress, but if the serial port is idle, the program will be given use of the serial port. Any program waiting for incoming calls on the same port will stay suspended while the dial-out program is running. When the dial-out program exits, any program sleeping on the dial-in line will again be able to answer the line if an incoming call arrives.

System Specific Information

Some UNIX systems do things a little (or, in some cases, a lot) differently than the mainstream. Although we've tried to keep the information in this section as accurate as possible, UNIX releases can change much faster than books are published. Be sure to read through the documentation (and online manual pages) that come with your system. Most vendors also have "cookbook" instructions for setting up serial ports and modems that are available from their Web sites, faxback services, or customer support staff.

---

[*] Solaris uses somewhat different names for its devices, like */dev/cua/a*.

Configuring AIX serial ports

On most systems, the special files are automatically created for you when the operating system is installed. But IBM's AIX requires you to run a configuration command to create the *tty* special files. Running **smit tty** brings up a menu that allows you to add, remove, or change serial ports. Pay careful attention to the hardware port number on the configuration screens, since AIX will happily let you configure *tty0* to point to any of the available serial ports on the system, regardless of their physical port number.

When configuring an AIX serial port, you should also specify the default baud rate for the port (use a comma-separated list if you want to allow incoming calls at more than one baud rate). AIX versions 4.1 and up also let you enable RTS/CTS flow control, but AIX version 3 does not have any direct way of doing so. (The AIX online documentation, *Info Explorer*, contains a sample program for enabling RTS in AIX 3.)

These menus also let you control whether a **getty** will run on the line; look for the "TTY Program" parameter (should be set to **/etc/getty**), the "Enable program" parameter (should be set to "respawn"), and the "Enable login" parameter (should be set to "enable" for normal dial-in ports, "disable" for dial-out ports, and "delay"—**uugetty** mode—for bidirectional ports).

If you're not fond of **smit**, you can use the commands that **smit** would call on your behalf: **mkdev** and **chdev**, which create and modify device definitions. But resist the temptation to edit **/etc/inittab** directly; although it will seem to work as expected, at the next system reboot, all of your changes will be erased.

Configuring Solaris serial I/O

With Solaris, terminal lines are handled by the Service Access Facility (SAF) in a very different manner than other UNIX systems. You can avoid dealing with its complexity by using the **admintool** system administration interface. We also recommend the tutorials written by Celeste Stokely of Stokely Consulting at *http://www.batnet.com/stokely/index.html*.

SunOS and Solaris flow control

The serial ports on Sun CPU boxes have a bad reputation for supporting hardware flow control in only one direction (on data transmitted from the workstation). This is insufficient for today's high-speed modems, which need hardware flow control in both directions. Sun has released patches for both Solaris and SunOS that are supposed to support bidirectional hardware flow control. Other options include purchasing a serial port expansion card that supports hardware flow control or upgrading to Taylor UUCP (assuming that your UUCP neighbors also have it), which has protocols that can run over a link using software (XON/XOFF) flow control.

SunOS has a special chat script sequence that can be used in the Dialers or Systems file for turning on hardware flow control (or any other *tty* device setting). For details, see the discussion following Table 10–1 in Chapter 10, *Setting Up a UUCP Link*.

Configuring Linux serial ports

Linux supports all the normal serial port hardware you're likely to have on your IBM PC-compatible.* This includes the standard 8250/16450 UARTs found on older PCs (and emulated in older, slower internal modems), and the 16550A and compatible UART used in high-speed serial ports (and emulated in high-speed internal modems). Many manufacturers of multiport serial boards also provide Linux drivers for their products.

A good resource for explaining the ins and outs of setting up serial ports on Linux can be found in the "Linux Serial HOWTO" that should be on your Linux distribution CD (it is also posted regularly to the newsgroup *comp.os.linux.answers*).†

Linux serial ports use the "split device" scheme, with separate device names for incoming and outgoing calls on the same physical port. The "incoming" device names start at */dev/ttyS0* and the "outgoing" device names start at */dev/cua0*. Some Linux distributions also create a symbolic link */dev/modem*, which points to the dial-out device; this has been known to cause confusion on some systems when the lock file for the dial-out device is not created properly.

To configure the interrupts, port addresses, and other low-level settings of the serial port driver, use the **setserial** command. You'll need to use **setserial** if you are using serial ports with nonstandard interrupts or port addresses, such as a third or fourth directly-attached serial port (COM3 and COM4 in DOS, */dev/ttyS2* and */dev/ttyS3* in Linux). If you're brave, you can ask **setserial** to probe your hardware and try to guess the correct configuration.

---

* At publication time, pre-release versions of Linux were also available for DEC Alpha computers and Apple Macintosh PowerPC systems. We have not yet had a chance to play with these systems, so we will limit our discussion of Linux serial ports to the IBM PC-compatible world.

† The Linux Serial HOWTO is copyright (C) 1993 - 1995 by Greg Hankins.

setserial is also used to control baud rates. If a Linux program does not know how to use a baud rate over 38400, with **setserial**, you can trick a program using a serial port at 38400 to use a higher rate instead.

Linux getty and stty

There are several different versions of **getty** available for Linux. We suggest you use either the **uugetty** supplied with your Linux distribution (which probably comes from the **getty_ps** package), or **mgetty** (part of the **mgetty+sendfax** package), which has support for modems and UUCP logins, as well as for receiving data and fax calls on the same modem.

To enable hardware flow control on a serial port, use the **stty** command:

```
# stty crtscts < /dev/cua0
```

To see whether hardware flow control is enabled on a port, try:

```
# stty -a < /dev/cua0 | grep rts
```

If you see the setting **crtscts**, hardware flow control is enabled; if you see **–crtscts** (with a leading hyphen), it is disabled.

You should place serial port initialization commands into one of the Linux start-up scripts. On Slackware, the ideal place is */etc/rc.d/rc.serial*.

IRIX serial ports

IRIX on Silicon Graphics machines uses different names for the same serial port to select whether modem control and flow control signals are enabled. The scheme works as follows:

- Devices with names beginning with */dev/ttyd* are for directly connecting a dumb terminal or other simple-minded serial device. Only TD, RD, and signal ground are used.

- Devices beginning with */dev/ttym* are for modems or terminals that use modem control signals. DCD and DTR are also supported.

- Devices beginning with */dev/ttyf* support all signals on the SGI serial port. Use the */dev/ttyf* device names if you want hardware (RTS/CTS) flow control on a port.

For more information, see the *serial* man page.

Configuring an HP-UX serial port

HP-UX has a more complex convention for naming its serial ports. The modem(7) man pages explain why. We recommend that you use the **sam** system administration tool to configure serial ports.

Table 9–4 gives naming conventions. You only need to be concerned with the "Convio 10.x" device names, unless you are trying to compare old with new names.

Table 9–4: Converged IO Filenames: TTY Mux Naming

General Meaning	S800 9.x	S700 9.x	Convio 10.x
tty* hardwired ports	tty<X>p<Y> diag:mux<X>	tty<YY>	tty<D>p<p> diag:mux<D>
ttyd* dial-in modems	ttyd<X>p<Y> diag:ttyd<X>p<Y>	ttyd<YY>	ttyd<D>p<p> diag:ttyd<D>p<p>
cua* auto-dial out	cua<X>p<Y> diag:cua<X>p<Y>	cua<YY>	cua<D>p<p>
cul* dial-out	cul<X>p<Y> diag:cul<X>p<Y>	cul<YY>	cul<D>p<p>

The table above uses the following abbreviations:
<X>= LU (Logical Unit)
<Y> or <YY> = Port
<D>= Devspec (decimal card instance)
<p>= Port

On all HP-UX 10.x versions, **mksf** is the preferred command to configure serial devices (rather than **mknod**). To configure devices, follow these steps:

1. Invoke **/usr/sbin/ioscan −f** to determine which interface card or MUX you are adding to the terminal or modem. For example:

   ```
   /usr/sbin/ioscan -d mux4 -fn
   ```

2. Find the hardware path of the serial interface to be used. You can find potential ports by typing:

   ```
   /usr/sbin/ioscan -C tty
   ```

   or

   ```
   ls -l /dev/tty#p*
   ```

   where # is the mux card instance.

3. Typically for terminals, special device files have already been created for terminals at each serial port, like */dev/tty0p0* or */dev/tty0p1*.

4. You can see the device file's characteristics by typing:

```
/usr/sbin/lssf /dev/tty0p1
mux4 card instance 0 port 1 hardwired at address 56.0 /dev/tty0p1
```

By comparing the output with **ll** output:

```
ll /dev/tty0p1
crw--w--w-   1 bin        bin        178 0x000000 Nov  8 09:50 /dev/tty0p0
```

you can see which port number corresponds to which bits in the minor number.

5. For terminals, you can just physically connect them now if no interface card is required.

6. For modems, execute **ioscan −C tty −fn** to identify card instance, hardware path, and port number for the modem port. The device files have the following format:

Access Mode	Port Access	Device File Format
0	direct connect	/dev/cua(instance#)p(port#)
1	Dial-out port	/dev/cul(instance#)p(port#)
2	dial-in modem	/dev/ttyd(instance#)p(port#)

(The instance number is from **ioscan −f** output; use the card instance shown for the *tty* class as the interface card to which the modem is being attached.)

In these examples, one file each is being created for direct connect (−a0), dial-out (−a1), and dial-in modem (−a2).

On the series 700:

```
/usr/sbin/mksf -d asio0 -H 2/0/4 -a0 -i -v
making cua0p0 c 1 0x000000
/usr/sbin/mksf -d asio0 -H 2/0/4 -a1 -v
making cul0p0 c 1 0x000001
/usr/sbin/mksf -d asio0 -H 2/0/4 -a2 -v
making ttyd0p0 c 1 0x000002
```

On the series 800:

```
/usr/sbin/mksf -d mux2 -I 0 -a0 -p2 -i -v
making cua0p2 c 193 0x000201
/usr/sbin/mksf -d mux2 -I 0 -a1 -p2 -v
making cul0p2 c 193 0x000201
/usr/sbin/mksf -d mux2 -I 0 -a0 -p2 -v
making ttyd0p2 c 193 0x000202
```

7. You can verify the creation of the device special files by using the **lssf** command.

Hardware flow control on HP-UX

Hardware flow control is available only on interfaces that support modems, and require a special device file setup. Consult your HP-UX documentation for more information.

Communications Settings

In order to communicate over a direct serial connection, both devices on the link must be using the same communications parameters. The important parameters are:

- Speed—the bit rate of both devices must be the same, or they will wildly misinterpret each other's data.

- Parity—both sides must agree on whether or not to use parity checking. Usually, they agree to turn it off.

- Word length—this is almost always eight bits.

- Stop bits—both sides usually use one stop bit. RS-232 devices can use two stop bits if asked, but this is obsolete.

Information about these four (and some less crucial) settings must be given to **getty** or **uucico** so that they can set the serial port up for proper communications with the other RS-232 device. The argument to **getty** specified in */etc/inittab* or */etc/ttytab* is a pointer to yet another configuration file that contains the information for these parameters.

As you will see, some of these options are outdated and no longer used, but since RS-232 hardware still supports them, we must make sure they are set properly.

Baud Rate vs. Bits Per Second

The speed is specified in bits-per-second (bps). This is often called the *baud rate*, a holdover from the Baudot code used in telegraphy. Properly speaking, the baud rate is the number of signals per second on the communications line. It is equivalent to bits-per-second only if one bit is encoded per electrical signal. This is true for all RS-232 links, such as a direct computer-to-computer link or the connection between your computer and modem. But all modem-to-modem protocols above 300 bps send multiple data bits with each electrical signal. For example, a 2400-bps modem actually operates at 600 baud (signals per second), and sends four bits of data with each signal to the remote modem. Thus, it would be erroneous to call a V.32 modem a "9600-baud modem," even though you might connect to it over a 9600-baud serial link.

Choosing a Line Speed

For a direct connection between two computers, set the line speed to the fastest speed that both devices can comfortably support—speeds of 38400 bps are standard on many systems. If one or both sides do not have flow control, you may need to slow them down if you experience overrun errors that interfere with data transfer.

For a connection to a modem, things aren't so simple. If your modem supports automatic speed conversion, use the highest speed that the modem supports. If the modem makes a connection to a slower modem, it will still feed you data at the higher speed. You must have hardware flow control configured on the modem and on the computer for this to work properly.

If your modem doesn't have flow control or automatic conversion, you can still set your computer to the highest speed supported by the modem, but you'll need to worry about falling back whenever the modem makes a slower-speed connection. For incoming calls, this is accomplished via the **getty** configuration files. For outgoing calls, the communications program (or the human trying to use it) must change the baud rate when the modem suddenly downshifts after making the connection.

Bits and Bytes

Serial communication occurs as a series of clocked voltage pulses over lines 2 and 3 of a serial cable. If a modem is involved, these pulses are converted to audible tones (modulated) for transmission over the telephone line; they are then converted back into serial pulses (demodulated) by the modem at the other end.

The basic data unit is a byte, or eight bits—in this case, eight serial pulses.[*] A byte is accompanied by two or three additional bits: a start bit and either one or two stop bits.

When no data is being transmitted, the signal on pin 2 (or the carrier tone on a modem) is equivalent to a continuous stream of binary ones. In a

---

[*] We really ought to call it an "octet," but old habits die hard.

holdover from the early days of telegraphy, this is referred to as the MARK state. (In those days of electromechanical relays, constant negative voltage was the preferred idle signal; it resulted in the stylus making a continuous mark on a roll of paper, hence its name.) The start bit is a voltage equivalent to binary 0. By contrast to MARK, this state is often referred to as SPACE. After the start bit is received, both devices count the desired number of data bits and look for the stop bit, which is always binary 1 (MARK). Two stop bits are usually used at lower speeds such as 110 baud.

Since the U.S. ASCII character encoding scheme uses only seven of the eight bits in a byte, it is possible to exchange useful data in the United States over a communications line with a word size of seven bits. Although no one does this any more, seven-bit history lives on in network limitations and our ASCII display terminals. For example, eight-bit character codes in electronic mail and Usenet news articles sometimes get changed in transmission. Eight-bit character sets such as ISO 8859-1 are vital for European computing, though, so using seven bits is a parochialism all Americans have cause to regret.[*]

Serial links also have the option of using a simple form of error checking known as *parity*. Parity checking uses one of a byte's eight bits to verify that what is sent out is the same as that received. The remaining seven bits are available for data, so only seven-bit characters may be used. There are five possible parity settings:

Odd   The value of the parity bit, plus the value of the data bits, must always add up to an odd number.

Even   The value of the parity bit, plus the value of the data bits, must always add up to an even number.

Mark   The parity bit is always one.

Space   The parity bit is always zero.

None   No parity bit is sent.

Even and odd parity are the only settings that provide any error protection. The sending computer sets the parity bit to 0 or 1, depending on the value of the data bits. The receiving computer checks to make sure that the parity came out as advertised: odd or even. If line noise (e.g., on a telephone line)

---

[*] A workaround has been provided by the ISO 2022 code extension, which provides for encoding eight-bit characters in seven bits. This can cause problems of its own, if the characters don't get converted back properly.

causes one data bit to be changed (appear 0 or 1 when it's not sent out that way), the parity will not come out right.

An even number of simultaneous errors in the same byte, however, will cancel each other out. Since line noise usually occurs in bursts, parity is relatively useless as an error checking mechanism, and has been superseded by various types of more complex error checking implemented in software. Nonetheless, parity is a feature of serial communications that cannot be overlooked because a parity mismatch will prevent any communication from occurring.

One more important concept is that of the BREAK, which is sometimes referred to as a character but is in fact an interruption in the normal framing of characters (start bit, data bits, stop bit). A BREAK is a SPACE state that extends past the length of time normally required to transmit a character. Some terminals have a BREAK key that generates this condition, and on most UNIX systems, UUCP can generate a true BREAK. A few older UNIX systems simulate a BREAK by changing the speed to a very low rate, sending NULL characters (all zeros), and then restoring the old speed in order to "break the frame" (i.e., keep the stop bit from being detected).

Serial Port Configuration Files

Some UNIX systems use one start bit and one stop bit, eight data bits, and no parity; others use seven bits, and even parity. However, whenever **uucico** starts up, it automatically switches the line to eight bits, and no parity. The simple error checking provided by parity is far inferior to the more complex error checking algorithms implemented in software by communications protocols like UUCP.

What this means is that all you normally need to do is specify the correct speed in either */etc/inittab* or */etc/ttytab*. The rest of the settings should be set correctly without any intervention on your part. If any system with which you are communicating uses nonstandard communications parameters, though, you may need to create new entries in the file */etc/gettydefs* (System V), */etc/gettytab* (SunOS or BSD 4.3), or */etc/ttydefs* (Solaris).[*]

A brief discussion of these two files is given below. See your UNIX system documentation for additional details on how to set communications line parameters. Some good places to start are the reference manual pages for

---

[*] Except in AIX, where all the communications parameters, including the I/O control codes detailed below, are configured via the same **smit** menus that create or modify serial ports.

gettydefs(5) or *ttytab*(5), *ttys*(5) on older SunOS and BSD systems, *termio*(7) (*termio*(4) on some systems), *tty*(4), and *stty*(1).

/etc/gettydefs (System V)

On systems that use System V-style terminal handling, the file */etc/gettydefs* contains the definition of the communications parameters for a serial line. Each entry in the file has five fields separated by hash marks (#), and looks something like this:

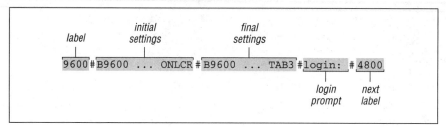

Figure 9-9: /etc/gettydefs

Field	Function in */etc/gettydefs*
label	The label that is used in */etc/inittab* to tell the **getty** process which *gettydefs* entry to read. This field is often, but not always, filled in with the baud rate of the entry. However, it can be any label that you find convenient, as long as there is a matching entry in both files.
initial settings	The *termio* I/O control codes that will be used by **getty** to initialize the line. These codes will be used until the *login* process takes over. Some of the codes you may need to change are listed in Table 9-5.
final settings	The *termio* I/O control codes that **getty** sets for the line before turning over control to the **login** program. These are the settings that will be in effect when the user logs in. The user can change settings with the **stty** command, or in case of **uucico**, via direct program calls.

login prompt   The prompt that **getty** will display on the screen. This prompt can include newlines by embedding the escape sequence **\n**. For example:

```
O'Reilly & Associates, Inc. CTIX 3.2\n\nlogin:
```

next label   The label to be used if the remote system—or user trying to log in—sends a BREAK, or there is a framing error on the line. This may indicate a possible speed mismatch: a user pressing the RETURN key when the two sides are at different speeds often appears as a particular kind of error on the receiving side. Many systems use this mechanism to create a linked list of entries, at different speeds, so that a dial-up line can be used by callers with modems at different baud rates. For example:

```
19200#B19200...IGNPAR#B19200...IGNPAR#login:#9600
9600#B2400...IGNPAR#B9600...IGNPAR#login:#2400
2400#B9600...IGNPAR#B2400...IGNPAR#login:#19200
```

The line will first be set to 19200 baud. If a user dialing in sends a BREAK, or if **getty** detects framing errors, the speed will switch to 9600. If another BREAK or framing error appears, the speed will go to 2400, then back to 19200. Assuming the autoanswer modem has also been set up to support all these baud rates, this line can service incoming calls at any of the three speeds.

Baud rate cycling (as shown above) is going out of style, as modern modems all support automatic speed conversion. Automatic speed conversion allows the modem and the computer to be set to a fixed baud rate (usually as high as possible) and the modem converts any calls that connect at the slower rates to the fast modem-to-computer rate. You need hardware flow control for this to work properly.

You should not generally need to write a new *gettydefs* entry, and if you do, you may just want to copy one of the existing lines and modify a few parameters.

We don't have space here to discuss all of the possible I/O control codes you can use in this file. (See the man pages for *stty*(1) for more information.) Table 9–5 lists a few of the codes that might come up if you are trying to establish a telephone link with another system (especially a non-UNIX system that may not use the same default communications parameters).

Table 9-5: I/O Control Codes in gettydefs

I/O Code	Meaning
B*nnnn*	Baud rate (e.g., B9600 for 9600 baud).
CLOCAL	Ignore the CD signal—do not block waiting for Carrier Detect when opening the port. This can be used for direct connections, but is not needed if your cabling is set up properly.
CS*n*	Character size in bits—usually CS7 or CS8.
CSTOPB	If set, use two stop bits. If not set, use only one stop bit.
HUPCL	Terminate program if device is closed. Be sure to use this on dial-up lines.
IXANY	Allow any character to restart output stopped with CTRL-S (default is only CTRL-Q).
IXON	Enable XON/XOFF (CTRL-S/CTRL-Q) flow control. See **IXANY** above.
PARENB	Parity is enabled. If set, default is EVEN parity.
PARODD	If **PARENB** is enabled, use ODD parity.
SANE	Use default settings for a variety of options.

You should be extremely careful in modifying */etc/gettydefs*, since a corrupted file can make it impossible to log in to your system from any terminal. (One trick is to keep a stray window or a spare terminal logged in while making the changes.) Do not modify the I/O control codes in any existing entry unless you are sure you know what you are doing.

Instead, copy the *gettydefs* file, and test that the entry you have created is legal by invoking **getty** manually with the **-c** (*check*) option, like this:

```
# /etc/getty -c file
```

It still may be a good idea to create a new entry and test it with a single serial line rather than replacing the entry used by all of your terminal lines.

/etc/gettytab (SunOS and BSD)

SunOS, BSD 4.3, and BSD 4.4 systems use the file */etc/gettytab* to describe the characteristics that will be assigned to serial lines. The *gettytab* file uses a format similar to the terminal database */etc/termcap*. That is, it defines a series of codes that describe the line characteristics. Some of the codes simply indicate the presence or absence of a characteristic, others assign a string or numeric value.

Certain line characteristics are assumed by **getty**; others are set by an entry in */etc/gettytab* labeled "default" that is read before any speed-selected entry.

The syntax of the *gettytab* file is far too complex to describe here. However, to give you a feeling for what the entries look like, a sample of several entries from a SunOS 4.1 system is shown here:

```
default:\
        :ap:lm=\r\n%h login\72 :sp#9600:

2|std.9600|9600-baud:\
        :sp#9600:

D2400|Fast-Dial-2400:\
        :nx=D1200:tc=2400-baud:
```

Each newline must be escaped, since each entry is actually a single line. Individual characteristics are separated with a colon. Unlike many other examples shown in this book, the backslashes at the end of each line do actually appear in the file.

The first line of each description contains the name(s) by which the description can be referenced. Multiple names can be separated by vertical bars (|).

For example, as shown in Table 9–2, an entry of *2* in an */etc/ttys* entry points to the 9600-baud entry shown above.

In the default description, the capability **ap** says that it is OK to use any parity. The **sp#** capability specifies the speed. Other capabilities that are available include:

- **im**—Print initial banner message before the login prompt
- **lm**—Customize the login prompt
- **nx**—Chain one entry to another for switching speeds on incoming calls
- **to**—Specify how many seconds **getty** will wait for the user to log in
- **hc**—Cause a hangup on close, like HUPCL in System V

You should not need to write *gettytab* entries. If you do, see *gettytab*(5) in your UNIX documentation for details.

10

Setting Up a UUCP Link

This chapter describes how to get your computer talking to another via UUCP. To get UUCP running, you need to tell the UUCP daemons about the following:

- What physical devices UUCP will use for its conversations: serial ports, modems, and/or network connections.

- The UUCP network name of the local system, and of the remote system(s) with which the local system will be conversing.

- How to contact the remote system—i.e., phone numbers, login names and passwords, or network connection information such as IP hostnames and service numbers for TCP/IP connections.

For modem and network links, you may also need to take extra configuration steps, such as setting up the modem for UUCP conversations or editing network configuration files. After you get the link up and running (see Chapter 11, *Making Sure the Link Works,* for how to test the UUCP link), you'll want to set up file access and other restrictions so that your UUCP connections won't threaten your computer's security and integrity (see Chapter 12, *Access and Security Considerations*).

Although this might seem like a lot of work, it's only the case for the first one or two UUCP connections; after that, adding a new system or device to the UUCP configuration is a fairly straightforward task.

Preparation

Before making any changes to your UUCP configuration, take a moment to see how your system's UUCP has been installed. In particular, you should find the directories used by UUCP, which vary depending on the version you have.

BNU Configuration Files

Older versions of BNU kept UUCP utility programs, **uucico**, and the configuration files (*Devices*, *Systems*, *Permissions*, *Dialers*, etc.) all in the */usr/lib/uucp* directory. Modern versions move the configuration files to another directory, usually */etc/uucp*, so that */usr/lib/uucp* can be shared across multiple machines. Most BNU installations have symbolic links in */usr/lib/uucp* for the files that have moved to the configuration directory.

The spool directory, */var/spool/uucp* (*/usr/spool/uucp* on older BNU systems), contains numerous hidden subdirectories such as *.Admin*, *.Log*, and *.Status* under which various control files, log files, and status files are kept, as well as the temporary workspace used during file transfer and execution of remote requests.

Taylor Configuration Files

Taylor UUCP can be configured to use any or all of three different kinds of configuration files: the "native" Taylor-style setup files, BNU-style, or Version 2. The location of the configuration directories is set at compile time; it can be found in the Makefile that comes with your Taylor UUCP source distribution. The default is */usr/conf/uucp* for Taylor configuration files, and */usr/lib/uucp* for HDB or Version 2 configuration files. One notable exception is the Slackware 2.3 Taylor UUCP setup: it reads Taylor-style *config* files from */var/lib/uucp/taylor_config*, and BNU-style *config* files from */var/lib/uucp/hdb_config*. Whether or not Taylor UUCP reads in older-style configuration files depends on the compile-time options in the *policy.h* file (see the Taylor UUCP source distribution). You can override this setting (and many other things) in the Taylor *config* master configuration file.

The location of the Taylor spool directory is also controlled by *policy.h* (or *config*), along with options to use either a native Taylor spool directory setup, or to emulate any of several spool directory formats used by other versions of UUCP (including BNU, BSD 4.3, BSD 4.2, and older Version 2). You might use these if you want Taylor UUCP to be compatible with an existing vendor version of UUCP already running on your system.[*] Unless you need this feature, we recommend that you configure Taylor UUCP to use its "native" configuration file, log file, and spool directory formats. This is easier in the long run, and it's worth learning the Taylor configuration file format, since there are important features of Taylor UUCP that can only be configured using the "native" configuration files. If you decide to use the BNU or Version 2 compatibility modes, you may run into minor but annoying differences in Taylor UUCP's interpretation of the configuration files. You can use the **uuconv** command to help you convert your configuration files to or from the Taylor UUCP "native" format.

Version 2 and BSD/OS Configuration Files

BSD 4.3 UUCP and its Version 2 ancestors keep all configuration files in the */usr/lib/uucp* directory; the spool directory is */usr/spool/uucp*. BSD/OS UUCP keeps configuration files in */etc/uucp*, and the spool directory is */var/spool/uucp*.

Start Keeping Records

Once you've found these directories, list them out with the **ls −alR** command and save the output someplace. Some of the files or directories may be symbolic links—be sure to include those files and directories in your listing. If file permissions or ownerships get accidentally changed in the flurry of editing, you'll be able to revert to the original settings. You should also save copies of all configuration files, especially if your system already has a working UUCP connection. You can do this all at once by making a backup of the UUCP directories. For example, on a typical BNU system, you could back up the UUCP configuration with:

```
# cd /
# find etc/uucp usr/lib/uucp usr/spool/uucp -print |
>     cpio -ocv > /save/me/somewhere/uucpconf.orig.cp
```

---

[*] These options let you install Taylor UUCP on a system with an active BNU or Version 2 UUCP spool. All configuration files, pending jobs, sequence numbers, and other state information should get picked up by the Taylor UUCP programs. This is an attractive option for upgrading older systems when you need the extra functionality of Taylor UUCP but don't want to rewrite your configuration files or lose any pending jobs.

Experienced system administrators use a source-code control system such as
SCCS (or its publicly available counterpart, RCS) to keep a trail of all
changes to important configuration files; this is a good idea for any UNIX
configuration file, not just UUCP.

Configuration File Basics

All of the UUCP configuration files adhere to the following conventions:

- A line beginning with a hash mark (#) is a comment (except in the most
  ancient versions of UUCP).

- The field separator is a space or tab. Spaces and tabs are not allowed
  within fields.

- Unused fields in BNU or Version 2 configuration files should contain a
  hyphen.

- Long lines can be continued with a backslash at the end of the line (followed immediately with a newline), except in older implementations of
  Version 2 UUCP.

- BNU UUCP will ignore any lines in a configuration file that begin with
  spaces or tabs. Taylor UUCP will accept such lines, but it will first truncate the leading white space.

BNU and Version 2 configuration files usually consist of a row of fields on a
line, such as:

```
ACU cua2 - 38400 hayes
```

Note the use of the hyphen (-) as a placeholder to mark an empty or unused
field. This style of configuration file is easy for a computer program to parse,
but disconcerting for most humans, since it's hard to remember what the
individual fields mean, or the correct order.

Taylor UUCP configuration files usually consist of a single item on each line,
containing a keyword and a value:

```
port    com3
type    modem
device  /dev/cua2
speed   38400
```

In the *port* and *sys* Taylor configuration files, groups of lines together define
a particular device or system, the same way a single-line entry with multiple

fields describes a device or system in BNU and Version 2. These groups of lines are often called *stanzas*, as if they were verses in a poem.[*] A new stanza is introduced by a specific command, such as the **port** command in the example above. Any commands at the top of the file, above the first stanza, set defaults for all stanzas. For example, the *port* file reads like this:

```
speed 38400
type modem

port com2
device /dev/cua1

port com3
device /dev/cua2
speed 19200
```

This file sets the default speed for all ports to 38400 bps, and the default type to "modem." You can override a default by specifying the desired attribute in the stanza itself, as we do with the "speed" command in the "com3" stanza above.

The Taylor UUCP *sys*, *port*, and *dial* file all use stanzas and accept default commands this way.

The Administrative Login

As noted previously, the */etc/passwd* file on your system probably has one or two UUCP logins already installed. Here's a sample:[†]

```
uucp:*:10:14:UUCP admin:/usr/lib/uucp:/bin/sh
nuucp:*:400:14:Unix-to-Unix Copy:/var/spool/uucppublic:/usr/lib/uucp/uucico
```

You can assign the UUCP administrative user a password and perform configuration tasks while logged in as *uucp*. Some system administrators prefer to disable the UUCP administrative login and do all UUCP configuration as the *root* user. See Chapter 12, *Access and Security Considerations*, for more information.

---

[*] However, we do not recommend that you read your Taylor UUCP configuration files at local poetry society meetings.

[†] On some systems, the default UUCP administration user is called *uucpadm*.

Automated Configuration Checking

All versions of BNU UUCP come with the **uucheck** command, which does a few consistency checks, inspects your *Systems* and *Permissions* files, and explains what kinds of access will be permitted during UUCP conversations. Taylor UUCP supplies a similar command, called **uuchk**. After creating or changing configuration files, you should run these commands to make sure that both you and UUCP have the same idea about what the configurations are telling UUCP to do. **uucheck** and **uuchk** are covered in more detail in Chapter 12, *Access and Security Considerations*.

UUCP Installation Tools

Some vendors provide menu-driven tools of varying degrees of user-friendliness that can help with UUCP configuration. These tools edit the UUCP configuration files for you, and help prevent syntax errors or inconsistent entries. You will still need to understand what goes into the configuration files, as it may be necessary to fine-tune them by hand.

The uucpadm tool (AIX)

In AIX, the command **/usr/lib/uucp/uucpadm** brings up an interactive menu that lets you edit the main UUCP configuration files. However, **uucpadm** is clumsy to use, mostly due to its quirky interpretation of control characters. For example, in most AIX environments, CTRL-U deletes a line of text. But in the **uucpadm** tool, it updates and saves an entry. Pressing CTRL-U in **uucpadm** when you make a mistake will permanently save the mistake to disk instead of erasing it.

The sam configuration tool (HP-UX)

sam is the general system administration and configuration tool for HP-UX, and includes UUCP configuration commands. You should start configuring UUCP using **sam**, and if needed, edit the configuration files (in */etc/uucp* or */usr/lib/uucp*) afterwards by hand.

The uusetup configuration tool (Digital UNIX)

The **uusetup** command in DEC OSF/1 (now called Digital UNIX) prompts you, one question at a time, for information that it will deposit in the UUCP configuration files. It also helps with some of the non-UUCP housekeeping, such as changing */etc/inittab* to set up incoming lines or reminding you to edit the */etc/passwd* file for UUCP logins.

The uuinstall configuration tool (SCO)

SCO UNIX provides the **uuinstall** command for editing UUCP configuration files. It will also edit */etc/inittab* for enabling and disabling incoming logins on a particular *tty* port, and let you set the local UUCP nodename.

Giving Your System a Name

Every system in a UUCP network needs a unique name. If you are building a private UUCP network, you can name your system anything you want. But if you want your system to be in the world-wide UUCP directory (known as the UUCP Mapping Project), you need to pick a name that isn't already in use. "Getting on the map" used to be required if you wanted to advertise a reasonably uncomplicated electronic mail address, but today most ISPs can give you an even simpler Internet-style mail address.

If you decide to register your system with the UUCP Mapping Project, you can browse through the database by reading articles in the Usenet newsgroup *comp.mail.maps*. You can also look up individual entries on the map interactively from the Web URL *http://www.uucp.org*. See Appendix G, *The UUCP Mapping Project*, for more information.

If your system is already on a TCP/IP network, you can usually use your TCP/IP hostname as your UUCP name. For example, the system *koshka.feelines.com* might use the UUCP name of *koshka*. Most BNU UUCP versions will insist on resolving a UUCP system name as if it is a TCP/IP hostname. If the other side of the link is not in the same domain, you will need to put the other side's numeric IP address into your */etc/hosts* file. Taylor, BSD, and SunOS UUCP do not have this problem, because they allow you to specify the TCP/IP hostname or the IP address in the UUCP systems configuration file.

The UNIX Nodename

Historically, UUCP gets the local system name from the UNIX kernel, where it's called the *nodename*. Every different version of UNIX seems to have its own way of setting up the nodename. System V-based versions install it at boot time via the **uname** −S*name* or the **setuname** command. Many systems, including BSD, SunOS, and Solaris, will take the system's TCP/IP hostname (returned by the **hostname** command) and convert that into the nodename. Some systems keep the nodename in a separate file such as */etc/sys_id* or */etc/HOSTNAME*, but read it in only when the system is rebooted.

Consult your system documentation for the exact details on changing your system's nodename.

Several versions of UUCP let you set the nodename via UUCP configuration files. For example:

- In Taylor UUCP, you can override the system nodename with the **node-name** keyword in the *config* setup file.

- In BSD/OS UUCP, you can define UUCP's local name by setting the NODENAME parameter in */etc/uucp/CONFIG*.

- In Solaris, you can set the UUCP nodename by creating the file */etc/uucp/Sysname*. The file should have only one line, containing the desired local UUCP name.

Displaying the Nodename

To make sure your nodename is set properly, or to see what it is currently set to, run the **uname** and **uuname** commands:

```
# uname -n
tabby
# uuname -l
tabby
#
```

uname reports name information from the operating system, while **uuname** reports information from the UUCP configuration. If you have set the local UUCP name via a UUCP configuration file (Taylor *config* or BSD/OS *CON-FIG*), only the output of **uuname -l** matters.

Length of Nodenames

Taylor, BNU, and BSD UUCP all support names of up to 14 characters. You should always use all-lowercase UUCP names. Many non-UUCP programs (especially mail-related ones) believe that all hostnames are case-insensitive. Older versions of UUCP truncate all system names to the first 7 characters.[*] You can use longer names, but the truncated name will appear in messages, in log files, and in the internal files used in the spool directory.

---

[*] Some very old versions of UUCP truncated names to the first 6 characters.

Quick Setup Examples

Here's how to configure a simple UUCP connection. Our example will be a dial-up link from the local system *tabby*, over a modem directly connected to one of *tabby*'s serial ports, to the remote system *fatcat* (which also has a modem directly connected to a serial port). The modem on *tabby* for this example is Hayes-compatible, with a maximum speed of 9600 bps.

The configuration files you need to edit are different for each different version of UUCP, but the core concepts are the same. You will need to supply UUCP with the remote system's name, phone number, how to detect the login prompt and sign on (known as the *chat script*), what kind of modem to use, and what serial port it is connected to.

A BNU Example

First, we visit the BNU *Systems* configuration file. This file contains a list of other systems that can have UUCP communications with the local system. For our sample connection, we would add a line like this:

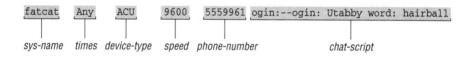

As you can see, a lot of information is stuffed into one line. Here is what the individual parts mean:

Field	Meaning
system-name	The UUCP name of the remote system (in this case, *fatcat*).
times	What times of day (or the week) UUCP is allowed to call this system. Here we use Any, meaning that UUCP may place an outgoing call whenever it wants to.
device-type	The type of device to use for conversations with this system. ACU stands for Automatic Call Unit, which is UUCP's old fashioned (but still charming) way of saying "modem."
speed	The speed that you want used for connections to *fatcat*.
phone number	The phone number of the remote modem that is attached to *fatcat*).

| chat script | The chain of "look for this, then transmit that" sequences, known as *expect-send* sequences, used to log in to *fatcat*. The administrator on the remote system has presumably assigned us the account *Utabby*, with password *hairball*. Details for using chat scripts appear later in this chapter. |

You'll notice that we still haven't told UUCP how to find the 9600 bps modem on */dev/tty01*. In BNU, this is done by editing the *Devices* configuration file, which contains entries telling UUCP what physical devices it can use for making outgoing UUCP calls:

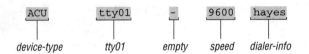

Field	Meaning
device-type	The type of device, in this case *ACU* for a modem. You can define your own device types if desired.
tty-name	The name of the device special file in the */dev* directory to use for this communications link. Note that you don't have to specify */dev*, just the rest of the file name.
empty	Not used with modern modems—leave a hyphen in this field.
speed	The speed of the modem. When calling a remote system, UUCP must be able to match the speed it finds in the *Systems* file with an entry in *Devices*. Otherwise, it can't make the call.
dialer-info	The dialer type—in this case *hayes*—that uses the modem description of that name in the *Dialers* configuration file.

The *hayes* dialer type should be pre-defined in the *Dialers* configuration file, but for completeness, here's a sample entry:

```
hayes  =,-,   "" ATE1V1X1Q0S2=255S12=255 OK ATDT\T CONNECT
```

You can read a detailed analysis of this gobbledygook in Appendix I, *Setting Up a Modem*. The *hayes* dialing entry supplied with your version of BNU should be enough to get you started. More information on fine-tuning these dialing descriptions can be found later in this chapter, and in Appendix I.

Finally, you should create an entry in the *Permissions* file to control what files and commands the remote system may access:

```
LOGNAME=Ufatcat VALIDATE=fatcat REQUEST=yes SENDFILES=yes
MACHINE=fatcat REQUEST=yes COMMANDS=rmail:rnews
```

The *Permissions* file is explained in more detail in Chapter 12, *Access and Security Considerations*.

A Taylor UUCP Example

For Taylor UUCP, the list of systems to call is named *sys*. Here's how the information for our sample connection would be written for the *sys* file:

```
system    fatcat
time      Any
speed     9600
port      hayes9600
phone     5559961
chat      ogin:--ogin: ULabby word: hairball
commands  rmail rnews
called-login Ufatcat
```

The meanings of these fields are almost all the same as their BNU counterparts in the previous example. Since the **port** command uses a device type defined by the user, we need to add an entry into the *port* configuration file:

```
port      hayes9600
type      modem
device    /dev/tty01
speed     9600
dialer    hayes
```

Note that we could have called this port definition "my_modem" or whatever else struck our fancy, as long as we used the same name in the *sys* file entry.

Finally, we need to set up the *dial* file with an appropriate dialing entry. Here's an example:

```
dialer  hayes
chat    "" ATE1V1X1Q0S2=255S12=255 OK ATDT\T CONNECT
```

A BSD/Version 2 Example

Version 2 UUCP is an ancestor of BNU, and uses a similar format for its configuration files. The file with information on remote systems is called *L.sys*. The file with information on devices is called *L-devices* (note the hyphen).

The BSD 4.2, 4.3, and BSD/OS UUCP are compatible enough with BNU that you can use the preceding BNU example, but edit the files *L.sys* instead of *Systems*, and *L-devices* instead of *Devices*. Since BSD UUCP versions have limited dialing support, there is no dialer configuration file; use the hard-coded dialer types *hayes* or *hayes2400* in *L-devices*.

A TCP/IP Example

Most versions of UUCP support conversations over a TCP/IP network connection. You can connect via a local LAN, a SLIP/PPP dial-up link, or two systems connected to the Internet.

For all versions of UUCP, you should first make sure your network configuration has the information UUCP needs to make its connections.[*]

Service number

The file */etc/services* must have the correct TCP/IP port number for the *uucp* service (540 is the standard service number). For example:

```
uucp      540/tcp      uucpd      # uucp daemon
```

This information should already be in your */etc/services* file; if it is not, add it in yourself. Always use port 540 unless you like trouble—some UUCP versions will not talk over any other port number.

If you are using the Network Information System (NIS, *nee* Yellow Pages), you may want to make these changes in your NIS maps instead.

Answering a call

To receive incoming calls over TCP/IP, the **inetd** daemon should be configured to start the UUCP server daemon **uucpd** when a remote host attempts to open a connection on port 540. The configuration file for **inetd** is usually */etc/inetd.conf*, and the entry usually looks like:

```
uucp  stream  tcp  nowait  root /etc/uucpd uucpd
```

Note that the exact file path to the **uucpd** daemon (field 6 in the example above) will vary depending on your UNIX vendor: some systems use */usr/etc/in.uucpd* or */usr/sbin/uucpd*.

---

[*] Although these examples show how to edit the */etc/services* and */etc/inetd.conf* files, on IBM's AIX you should use the **smit** tool to make these changes for you. Otherwise, your changes may vanish upon the next reboot.

uucpd is essentially a stripped-down login daemon. It will provide a login and password prompt to the calling host, but it will permit logins only for user accounts that have **uucico** as their login shell.

Taylor UUCP does not come with **uucpd**.[*] Instead, **uucico** is invoked with the −l option, which will cause it to issue a login/password prompt to the remote caller. However, unlike **uucpd**, Taylor **uucico** will not use the standard system password file */etc/passwd*; instead, it will use the Taylor password file, by default stored in */usr/conf/uucp/passwd*. We discuss the reasons for this (and its implications) in Chapter 12, *Access and Security Considerations*. Here's a sample *inetd.conf* entry for Taylor UUCP being invoked this way:

```
uucp  stream  tcp  nowait  uucp  /usr/lib/uucp/uucico uucico -l
```

After changing *inetd.conf* you need to reset the **inetd** daemon so that it will read in the changes. The usual way to do this is to find the process ID of the currently running **inetd**, and send it the hangup signal like this:

```
# kill -HUP pid-number
```

Some systems also have vendor-specific ways of resetting **inetd**. In AIX, you would issue the command **refresh −s inetd**; in HP-UX, you could use **/etc/inetd −c**.

If you have the **tcpd** command (from the TCP Wrappers[†] package) installed on your system—and you should—your *inetd.conf* entries will be slightly different than the examples shown here. Make sure the */etc/hosts.allow* and */etc/hosts.deny* files instruct **tcpd** to permit only the desired remote hosts to use your UUCP service.

Name resolution

In order to place an outgoing call, UUCP will need the IP address of the remote host. Taylor and BSD let you specify the IP number or hostname in their configuration files, but most BNU versions insist on trying to use the UUCP nodename as an Internet hostname. This will probably work between two hosts in the same domain; otherwise, you will need to obtain the

---

[*] But if you install Taylor UUCP on a system that has an existing implementation of **uucpd**, that **uucpd** should work as long as you make sure that the original system path for **uucico** (usually */usr/lib/uucp/uucico*) points to the Taylor **uucico**.

[†] TCP Wrappers is an access control mechanism that restricts which hosts can use the network services under the control of **inetd**. For more information, see the files in *ftp://ftp.cert.org*

numeric IP address of the remote system and add a host resolution entry
into your network configuration by editing */etc/hosts* like this:

```
10.1.2.3    fatcat.feelines.com  fatcat  # alias for UUCP connections
```

If you are using a name server or NIS, you may need to edit one of the
name server configuration files (such as */etc/resolv.conf* or
/etc/nsswitch.conf) to remind your system to check the local */etc/hosts* file for
name resolution.

BNU setup for TCP/IP (except SunOS)

In most BNU systems, you would add the following line to the *Systems* file:

```
fatcat Any TCP - - ogin: Utabby word: hairball
```

Note that the chat script is simpler (we don't have to worry about modems
synchronizing or losing characters at the beginning of the connection). Also,
note the reference to the **TCP** device. If there is not already a **TCP** entry in
your *Devices* file, you'll need to add one. The exact entry you'll need varies
slightly from one BNU version to the next. Here are a few that we know
about:

```
AIX and HP-UX: TCP     -    - -    TCP

Solaris:       TCP,et -    - Any  TCP -

IRIX:          TCP    -    - Any  TCP uucp

SCO:           TCP TCP,e - Any  TCP 540
```

In AIX, you may also need to add a line to the *Dialers* file:

```
Dialers: TCP
```

Finally, for all versions, make sure you have an entry in the *Permissions* file
for the system with which you'll be communicating:

```
LOGNAME=Ufatcat VALIDATE=fatcat REQUEST=yes SENDFILES=yes
MACHINE=fatcat REQUEST=yes COMMANDS=rmail:rnews
```

Taylor setup for TCP/IP

In Taylor UUCP, your configuration files should look like this:

sys:

```
system   fatcat
address  fatcat.feelines.com
time     Any
```

```
port      TCP
chat      ogin: Utabby word: hairball
commands  rmail rnews
called-login Ufatcat
```

port:

```
port    TCP
type    tcp
```

Note that the **address** command in the *sys* file lets you specify either the IP address, or the hostname of the remote site. There's no need to put entries in */etc/hosts*.

BSD and SunOS setup for TCP/IP

SunOS, BSD 4.3, and BSD/OS all put the TCP/IP specific information for connecting to a remote host into otherwise meaningless fields in the *Systems* (*L.sys*) file. Instead of the *speed* field, insert the TCP port number or service name, and instead of the *phone-number*, put in the TCP/IP host name or IP address:

```
fatcat Any TCP uucp fatcat.feelines.com ogin: Utabby word: hairball
                │    │
            TCP-service  TCP-hostname
```

None of the BSD versions requires any entries in the *L-devices* file for a TCP/IP connection—all of the necessary information is in *L.sys*. In SunOS 4, you may need to add this line into *Devices*:

```
TCP,et  -  -  Any  TCP -
```

UUCP Configuration Concepts

As you can see from the previous examples, most of the setup for UUCP links is done by adding entries into UUCP's configuration files. (The frustrating part comes when you try to get your UUCP connections running, but we'll cover that in the next chapter.)

Before we go into the gory details of what you can put in your UUCP configuration files, let's briefly discuss what systems information UUCP wants before it can make an outgoing connection, and how it organizes the information in its configuration files. We'll go into each of these subjects in more detail in the UUCP version-specific sections later in this chapter.

How UUCP Finds Its Way

uucico has a whole pile of preparations to make before it can start talking to another system. These tasks are the same in all versions of UUCP, even though the individual details may differ.

Is the time right?

Before doing anything else, **uucico** parses the "times to call" information associated with the remote system. In the examples above, we've used "Any" so that calls may occur at any time of day, but this field could be an elaborate combination of time and day-of-week specifications that will limit when UUCP will place outgoing calls.

Device and speed classes

Every *Systems* (*sys*, *L.sys*) entry also specifies a type of device that will be used to reach the remote system. **uucico** looks through the device files (*Devices*, *port*, or *L-devices*) to find a matching device type.

The most common device type is a modem. A site with many serial connections, or with serial connections to a terminal server or other network front end (such as an X.25 PAD interface), could define device types for each type of gizmo hanging off a serial port. BNU UUCP requires that you define direct serial links to other systems as a separate device type.

uucico must also match the *speed class* requested in the systems entry for the remote host. UUCP treats multiple entries of the same device type and speed as equivalent: you can define multiple modems at a particular speed, and when UUCP tries to make a call that needs one of those modems, it will grab the first one available.

BNU and Version 2 UUCP's definition of speed has an extra wrinkle: if you have two modems (or two directly connected serial ports) that are the same speed but connect to things that aren't interchangeable, then you can segregate them into different classes by prefixing a letter in front of their baud rate. For example, a site might have two 9600-bps modems: one a Telebit modem that uses the proprietary PEP protocol, and the other a more mainstream modem that uses the V.32 protocol. These two types of modems are not compatible with each other. If you call a site that has a PEP modem with your V.32 modem, the two modems will be able to communicate only at 2400 bps. By putting the two modems into separate speed classes (call one of them "T9600," and the other "V9600"), UUCP will always use the right type of modem to call a particular site.

For outgoing network calls, things are much simpler. A TCP/IP network has all the virtual circuits that UUCP could want and the network always runs at the same speed. However, most versions of BNU UUCP still expect to find a device entry for the "TCP" device.

If UUCP cannot find an available device, it will not make the call. It may be that the device you need is in use by another system process, or it may also be that you haven't defined the right device (or any devices) in the configuration files.

Dialing away

Interacting with a modem in order to dial a call is yet another task for **uucico** to perform before it can get on to the big show. BNU and Taylor UUCP have generalized this problem by allowing you to define *dialer scripts*, which are basically the same as chat scripts, but they interact with the modem (or other device that appears before the connection is complete) instead of the remote system.

At a site with modem pools, X.25 PAD interfaces, intelligent port switches, or other network front ends, making a UUCP connection between two systems may not only mean dialing a modem, but also interacting with other switching devices along the way. BNU and Taylor allow you to write separate dialing scripts for each intermediary you need to deal with; they also permit you to use multiple dialing scripts in any order needed for a particular connection.

The "modern" Version 2 UUCP supplied with BSD 4.3 does not support dial scripts as a separate entity, but permits you to define them on a per-device basis in the *L-devices* file. Some implementations of UUCP, including Taylor, also support calling an external program to perform dialing functions.

Time for a chat...

The interactions needed to finally log on to the remote system and start talking UUCP-speak are defined by the chat script. A chat script (or a dialer script) is defined with "expect send" pairs of the form. For example:

```
expect_sequence[-sub_send-sub_expect]  send-sequence
```

uucico waits for the expect sequence (a string of characters) to be received on the connection, and then sends the send sequence (another string of characters). If the expect sequence is not received within a certain timeout, the optional *subsend sequence* is sent, which is marked off by hyphens within the expect sequence. After the *subsend sequence* is sent, a new expect subsequence is awaited. An expect sequence can have multiple sub-sequences, which can make chat scripts hard to read but quite persistent when trying to contact another system.

One confusing aspect of chat scripts is what they *don't* seem to do. By default, all send sequences are suffixed with a carriage return (decimal 13) character.* So a chat script like this:

```
ogin:--ogin: Utabby  word: hairball
```

not only sends a carriage return after the login name "Utabby" or the pass-word "hairball," but also sends a carriage return as part of the subsequence triggered if the pattern "ogin:" is not received in time. In this case, the sub-sequence between the two hyphens is null (zero length), but the carriage return will still be sent "afterwards," unless you explicitly disable it.

If the expected pattern does not appear on the line, and any supplied sub-sends and subexpects also fail, the chat script fails and the connection is aborted. If the chat script executes successfully all the way to the end, it is declared successful and **uucico** proceeds to the next stage of the connec-tion—namely the UUCP session.

Passive Systems

It is possible to set up one side of the link as a *passive* system; that is, one that can be called but will never originate calls of its own. This is often used by ISPs or other providers of paid UUCP service, because they expect their customers to always pay for phone calls. This greatly simplifies the UUCP setup for the passive side of the link, since you don't need to specify phone numbers or other contact information.

Systems and L.sys Files

The BNU *Systems* file and the Version 2 *L.sys* file have a similar format. Each line in the file represents one system that can be called by the local UUCP programs. If you want to supply multiple paths to a system, for example, two different phone numbers that should be tried in succession, you can create multiple entries for the same system.

---

* Some older Version 2 implementations send a newline (decimal 10) instead.

The general format for a *Systems* or *L.sys* entry is:

```
system_name  schedule  device  speed  phone_number  chat_script
```

Field   **Function in *Systems* and *L.sys***

system_name   The nodename of the remote system. The name can be up
                     to 14 characters long, but for compatibility reasons should
                     be unique to the first 7 characters.

schedule   When the local system is allowed to call the remote system.
                     Any means any day of the week. See below for details.

device type   The type of device to be used for the call. See below for
                     details.

speed   The speed in bits per second for the device. You can also
                     specify a range of speeds (e.g., 2400-38400) when connect-
                     ing to a modem that adjusts its speed to match the modem
                     that answers on the other end. Speed classes can be created
                     by combining an initial letter with the speed (e.g., "H9600").
                     In BSD and SunOS, if the device is "TCP" for a TCP/IP net-
                     work connection, this field should contain the TCP service
                     number or name.

phone_number

                     The dialer sequence that will be used by the modem to call
                     the remote system. This is usually a phone number, but
                     might be some other kind of string if you have a port switch
                     or an X.25 PAD with which to connect (such as a menu
                     choice or an X.25 destination ID). In BSD and SunOS, if the
                     device is "TCP" for a TCP/IP network connection, this field
                     should contain the IP address or hostname of the remote
                     system.

chat script   A string describing the initial conversation between two
                     machines. It contains the login ID, the password, and any
                     other character sequences needed to complete the login
                     procedure (see below).

When **uucico** is invoked, it first scans the system file for the name of the
system to be called. It then checks that the current time is a valid time to
call. If so, it checks the *device type* and *speed* fields and goes to the device
configuration file for a device that matches. **uucico** then checks to see if the

device is already in use. If so, **uucico** checks to see if there is another device of the requested type and speed available, and uses it.

If no device is available, **uucico** returns to the system file to see if there is another entry for the system in question. If so, the process is repeated. If not, the call is terminated. Once an available device is located, **uucico** uses the telephone number (if appropriate) and chat script to actually make the connection.

schedule

The *schedule* field indicates when the local system can call the remote system. It has several subfields: the *day* of the week, an optional *time* of day when the system can call, and an optional minimum *retry* period for calling in when an attempt fails. BSD 4.3 and most versions of BNU allow an additional *grade* subfield that allows you to control what type of transfers go out at a specific time.

The *day* and *time* subfields are written with no intervening spaces. The retry subfield is set off with a semicolon in BNU and BSD 4.3, and a comma in older implementations of Version 2.

The *day* subfield must be present. It can be any one of the following:

Any   The system can call on any day.

Never The system should never call; the other system will call instead.

Wk   Any weekday. You can also specify individual days of the week using one or more of the keywords **Su, Mo, Tu, We, Th, Fr,** and **Sa.**

The *time* subfield is specified by two 24-hour clock times separated by a dash (-). For example, 1900-2300 means that a system can be called only from between 7 and 11 o'clock in the evening. The range can span 0000, so that a range of 0700-0500 means that the local system can call between 7 a.m. each day and 5 a.m. the next morning; that is, any time **except** from 5 to 7 a.m.[*] If the time subfield is omitted, the local system can call any time of the day.

---

* This is not exactly correct. **uucico** actually interprets this figure on a same day basis, so 0700-0500 actually means from 0000-0500 and from 0700-2359 on the same day. This is a fine distinction, which really has impact only when combined with a day specification. For example:

```
Wk2310-0750
```

means 0000-0750 and 2310-2359 Monday through Friday—not 0000-0750 Saturday morning.

A direct link would most likely be set up to run at **Any** time. However, for a dial-out line, you may want to restrict outgoing calls (particularly to systems outside your local area) to non-peak hours to take advantage of lower telephone rates. (Be aware that your computer's clock may not match the telephone company's clock; you'll probably want to give yourself a few minutes of leeway on either end.)

For example, to limit outgoing calls to system *farcat* to 11:10 p.m. until 7:50 the following morning any weekday (when American telephone rates are cheapest), you would write:

```
farcat Wk2310-0750 ...
```

Users can still invoke **uucp** or **uux** during any time they want, but all requests will be spooled and not executed until the permitted time.

In older implementations of Version 2, you cannot specify different times for individual days (e.g., weekday evenings, but all day Saturday and Sunday) except by creating multiple *L.sys* entries for a system, each with a different schedule field.

```
farcat Wk1800-2400...
farcat SaSu...
```

In BNU and BSD 4.3, you can do this by separating day/time pairs with a comma. For example:

```
farcat Wk1800-2400,SaSu ....
```

A few implementations of Version 2 UUCP support a similar mechanism, using a vertical bar (|) as the delimiter instead of a comma.

In BSD 4.3, the keyword *Evening* is equivalent to *Wk1700-0800,Sa,Su* and *Night* is equivalent to *Any2300-0800,Sa,Su0800-1700*. These correspond to the time ranges where telephone calls within the United States are usually billed at lower rates. BSD 4.3 also defines the keyword *NonPeak* as equivalent to *Any1800-0700,Sa,Su*, to match the off-peak hours of the American X.25 public data networks. However, those networks have changed their procedures substantially since that keyword was implemented, so it may no longer be relevant.

Grading

Most versions of BNU (along with BSD 4.3) allow the day or time subfield to be followed by a maximum *grade* specification, set off by a slash. The grade is a either a single numeric digit, or an upper or lower case letter. The grades are valued like this:

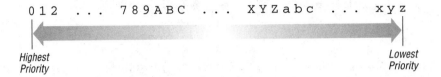

```
0 1 2   . . .   7 8 9 A B C   . . .   X Y Z a b c   . . .   x y z
```

Highest   Lowest
Priority   Priority

That is, grade 0 (zero) has the highest priority, and grade z the lowest. Grade specifications can be used to allow high-priority jobs to be transferred as soon as possible, or to hold low-priority traffic until an off-peak hour arrives.

uucico normally processes work files (see Appendix B, *The Spool Directory/Working Files*) in grade order. The default grade for various types of requests varies from system to system, but is generally highest for **uux** requests, followed by mail, then news, and **uucp** requests last.* Grading is used automatically to control the order in which UUCP requests, mail, and news are transferred. However, by setting a grade specification in the time subfield, you can actually keep certain classes of requests from being sent.

This feature allows you, for instance, to transfer mail messages even at peak times, while only transferring Usenet news articles at night. For example, the schedule field:

```
    bloom-beacon Any0900-1700/C . . .
```

will allow only grade C or better to be sent during business hours.

Note, however, that setting the grade controls only what your site *sends*, not what it *receives*.† For example, consider a UUCP connection between sites *ora* and *bloom-beacon*. Assume *ora* has some jobs queued for *bloom-beacon* at grade C (mail) and some at grade m (news). If *ora* calls *bloom-beacon* with the grade set to C, only the mail will be transferred from *ora* to

---

* The default grade for uux is generally A, for mail C, for news d, and for **uucp** n. If **rmail** is executed by **uux**, the grade for mail will be A. However, **sendmail** normally sets the grade to something lower, typically C.

When you queue a UUCP job with **uux** or **uucp**, you can change the grade of your transfer with the **−g** option.

† Except in Taylor UUCP, which allows you to set up grade restrictions in both directions. However, the restrictions are not effective when receiving files unless both sides are running Taylor UUCP.

bloom-beacon. But, any transfers waiting on *bloom-beacon* for *ora* will be sent, no matter what their grade.

In BSD 4.3 and BSD/OS, you can also invoke **uucico** with the *–ggrade* option, where *grade* specifies the lowest grade to be transferred during that session. On older UUCPs that do not support grading, you may find the system dialing every time a user sends mail. In order to keep this from happening, set the time field to *Never* and use **cron** to periodically invoke **uucico** with the **–S** option (which overrides the time field).

How often to retry?

The optional *retry* field indicates the minimum waiting period (in minutes) after an unsuccessful call to the remote system. The local system cannot try calling the remote system again unless the minimum waiting period has expired. BNU and BSD 4.3 UUCP use an "exponential backoff" retry strategy, starting with 5 minutes and growing larger as the number of unsuccessful attempts increases. Older Version 2 UUCPs will wait a fixed interval, either 55 minutes or an hour, before retries are allowed.

To specify a retry period, put a semicolon (or a comma in older Version 2 UUCPs) at the end of the *schedule* field if you want to override these defaults. For example:

```
japan SaSu;60 ...
```

This entry limits overseas calls to system *japan* to weekends. If UUCP fails to log in on the first call, it must wait at least 60 minutes before it can try calling *japan* again.

You may want to have a shorter retry time for direct links than for dial-up links. Be aware, though, that shortening the retry period may cause you to reach the maximum number of retries (default is 26) before a remote system comes back on line. Note also that changing the retry period will not cause **uucico** to be invoked any sooner. That's under the control of a **cron** table entry or other external force.

device type

This describes the device that UUCP will use to connect to the remote system. In BNU, the device type is a keyword that will be looked up in the *Devices* file. Version 2 is less consistent: some device types require a corresponding entry in the *L-devices* file, while others do not.

Type	Meaning
ACU	A dial-up modem.
TCP	A TCP/IP network connection.
system_name	A direct serial link to the named system (BNU only).
DIR	A direct serial link. The name of the serial port must be specified in the phone number field, as well as in *L-devices* (BSD 4.3 only).

Some systems have other keywords that you can put here, for pre-defined devices supported by their particular UUCP version. See your documentation for more details. In BNU, you may also define your own device names. Some people use this feature to reclassify a particular modem (perhaps to reserve it for a particular system or group of systems), or to group serial ports by the kind of device with which they connect (such as a port switch or X.25 PAD).

Protocol selection

In BNU, you can append to the device type a comma followed by a list of protocols that UUCP should use for communications with the system specified by this entry. Protocols are discussed more fully in Appendix J, *UUCP Protocol Internals*. You may want to override BNU UUCP's default protocol selection mechanism to improve efficiency when you place a call over an error-correcting modem or other low or no-error connection. You can also specify a protocol in the BNU *Devices* file; this is a good idea because you can link devices with the particular protocols that are best suited for them.

phone number

In the fifth field, you specify a telephone number for the remote system. In BNU, this field can be used for any system-specific contact information that is needed by a dialing script. For directly connected systems or TCP/IP links, put a hyphen here as a placeholder.

In Version 2, this field is reused for different kinds of links. For a direct link, put the device special filename (i.e., *tty01*) here; for a TCP/IP link (in SunOS and BSD), insert the Internet hostname or IP address of the remote site.

Telephone numbers can undergo additional processing before they are given to the modem for dialing: UUCP attempts to translate the hyphen (-) into the appropriate command to make the modem pause for a second or two, and the equal sign (=) into the command to make the modem wait for a second dial tone. In addition, UUCP can perform dialcodes processing on a file. Dialcodes is a macro-processing feature for phone numbers that, if used properly, allows you to share a systems file with systems in different area codes or with different office phone systems. Dialcodes are described in further detail later in this chapter. Depending on the device type, other device-specific connection information may go in this field. Again, check your system documentation for details on how to "place calls" using that device.

chat script

The remainder of the line following the phone number contains a string of text called the *chat script*. The chat script defines the login "conversation" that will occur between the two systems. It consists of "expect-send" pairs separated by spaces, with optional "subexpect-subsend" pairs separated by hyphens, as shown in Figure 10-5.

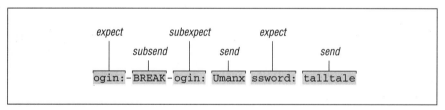

Figure 10-5: Components of a chat script

This line defines what the local system *expects* from the remote system and what it should *send* as a reply to the remote system, if the correct string is received.

The "expect" portion need contain only part of what is really expected. For example, if system *fatcat* displays the following banner and login prompt:

```
Fee Lines, Inc. (fatcat)
login:
```

the *expect* field may contain only the trailing portion of the login prompt, such as "ogin:" or even "in:". This is done to prevent failure if the remote system prompts "Login:" or "Password:" instead of the more common lower-case prompt. (Note that **uucico** actually will stop looking when it finds any part of the *expect* string. For example, "login" without the colon would also work. It is customary to use the last part of the string to make sure that the *send* string is not sent out too soon.)

A second or so after the expect string is received, the next send string is sent out. Unless explictly suppressed, each send field is followed by a carriage return.[*] A very simple chat script might look like this:

```
ogin: Utabby ssword: patches
```

In other words, expect ... **ogin:**, send **Utabby<CR>**, expect ... **ssword**, send **patches<CR>**.

In Chapter 11, we will show you how to watch the progress of this conversation. It goes something like this:

```
wanted ogin:
got that
Utabby
wanted ssword:
got that
```

In actual practice, such a simple chat script is rare. For most devices, the chat script should always use an optional "subexpect-subsend" sequence to give **uucico** more than one chance to log in. For example, assume that noise on the line was received by either system as real data before the login sequence was initiated. The simple chat would fail, where a script like the following might not:

```
ogin:--ogin: Utabby ssword: patches
```

This script says: expect "ogin:"; if you do not get it in a certain time, send a carriage return (the -- here indicates a null subsend, with the default carriage return afterwards), and look again for "ogin:".

The difference between a normal "expect-send" sequence and a "subexpect-subsend" sequence is that a send occurs if the expect string *is* received, and a subsend occurs only if the preceding expect string *is not* received.

In order to create a chat script for logging in, you need at the very least to get the UUCP login name and password from the system administrator of the remote system.

In addition, you may need to use one or more special character sequences if the remote system has any peculiarities in its login sequence. The escape sequences used in expect or send strings are listed in Table 10-1.

---

[*] Some older Version 2 UUCP's send a newline (decimal 10).

Note that you can use a null string delimited by double quotes ("") as an expect string, which will immediately match and send the send string. You can also use the null string as a send string, which will send only the trailing carriage return. For a truly null send string that sends nothing, use \c as the send string. (See Table 10–1.)

Table 10–1: Chat Script Escape Sequences

Escape Sequence	Description
EOT	Send the end-of-transmission character, ^D (decimal value 4).
BREAK	Cause a BREAK. This is sometimes simulated using line speed changes and null characters. May not work on all systems.
\b	Send a backspace character. On BSD 4.2 systems, send a BREAK.
\c	Suppress the default carriage return at the end of the *send* string.
\d	Delay for 1 second.
\K	Insert a BREAK (BNU and Taylor).
\n	Send a newline or linefeed character.
\N	Send a null character (BNU and Taylor). Use \0 to send a null in Version 2.
\p	Pause for 1/10th of a second (BNU and Taylor).
\r	Send a carriage return.
\s	Send a space character.
\t	Send a tab character (not implemented in BSD 4.3).
\\	Send a backslash (\) character.
\E	Turn on echo checking (BNU and Taylor). For the remainder of the characters in the send string, after sending each character, wait for it to be echoed by the remote side. Echo checking must be re-enabled for each send string where it is desired.
\e	Disable echo checking (BNU and Taylor).
\ddd	Collapse the octal digits (*ddd*) into a single ASCII character and send that character.

BSD, SunOS 4.1, and Solaris systems add a few more keywords that can be used as a send string. In particular, *P_ZERO* causes the following send strings to be sent with their parity bit set to zero, instead of the default even parity. The keywords *P_EVEN*, *P_ODD*, and *P_ONE* are also available to set even parity, odd parity, or to force the parity bit to one.

SunOS and Solaris allow another send string escape that lets you set terminal modes on the communications device. This can be used in either the *Systems* or the *Dialers* file:

```
hayes    =,-,    "" AT OK ATDT\T CONNECT STTY=crtscts
```

The **crtscts** terminal mode turns on hardware flow control.

A limitation on many UUCP versions is that you cannot use a hyphen as part of a chat script. Some versions let you use \055.

If you're calling a system with a complicated login sequence, with any luck the remote system administrator has already solved this problem and can supply you with a working chat script. If not, then you should use **cu**, **tip**, or another telecommunications program to log in to the remote system. Watch very closely what happens, or better yet, save the session to a file (see Chapter 5, *Logging In on a Remote System*). For example, do you get a login prompt right away or do you have to press RETURN one or more times? Does the remote system always answer at the same speed? (As we saw in Chapter 9, *The Physical Connection*, it is possible to set up a line so that **getty** cycles through a number of possible baud rates until it finds one that matches. If this is the case, the user manually dialing in normally needs to send a BREAK or RETURN to switch speeds.)

For irregularities beyond the initial login, you may need to invoke **uucico** in a special debugging mode to see exactly what is going wrong.

Chapter 11, *Making Sure the Link Works*, includes a detailed discussion and examples of how to figure out the chat script for a neighboring system.

Several examples of BNU *Systems* file entries follow, including chat scripts:

```
venus Any venus 9600 - "" \n in:--in: Umars word: mirror
roma Any;3 roma E9600 - "" \r\d\r\d\r ogin:-BREAK-ogin: nuucp word: milan1
test1 Any ACU 38400 9991212 "" \r\d\r ogin:-BREAK-ogin: test1 word: itsdone
```

And here's an example with the same system listed twice, so that a second phone number can be tried if the first is busy:

```
catnip Any ACU 38400 5554737 "" \d ogin:--ogin: Utabby word: barehall
catnip Any ACU 38400 5552454 "" \d ogin:--ogin: Utabby word: barehall
```

The Taylor sys File

The Taylor *sys* file has more or less the same purpose in life as the BNU *Systems* or Version 2 *L.sys* files, but it uses the Taylor "keyword value" syntax, with each system entry described in a multi-line stanza. Here's an example:

```
system  fatcat
time    Any
port    fastmodem
speed   38400
phone   5550123
chat    ogin:--ogin: Utabby word: hairball
```

Although we chose to list these lines in the same order as in a *Systems* file, they can be ordered any way you like. A new stanza starts with another **system** command. Any commands before the first **system** command will be used as file-wide defaults.

Nearly all the values in a Taylor *sys* file take the same form as their counterparts in *Systems* or *L.sys*. For example, the format for time strings, baud rates, and chat scripts are all nearly the same as described for BNU and Version 2, with exceptions noted below.

system *sys_name*

> Names the system for this entry.

time *schedule* [*retry_time*]

> When the remote system may be called. The *schedule* is a standard UUCP time string. The optional *retry_time* is the number of minutes before another call may be made if this attempt fails, as in BNU. You can specify multiple time strings by combining them with either the comma (,) or the pipe (|) character. You can also specify multiple time strings with multiple **time** commands; in which case, you can specify a different *retry_time* on the different **time** commands to change the retry time based on when the failed call was made.

timegrade *grade schedule* [*retry_time*]

> Specifies that jobs of grade *grade* or higher may be transferred on an outgoing call during the times described by *schedule* (a time string as in the **time** command). The optional *retry_time* is used as with the **time** command. This command may also be specified multiple times, controlling the grades allowed at certain times.

called-timegrade *grade schedule*

> Like the **timegrade** command, but controls jobs by grade on incoming calls.

max-retries *count*

> The maximum number of times this system may be retried. The default is 26.

success-wait *seconds*

> A retry time, in seconds, that applies only after a *successful* call. This is used to limit how often a system is called. You might want to do this if the link was through an expensive dial-up call. The default is zero, meaning no limit.

port *port_name*
port *port-file-command*

> Name a particular port or class of ports to use for calling the remote system. Ports are defined in the *port* configuration file. You can also use this command to put "in-line" any commands that would otherwise appear in the *port* file. This lets you bypass the *port* file completely for simple configurations.

speed *number*
baud *number*

> For serial links, the speed (i.e., baud rate) at which to call the remote system. The BNU and Version 2 speed classes (baud rates prefixed with a single letter) are not supported (except when Taylor UUCP is reading BNU or Version 2 configuration files).

phone *phone_number*

> The telephone number to dial when using a modem port. Telephone numbers are translated with pauses (= or − characters) and dialcodes as in BNU/Version 2.

address *host_name*

> The remote host name (or IP address) to use when calling over a TCP/IP network connection.

chat *expect / send pairs*

> The chat script used to contact the remote system after the connection has been established. Table 10-1 lists the allowable chat script escapes. Taylor chat scripts have a few extra escape characters that can be used:

\W*nn*   Change the chat script timeout to *nn* seconds for the expect string that the \W escape appears in. The \W escape is allowed only at the end of an expect string.

\x*hh[hh]* . . . Translate the hexadecimal sequence *hh* into character data. Hex characters will be read in until a non-hex character is encountered.

\L and \P   Insert the login or password defined by the **call-login** and **call-password** commands, or from the *call* file. You can use these commands to separate authentication information from the chat script.

call-login *string*
call-password *string*

Specify the login name (and password) to send with the \L or \P escapes in the chat script for this system. If *string* is an asterisk (*), the login name or password will be fetched from the *call* configuration file.

chat-timeout *seconds*

The number of seconds to wait for an expect string to be received before timing out and sending the next subsend sequence, or aborting the script entirely. The default value is 10 seconds for a login chat, or 60 seconds for any other kind of chat. This can be overridden on a per-expect string basis with the \W escape.

chat-seven-bit *boolean*

If true, all incoming characters are stripped to seven bits when being compared to the expect string. The default is true, to avoid confusion when calling systems that generate parity bits during the login prompt.

chat-fail *expect_sequence*

If the *expect_sequence* is received at any time during the execution of a chat script, the script is aborted. This is useful for immediately detecting a failure condition, such as a modem responding with "BUSY" or "NO DIALTONE."

chat-program *progname args*

Run an external program before executing any chat script. This can be used for dialing or any other connection initialization needed. A few escape sequences are recognized in the program arguments *args*:

\Y   Expand into the port device name.

\S   Expand into the port speed.

\Z   Expand into the name of the system being called.

\L and \P   Expand into the login name or password defined by the **call-login** and **call-password** commands.

\\   Place a single backslash character into the arguments.

debug *debug-levels*

Turn on debugging for conversations with this system. This can be used to enable debugging on incoming calls. Table 10–2 shows the debug levels supported by Taylor UUCP.

max-remote-debug *debug-levels*

On an incoming call, a remote system may request debugging to be turned on. Since the debugging messages can affect performance or fill up disk space on the local system, this command lets you restrict remotely-requested debugging to the specified debug levels. (See Table 10–2.) To prohibit any remotely-requested debugging, set *debug-levels* to the word **none**. The default remote debugging levels permitted are **abnormal**, **chat**, and **handshake**.

Table 10–2: Taylor UUCP Debug Levels

Debug Level	Action
abnormal	Show abnormal situations, such as recoverable errors.
chat	Show the chat script dialogue.
handshake	Show the interaction of the initial UUCP handshake.
uucp-proto	Show the UUCP session protocol.
proto	Show the individual link protocols.
config	Show reading the configuration files.
spooldir	Show actions in the spool directory.
execute	Show command execution activity.

Table 10-2: Taylor UUCP Debug Levels (continued)

Debug Level	Action
incoming	Show all data received from the remote system.
outgoing	Show all data transmitted to the remote system.
all	All of the above.

alternate [*name*]

Start an alternate definition for how to contact the remote system. Set whatever parameters are different (i.e., a different phone number, serial port, etc.) in the keywords following the **alternate** line. An optional *name*, if specified, will be used in the log file when logging use of this alternate connection path.

Here's a sample *sys* entry that uses an alternate to specify a TCP/IP path to use if the modem connection fails:*

```
system    fatcat
time      Any
port      fastmodem
speed     38400
phone     5550123
chat      ogin:--ogin: Utabby word: hairball

alternate fatcat-tcp
port      TCP
address   fatcat.feelines.com
chat      ogin: Utabby word: hairball
```

The call File

As an added convenience, Taylor UUCP lets you segregate all login and password information into a separate file. This simplifies UUCP security, because there is only one file you need to keep your local users from examining (the *call* file with the logins and passwords within), and all other Taylor UUCP configuration files can be world-readable. All your chat scripts must use the \L and \P escapes to send the login and password and you must have the **call-login** and **call-password** commands in your configuration to select the *call* file as the source of logins and passwords.

---

* In case you're wondering why, you could use this setup from a home system with only one modem that is usually in use for PPP or SLIP. If UUCP's first attempt fails, it's probably because the modem is online with a dial-up IP link; in which case, the TCP/IP connection should work.

To use the *call* file, first put these lines at the top of your *sys* file:

```
call-login *
call-password *
```

This sets the default so that all chat scripts will use the *call* file. Here's a sample *call* file:

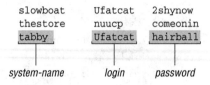

To get these logins and passwords from the *call* file into your chat script, put the \L and \P escapes in place of the login name and password, respectively. Taylor UUCP has the following pre-compiled default chat script that does this:

```
chat "" \r\c ogin:-BREAK-ogin:-BREAK-ogin: \L word: \P
```

This script is used whenever you do not explicitly use the **chat** command in a systems entry. You can also create your own default by placing a single **chat** command at the top of your *sys* file, before the first **system** entry.

Using Defaults

You can use Taylor UUCP defaults to simplify your configuration files. As we showed in the preceding section, you can set up a default chat script so you won't have to repeat it in each system stanza. What do you do if you need a different chat script for the 20 TCP/IP systems with which you connect? Since Taylor UUCP allows you to specify multiple *sys* files (via the *config* master configuration file described later in this chapter), you can separate your dial-up and your TCP/IP systems descriptions into two different files, and set a different default chat script for each. You can use defaults and multiple files for the other Taylor UUCP configuration files (*port* and *dial*).

Devices, Modems, and Networks

All versions of UUCP support (to varying extents) the concept of a *device class*, where more than one device can be used by UUCP for the same purpose. For example, on a system with more than one modem available, you usually want UUCP to use the first available modem for an outgoing call.

Likewise, on a system with multiple hardwired links to a port switch, you would want UUCP to use any port available.

Each version of UUCP has its own requirements for its device configuration files.

Creating Devices File Entries (BNU)

In BNU UUCP, the *Devices* file contains information for direct links, automatic call units (i.e., modems), and network connections. Each entry in the *Devices* file is a group of fields separated by white space, as shown in Figure 10–7.

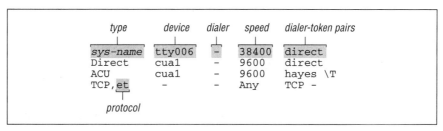

Figure 10–7: Entries in the Devices file

Field	Function in *Devices*
type	The *type* field describes the type of link. You can define your own types if you like. The following keywords are commonly used:

       ACU   For links made through a modem. The modem may be directly connected to a local serial port, or indirectly through a modem pool or other kind of port switch hooked up to the local serial port.

       Direct   Indicates a direct serial port connection that can be used by the **cu −l** *line* command. This is needed when you want to use **cu** to talk directly to a modem without dialing first (as you would want to do when setting up a modem or dialing by hand). This means you often need two lines in the *Devices* file for each modem: one with an ACU type, and another with a **Direct** type. Note the uppercase **D** in **Direct**: getting the case wrong here will confuse both you and UUCP.

TCP   For links made through a TCP/IP network. This tells UUCP to use a TCP/IP socket connection over the network rather than a serial port. Other networks may be supported by individual vendors. You may want to consult your documentation to see if this is the case.

sysname   For direct links to a particular machine, where *sysname* is the remote machine name. This indicates that the line associated with this *Devices* entry is hard-wired to a particular system. There must be a corresponding entry for this system in the *Systems* file.

The *type* field can be followed by a comma and a list of protocols to be used for that device. Usually the choices are *g*, *t*, and *e*, and some systems may also support the *f* and *x* protocols. See Appendix J, *UUCP Protocol Internals*, for more information about UUCP protocols.

device   The device name of the serial port to be used for making the connection. For direct serial links and modems, this is the name of the special file in */dev* for the desired serial port. For network connections, put a hyphen here as a placeholder.

dialer   For the device name of an outboard dialer. See Chapter 8, *How UUCP Works*, for a brief history lesson on dialers. Since these dialers are obsolete in the age of smart modems, put a hyphen here as a placeholder.

speed   For devices that refer to serial ports, this field contains the speed of the device. You can also use the keyword **Any** in this field, in which case the line will match any speed requested in the *Systems* file. If the device supports multiple speeds, you can specify a range (e.g., 1200-9600). If there are different types of devices, which may be used to place different types of calls at the same speed, you can precede the speed with a key letter (as long as it matches the

Systems file entry). For example, I9600 and S9600 might be used to distinguish between calls placed over an ISDN terminal adapter and another kind of network switch. You can also define a new device class to segregate different kinds of devices.

For a TCP/IP network link, put a hyphen in this field as a placeholder.

dialer-token pairs

The remainder of the line contains pairs of dialer names and "tokens." Each pair represents a dialer and an (optional) argument to pass to that dialer.

In most instances, the computer is directly connected to the modem, so there is only one dialer-token pair needed, and the argument \T will be expanded into the phone number to dial (supplied from the *Systems* file, described below).[*] However, if there is a port switch or other gateway device to be dealt with, one could implement this with two or more dialer-token pairs: one for each phase of the dialogue needed to make the ultimate connection to the remote UUCP host. An example of this kind of environment is in Chapter 11, *Making Sure the Link Works.*

Some dialer types are pre-installed in the *Dialers* file (see below). The one you're most likely to use is the **hayes** modem type; this will work for most outgoing calls. You can easily add new descriptions to the Dialers file to suit your own needs.

For a direct serial connection with no modem, put the word **direct** in this field to reference the appropriate entry in the *Dialers* file for connecting to a direct link (which is usually a null dialing script). Note the lower case **d** in **direct**—do not confuse it with the device type **Direct** (upper case **D**) that can be used in field 1.

---

[*] The argument \D is also available. This is converted into the telephone number from the *Systems* file, but without expansion of any dialcodes. Use \D when the argument being passed to the dialer is not a telephone number (like when dialing in through a terminal server or network switch).

For a TCP/IP connection, put in the word **TCP**. In SCO
UNIX, HP-UX, and IRIX, you can specify a TCP port number
in the last field.

There may be other network-specific dialers that you can
use. Check your system documentation (and any comments
in the installed *Dialers* file) for more information.

In SCO UNIX, another possible choice for the dialer name is
the path of an external binary program that knows how to
dial a particular modem. Since SCO also supports the
Dialers file, you shouldn't need this feature very often. But
if you did, here's an example:

```
ACU ttynn - 2400-19200 /usr/lib/uucp/dialTBIT
```

This uses the dialTBIT program to dial a Telebit Trailblazer
modem.

Creating port File Entries (Taylor)

The Taylor UUCP *port* configuration file uses multi-line stanzas to describe a
port, as shown in this example:

```
port       com1
type       modem
device     /dev/cua0
speed      38400
```

A port definition starts with the **port** command, and continues until the next
appearance of a **port** command (or the end of file). You can create defaults
or let attributes of a port be defined by the system defaults, but we recommend that you specify all the attributes of a port for each port in the *port*
file. This way the file will be easier to read when making changes or solving
problems.

The commands that you're most likely to need are:[*]

port *name*

Start a port entry. The *name* can be anything you want; it will be
used by a **port** command in the *sys* file.

---

[*] For the details on the lesser-used commands not listed here, consult the Taylor UUCP documentation.

type *port-type*

>   Define the type of port. This command must appear immediately
>   after the **port** command. Supported values of *port-type* are:

> | | |
> |---|---|
> | modem | The port is attached to a modem. |
> | direct | A direct connection to another system. |
> | tcp | A TCP/IP network connection. |
> | tli | A TLI (Transport Layer Interface) network connection. |
> | pipe | A pipe to another program. It can be used to support connections via **rlogin** or a user-supplied networking program. |
> | stdin | Indicates the connection will be via standard input and standard output, like when **uucico** is invoked on an incoming call. |

device *filename*

>   For devices of type **modem** or **direct**, the special filename (i.e.,
>   */dev/tty0*) for this port. If not supplied, the port name will be
>   used instead.

speed *number*

speed-range *number number*

>   Specify the speed of the port, either a fixed speed or a range of
>   speeds. The commands **baud** and **baud-range** also work.

carrier *boolean*

>   Indicates whether carrier detect (DCD) sensing is supported on a
>   serial port. If false, carrier detect will always be ignored on this
>   port.

hardflow *boolean*

>   If true (the default) hardware flow control will be turned on for
>   this port, provided that it is available on this system.

dialer *dialer-name*

>   Name a dialer to use for this port. A corresponding dialer defini-
>   tion must be in the *dial* configuration file.

dialer-sequence *dialer-name token* . . .

>   Define a chain of dialers and phone numbers (or other contact
>   information) to use. Each dialer will be executed in the order
>   listed, with the argument supplied. The last dialer, if no *token* is

supplied, will be given the phone number from the *sys* file for
the system being called.

service *service-info*

For a TCP/IP port type; specifies the service name or number to
use. The default is the *uucp* service (port 540).

protocol *protocol-list*

Supplies a list of UUCP protocols that should be used over this
connection. The available protocols are described in Appendix J,
UUCP Protocol Internals.

reliable *boolean*

If false, forces the negotiation of a protocol that will work across
an unreliable communications link.

seven-bit *boolean*

If true, forces the negotiation of a protocol that will work over a
seven-bit link.

command *path args*

For the **pipe** port type only, the name of the command (and
arguments) to invoke. Either **uucico** or **cu** will run the command
and communicate with it via a pipe. This lets you call systems
that are connected via proprietary or nonstandard networks. It
also lets you call a TCP/IP connected system that does not support the regular *uucp* service (port 540). On a Linux or BSD 4.4
system, you can make Taylor UUCP use the *rlogin* service by
specifying the following:

```
/bin/rlogin -E -8 -l login-name system
```

as the pipe command.

Creating L-devices Entries (Version 2)

Version 2 UUCP's *L-devices* file is an ancestor of BNU. The formats are similar, but they're a bit simpler and have a few less features.

An entry in *L-devices* is displayed in Figure 10–8.

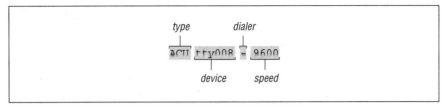

Figure 10–8: An L-devices entry

Field	Function in *L-devices*
type	The type of link: usually **DIR** for a direct link and **ACU** for a modem connection, although additional types are sometimes supported. If there are multiple links of either type, additional lines with the same type label can be used. In BSD documentation, this field is referred to as the *caller*.
	For a TCP/IP network link, use the keyword **TCP**. Other types of links may be supported, depending on the version—see your documentation for details.
device	The name of the special file (such as *tty007*) in the */dev* directory that corresponds to the serial port used for the UUCP link.
dialer	The device name of an external dialer—not relevant for modern modems. Put a hyphen here as a placeholder.
speed	The baud rate of the port for modems and direct links. It may have an initial letter to distinguish a particular speed class.

In BSD/OS, BSD 4.2, and BSD 4.3, there is a fifth field that specifies the type of dialer. The dialers are built-in to UUCP and cannot be defined by the user. The only dialer types defined that are recognizable to modern users are **hayes** and **hayes2400** (intended for the Hayes Smartmodem 1200 and 2400 respectively). You can also use **hayespulse** and **hayes2400pulse** to force pulse dialing.

In BSD/OS and BSD 4.3, you can also supply a chat script after the dialer field that will act as a dialing script to be run before the *L.sys* chat script.

Dialing the Modem

BNU and Taylor UUCP both support user-definable dialer definitions. For reliable high-speed communication, you will often need to modify the dialer script to set modem parameters unique to your particular brand of modem. The BNU *Dialers* file is basically another type of chat script customized for modems; Taylor UUCP provides a rich set of dialing operations and parameters that should make it possible to connect properly no matter how stubborn your modem is.

BNU Dialers File

Each entry in *Dialers* has the form shown in Figure 10–9.

Figure 10–9: Dialers

Field	Meaning
dialer-name	The name of the dialer entry. A name used in the fifth field of the *Devices* will be looked up in *Dialers*. In addition, any odd-numbered fields in **Devices** after the seventh field (optional additional dialer-token pairs) will also refer to entries in the *Dialers* file.
dialtone wait and pause chars	UUCP supports two generic commands in telephone numbers: the equal sign (=) to wait for another dial tone, and the hyphen (–) for a pause of a few seconds.[*] Assuming that your modem accepts special characters in a phone number as dialing commands (nearly all do), this field will translate the two generic dialing commands into the commands required by this particular modem. The first of each pair of characters in the translation string is mapped to the

---

[*] Actually, they're specific to the Bell 801 dialer, which was the only dialer supported by the first version of UUCP.

second of the pair. In the sample entry above, the = is translated into **W**, and the hyphen is translated into a comma
(the Hayes modem commands for waiting for secondary dial
tone and pausing, respectively).

If you are creating a dialing entry for a device that does not
support these commands, use two double quotes ("") as a
placeholder.

dialer-chat A chat script for setting up the modem, dialing out, and rec-
ognizing whether the connection is successful. In addition
to everything allowed in a regular BNU chat script (see
Table 10–1), a few more escapes are supported:

\T   Inserts the telephone number from the *Systems*
            file entry for this system. Any dialcode transla-
            tion (see below) is performed first.

\D   Inserts the telephone number from the *Systems*
            file entry without any dialcode translation. Use
            this escape when dialing through a port switch
            or other device, with which the addressing infor-
            mation in the *Systems* file entry is not a phone
            number.

\M and \m

            Turn carrier detect sensing off (\M) or on (\m).
            This is done by toggling the CLOCAL terminal
            mode. This is only supported in SunOS and
            some SVR4 BNU versions.

~*nn*   Change the expect timeout from the default 45
            seconds to *nn*. This escape is only permitted at
            the end of an expect string (some SVR4 BNU
            versions only).

A few SVR4 versions of BNU support additional escapes in
the chat script. The special expect-send sequence "ABORT
BUSY" aborts the call if the string "BUSY" appears during
the subsequent dialogue. You can have up to five of these

special ABORT sequences. Here's a sample from an IRIX 5.3
Dialers file:

```
telebit  =W-,  ABORT BUSY ABORT NO\sCARRIER ABORT NO\sDIALTONE \
" " \dAT\r\c OK\r~2-AT\r\c-OK\r~2 ATs0=0s110=0\r\c OK\r \
ATdtw\T\r\c CONNECT~90
```

We deconstruct the *dialer-chat* portion of *Dialers* entries further in Appendix I, *Setting Up a Modem.*

Taylor dial File

Taylor UUCP provides complete functionality for tending to your modem or
other dialing device. This allows you to run external programs if needed, or
to run chat scripts to reset the modem after a call is over.

dialer *dialer_name*
> Start the definition for a dialing entry, with the name
> *dialer_name.*

dialtone *string*
> Translate the = character (the wait for another dialtone com-
> mand) into *string.*

pause *string*
> Translate the comma (,) character (the pause during dialing com-
> mand) into *string.*

carrier *boolean*
> If true (the default), then the device being dialed supports the
> RS-232 carrier detect (DCD) signal. **uucico** will try to wait for
> DCD to be asserted after the phone number is dialed.

carrier-wait *seconds*
> If the port is supposed to wait for carrier, how many seconds
> **uucico** should wait for carrier to appear. Only some operating
> systems support this feature.

dtr-toggle *boolean* [*boolean*]
> If the first argument is true, toggle the Data Terminal Ready
> (DTR) signal on the serial port before using the device. The
> optional second argument, if true, causes a one-second sleep
> after toggling DTR. The default is no DTR toggling.

chat *expect_send pairs*
chat-timeout *seconds*
chat-fail *expect_sequence*
chat-seven-bit *boolean*
chat-program *progname args*

> Define the chat script for dialing the device. The commands are the same as those used in the *sys* file, with these additional escapes allowed in send strings:

> | | |
> |---|---|
> | \D | Send phone number without dialcode translation. |
> | \T | Send phone number, performing dialcode translation first. |
> | \M | Do not require carrier detect. |
> | \m | Fail if carrier detect not present. |

complete-chat *expect_send pairs*
complete-chat-timeout *seconds*
complete-chat-fail *expect_sequence*
complete-chat-seven-bit *boolean*
complete-chat-program *progname args*

> Define a completion chat script that will be run after a call has completed normally. This is used to reset the modem after a call.

complete *send_sequence*

> A shorthand for defining a simple completion chat script. The *send_sequence* will be sent to the modem after a call finishes normally.

abort-chat *expect_send pairs*
abort-chat-timeout *seconds*
abort-chat-fail *expect_sequence*
abort-chat-seven-bit *boolean*
abort-chat-program *progname args*

> Define a chat script that will be run after a call fails. This is used to reset the modem after a call is aborted.

abort *send_sequence*

> A shorthand for defining the abort chat script; the *send_sequence* will be sent to the modem after a call fails.

Version 2 dialing

We've already covered the dialing capabilities of the BSD 4.3 UUCP (see "Creating L-devices Entries"). Some older Version 2 implementations also have dialing abilities, but they vary from vendor to vendor. Some UNIX vendors, before the release of BNU UUCP, made custom changes to their distributions to support the then-new breed of smart modems. You might find the modem definition files *acupcap* or *modemcap*, which use a syntax similar to the inscrutable *termcap* terminal information database. Some versions can call user-written dialing programs (a feature still supported in SCO UNIX and Taylor UUCP).

Consult the documentation for your particular UNIX distribution to find out what dialing support is available. Consider installing Taylor UUCP on your system, which will give you much better dialing and device support.

If you get stymied by your UUCP version's lack of dialing capabilities, you can "punt" and put the dialing instructions in the *L.sys* file. If you have only one or two modems, this solution usually works quite well. The trick is to tell UUCP that your modem is not an ACU, but a direct serial link, and put the dialing instructions in the chat script like this:

```
fatcat Any tty01 9600 tty01 "" ATZ OK ATDT5559977 CONNECT
    ogin:--ogin Uoldcat word: furcoat
```

Note that although the above example is printed over two lines due to space limitations, it should be only one line in an *L.sys* file.

This systems entry tells UUCP that the remote system *fatcat* is hooked up by a direct link on line *tty01* at 9600 bps. When it comes to the chat, expect nothing, send "ATZ," expect "OK," send "ATDT" followed by the telephone number, expect "CONNECT," and then login to the remote system with the userid "Uoldcat" and password "furcoat."

If the chat script times out before the modem finishes handshaking with the other side, try putting some extra delays in the phone number. For example:

```
ATDT5559977\r\d\d\d\d\d\c CONNECT
```

This causes UUCP to send the phone number (note the forced carriage return with the **\r** escape), and then spend a few seconds delaying (the **\d** escape) before starting to search for the **CONNECT** response. Note the **\c** escape to suppress a trailing carriage return. Without this escape, the extra character sent at that moment would abort the modem's dialing.

This solution does not scale well if you have more than one modem or many sites to connect to, but it can get your link running without too much pain and frustration. On a Version 2 system without decent dialing support, it might be the only way to get UUCP to work properly with some modems.

Dialing Prefixes

UUCP supports a "portable" systems file, in which you can abbreviate prefixes of phone numbers and store the abbreviations in a separate configuration file. This allows you to organize the phone numbers in the systems file so that the same file can be distributed to machines in different area codes, or with different office phone systems, and all still dial each other.

Thankfully, the dialcode files in all known versions of UUCP use the same format. The file names are slightly different, though: BNU calls it *Dialcodes*, Taylor uses *dialcodes*, and BSD/Version 2 uses *L-dialcodes*. Each line of the dialcodes file has two entries. For example:

```
         abbrev     expansion
           |           |
          nyc       9=1212
          dc        9=1202
```

In this example, a phone number in the systems file entered as "nyc5552468" will be expanded to "9=12125552468" when dialed by UUCP.* A system lucky enough to be in New York City would have a different dialcodes file, which expanded the "nyc" entry to only "9=", so that no area code prefix would be dialed when calling local numbers.

The BSD 4.3 documentation suggests encoding all phone numbers in the dialcodes file with the name of the system that they connect to, so that the telephone numbers remain public (presumably for use by the **cu** command) while the *L.sys* file containing login and password information can be kept off-limits to normal users. You can do this more elegantly in Taylor UUCP with the *call* file, which can keep the login and password information completely separate from all other configuration files.

---

* The = sign tells UUCP to command the modem to wait for a second dial tone, which is often needed on office phone systems.

Aliases

Taylor UUCP, BSD/OS, and BSD 4.3 support alternate names for their UUCP
neighbors. If a neighboring site changes its name, an alias can be set up so
that users on the local system refer to it by its old name.

For example, if the system *leninvax* changed its name to *petrovax*, the system administrator on a neighboring Taylor UUCP system could create an
alias by adding an alias command to the *sys* file entry for *petrovax* like this:

```
system    petrovax
alias     leninvax
```

And on a BSD/OS or BSD 4.3 system, one would add an entry to the
L.aliases file like this:

```
petrovax    leninvax
```

Aliasing allows users on the local system to enter **uucp** or **uux** commands
using the old system name, and the UUCP daemons will automatically convert it to the new name. However, mail or Usenet news servers would have
to be configured separately to also use the alias.

Master Configuration Files

In Taylor UUCP, most versions of BNU, and BSD/OS, you can create a master configuration file that tells UUCP where to find all other configuration
files. In Taylor and BSD/OS, the master configuration file can also controls
other facets of UUCP's behavior.

The BNU Sysfiles File

Most versions of BNU support a configuration file called *Sysfiles* that allows
you to specify pointers to multiple sets of configuration files. While *Sysfiles*
is designed to allow different dialing procedures for **uucico** and **cu**, it can
also be used to split large *Systems* files into more manageable chunks.

The file includes two "service" definitions (one each for **uucico** and **cu**), as
follows:

```
service=service name      systems=systems file list \
                          devices=devices file list \
                          dialers=dialers file list
```

where *service name* is either **uucico** or **cu**, and the various file lists are colon-separated lists of filenames. Each service definition must be placed on a single line; however, escaped newlines are acceptable, as shown in the example.

Filenames are relative to the UUCP configuration directory (i.e., */usr/lib/uucp* or */etc/uucp*) unless you specify a full pathname. If no file list is specified for any of the three keywords (**systems**, **devices**, or **dialers**), the standard files are used by default. If multiple files are specified in a file list, they are searched in order.

For example:

```
service-uucico  systems=Systems.uucico:Systems \
                dialers=Dialers.uucico:Dialers
service=cu      systems=Systems.cu:Systems \
                dialers=Dialers.cu:Dialers
```

In this example, when **uucico** is invoked, it will first search the *Systems.uucico* file, then the standard *Systems* file; it will do the same for *Dialers.uucico* and *Dialers*. By contrast, **cu** will start with *Systems.cu* and *Dialers.cu* before going on to the standard files.

To use *Sysfiles* merely to segment a large *Systems* file, specify the same file lists for both the **uucico** and **cu** services, and specify a search list of *Systems* files. For example, the following *Sysfiles* searches local, company-wide, and global *Systems* files, in that order:

```
service=uucico  systems=Systems.local:Systems.company:Systems
service=cu      systems=Systems.local:Systems.company:Systems
```

If your system supports the *Sysfiles* file, there should be a sample *Sysfiles* in the UUCP configuration directory with all lines commented out to prevent it from being used. If your Taylor UUCP is set up to accept BNU configuration files, it will also support *Sysfiles*.

The Taylor config File

The Taylor UUCP master configuration file is called *config*. It can control numerous things, including everything done by the BNU *Sysfiles* file. The *config* file is optional: all of its parameters have defaults that will be used if you do not create it.

In this section, we'll discuss only the options relevant to initially setting up UUCP. Other options for fine-tuning a running UUCP system are described in Chapter 13, *UUCP Administration*.

nodename *name*
hostname *name*
uuname *name*

> These commands are all equivalent: they set the local UUCP
> name. The default is to use the *gethostname(2)* or *uname(2)* sys-
> tem calls.

spool *dir-name*
pubdir *dir-name*

> Specify the pathname of the spool or public directory. This over-
> rides the default settings in *policy.h.*

v2-files *boolean-val*
hdb-files *boolean-val*

> If the Taylor package is compiled to read in V2 or BNU (HDB)
> configuration files, a value of "false" or "f" will prevent them
> from being read. A value of "true" or "t" (the default) enables
> reading in these configuration files.

sysfile *file-list*
portfile *file-list*
dialfile *file-list*
dialcodefile *file-list*
callfile *file-list*
passwdfile *file-list*

> These commands control the locations of the various configura-
> tion files. *file-list* is either one filename or a list of filenames. You
> can also repeat the command multiple times to specify multiple
> filenames.

If that isn't enough configurability, you can also prefix any command in
config with either of the keywords **cu** or **uucp**, which will limit the programs
that read in those commands. A command prefixed with **cu** will only be
read by the **cu** program, and a command prefixed with **uucp** will *not* be
read by the **cu** program. This lets you use separate configuration files for **cu**
and for the rest of the UUCP package, similar to (but more ornate than) the
Sysfiles configuration file in BNU.

The BSD/OS CONFIG File

BSD/OS UUCP uses the file */etc/uucp/CONFIG* to control the location of the
other configuration files, as well as dozens of other configuration parameters. You can set the nodename (the **NODENAME** parameter), set system
timeout and other parameters, and many other features.

Space considerations prevent us from listing out the many different settings available in the *CONFIG* file, but you can get a complete description from the BSD/OS online documentation with this command:

```
$ man 5 uuparams
```

You can also use the **uuparams** command to display settings in the master configuration file and to check for inconsistencies.

11

Making Sure the Link Works

Testing the connection to make sure you've configured it correctly is the final step in installing a UUCP link to another system.

Before you try your first UUCP request over a modem link, you should try dialing the remote system with **cu**, or another telecommunications program, to make sure you can log in manually. If anything goes wrong during this stage, you need to check your modem, serial port, or device configurations. If you successfully connect but the login and password are rejected, you'll need to get the remote site's administrator to help you.

You can do rudimentary testing of a TCP/IP link with the **telnet** command or the Taylor version of **cu**. Either way, you should be able to tell if the remote side is providing the login prompt that your UUCP software expects to find.

Once you've confirmed that the basic connectivity to the remote site is in place, you are ready to test whether **uucico** is able to negotiate the chat script and successfully log in automatically.

If you are fairly confident that everything has been set up correctly, you can test the link by queuing a UUCP job to the remote site, such as:

```
$ uucp some.file fatcat!~
```

If you're in good shape, the UUCP daemons will connect to the remote site and transfer the file.

If the file does not get through or if you are interested in getting a better understanding of how UUCP works, you should run **uucico** manually, using the debugging option (**−x**) to log the progress of the UUCP connection attempt. The messages are fairly obscure, but once you become familiar with them, they can be deciphered. More understandable messages are written to the logfile that **uucico** keeps for each transfer.

Different versions of UUCP have different types of error and log messages. In the discussion that follows, we have focused on BNU and Taylor UUCP. (Version 2 messages are generally similar to BNU, but more obtuse.) In all versions, the process that **uucico** goes through to connect a call and transfer files is substantially similar. For a detailed listing of the messages that you might find in a UUCP logfile (and what they mean), see Appendix C, *Status and Error Messages*.

Testing with cu

Except for BSD/OS and older BSD systems (which don't supply **cu**),[*] you can use **cu** to test whether you have properly defined your modems and serial ports to UUCP. If **cu** can connect over a serial port to your modem and dial your modem to reach the remote system, **uucico** will also be able to perform these tasks.

Testing Serial Port Links

The first step in testing your serial port links is to see if you can talk to your modem. In BNU UUCP, assuming that you wanted to test a modem attached to */dev/tty01*, you would test this out with something like this:

```
# cu -l /dev/tty01
```

If **cu** successfully connects, try sending modem commands (such as the command to list out the modem status, usually **AT&V** with Hayes-compatible modems) to see if you are successfully communicating with your modem. To further test things, try specifying a baud rate with the −s option (i.e., −s 38400) to make sure you're accessing the modem at the baud rates you intend to use for dial-up connections.

---

[*] You can use **tip** or other telecommunications software, such as **kermit** or **seyon**, to test that your serial port and modem are working properly (see below).

If the **cu** command fails,[*] and you get this message:

```
Connect failed: NO DEVICES AVAILABLE
```

you may not have defined the serial port correctly in *Devices*. In order to use **cu** to connect to a modem (rather than having UUCP automatically dial the modem), BNU requires you to define the port a second time as type "Direct" in *Devices*. For example:

```
ACU    tty0 - 38400 hayes
Direct tty0 - 38400 direct
```

With Taylor UUCP, you don't need the extra entry in the device configuration file, even if you are using BNU-style configuration.

If you still get a message like "NO DEVICES AVAILABLE" (or a file open error from Taylor **cu**), you may have a file ownership or permission problem. Taylor **cu** prints the actual error code before exiting (along with a usually bogus message about the device being in use), but for other versions of **cu**, you may need to invoke them in debug mode (the **−d** option) to find out exactly the file or device that cannot be opened.

Under most circumstances, a device special file to be used by UUCP should be owned by the *uucp* user, and have at least read-write permissions for the owner.

Once you have established communications with your modem, it's a good idea to configure the modem for use with UUCP. If the modem will be used only for outgoing calls, the easiest way to do this is by adding any required modem configuration commands into the UUCP dialing script. If the modem will be used for both incoming and outgoing calls, you need to program the modem so that it "wakes up" in a state that works for both kinds of calls, and returns to that state after the call is over. Both of these configurations are described in Appendix I, *Setting Up A Modem*.

If you have more than one modem attached to your computer, it's a good idea to watch the modem status lights while you are testing to make sure you are connecting to the right modem. At this point, you should also issue a few modem dialing commands to make sure the telephone line is connected properly and that the modem can connect to remote systems.

---

[*] On an AIX system, invoke **cu** with the **−m** option if you get the message "Carrier Lost" when trying to access the modem.

Testing Modem Links

An important test is to see if UUCP can dial properly. Here's an example of a way to test this:

```
# cu phone_number
```

For the first dialing try with a new setup, call a phone number you know will answer with another modem, or a voice number that will ring within earshot (in the latter case, after you hear the phone ring, abort the dialing with the interrupt character, usually Control–C).

If you have more than one modem on your system, select the modem you'd like to use by specifying the serial port with the –l option, like this:

```
# cu -l tty_line phone_number
```

tty_line is the serial port connected to the modem you want to test.

If cu does not dial properly (but direct connections to the modem work OK), check your dialing script. You can monitor the dialogue between UUCP and your modem by adding a debug option to your cu command. In BNU, you would use the –d option, and in Taylor, –x chat. Here is a sample listing of a dialing attempt with BNU cu in debug mode:

```
# cu -d 17185439901
altconn called
Device Type ACU wanted
errno: 17 link(/etc/locks//LTMP.30845, /etc/locks/LCK..tty0)
ttylock file /etc/locks/LCK..tty0
kill pid (11844), returned -1--ok to remove lock file (/etc/locks/LCK..tty0)
ttylock tty0 succeeded
Attempting to open /dev/tty0
fixline(7, 38400)
Changing tty c_cflags from 03602277
Changing tty c_cflags to   03606277
gdial(hayes) called
expect: ("")
got it
sendthem (DELAY
nap(200) ATQ0^M<NO CR>)
expect: (OK)
^M^JOKgot it
sendthem (PAUSE
nap(25) ATDT17185439901^M<NO CR>)
expect: (CONNECT)
^M^J^M^JBUSY^M^Jtimed out
getto ret -1
Connect failed: CALLER SCRIPT FAILED
call cleanup(1)
call _mode(0)
```

In this case, we see near the bottom of the debug output that the dialing attempt failed because the telephone number dialed was busy. We also see (at the top of the debug output) that BNU is smart enough to test for an "orphaned" lockfile—a lockfile created by another process that forgot to remove it—and handles it accordingly. Older versions of UUCP often have trouble with stale lockfiles, and require you to remove them by hand.

Here's a similar debugging session with Taylor UUCP:

```
# cu -x chat 17185439901
cu: fcsend: Writing sleep "ATE1Q0\r"
cu: icexpect: Looking for 3 "OK\r"
cu: icexpect: Got "ATE1Q0\r\r\nOK\r" (found it)
cu: fcsend: Writing echo-check-on "ATDT" \T "17185439901\r"
cu: icexpect: Looking for 7 "CONNECT"
cu: icexpect: Got "\r\nBUSY\r\n" (timed out)
cu: Timed out in chat script
```

The next test is to see if **cu** will dial a system by name. Here's the syntax:

```
# cu system_name
```

cu attempts to dial the remote system based on the information in the systems configuration file. If this fails, you should run **cu** again with debugging options to find out why it didn't work.

If you've dialed in successfully (**cu** prints the terse message "Connected"), the next step is to bring up the remote system's login prompt. On some systems, it appears immediately; on others, you will have to press the RETURN key, or other sequences (such as sending a BREAK signal) before getting the prompt. Take careful notes here, since whatever you do to raise the login prompt will also need to be done in the **uucico** chat script for this system.

Once you are presented with the login prompt of the remote system, type in the user ID and password assigned to you by the remote system's administrator. If the login works, you should see a few login messages followed by an enigmatic message along these lines:

```
Shere=fatcat
```

This is the opening salvo of the UUCP protocol exchange. The remote system (*fatcat* in this case) starts the session by announcing its UUCP nodename. Since you need to use the UUCP communications protocol to get any farther, hang up the line (with the RETURN ~. RETURN command) and proceed to testing with **uucico**.

If you can't bring up the login prompt no matter what you try and you're sure you're dialing the correct phone number, and that your modem is handshaking at the correct baud rate, contact the remote system's administrator and ask for assistance.

Testing TCP/IP links

Of all the versions of UUCP, only Taylor **cu** easily connects over network ports.* If you are testing a UUCP over a TCP/IP connection, you should be able to use Taylor **cu** to log in by hand. For example:

```
# cu -x3 fatcat
Connected.
login: Password: Shere=fatcat
```

Note that **cu** does not echo your typing, nor perform carriage return/newline processing. However, it's enough to test whether you've properly defined the TCP/IP link to UUCP, and that the login and password you've been provided with work.

If you're not using Taylor UUCP, you can use **telnet** to try logging in by hand. Since UUCP links do not use the default TCP/IP service number for **telnet** (port 23), but rather the UUCP service number (port 540), you'll need to specify the number or the standard service name *uucp* on the command line. For example:

```
# telnet fatcat uucp
Trying...
Connected to fatcat.
Escape character is '^]'.
login: Utabby
Password: meow
Shere=fatcat
user types escape character control-]
telnet> q
Connection closed.
#
```

If the login/password combination fails, don't despair. **telnet** sends extra, invisible (to you) data during a connection attempt, and some versions of **uucpd** (the daemon that listens for incoming UUCP connections over TCP/IP) get confused by these messages. Try connecting with **uucico** to confirm that the login/password you've been given work properly.

---

* The BNU UUCP supplied with a few SVR4 systems also supports using **cu** over a TCP/IP link, but it requires configuring the enigmatic TLI interface to TCP/IP, which is not easy.

Testing with tip

On all BSD systems except for FreeBSD and NetBSD, **cu** does not really exist. If provided, **cu** is just a link to **tip**, which is the BSD telecommunications command.* Although you can use **tip** to test whether your serial port and modem are functioning properly, since **tip** does not use any UUCP configuration files, you are only testing your hardware, not the UUCP configuration itself. **tip** is still useful for connecting to a remote system, and manually verifying the login sequence.

To get **tip** to talk to your modem, you can either add a system-specific entry to the *tip* configuration file */etc/remote*, or, if it exists, you can use the *hardwire* entry to connect directly to the modem. Here's an example of a hardwire entry:

```
hardwire:dv=/dev/cua0:br#9600
```

When you issue the command **tip hardwire**, you will be connected to the device on */dev/cua0*, at 9600 bps. You can then issue commands to the modem to dial another system.

Testing Incoming Calls

If you are setting up your system for incoming calls, it's only polite to test your configuration before inviting other UUCP sites to call you. If you have two modems, this is easy: use **cu** to call your own system, and try to log in with the UUCP account that you are setting up. If the remote node will be calling in over TCP/IP, use the instructions provided earlier in this chapter for testing a TCP/IP link to test your configuration. Substitute your own hostname or IP address when using **telnet** or Taylor **cu** to test the link. You can also test using the TCP/IP loopback address, 127.0.0.1.

Testing with uucico -x

Although **uucico** is usually invoked by a **cron** job or as an after-effect of a **uux** or **uucp** command, you can also run **uucico** manually like any other program. It does not matter whether there is any work pending for the remote system; if you invoke it, **uucico** will do as it is told and attempt to place a call to the remote system.

---

* Since FreeBSD and NetBSD come with Taylor UUCP, they provide the Taylor **cu**.

When using **uucico** to test a link, you usually run it in debug mode. In BNU, BSD, and Version 2, the **−x***nn* option lets you set a debugging level from 1 through 9: the higher numbers supply more and more debugging information, such as every byte of data sent or received on the link. Taylor UUCP also supports the **−x** option, but you can use numbers up to 11. Taylor also supports mnemonic names for the different debug levels, and unlike the other versions, lets you pick the levels you want. The debug levels are listed back in Table 10–2, in Chapter 10, *Setting Up a UUCP Link*.

In BNU and Version 2, **uucico** writes its debug output to standard output, letting you view the actions of **uucico** in real-time. You can also put **uucico** in the background and direct its output to a file, a function that is performed for you automatically by the **Uutry** script supplied with BNU. Taylor UUCP always writes its debug output to a specific file, such as */usr/spool/uucp/Debug* (the default when compiled with Taylor logging mode) or */usr/spool/uucp/.Admin/audit.local* (when compiled with BNU logging mode).

Access to Debugging Information

The logins and passwords in a UUCP systems configuration file are generally considered sensitive; a malicious person could use this information to gain access to a system's UUCP neighbors and possibly divert UUCP traffic. Since any user can invoke **uucico** in debug mode and since the debugging output shows the logins and passwords used by UUCP, most versions of UUCP take steps to prevent unauthorized users from seeing this information.

The Taylor debugfile is created with permissions allowing only the *uucp* user access, which prevents normal users from reading it. This effectively keeps all debugging information out of the hands of regular users.

BNU and Version 2 are more permissive: they let users see debugging output of **uucico**, but they suppress debug output of send strings in chat scripts in an attempt to hide logins and passwords from prying eyes. If you run **uucico −x** as the super-user, you'll always see complete debug output. When a normal user tries **uucico −x** however, the debug output will be slightly "censored" during the chat script phase, excising the trace of send strings from the output.

Different versions of BNU and Version 2 use different schemes to decide whether to hide the send strings. On some versions, the decision is based on whether the *Systems* or *L.sys* file is world-readable or not and in some older Version 2 systems, it depends on whether the invoking user's UID is less than some "magic" value. On still other versions, access depends on whether the user is *root* or what group privileges the user has.

If you are concerned about keeping local users from seeing login and password information, you should test **uucico** in debug mode from a regular user's account to see what information is displayed.

Invoking uucico

To run **uucico** on a specific system, you need to specify the name of the system to be called with the **−s** *name* option. To start up **uucico** in Master mode (that is, as the calling system), you must also specify the **−r1** option. And to turn on debugging, pick a debug level like **−x4**, which usually shows you enough information to figure out what's going on.

For example:

```
$ /usr/lib/uucp/uucico -r1 -x4 -sfatcat
```

This entry runs **uucico** in Master mode with debug level 4, and attempts to contact the system *fatcat*. The debug messages will be printed on your terminal. Since **uucico** disables most keyboard interrupts, if you decide to abort the connection attempt, the only way to do so is to suspend the program with control−Z (assuming your system supports job control), or to log in via another session and issue a **kill** command.

BNU UUCP comes with the **Uutry** script, which invokes **uucico** for you, places it in the background, and sends the debug output into a file. **Uutry** then runs the **tail −f** command so that you may see the debugging messages as they are written to the output file. When **uucico** finishes (or sooner, if you get tired of reading the debug output), you must break the **tail** program with an interrupt (usually Control−C) to return to your shell prompt.

Invoking **Uutry** is fairly straightforward, as Unix commands go. For example:

```
# /usr/lib/uucp/Uutry fatcat
```

Uutry will run **uucico** for the specified system (**−s fatcat**), in Master mode (**−r1**), with a debug level of 5 (**−x5**). You can specify a different debug level as an option to **Uutry**. You can also specify **−r** on the command line to tell **Uutry** to remove the UUCP status file for the specified system.

Whatever level of debugging you specify, on all but Taylor systems, the output of **uucico** always shows the following phases of a UUCP conversation:

- Connection setup and login
- Protocol negotiation
- Data transfer (if any)
- Shutdown

On a Taylor system, you see only what you ask for with the **−x** (or **−debug**) option. The **−x4** debugging level gives you the same basic information listed above.[*]

Debugging Incoming Calls

So far, we've only discussed turning on **uucico** debugging when making outgoing calls. But it is also possible to turn on debug messages on incoming calls. This is easy to do in Taylor UUCP: add a **debug** command into the *sys* file for the system you want to trace. (See Chapter 10, *Setting Up a UUCP Link*, for more details.)

In other versions of UUCP, there's no direct way to turn on debugging for an incoming call. All incoming UUCP calls must use an account that has **uucico** as a login shell, and when **uucico** is invoked this way it is called without any command-line options. A typical */etc/passwd* entry for one of these accounts looks like this:

```
Utabby:*:900:14:Tabby UUCP:/var/spool/uucp:/usr/lib/uucp/uucico
```

What we'd like to do is run **uucico** with the **−x4** option. Some UNIX versions support command-line arguments to the login shell in */etc/passwd*; if yours is one that does (check your online documentation or just experiment), you can add the **−x4** option to the login shell field of the UUCP account that you want to debug. For example:

```
Utabby:*:900:14:Tabby UUCP:/var/spool/uucp:/usr/lib/uucp/uucico -x4
```

If your UNIX system does not support login shell arguments in */etc/passwd*, you can compile the following short C program (*uudebug.c*) and use it as a login shell:[†]

---

[*] Instead of **−x4**, you could verbosely request the same debugging output with:

```
-x abnormal,chat,handshake,uucp-proto
```

[†] This kind of program is known as a *wrapper*, because it is a thin protective layer around another program. Other wrappers mentioned in this book include the TCP wrapper (**tcpd**), which protect a UNIX host's network services, and the Sendmail wrapper **smrsh**.

```
/* uudebug.c -- invoke uucico with debugging */
/* use as a login shell to debug incoming UUCP calls */

#include <stdio.h>
#include <unistd.h>

extern char **environ;
extern int errno;

main()
{
        execl( "/usr/lib/uucp/uucico", "uucico", "-x4", NULL);
        printf("Can't exec uucico: error %d\n", errno);
}
```

You would then install this program in some directory, perhaps in
/usr/lib/uucp/uudebug, and put the full path of **uudebug** in the login shell
field of the appropriate */etc/passwd* entry.

In all versions of UUCP, when debugging is turned on for incoming calls,
the messages are written to the *audit* file in the spool directory. The path
within the spool directory will be *.Admin/audit* in BNU, *Debug* in Taylor,
and *AUDIT* in BSD or Version 2.

Status Files and Retry Times

Whenever **uucico** finishes a conversation (or an attempt at conversation), it
writes a status file containing the date, time, and system status. (In BNU and
Taylor, the status file is kept in the *.Status* subdirectory of the spool directory, with the name of the remote system. In Version 2, the status file is in
the spool directory, with the name *STST.sysname*.)

Subsequent invocations of **uucico** will look at this status file before calling
the system again. If **uucico** sees that one of its previous incarnations tried to
contact that system and failed, it will not make another attempt until the
appropriate time period has elapsed. This can be either the default retry
time (usually 55 minutes), or an interval for that particular system specified
in the UUCP configuration files.

This behavior of **uucico** is intended to keep a phone line from being tied up
with multiple calls to a system that won't answer. But when debugging a
connection, you often want to make several attempts in a row, as you fix
configuration files and try to test each change. The traditional way of preventing **uucico** from rejecting your connection attempts is to manually

remove the status file. In modern UUCP configurations, this is no longer necessary. For example:

- In BNU, the **Uutry** script automatically removes the status file for you if you invoke it with the **−r** option.

- The Taylor **uucico** ignores the status file if you give it the **−f** option, or if you say **−S** *system* (upper case S) instead of **−s** *system*.

- BSD/OS and BSD 4.3 **uucico** ignore the status file when invoked with debugging (the **−x** option).

Analyzing uucico Debug Output

A successful connection generates a large amount of output. To simplify our explanations in this chapter, we have broken the output into sections, with each section followed by a brief discussion.

The specifics of debug output from **uucico** varies widely between the different versions of UUCP. The following examples include excerpts from both BNU and Taylor UUCP. The exact messages you get from your system may be different, depending on your UUCP version, your chat script, what device you are using to place the call, and so on. However, the phases of transfer will always be the same.

Below we show a successful attempt to transfer a short test file from a system running BNU UUCP (called *tabby*) to the public directory on system *fat-cat*. The file to be transferred is spooled using **uucp**'s **−r** option, which says to spool the file but not to start up **uucico**. This allows us to start up **uucico** manually, with debugging enabled. For example:

```
# uucp -r testfile fatcat\!~
# /usr/lib/uucp/uucico -r1 -x4 -sfatcat 2> debug &*
# tail -f debug
```

----

* Instead of invoking **uucico** directly, we could have used **Uutry**:

```
# /usr/lib/uucp/Uutry fatcat
```

with the same effect.

Connection Setup and Login

The first part of the debugging output shows the execution of the dialing procedure and chat script. The device is opened, then the dialing instructions and telephone number are sent to the modem. After the modem dials, the chat script is executed.

The output from **uucico** is a little hard to read at first, since the "reads" and "writes" are jumbled together and various nonprinting characters may show up as their octal or hexadecimal equivalents (e.g., \015 or <0xd> for carriage return, \012 or <0xa> for line feed, \0 or <0x0> for null). But with a little practice, you can pick out what is happening, especially if you know what you are looking for. In our sample BNU output below, the nonprinting characters are shown in "control" notation, after the corresponding ASCII control character (i.e., ^M (Control−M) for carriage return, ^J (control−J) for linefeed, etc.).

Let's look at the output from **uucico**:

```
mchFind called (fatcat)
conn(fatcat)
Device Type ACU wanted
ttylock tty0 succeeded
Attempting to open /dev/tty0
Changing tty c_cflags from 03602277
Changing tty c_cflags to   03606277
```

uucico's first order of business is to find a device that will connect to *fatcat*. We see from this debug output that **uucico** first looks for a device from the logical class "ACU," and opens a free device that is in that class, namely */dev/tty0*. After initializing the *tty*, it's time to dial the modem:

```
gdial(hayes) called
expect: ("")
got it
sendthem (DELAY
nap(200) ATQ0^M<NO CR>)
expect: (OK)
^M^JOKgot it
sendthem (PAUSE
nap(25) ATDT917185559977^M<NO CR>)
expect: (CONNECT)
^M^J^M^JCONNECTgot it
Changing tty c_cflags from 03606277
Changing tty c_cflags to   03602277
getto ret 5
```

The dialing script for this device (from the *Dialers* file) is "hayes." It looks like this in the *Dialers* file:

```
hayes   =,-,    "" \dATQ0\r\c OK \pATDT\T\r\c CONNECT
```

The author of this dialing script chose not to use UUCP's default "send a carriage return" feature; it is turned off with the \c at the end of each send string, and the author uses the \r escape so that it is explicitly clear to anyone reading the dialing script what characters it sends. UUCP shows this in the debug output by printing <NO CR> to show that it is not adding the carriage return that it usually appends to each send string. Note that there are two different delay escapes in the dialing script (\d and \p), and they both show up in the debug output as a *nap()* call.

We see that the first command is **ATQ0**, which turns on modem responses (this would be needed if they were turned off by default, as they often are in a bidirectional modem). The script waits for a response from the modem (**OK**), and then dials the phone number. When the desired response from the modem is received (**CONNECT**), the chat script ends. **uucico** changes the *tty* settings again, and gives control of the line to the chat script. It looks like this:

```
expect: (ogin:)
 38400^M^J^[[;H^[[2J^M^M^JWelcome to Linux 1.2.8.^M^J^M^Jfatcat login:got it
sendthem (Utabby^M)
expect: (word:)
 Utabby^M^JPassword:got it
sendthem (meow^M)
Login Successful: System=fatcat
msg-ROK
 Rmtname fatcat, Role MASTER,  Ifn - 5, Loginuser - root
```

We have a cooperative system here: it prints the login prompt soon after the modems connect, making life easier for the calling **uucico**, which immediately recognizes the **ogin:** string and sends the login ID. Note that *fatcat*'s echoing of the strings sent by *tabby* appears in the data stream as *tabby* tries to decipher the received characters, and looks for the next prompt. When *tabby* finds it (**word:**), it sends the password. Here's the chat script for this dialogue in the *Systems* file:

```
ogin:--ogin: Utabby word: meow
```

If the login is successful, the called system will run **uucico** in Slave mode. The Slave (*fatcat* in this instance, since it is on the receiving end of the call) starts the UUCP dialogue by sending this message:

```
Shere=nodename
```

where *nodename* is its nodename (hostname), as described in Chapter 10, *Setting Up a UUCP Link*.

The Master (the calling system) replies:

```
Snodename  -Qseq  -xnum
```

where *nodename* is its nodename (hostname), *seq* is the sequence number (see Chapter 12, *Access and Security Considerations*) or 0 if unused, and *num* is the level of debugging in effect.[*] Taylor UUCP and some of the later BNU versions may send information about other capabilities that they support, such as the maximum grade permitted for jobs transferred during this call (−v*grade* or −p*grade*) or the ability to restart a previously aborted file transfer (−R).

If the Slave decides to accept the call, it responds with "ROK." But the Slave might want to reject the call. Table 11−1 shows a quick list of the messages, with explanations and the most likely ways to fix a given problem:

Table 11−1: UUCP Login Responses

Message	Meaning	Possible Solution
ROK	Slave accepts the call.	No problem.
RCB	Slave will call back; both sides must hang up first.	No problem.
RLOGIN	The Master has used the wrong login name. The login name may belong to another system, or not allowed to use UUCP at all.	Fix the UUCP configuration files on the Slave to allow this login name, or give the Master the right login name to use.
RYou are unknown to me	The Master's UUCP nodename is not one of the Slave's known neighbors.	Add the Master to the Slave's system configuration file.

---

[*] Note that, as always, this conversation can vary depending on the systems involved. For example, older Version 2 UUCP's announce themselves in Slave mode with just "Shere," without specifying the hostname, and send just "S*hostname*," without any other information, during the initial handshake in Master mode.

Table 11–1: UUCP Login Responses (continued)

Message	Meaning	Possible Solution
RLCK	The Slave thinks it is already talking with the Master (i.e., a lockfile is present).	Use **uustat –p** on both sides to look for other UUCP processes that may be using the link.

Another possible diversion: the Master might notice that the name of the system announced by the Slave is not the name of the system that the Master thought it was calling. If this happens, the Master hangs up and issues an error like this:

```
WRONG MACHINE NAME
```

Although not shown here, the messages in this phase of the UUCP conversation are preceded by a synchronization character (decimal 16), and ended with a null character (decimal 0) or newline (decimal 10). Since these characters are easily generated by the keyboard, you can often "type your way" through the first two UUCP handshake messages if you are so inclined. For example, if you are testing a link where *tabby* calls *fatcat* with **cu** or **telnet**, and you get to the Shere= prompt, you can try finishing the UUCP handshake by hand like this:

```
remote system sends: Shere=fatcat
       user types:  Control-P Stabby Control-J
remote system sends: ROK
```

You can abort the handshake at this point by typing CTRL-P CTRL-J. This is an empty message. The remote **uucico** should abort the call immediately. Some versions of **uucico** will crash when given an empty message, which also has the effect of immediately ending the call.

Protocol Negotiation

The two **uucico** programs now try to agree on a communications protocol. For example:

```
rmesg - 'P' got PiagGjfv
wmesg 'U'g
Proto started g
```

The Slave first offers its list of available protocols. Each protocol has its own low-level handshaking, error-checking, and data transfer methods that are intended for a particular kind of device, such as a modem or network link. The Slave sends a list of the protocols it supports (the "P" message, or "protocol list"). The Master compares the Slave's protocols against its own supported protocols, and picks the one that is best for the device being used for the link.

In this example, the Slave system, which is running Taylor UUCP, has eight protocols available. Taylor UUCP supports other protocols, but since this session is held over a telephone line, Taylor UUCP doesn't offer its repertoire of protocols that are more suitable for "reliable" links.

A complete description of the numerous UUCP protocols available is found in Appendix J, *UUCP Protocol Internals.* In most cases, UUCP over telephone links will use the *g* protocol, unless both sides are running Taylor UUCP, in which case they will choose the faster *i* protocol. BNU and Taylor UUCP let you fine-tune the protocols chosen over a particular device (or with a particular system) via the configuration files.

Data Transfer

Once the two sides have agreed on a protocol, they are ready to start transferring data. For example:

```
*** TOP ***  -  role=MASTER, setline - X
Request: tabby!/tmp/testfile --> fatcat!~ (root)
setline - S
wrktype - S
 wmesg 'S' /tmp/testfile ~ root -dc D.0 644 root
rmesg - 'S' got SY
role=MASTER, PROCESS: msg - SY
SNDFILE:
-> 3001 / 3.160 secs
rmesg - 'C' got CY
role=MASTER, PROCESS: msg - CY
RQSTCMPT:
mailopt 0, statfopt 0
notif 0
```

During the work processing phase, four messages are used. These are specified by the first character of the message:

S   send a file

R   receive a file

C   copy complete

X   execute a command

In the preceding example, the Master asks to send the file (*wmesg 'S'* */tmp/testfile*) and the Slave acknowledges ("SY"). If for any reason the file cannot be transferred (e.g., wrong permissions), the Slave would reply "SN."[*] While data is being transferred, it is stored in a temporary file in the spool directory, whose name begins with the letters TM. Once the transfer is complete, you should see a message like this:

```
-> 320 / 1 seconds
```

This entry shows the direction of the transfer, the number of bytes transferred, and the length of time it took.

The Master then awaits confirmation, in the form of a C message. The Slave sends CY ("Yes, the file made it across"), once the data has been copied from the temporary file to its final destination.

Role Reversal and Shutdown

When the Master finishes sending all queued files, it sends an **H** command, which asks the Slave to hang up the line. For example:

```
*** TOP *** - role=1, setline - X
Finished Processing file: /usr/spool/uucp/C.fatcatnA5148
wmesg 'H'
rmesg - 'H' got HY
 PROCESS: msg - HY
HUP:
wmesg 'H'Y
cntrl - 0
send OO 0,exit code 0
```

If there are jobs queued in the other direction, the Slave answers "HN" (for No), and the roles are reversed.

If the Slave does not have any files to send to the Master, it responds "HY" (for Yes). The connection ends with an "OO" message (over and out), as shown in the example above.

Role reversal is less meaningful when the two sides are using the Taylor UUCP *i* protocol. There's no need to "turn around" the line, because both

---

* Any "No" message (SN, RN, CN, or XN) may optionally be followed by a number indicating the reason for the refusal. The most common values are:

2 Remote access to path/file denied.

4 Remote system cannot create the TM file—usually means there is not enough space on the remote system.

5 Cannot copy the TM file to the requested destination. Depending on the system, the file may be put in the public directory, left in the spool directory, or deleted.

sides can send files simultaneously. When one side finishes sending all its files, it sends an "H" message. The other side will send "HN" if it is still transmitting data, otherwise it sends "HY" (and the line is shut down).

Checking the Logfile

Throughout the entire transfer, **uucico** writes messages into a logfile in the spool directory. (The exact name and location of this file may vary from version to version of UUCP. See Appendix B, *The Spool Directory/Working Files*, for details.) Normally, these messages are fairly terse, stating only that a remote system was called and that a transfer was made. On some systems, if debugging is turned on, the messages in the logfile also get more extensive.

For example, the logfile messages for the preceding transfer are as follows:

```
root fatcat fatcatmN05bf (2/4-23:49:01,36025,0) QUEUED (tabby!/tmp/thing -->
  fatcat!~)
uucp fatcat  (2/4-23:50:45,14286,0) SUCCEEDED (call to fatcat)
uucp fatcat  (2/4-23:50:47,14286,0) OK (startup)
root fatcat fatcatmN05bf (2/4-23:50:47,14286,0) REQUEST (tabby!/tmp/thing -->
  fatcat!~ (root))
uucp fatcat  (2/4-23:50:51,14286,1) REMOTE REQUESTED (fatcat!/etc/motd -->
  tabby!~ (root))
uucp fatcat  (2/4-23:50:53,14286,2) OK (conversation complete tty0 56)
```

The first line is a record of the original **uucp** or **uux** job request. It shows the destination system and the login user who made the request, the date and time, the **uucp** job ID, the action that occurred (QUE'D), and the name of the work file in the spool directory. The remainder of the lines were written by **uucico**. Since BNU stores log messages from **uucico**, **uux**, and **uucp** each in separate files, the above listing is combined from multiple log files.

On some systems, you may find it useful to correlate the messages shown in the UUCP logfiles with the debugging output of **uucico**. Another tactic is to compare the debug output on your local system with the debug output of the remote system (if available). For example, here's the debugging log from the called system in the previous example (a Taylor UUCP system):

```
uucp tabby (2/4-23:50:37,4526,0) Setting debugging mode to 07
uucp tabby (2/4-23:50:37,4526,0) DEBUG: fsend_uucp_cmd: Sending "ROK"
uucp tabby (2/4-23:50:37,4526,0) DEBUG: fsend_uucp_cmd: Sending "PiagGjfv"
uucp tabby (2/4-23:50:37,4526,0) DEBUG: zget_uucp_cmd: Got "\020Ug\000"
uucp tabby (2/4-23:50:37,4526,0) DEBUG: fgprocess_data: Got control INITA 3
uucp tabby (2/4-23:50:37,4526,0) DEBUG: fgsend_control: Sending control INITA 7
uucp tabby (2/4-23:50:37,4526,0) DEBUG: fgprocess_data: Got control INITB 1
uucp tabby (2/4-23:50:37,4526,0) DEBUG: fgsend_control: Sending control INITB 1
uucp tabby (2/4-23:50:38,4526,0) DEBUG: fgprocess_data: Got control INITC 3
```

```
uucp tabby (2/4-23:50:38,4526,0) DEBUG: fgsend_control: Sending control INITC 7
uucp tabby (2/4-23:50:38,4526,0) Handshake successful (login Utabby port ttyS0
 protocol 'g' sending packet/window 64/3 receiving 64/7)
root tabby (2/4-23:50:38,4526,0) Receiving /var/spool/uucppublic/thing
root tabby (2/4-23:50:39,4526,0) DEBUG: fgprocess_data: Bad checksum: header
 0x46b8, data 0xa07c
root tabby (2/4-23:50:39,4526,0) DEBUG: fgsend_control: Sending control RJ 6
root tabby (2/4-23:50:39,4526,0) DEBUG: fgprocess_data: Got packet 1; expected 7
root tabby (2/4-23:50:39,4526,0) DEBUG: fgprocess_data: Got packet 2; expected 7
root tabby (2/4-23:50:39,4526,0) DEBUG: fgprocess_data: Got packet 3; expected 7
root tabby (2/4-23:50:39,4526,0) DEBUG: fgprocess_data: Got packet 4; expected 7
root tabby (2/4-23:50:39,4526,0) DEBUG: fgprocess_data: Got packet 5; expected 7
uucp tabby (2/4-23:50:43,4526,0) DEBUG: fgsend_control: Sending control CLOSE 0
uucp tabby (2/4-23:50:43,4526,0) DEBUG: fgsend_control: Sending control CLOSE 0
uucp tabby (2/4-23:50:43,4526,0) Protocol 'g' packets: sent 8, resent 0,
 received 53
uucp tabby (2/4-23:50:43,4526,0) Errors: header 0, checksum 1, order 2, remote
 rejects 0
uucp tabby (2/4-23:50:43,4526,0) DEBUG: fsend_uucp_cmd: Sending "OOOOOOO"
uucp tabby (2/4-23:50:43,4526,0) DEBUG: fsend_uucp_cmd: Sending "OOOOOOO"
uucp tabby (2/4-23:50:43,4526,0) DEBUG: zget_uucp_cmd: Got "\020\011\n"
uucp tabby (2/4-23:50:44,4526,0) DEBUG: zget_uucp_cmd: Got "* \011\020\011
 \"*\010\011\020\011\"*\010\011\020OOOOOO\000"
uucp tabby (2/4-23:50:44,4526,0) Call complete
```

If you want to better understand this level of debug output, read through
Appendix K, *The UUCP g Protocol*, or Ian Taylor's *UUCP Internals Frequently
Asked Questions* file (available on the Usenet newsgroup *comp.mail.uucp*
and elsewhere).

Another file to look at is the statistics file in the spool directory, which logs
the byte counts of file transfers between systems. In BNU, this file is stored
in the *.Admin* subdirectory of the spool directory, with the name *xferstats*.
In Version 2, it is stored in the spool directory under the name *SYSLOG*, and
in Taylor, it is also in the spool directory, but named *Stats*.

From our previous example, the *xferstats* file on *tabby* showed:

```
fatcat!root M (2/4-23:50:50) (C,14286,1) [tty0] -> 3001 / 3.160 secs
```

And on *fatcat* (the Taylor UUCP system), you'll see this:

```
root fatcat (1996-02-04 23:50:42.76) received 3001 bytes in 3.522 seconds
 (852 bytes/sec) on port ttyS0
```

The transfer statistics file is useful if you want to know what throughput you
are getting out of your UUCP links, or for a quick look at what files are
being transferred to or from your system.

Fine-Tuning a Chat Script

In writing the chat script, you have to simulate the process of manual login. If the system administrator of the remote system cannot tell you from experience what the chat script ought to be, then you should use **cu** or **tip** to log into the remote system, as discussed in Chapter 10, *Setting Up a UUCP Link*. Pay attention to the keystrokes required before a login prompt appears on your screen.

Return to Sender

For example, to get a login prompt on one system, you might first need to press RETURN twice. Your chat script would begin like this:

```
"" \r\r ogin:
```

That is, expect nothing (""), send a pair of RETURNs (\r\r), and expect to get "ogin:". (\r\r will actually send three carriage returns,[*] because of the "default" carriage return sent at the end of every send string. To send exactly two carriage returns, use the send string \r\r\c.)

Some systems support dial-up lines at more than one speed. As we saw in Chapter 9, *The Physical Connection*, the **getty** process that controls the speed of the serial line can be set up to cycle through a series of different speeds each time it receives a break character.

So, for instance, this expect sequence:

```
ogin:-BREAK-ogin:
```

waits for "ogin:". If it gets it, **uucico** goes right on to the next send (e.g., "nuucp" in our first example). If it does not get it after a certain amount of time, it sends a BREAK, which should cause the remote system to cycle through to the next speed. It then waits for the next subexpect ("ogin:" again), which hopefully this time it will get. On a system that supports multiple speeds from 1200 to 9600, you might want to have four or five chances to cycle to the correct speed, hence this expect sequence:

```
ogin:-BREAK-ogin:-BREAK-ogin:-BREAK-ogin:-BREAK-ogin:
```

---

[*] Or, on some older systems, two carriage returns followed by a linefeed.

The Pause That Refreshes

When creating a chat script, it's easy to overlook the pauses and delays associated with a manual login to a system. For example, if you typed two carriage returns to wake up the remote system, there is probably at least a tenth of a second's delay between the two characters. Although such a short interval would go unnoticed by a human, that's a pretty significant amount of time to a computer. When **uucico** sends two consecutive carriage returns, they go out at the full speed of the link, which even on a 2400-bps connection is less than a millisecond between each character.

Why does this matter? Some kinds of equipment, such as smart port switches or the front end processors of public data networks, use the time delays between characters to auto-detect the baud rate of the line. When a computer sends the characters without delays between them, these switches get hopelessly confused.

So to send two carriage returns as if a human was typing it, you would use this send string:

```
\r\d\r\c
```

This entry sends one carriage return, waits for one second, then sends the second carriage return.

Another example is the eccentric **getty** that answers the line on many SCO UNIX systems. After it prints the login prompt, it does a little internal book-keeping, and then discards any characters received during that processing interval. When a human logs in, they usually don't notice, because it takes a human being a moment or two to react to the login prompt. When **uucico** calls, it has a much shorter reaction time, and the first few characters of the login name get lost. If you're calling one of these systems, use a chat script with a delay escape in front of the login name like this:

```
ogin:--ogin:--ogin: \d\dUfatcat  word: whiskers
```

Is There an Echo in Here?

A more subtle version of the delay problem occurs when **uucico** is trying to chat with a device that prefers to deal with a slow human rather than a fast computer. For example, a device with a command line interpreter might not have the buffer space to accept characters transmitted at the full line speed. BNU and Taylor have a feature for these situations, called *echo checking*.

Echo checking, when turned on, causes **uucico** to wait for the remote device to echo the last character sent before sending the next character. This slows down the conversation enough to avoid overrunning the remote device. Usually, you turn echo checking on at the beginning of a send string (the **\E** escape) and turn it off at the end (the **\e** escape). For example:

```
Request: \Edialout\e Connected AT OK ATDT\T CONNECT
```

This script waits for the modem server's prompt, and sends the command "dialout" with echo checking on (followed by a carriage return).

Chat between uugettys

If two systems running BNU are both using **uugetty** with the **−r** option to allow a single line to be used for both dialin and dialout, several carriage returns must be sent before **uugetty** will respond with a login prompt.

The chat script on each system should begin with the following sequence:

```
...  ""  \r\d\r\d\r\d\r\c  ogin:--ogin: ...
```

That is, expect nothing; send return, delay, return, delay, return, delay, return before expecting the login prompt.

uugetty requires this "wakeup sequence" to minimize the chance of getting into a data loop with the other **uugetty**, where each side sees the other's login prompt and thinks it is receiving a username and password.

Multiple Dialing Scripts

BNU and Taylor UUCP support chaining of dialing scripts. In an environment with different kinds of devices that are interconnected, this feature can greatly simplify configuration files.

In some corporate environments, rather than have a modem and analog phone line on each employee's desk, a bank of modems for shared use is set up. Each employee's computer is wired via a serial cable to a port switch in the basement, which controls access to the modems. Usually these "modem pool" arrangements require the calling computer to send a few commands, perhaps even logging in with a username and password, so that the data call can be billed to the appropriate user.

We'll pretend for a minute that Fee Lines, Inc., has such a system, and that a typical dialogue looks like this:

```
User sends:          <return> <delay> <return>
Switch responds: Please enter your username:
User sends:          joe <return>
Switch responds: Please enter your password:
User sends:          billme18r <return>
Switch responds: Enter request:
User sends:          dialout <return>
Switch responds: Connected
```

At this point, the switch connects the user's computer to a modem in the pool and the user can proceed as if the modem was directly connected to his computer, namely by sending AT commands to set up the modem and place a call.

Since we have two different devices (the port switch and the modem) it makes sense to write two different device handling scripts. They might look like this (in the BNU *Dialers* file):

```
# NakWell modems in modem pool
Nakwell  =W-,  "" ATQ0E1X4 OK  \EATDT\T\e CONNECT

# DataLoss port switch
Dataloss ""    "" \d\r\d\r\c username: joe  word: billme18r  quest: \D
```

Note that the modem dialing script uses the **\T** escape for inserting the dialing token (in this case, a telephone number) with dialcodes translation, while the port switch script uses the **\D** escape for the dialing token with no translation.

To chain these two scripts together, we need a definition in the BNU *Devices*[*] file that has both "dialer-token pairs" in the device definition. For example:

```
Pool tty00 - Any Dataloss dialout Nakwell \T
```

The command "dialout" becomes an argument to the "Dataloss" dialing script, which will send it in place of the **\D** escape.

And in the BNU *Systems* file, a system definition might look like this:

```
fatcat Any Pool 9600 97185554737 "" ogin:--ogin: Utabby word: meow
```

When **uucico** tries to contact *fatcat* now, it will first use the *Dataloss* script to obtain a modem from the port switch, use the *Nakwell* script to dial the phone number, and then log into *fatcat* with the chat script supplied in the *Systems* file.

The benefit of organizing dial scripts this way becomes apparent when you want to add another destination to the UUCP configuration. To reach the company's mail server, you need to supply the "mailhost" command instead of "dialout." The required configuration entries would look like this:

```
Devices:  Mailconn tty00 - Any Dataloss mailhost
Systems:  mailhost Any Mailconn 9600 - ogin:--ogin: Utabby word: furr
```

We didn't need to rewrite any of the dialing scripts, we only had to call them a different way.

Now let's suppose that Fee Lines, Inc. has reorganized its operations, moving Joe and his workstation to a field office in another state. They were kind enough to give him a Nakwell modem for dialing back to the main office, and also converted a few modems in the pool to act as incoming lines for the port switch; this allows an outside employee like Joe to use the port switch to contact other machines in the main office. Our new configuration entries for picking up the mail look like:

```
Devices:  Homebase tty00 - Any Nakwell \T Dataloss mailhost
Systems:  mailhost Any Homebase 9600 12125558800 ogin:--ogin: Utabby word: furr
```

And now **uucico** will dial the modem first, log into the port switch, tell the port switch to connect to the mail host, and then sign on to the mail host.

These features are also supported in Taylor UUCP: after adding the dialing scripts to the *dial* file, use the **dialer-sequence** command in the *port* file to set up the chain of scripts.

12

Access and Security Considerations

So far, the other chapters in this book have been about how to provide access to UUCP for file transfer and command execution on a local or remote system. In this chapter we turn things around, and talk about how to *deny* access rather than provide it.

The goal of this discussion is to explain how to set up UUCP so that it provides the services that you want to provide, and nothing else. We also discuss how to secure related aspects of the UUCP environment: the login accounts of your UUCP neighbors, the UUCP administrative login, UUCP configuration files, and the working directories.

A security review of your UUCP installation is important. If your UUCP configuration is too permissive, someone might be able to use the UUCP system to gain unauthorized access to your computer. The services you use UUCP for (like news and mail) could be tampered with or rerouted. If your system is compromised, the UUCP neighbors that you connect with might also be placed at risk. And good security protects against accidents such as a mistyped command at a remote site that might otherwise overwrite files on your system.

As part of the security review, look at the way you use the UUCP programs. If you or your users are fond of using the public directory for file transfers or you use the BNU or Version 2 **cu** command for remote logins, you should learn some new habits that are less susceptible to outside interference.

UNIX Security Overview

The UNIX operating system delegates all control of who may access the system to programs (daemons) running with root privilege. (The most famous of these daemons is **/bin/login**.) There are different programs for different kinds of access, and they often use different information to decide whether to let someone in. This decentralization of access control makes it easy to add new services and features into UNIX, but it leaves many avenues open for people who want to use your system without your permission.

Because of the myriad ways that UNIX can be compromised, even small, individual lapses in security could endanger the entire system. On some systems, if an intruder obtains a copy of your */etc/passwd* file, within a few hours or days he will be able to call back with valid passwords for your machine. On systems connected to TCP/IP networks, a change in the contents of a single file such as */etc/hosts.equiv* could suddenly let users from all over your network (or the world, if you're connected to the Internet) access your system.

Although we can't tell you how to secure your system against all possible threats (that would be the subject for another book, such as *Practical UNIX and Internet Security*, also published by O'Reilly & Associates), we can tell you how to keep UUCP from adding to them.

User Logins

The primary way people access a system is by logging in. Incoming UUCP calls use a similar method: they usually have a login account on the system that they are calling, ordinarily used only for UUCP. As you've seen from previous chapters, UUCP logins don't seem to be much good for anything besides UUCP. You can login by hand with a UUCP login and password, but all you get for your trouble is a "Shere=" prompt. However, if your system is on a TCP/IP network (even if it supports only the dummy "loopback" network), there are suddenly six or seven different ways of logging in, some of which can be used with a UUCP login/password to gain access.

Directory and File Protections

The UNIX file protection mechanism is one of the most reliable security features on a UNIX system. Via the file and directory permission bits, you can control who can read, write, or list out the files within. Careful attention to file ownerships and permissions is important for UUCP configuration files to prevent local users from reading the UUCP logins and passwords of the sites with which you communicate, and to prevent anyone from modifying the UUCP configuration to their own ends.

UUCP Application Security

The UUCP configuration files give you several features related to UUCP security:

- By setting up separate login IDs for each of your UUCP neighbors, and having UUCP double-check that callers are using their assigned login ID, you can minimize the chances that a third party will pretend to be one of your UUCP neighbors and try to access your system. (This kind of masquerade is called UUCP *spoofing*. Even local users on your system can engage in this trickery if you do not take steps to prevent it.)

- You can limit what commands your UUCP neighbors can run to a pre-approved list that you know are "safe."

- You can limit the access your UUCP neighbors have to your local filesystem to prevent any malicious (or accidental) changes to your system. This also prevents someone from snatching sensitive information from your system, such as your password file or the passwords you use for other UUCP connections.

- Your UUCP configurations files and directories should have their file permissions set to keep local users from changing files in UUCP directories, or from seeing the passwords used to access your UUCP neighbors.

- You can optionally require *callback* on a link, where one system will refuse an incoming call from a particular system, but immediately call it back. You are less likely to be spoofed if you always make the outgoing call; however, the system you are peering with will not have the same assurance, since only one side of a link can use callback.

- For extra protection against UUCP spoofing, most versions of UUCP support *conversation sequence* numbers, with which both sides of a UUCP link keep a counter that is incremented with each conversation. At connection time, the two sides see if their counters match. If they do not, it's assumed something is amiss and the line is disconnected. Conversation sequence numbers do not fully prevent spoofing, but they should let you know (after the fact) if it happens. They can be cumbersome to use, and may not be worth the extra administration overhead.

UUCP Login IDs

It's important to create a separate login ID and password for each of your UUCP neighbors. Older systems often used one UUCP login and password for multiple neighbors, which is extremely risky. Many systems still come with a *nuucp* user installed for this purpose and some vendor documentation still recommends using *nuucp* as a common login for your UUCP neighbors. This is a bad idea—even if you put a password on a multi-neighbor UUCP account, you won't be able to change it without notifying the administrators of all the remote systems. Common accounts make UUCP spoofing easier, and make it harder to detect abuse of a UUCP account.

Separate UUCP login IDs help prevent your UUCP links from interfering with each other and you can easily disable access for one system if a problem occurs, or if you decide to disconnect from one of your neighbors. We strongly recommend you use separate UUCP login IDs at all times. Common UUCP accounts should be used only when you are providing an "anonymous UUCP" site and you want "strangers" to be able to call up and use your UUCP services.

UUCP login names should be clearly distinguished from regular users. A common practice is to begin all UUCP user accounts with the letter "U" (capitalized), followed by the UUCP node name of the calling system.[*] This is the convention that we have used throughout this book, hence names like *Ufatcat* for the login ID used by the system *fatcat*. Using distinct names for UUCP users makes it easier to identify UUCP activity in system logs or when using the **ps** command, and calls attention to any discrepancies (such as seeing a UUCP user running a text editor or interactive shell).

Taylor UUCP allows the system administrator to create a separate password file that is used only for UUCP access. If your system is connected to the Internet or if you have many UUCP neighbors logging in, we strongly recommend that you use this feature. With the Taylor password file, you do not need to create any UUCP user accounts, which prevents many of the security exposures described here.

In the following discussion about user access, remember that some UNIX vendors have added extra user authentication and login restriction features into their code, which may give you more tools for managing UUCP logins. Features available on various systems include restricting logins to particular

---

[*] Or for long nodenames, the first seven letters, since most UNIX systems don't like usernames longer than eight characters.

port, preventing logins from being used over a network, disabling accounts after too many failed login attempts, and many others. Check your vendor documentation to see what is available on your particular system.

/etc/passwd

All logins on UNIX systems have entries in the */etc/passwd* file. Each entry in */etc/passwd* is a single line, separated into multiple fields delimited by the colon (:) character. The first field is the login name, and the last field is the program that will be executed when the user logs in. Here's a typical example:[*]

```
root:!:0:0:root:/:/bin/bash
bin:*:1:1:bin:/bin:
daemon:*:2:2:daemon:/sbin:
adm:*:3:4:adm:/var/adm:
uucp:*:10:14:uucp:/var/spool/uucppublic:
Ufatcat:!:12:14:Fatcat UUCP:/var/spool/uucppublic:/usr/lib/uucp/uucico
```

A UUCP login account is easily recognized by the pathname for **uucico** in the rightmost field (as in the *Ufatcat* entry in the above example). Note that an empty field (as in the *uucp* entry above) means to use the system default shell, usually **/bin/sh**.

The UUCP Administrative Account

Most systems are set up with a *uucp* account intended to be used for administering the UUCP configuration. But if you create and edit UUCP configuration files as the *uucp* user, all the files must be owned by *uucp*. This means that if someone finds a hole in your UUCP permissions, there is nothing to stop them from overwriting UUCP configuration files and taking over your UUCP environment.

Some system administrators prefer to do all UUCP administration as the *root* user to keep the UUCP configuration directories and files owned by *root*, and to change files to *uucp* ownership only when needed. This way, even if **uucico** is duped, it will be unable to tamper with any files owned by the *root* user (providing the directory permissions are also set up properly).

---

[*] This example shows a system with shadow passwords in use (encrypted passwords are kept in a separate, private file, such as */etc/shadow*). Most modern systems support a shadow password scheme. Shadow passwords are an excellent UNIX security feature and we strongly recommend them.

In any case, make sure that the *uucp* account's home directory (from the */etc/passwd* file) is *not* the public UUCP directory, nor any other directory accessible via a UUCP request. An attacker could create or change files such as *.profile* that will be automatically executed the next time the administrative user logs in. There are (far too many) other files in a home directory, that if created or modified by an attacker, could compromise your security. They include *.rhosts* (bypass passwords when logging in via TCP/IP), *.forward* (control delivery of a user's mail, possibly directing it to a program), and shell initialization files (*.kshrc*, *.bashrc*, and *.cshrc*).

Controlling Use of UUCP Logins

When you create a UUCP login, you expect it to be used for UUCP and only UUCP. Even if someone else has the login ID and password, you might think that an attacker would be limited to trying to spoof your UUCP sessions. But depending on what other software and network interfaces are on your system, a rogue with a UUCP login and password may be able to walk right in.

The biggest exposure is on a machine that provides TCP/IP networking services. Even if your machine has no network interface, it may still provide services over the TCP/IP "loopback" address of 127.0.0.1 (a dummy network interface designed to let two programs on the same computer communicate as if they were on a network). To check to see if you have TCP/IP services running, try this command:

```
# netstat -a | fgrep '*'
```

If you see any entries like this:

```
tcp     0     0    *.shell         *.*         LISTEN
tcp     0     0    *.login         *.*         LISTEN
tcp     0     0    *.exec          *.*         LISTEN
tcp     0     0    *.finger        *.*         LISTEN
tcp     0     0    *.time          *.*         LISTEN
tcp     0     0    *.telnet        *.*         LISTEN
tcp     0     0    *.ftp           *.*         LISTEN
```

your system is offering network services.

FTP access

The FTP file transfer daemon (**ftpd**) on many systems will allow anyone who has a UUCP login and password to sign on and transfer files. This lets them bypass all UUCP application security that would otherwise restrict the files they could read or write.

Most FTP servers have a way to disable access for specific users. If your system (and your FTP server) supports the *getusershell*(3) call, make sure that **uucico** is *not* listed in the file */etc/shells*. When supported, **ftpd** will automatically reject logins from users whose shells in */etc/passwd* are not also present in */etc/shells*. See the man pages for *getusershell*(3) and *ftpd*(8) for more information.

Another way of limiting access is to keep an */etc/ftpusers* file. This file contains a list of users who may *not* use FTP (this is counterintuitive to the file's name). See the documentation for **ftpd** on your system for more details. Unfortunately, this means adding each UUCP user one by one into the appropriate configuration file, a time-consuming process if you have many UUCP neighbors.

You may want to install the Washington University FTP daemon (**wu-ftpd**) in place of your vendor's **ftpd**. It supports *getusershell()* and */etc/shells*, and provides additional FTP access control features.

X11 access

If your system runs the **xdm** server (or its CDE equivalent, **dtlogin**), anyone with a UUCP login and password may be able to log into your system from an X terminal (or a computer that emulates an X terminal). Once logged in, one is able to use the system like any normal user.

If your system runs **xdm** or **dtlogin**, then you should test for this problem. Here are several ways to plug up this hole:

- Disable **xdm** if you don't need it.

- Limit **xdm** logins to the local console or other trusted terminals. This is usually done by editing the files */usr/lib/X11/xdm/Xaccess* and */usr/lib/X11/xdm/Xservers*.

- Edit the **xdm** session initialization script (usually */usr/lib/X11/xdm/Xsession*) to disallow UUCP logins.

For **xdm**, here are the changes needed for */usr/lib/X11/xdm/Xsession* (add this fragment near the top of the file):

```
# don't proceed if users have an invalid login shell

case ${SHELL:-} in
*uucico) echo "uucico login attempted by ${USER:-?} on 'date'"
        exit 3
        ;;
esac
```

```
case 'whoami' in
U*) echo "UUCP login attempt by 'whoami' on 'date'"
        exit 4
     ;;
esac
```

In systems with Common Desktop Environment (CDE), the **dtlogin** program performs the functions formerly held by **xdm**.[*] There are two scripts that control startup after logging in: */usr/dt/bin/Xsession* for normal logins and */usr/dt/config/Xfailsafe* for "fail-safe" logins used when the login user asks to have his or her login environment bypassed. If your **dtlogin** allows UUCP users to log in, the above changes must be added to both *Xsession* and *Xfailsafe*.

If you customize the **xdm** or **dtlogin** startup scripts, remember that operating system updates or patches may overwrite these files at a later date. Always test your changes to these scripts to make sure they work as intended.

rsh and rlogin

These services are famous for their willingness to let someone log on without a password if a file named *.rhosts*, with the proper contents, exists in a user's home directory. Although **rsh** and **rlogin** can be used to bypass password control, they cannot be used to run programs other than **uucico**.

To prevent abuse via **rsh** and **rlogin**, make sure all UUCP logins have different numeric user IDs (the third field in */etc/passwd*), that none of them has the same numeric user ID as the *uucp* user, and that the home directory specified in */etc/passwd* for each UUCP user (it can be the same for all) is not writable. In newer systems, you can turn off password bypassing in **rshd** and **rlogind**, usually by editing the */etc/inetd.conf* file and adding the appropriate option. Check your system documentation for **rshd** or **in.rshd** to see if this feature is supported.

Another trick is to create an empty or bogus *.rhosts* file (or subdirectory) owned by *root* in the home directory of *uucp*; this will also prevent password-less access.

---

[*] HP-UX 9.0 and later systems use **vuelogin**, which is similar, though not identical. Also, some systems may supply both **xdm** and **dtlogin**, although they cannot both run simultaneously.

UUCP Over TCP/IP

If you provide access for incoming UUCP calls via TCP/IP, you should set up access controls so only the hosts that you expect to call will be able to see your UUCP login prompt. The TCP Wrappers package (available from *ftp://ftp.cert.org*) will provide this protection for you. If your site is connected to the Internet, we recommend that you install TCP Wrappers for all possible network services, not just UUCP.

Mail to the uucp User

Many UNIX systems use **sendmail** as their system mailer. One of the many features of **sendmail** lets users redirect their mail to a program for processing. This feature is also the source of several security exposures.

A user can forward his or her email to a program by manipulating the *.forward* file in their home directory. If you set up a UUCP login ID with the public directory as its home, a user on the local system may be able to create a *.forward* file that can be used to trick **sendmail** into executing arbitrary commands.

If you run **sendmail**, you can protect against this problem by redirecting email for the *uucp* user in the */etc/aliases* file (**sendmail**'s alias database), which will prevent *.forward* processing for that user, and by using a unique numeric user ID for each UUCP login (as described earlier in this chapter for protecting against *.rhosts* attacks). You should also install the **sendmail** restricted shell program **smrsh**, which limits—to a pre-approved list—the programs that **sendmail** may execute on behalf of users.

BNU/Version 2 cu Vulnerability

The **cu** communications program as delivered in most BNU and Version 2 systems uses a naive file transfer method that is easily tricked. Lines of text from the remote system that begin with the sequence `~>:filename` can forcibly trigger the `~%take` feature of **cu**, providing an opening by which files can be written (or overwritten) in the home directory of the user running **cu**. We describe this problem in detail in Chapter 5, *Logging In on a Remote System*. The Taylor version of **cu** does not have this vulnerability: it uses a more sensible scheme for `~%take` file transfers.

If **cu** weren't so useful for testing UUCP configurations, we'd suggest removing it entirely from a BNU or Version 2 system. If anyone on your system is a regular user of **cu**, you should replace it with the Taylor version (but keep the original around somewhere in case you need it for debugging configuration files). You can also try demanding a fix from your system vendor; at publication time at least one UNIX vendor had promised to remove the ˜>:*filename* escape from future releases of **cu**.

Filesystem Security

The UNIX filesystem protection scheme is one of the few security mechanisms in UNIX enforced by the operating system, rather than by a user program or daemon. This means it cannot be easily bypassed, except by the superuser. By properly using file and directory permission bits, you can keep users from reading files, writing to files, or listing out directory contents.

You should use filesystem security to keep the UUCP configuration files from being modified by anyone but the superuser. The directories with UUCP configuration files (usually */usr/lib/uucp*, */etc/uucp*, or */usr/conf/uucp*) should be owned by *root* and have protection mode 0755 (read/write/searchable by the owner, read/searchable by the group, and read/searchable by the rest of the world).[*] The configuration files within directories should be owned by *root* and set to mode 0644 (read/write by owner, read-only to all others) if they are to be publicly available (such as the device or dialer information). Private files (those containing phone numbers, logins, and passwords) should be owned by *uucp* and set to mode 0400 (read-only to owner, inaccessible to all others). Since the main UUCP utilities (**uucico**, **uucp**, **uux**, etc.) are all *setuid* (set user ID upon execution) to the *uucp* user, they will be able to access the private files when needed.

A few systems make use of the *uucp* group to allow **uucico** and **cu** to access UUCP configuration files. On these systems, private configuration files are set to 0640 (read/write by owner, usually *root*, readable to the group, *uucp*, and inaccessible to all others). We've also seen configurations where **uustat** has *setgid* (set group ID) permissions to the UUCP group, which lets it kill pending jobs in the spool directory. For this to work, the spool directory must also be writable by the *uucp* group.

---

[*] A perhaps unwanted side-effect of this configuration is that it disables BNU and Version 2 conversation sequence numbers. See the discussion later on in this chapter.

The Spool Directory

The UUCP spool directory's contents include pending jobs, data files in transit, logfiles, debug output, and statistics files. Since UUCP is constantly creating and deleting files in the spool directory, it needs to be in charge of the directory and all its contents.

The spool directory and its subdirectories should be owned by *uucp*, and their permissions should be 0755, which allows *uucp* full access, and all others read-only access. All the files in the spool directory and its subdirectories should be owned by *uucp*. Some of the information in the spool directory is open to the public, like log files or the files containing pending UUCP requests. These files can be mode 0644 (read/write to owner, read-only to everyone else).

Other information should be private: the data files for pending jobs (which might contain electronic mail, or other data private to the users), the Taylor UUCP debug file or the BNU audit file (which contain debug information that might reveal logins, passwords, or the aforementioned user data), and the Taylor conversation sequence number files. All private files in the spool directory should be set to mode 0600 (read/write only by owner). If a directory contains only private files, it should be set to mode 0700 (read/write/search to the owner only).

A few files created by UUCP, such as status files, may be created with world-writable access. On some older systems, usually Version 2, the spool directory permissions are such that any user can remove a status file or any other file in the spool directory. This may open up opportunities for meddling with UUCP's pending jobs and is not recommended. Unfortunately, some older Version 2 systems may not work properly if you change the spool directory permissions to be more restrictive. If you are using one of these versions, you should upgrade to Taylor UUCP.

The Public Directory

As we described in Chapter 2, *File Transfer*, the public directory is a little too public for any secure use. Any other user on the local system, as well as any user on any of the UUCP neighbors of the local system, can read or write files in the public directory. Most sites set the public directory's permission to be 0777, letting anyone read or write files within.

You can disable the public directory completely by changing its directory protection to read-only (mode 0555), and its ownership to *root*. If this is too drastic, you can make a slight improvement in the security of the public directory by setting the "sticky" bit on the directory permissions (mode 01777). This will prevent UUCP or remote users from deleting or changing files in the public directory created by local users. It also prevents local users from removing any files copied into the public directory from remote systems via **uucp** or **uuto**.

Most systems set the sticky bit on the */tmp* directory to keep users from deleting each other's temporary files. A few systems (notably SunOS and Solaris) set the sticky bit on the UUCP public directory at install time.

BNU Security

Most of BNU's security features are controlled by the *Permissions* configuration file. *Permissions* controls what portions of your local filesystem are accessible to remote systems via UUCP, what commands may be executed by remote systems, and numerous other features. BNU also allows you to control whether anonymous UUCP is allowed on your system with the **remote.unknown** command.

The *Permissions* file has two types of entries:

* LOGNAME entries allow you to grant specific permissions for individual login IDs that are used *when remote systems call you*. They begin with the word "LOGNAME."

* MACHINE entries allow you to specify permissions for individual systems *when you call them*. They begin with the word "MACHINE."

While it is tempting to think that MACHINE entries set permissions for a remote machine on the basis of its nodename, this is not really the case. The same UUCP jobs may be subject to the restrictions of either a MACHINE entry or a LOGNAME entry, depending on which side of the link originated the call. This somewhat confusing approach was taken because the BNU UUCP authors felt that one can be more certain of a remote host's identity if the local host had placed the call, and that UUCP spoofing was more likely on an incoming call. This was more relevant back when systems commonly had generic UUCP login accounts shared by multiple UUCP login neighbors.

We recommend you control access by each individual machine by using combined MACHINE and LOGNAME entries, as described below. If you always use the VALIDATE option to confirm that the remote host is using the right UUCP login account, the distinction between outgoing and incoming calls is less important.

Whenever you create or change entries in the *Permissions* file, be sure to run the **uucheck −v** command to verify that your changes work as expected.

Permissions File Entries

Both MACHINE and LOGNAME entries consist of option/value pairs. You can have as many of these option/value pairs as you want, and can write entries for all or only some of the remote sites.

The options and their allowed values are listed in Table 12−1. In the table, the *Class* column uses the code **M** or **L** to designate whether an option can be used in a MACHINE entry, a LOGNAME entry, or both.

Table 12−1: Allowable Permissions Entries (and Options)

Option	Class	Description
LOGNAME		Defines one or more UUCP login IDs, and the associated permission options for them when they call in. Incoming calls with a login ID not listed in a LOGNAME= entry will be rejected.
MACHINE		Defines one or more UUCP nodenames, and the associated permission options for them when this system calls them.
REQUEST	M, L	Specifies whether the remote system can copy files from your computer. Default is "no."
SENDFILES	L	Specifies whether the local system should send jobs queued for the remote system. If set to "call" (the default), jobs for a remote system are sent to it only when the local system originates the call. If set to "yes," jobs are also sent out when the remote system logs in.
READ	M, L	Specifies the directories that **uucico** can use for requesting files. The default is the public directory.
WRITE	M, L	Specifies the directories that **uucico** can use for depositing files. The default is the public directory.
NOREAD	M, L	Exceptions to READ options or defaults.
NOWRITE	M, L	Exceptions to WRITE options or defaults.
CALLBACK	L	Specifies whether the local system must call back the calling system before transactions can occur. Default is "no."
COMMANDS	M	Lists the commands the remote system can execute locally. For example, "COMMANDS=rmail:rnews" allows only the **rmail** and **rnews** commands. Full pathnames may be used. The default is usually the **rmail** command. The keyword "ALL" allows a remote site to run any command on your system, subject to the usual file permissions.

Table 12-1: Allowable Permissions Entries (and Options) (continued)

Option	Class	Description
VALIDATE	L	VALIDATE=*system_name* links a LOGNAME entry to the corresponding MACHINE entry. All incoming UUCP calls that claim to be from the system(s) named in the VALIDATE option must use the login ID (or one of the login IDs) in the LOGNAME entry where the VALIDATE option appears.
MYNAME	M, L	Changes the local system's name (MYNAME=*newname*) during conversations with this machine.
PUBDIR	M, L	Specifies the directory for local access (e.g., */usr/spool/ uucppublic/loginA*). Default is the *uucppublic* directory.

Before we show you how to use these options, let's first lay down some ground rules for writing the *Permissions* file entries:

- Each option-value pair has the following format:

    option=value

    Blanks are not allowed before or after the equal sign (=). For many options, you can specify multiple values, delimited by the colon (:) character. For example:

    option=value1:value2:value3 . . .

- Each line corresponds to one entry. A line may be continued on to the next line(s) by a backslash (\) character.

- A blank is used to separate multiple option-value pairs on the same line.

- Comment lines begin with a hash mark (#), and end with a newline.

- Blank lines are ignored.

- Case matters. "REQUEST=yes" is a valid option, while "REQUEST=YES" is a syntax error and is silently ignored.

- Context matters. Options that are not meaningful for the entry they appear in are silently ignored. For example, if you specify a a COMMANDS= option in a LOGNAME= entry, it will not take effect, but it will not produce an error message either.

- Always run **uucheck −v** after editing *Permissions*, and review its output carefully.

When writing entries, you should keep in mind the following:

- All login IDs used by remote systems must appear in one and *only* one LOGNAME entry.

- If you do not want to grant permissions to each system by name, the entry MACHINE=OTHER will assign permissions to any system not mentioned by name in other MACHINE entries. This is useful if you have a lot of UUCP neighbors and don't want to specify separate permissions for each one.

- Although you can specify multiple login IDs in LOGNAME entries, and multiple machine names in MACHINE entries, it is better practice to use only one name per entry, especially if you are using VALIDATE.

Combining LOGNAME and MACHINE

You should combine MACHINE and LOGNAME entries into a single entry if the options are the same. For example, two separate entries like these:

```
LOGNAME=Utabby VALIDATE=tabby REQUEST=yes SENDFILES=yes

MACHINE=tabby REQUEST=yes SENDFILES=yes
```

can be combined into the following:

```
LOGNAME=Utabby VALIDATE=tabby MACHINE=tabby REQUEST=yes SENDFILES=yes
```

Many administrators prefer setting up *Permissions* this way: a single entry for each machine, regardless of who initiated the call. This is conceptually simpler and it is easier to read than using separate LOGNAME= and MACHINE= entries. This method for setting up *Permissions* does require that you create separate login IDs for each of your UUCP neighbors who call in, but for good security you need to do that anyway.

Permissions on Three Systems: An Example

The *Permissions* file can get quite confusing. The best way to explain how the options are used is by example. Figure 12-1 shows the *Permissions* files for three connected systems and discusses the permissions they grant. After the example, the individual options are discussed in more detail.

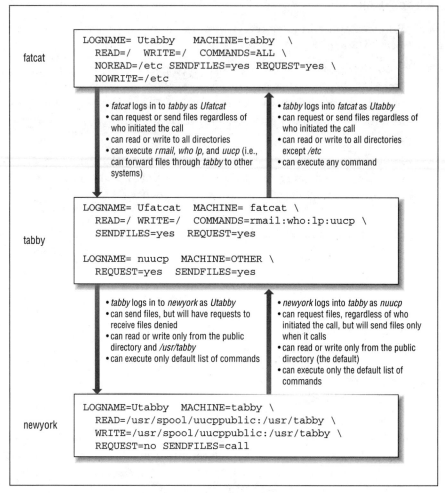

Figure 12–1: Permissions file on three systems

The Default Permissions

An entry similar to this:

```
LOGNAME=nuucp
```

allows any remote system to log in as *nuucp*. Since no other options are given, however, the default values for all other access controls are used, giving minimal remote access to the local system. This entry is equivalent to the following:

```
LOGNAME=nuucp \
READ=/usr/spool/uucppublic WRITE=/usr/spool/uucppublic \
SENDFILES=call REQUEST=no COMMANDS=rmail
```

These permissions allow the remote site to execute **rmail** and to transfer files into the public directory (or subdirectories within the public directory), and that's it.* But remember that a LOGNAME= entry controls only those conversations when the remote side has dialed into the local system. The other half, when the local system places the call, is controlled by MACHINE= entries. If you don't specify a MACHINE= entry for a site that is called, the following defaults apply:

- Local send and receive requests will be executed.

- The remote computer can send files to the local */usr/spool/uucppublic* directory.

- The commands sent by the remote computer for execution on the local system must be one of the default commands, usually just **rmail**.

Who Calls Whom?

The first line of defense in UUCP security is to give separate login IDs to each of your UUCP neighbors who call in to exchange UUCP traffic. Then, you may set up the VALIDATE, CALLBACK, SENDFILES, and REQUEST options to further control what kinds of requests may take place over your UUCP links.

The VALIDATE option allows you to crosscheck the nodename of a calling system against the login name it uses. For example:

```
LOGNAME=Uneeda VALIDATE=needa
```

This specifies that only a system using the login name *Uneeda* will be able to set up a UUCP link with the system name *needa*. If an incoming call logs in with any other login name and claims to be the system *needa*, **uucico** will refuse the connection (with the RLOGIN error message, as described in Chapter 11, *Making Sure the Link Works*).

---

* Some BNU versions have a slightly different default for the COMMANDS= option. For example, IBM's AIX also allows the **uucp** command. Consult your system's documentation for the exact details on your system.

CAUTION   To protect UUCP connections properly, *every one* of your UUCP neighbors must be referenced by a VALIDATE option within a LOGNAME entry. Any machine not mentioned, such as a passive neighbor who never calls your system, will not be protected. If you have UUCP links to machines that do not call in, create a fake LOGNAME entry for them along these lines:

```
LOGNAME=UNEVER VALIDATE=sys1:sys2:sys3
```

This will keep anyone—unless there's a user named *UNEVER* on your system—from calling in and pretending to be one of the named systems.

If you set CALLBACK to "yes," you can be more sure of the identity of the caller, since spoofing telephone numbers is much more work than discovering login IDs and passwords or temporarily changing a nodename. But it is not foolproof; phone numbers can be redirected with the "remote call forwarding" features available in the more modern telephone exchanges, and an incoming call at the right moment can fool a modem into thinking it has dialed someone.

CALLBACK also works with network connections. This gives you a way to verify that UUCP traffic for a particular node is always associated with the same network address.

CALLBACK has one nonsecurity use: it lets you decide who gets to pay the phone bill for data transfers. This would be useful when one side of the connection has access to low cost or flat-rate telephone service.

The SENDFILES option describes whether or not your system will send out locally queued work after a system that calls in has finished with its own business. This default value:

```
SENDFILES=call
```

means that your system will send out work only if it has initiated the call. That is, when a remote system calls in, finishes its business, and offers to hang up, your system will accept the offer instead of reversing roles and sending out the locally queued work. This feature is useful for limiting UUCP traffic to the hours that the local system is willing to dial out (set in the *Systems* file), since your local system will hold outgoing jobs until it is allowed to place the call itself.

The REQUEST option describes whether or not a remote system can request files from you. This default value:

```
REQUEST=no
```

means that all file transfer requests from your system must *originate* with your system.

If both of these options are set, your system is pretty much in the driver's seat with regard to file transfers queued with the **uucp** command.[*] Regardless of what READ and WRITE options are set, someone on your system must initiate a transfer to the remote system.

There are a number of not-so-obvious implications to these options. For example, if you require CALLBACK, the remainder of the permissions that will be in effect whenever you communicate with the other system are set by the relevant MACHINE entry (and by the remote system's LOGNAME entry for you), not by the LOGNAME entry. This is also true, to a lesser extent, if you specify SENDFILES=call.

Be careful not to accidentally set things up so no transfers can occur. The most obvious case is when both systems require CALLBACK of each other. Less obviously, if one system requires CALLBACK and the other SEND-FILES=call, the latter system will never be able to send out work of its own.

Controlling File Access

The READ and WRITE options define remote access to directories. Consider this entry:

```
LOGNAME=Ufatcat READ=/ WRITE=/ REQUEST=yes SENDFILES=yes
```

This entry grants the following permissions to systems that log in as *nuucp*:

- Files can be transferred to any directory (WRITE=/). Of course, UUCP is still subject to normal UNIX file permissions. In order for writes to occur in any directory, the directory must have owner of group **uucp** or must be writable by all.

- Files can be read from any directory (READ=/). Again, standard UNIX file permissions apply.

---

[*] However, if you're sloppy with the commands you allow to remote systems, they may still be able to snoop around via **uux** requests.

- Files can be requested from the local site (REQUEST=yes) by the remote system.

- Any locally queued jobs will be transferred during the conversation (SENDFILES=yes).

- The remote system can execute locally only those commands in the default set (COMMANDS not specified).

An entry such as this should be used only with tightly coupled systems in which you have complete confidence. Allowing remote systems this level of access would allow a remote system to read, and potentially replace files like *Systems* and *Permissions*. (Since these files are owned by **uucp** and the remote **uucico** is running set-user ID **uucp**, the normal UNIX file permissions will pose no obstacle.)

You can modify this example to restrict access to specific directories only. For example, it would not be wise to make the */etc* and */usr/lib/uucp* direc-tories open to writes. Doing this would make your */etc/passwd*, *Systems*, and *Permissions* files fair game to remote systems. In this case, you can use the NOREAD and NOWRITE options. For example:

```
LOGNAME=Ugossip  NOREAD=/etc:/usr/lib/uucp \
READ=/ WRITE=/work/rumors:/var/spool/uucppublic
```

This means remote machines that log in as *Ugossip* cannot read */etc* or */usr/lib/uucp*, but can read all other directories. They can also put files in */work/rumors* or the public directory.

One of the better features of the *Permissions* file is that read and write access are independent. In older versions of UUCP, you had to grant both read and write access, or none at all. This makes it possible, for instance, to set up a directory for software distribution. Any number of systems can read from this directory, but none of them (or only specially chosen systems) can write to it.

NOTE   When you use READ and WRITE entries, make sure you leave */usr/spool/uucppublic* readable and writable if you want the remote site to have access to the public directory. This directory is accessible by default only when READ and WRITE options are not specified; if you use them, you must explicitly name the public directory in the READ and WRITE options.

Allowing Command Execution

The commands that remote systems can execute locally are defined by the COMMANDS option. This keyword is an exception to the general rule that MACHINE entries apply to your system when it calls the named remote system. COMMANDS sets up the command list regardless of who originates the call. For example:

```
MACHINE=fatcat COMMANDS=rmail:/usr/bin/lp:rnews
MACHINE=OTHER COMMANDS=rmail
```

This entry allows **fatcat** to execute the **rmail, lp,** and **rnews** commands. Other machines can execute only **rmail**. For safety, you should always specify the full path to commands, as shown above for */usr/bin/lp*. Otherwise, a default path will be used, which usually includes */bin* and */usr/sbin*. To find out the default path on your system, check your vendor documentation, or try this command:

```
# strings /usr/lib/uucp/uucico | grep /bin
```

You should be very careful in selecting commands that can be executed locally by remote sites. A sufficiently general command like **tar** can be used to bypass UUCP's file access restrictions. Commands like **mail** or **mailx** that support shell escapes are also quite dangerous. **rmail**, however, is a restricted mail command specifically written to be safe for use by UUCP.

Here's an example using the "ALL" value:

```
MACHINE=Utrustme COMMANDS=ALL READ=/ WRITE=/
```

An entry like this gives the remote UUCP node complete access to your system, the same access someone would get if you gave them a regular user account on your system, plus the ability to meddle with the UUCP configuration and spool directories. Needless to say, we don't recommend this.

Forwarding

BNU UUCP forwards files by executing the **uucp** command on the remote system through which a file must be forwarded. If you want your system to be a conduit by which other systems can forward files between each other, you must include the **uucp** command in the COMMANDS= option for each system that is a potential source of forwarding requests. If the forwarding chain passes through other systems, they too must allow the **uucp** command to be executed by the requesting systems in the chain.

This implementation of forwarding is incompatible with the methods used in Version 2 and BSD UUCP, but it does interoperate with Taylor UUCP.

If a user on system *wrists* types this entry:

```
wrists$ uucp myfile carpal!tunnel!syndrome!/usr/spool/uucppublic
```

both *carpal* and *tunnel* must allow **uucp** in the COMMANDS option for the calling system. That is, assuming that all the systems in this example are running BNU UUCP, *carpal* must allow *wrists* to run **uucp** and *tunnel* must allow *carpal* to run **uucp**. Since *syndrome* is the ultimate destination and is not forwarding the file any further, it need not allow *tunnel* to run **uucp**.

One security worry with forwarding is that you are allowing remote systems to invoke **uucp** any way they please. You cannot control the systems to which a remote neighbor can forward. Another worry is that an attacker might find some way to run **uucp** on your system to copy out files that you don't want them to see. This can be prevented by minimizing the remote system's file access privileges with the READ= or NOREAD= options in that system's *Permissions* file entry.

If you want better control over UUCP forwarding, switch to Taylor UUCP, which lets you control forwarding destinations and does not require that you allow remote systems to execute the **uucp** command.

Assuming an Alias

Sometimes you want your system to be known by different names depending on who's calling. For example, if you supply anonymous UUCP services, it is prudent to present an entirely different face to unknown systems, including a different name. This could be done like this:

```
LOGNAME=nuucp MYNAME=freesys
```

Now the name *freesys* is used whenever a remote system logs in as the *nuucp* user. Another example is when one system takes on the UUCP connections of another one (perhaps temporarily), and needs to use the name of the original system when talking to some of its neighbors.

The MYNAME option can be used for testing purposes, since it allows a system to call itself. MYNAME can also be used for mischief, letting one machine masquerade as another. This, however, can be thwarted with judicious use of the VALIDATE option.

remote.unknown

By default, BNU will refuse to communicate with any system not listed in the local *Systems* file. This feature is turned on or off via the file */usr/lib/uucp/remote.unknown*.

The *remote.unknown* file is a shell script or program that records any login attempts by unknown systems in the file */usr/spool/uucp/.Admin/Foreign*. This file is scanned by the BNU administrative scripts, which sends email detailing the unknown login attempts. You may want to modify *remote.unknown*, if it's a shell script, to notify you in a more timely manner.

To allow unknown systems to log in, remove the execute permissions from *remote.unknown* (with the **chmod −x** command). Make sure you have limited the access permissions of unknown systems as much as possible via the MACHINE=OTHER option, and that all of your regular neighbors have VALIDATE= options in their LOGNAME entries so that an unknown system cannot use the anonymous UUCP login to spoof you.

Sequence Numbers in BNU UUCP

Most versions of BNU UUCP support conversation sequence numbers, but do not mention it in their system documentation.[*] Sequence numbers are stored in the *SQFILE* file, which lives in the configuration directory (*/etc/uucp* or */usr/lib/uucp*). The problem is that for secure operation of UUCP, the UUCP configuration directory should be owned by *root* and not writeable by anyone, including *uucp*; but, **uucico** wants to update *SQFILE* on every call, as well as create a temporary file in the configuration directory. As we've already mentioned, you're safer when UUCP *cannot* write files in its configuration directory, since an interloper might find a way to trick UUCP into changing permission or command execution restrictions.

You can tell if your version of UUCP supports conversation sequence numbers by using the **strings** command (see the example at the end of Chapter 14, *Troubleshooting UUCP*, for details). If you want to try using sequence numbers, change the ownership of the UUCP configuration directory to *uucp*, and the permissions to mode 0755, so that **uucico** will be able to write the sequence files as needed.

---

* Peter Honeyman, one of the original authors of BNU UUCP, notes that "sequence numbers add very little to uucp's password-based security and are prone to getting out of sync, an administrative headache. i should have killed them when i had the chance. i thought i had."

BNU sequence number support appears to be identical to sequence number support in Version 2 UUCP. (See the section on Version 2 later in this chapter for more information on using *SQFILE*.) Remember that sequence numbers provide only a little extra protection against spoofing, and are often an administrative headache because the numbers can slip out of sequence due to "natural causes."

The uucheck Command

No matter how long you stare at a BNU *Permissions* file, there's always a detail or two that you will miss. By running the **/usr/lib/uucp/uucheck –v** command, you can see UUCP's view of your *Permissions* entries. Here is a sample **uucheck** output for a *Permissions* file with a single entry:

```
# /usr/lib/uucp/uucheck -v

*** uucheck:  Check Required Files and Directories
*** uucheck:  Directories Check Complete

*** uucheck:  Check /usr/lib/uucp/Permissions file
** LOGNAME PHASE (when they call us)

When a system logs in as: (Utabby)
          We DO allow them to request files.
          We WILL send files queued for them on this call.
          They can send files to
              /usr/spool/uucppublic (DEFAULT)
          They can request files from
              /usr/spool/uucppublic (DEFAULT)
          Myname for the conversation will be fatcat.
          PUBDIR for the conversation will be /usr/spool/uucppublic.


  ** MACHINE PHASE (when we call or execute their uux requests)

When we call system(s): (tabby)
          We DO allow them to request files.
          They can send files to
              /usr/spool/uucppublic (DEFAULT)
          They can request files from
              /usr/spool/uucppublic (DEFAULT)
          Myname for the conversation will be fatcat.
          PUBDIR for the conversation will be /usr/spool/uucppublic.

Machine(s): (tabby)
CAN execute the following commands:
command (rmail), fullname (rmail)
command (uucp), fullname (uucp)
command (rnews), fullname (rnews)

*** uucheck:  /usr/lib/uucp/Permissions Check Complete
```

Unfortunately, **uucheck** does not check everything; in particular, it gives no indication whether the VALIDATE option is in effect for a particular machine. It also won't remind you to use the **−v** option. Without this option, **uucheck** will not check your *Permissions* file. In general, **uucheck** checks only syntax, not meaning, so you must always read **uucheck** output very carefully to make sure UUCP is interpreting the *Permissions* file the way you expect it to.

Taylor Security

Taylor UUCP supports all the security features of older UUCP versions, and throws in a few new ones for good measure. Our favorite feature is the ability to control a UUCP-only login and password database separate from */etc/passwd*, which lifts the burden of maintaining UUCP login IDs and all their attendant security risks. Taylor UUCP configuration files are also easier to understand than a BNU *Permissions* file, especially when it comes to the access and security commands.

Using UUCP-only logins

Taylor **uucico** has the ability to prompt for a login and password, similar to the **getty** or **uucpd** commands. You can use Taylor **uucico** as a direct port-answering daemon, giving it complete ownership of the incoming port; you can also have it cooperate with an enhanced version of the **getty** command—such as the **mgetty** package written by Gert Doering—that will pass UUCP logins to **uucico** while sending regular user logins to **/bin/login**. Taylor **uucico** can also replace **uucpd** in the */etc/inetd.conf* file, allowing **uucico** to be started directly by **inetd** when an incoming call arrives via TCP/IP.[*]

Like most Taylor features, support for the UUCP-only password file and its default location will vary depending on how your local version is compiled.

Taylor passwd file

The Taylor UUCP password file is an alternate database of usernames and passwords, which is used instead of */etc/passwd* to validate incoming UUCP connections. Its default location is */usr/conf/uucp/passwd*, but as with all configuration files in Taylor, this can be changed either at compile time or

---

[*] This is how UUCP over TCP/IP is supported in Linux, which does not come with **uucpd**.

via the *config* master configuration file. The format of a Taylor password file is quite simple. For example:

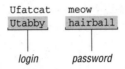

Passwords are usually stored in cleartext, as in this example. If the appropriate *crypt(3)* library call is available on your system, you can define HAVE_ENCRYPTED_PASSWORDS in the Taylor source file *policy.h* and use standard UNIX password encryption. Since Taylor **uucico** will also allow its password file to be delimited by the colon character (:), it is possible, with the right compile-time definitions and library support, to use the */etc/passwd* file format.

NOTE   Using encrypted passwords is much safer than keeping them "in the clear." If you have many UUCP neighbors, you should try to implement encrypted password support in the Taylor UUCP password file.

In order to use the Taylor password file for incoming UUCP calls, you must set up a nonstandard "login" path with which **uucico** is allowed to prompt the incoming caller for their password. Here are three different ways to do this:

- For a serial or modem port that will be devoted to UUCP traffic, have **uucico** run in "endless" mode; it then has complete control over the port. This prevents normal (i.e., non-UUCP) logins on that port.

- For a serial or modem port that will be used for regular logins as well as UUCP traffic, use the **mgetty** package to divert UUCP login IDs towards **uucico**, while normal users are sent to **/bin/login**.

- For incoming TCP/IP calls on the UUCP service number (port 540), have the **inetd** daemon start **uucico** in response to incoming connections.

After you have set up the login path, edit the Taylor password file to create the login IDs and passwords for your incoming UUCP users.

uucico as a login daemon

Taylor **uucico** supports an "endless" or "freestanding" mode, which refuses to exit once started. When an incoming call ends, **uucico** resets and waits for a new call on its port. Since only **uucico** is taking calls on this port, the port is dedicated to UUCP.

To invoke **uucico** in endless mode, use the following syntax:

```
# /usr/lib/uucp/uucico -e -l -p port_name
```

port_name is a port name defined in the *port* configuration file. If the port is attached to a modem, modem commands needed (such as putting the modem into "dumb" mode so that **uucico** doesn't try to use "CONNECT 38400" as a login name or password) must be defined in the configuration files as device chat scripts. Another complication when **uucico** is used as a modem handler is that callers get only one chance to supply their login ID and password. If a connection error or line noise error occurs, the login will fail and **uucico** will hang up.

uucico and mgetty

Standard UNIX **getty** programs can call only one program (usually /bin/login) to validate a user's password and let them into the system. One of the added features of **mgetty** allows a choice of login validation programs, based on the login ID supplied by the caller. The sample *login.config* file supplied with the **mgetty** package shows how to direct login IDs beginning with a capital "U" to **uucico**.

Incoming TCP/IP calls

To have **uucico** answer incoming TCP/IP calls, make sure the following entry is in */etc/inetd.conf*:

```
uucp   stream  tcp    nowait  uucp  /usr/lib/uucp/uucico  -l
```

You should also signal the **inetd** daemon with **kill −1**, so it rereads the changed configuration file. For more information, see Chapter 10, *Setting Up a UUCP Link*.

Configuration File Security Commands

All of the security, file permission, and access control features in BNU are also available under Taylor, albeit under different names.* Taylor UUCP also has a few additional features, such as commands that control access in both directions (unlike BNU, where you need to specify both LOGNAME= and MACHINE=), the ability to run chat scripts or external programs when answering calls, and control over the maximum file size that may be transferred.

Security-related configuration commands appear in the *config* master config- uration file and the *sys* system configuration file.

config file

The master configuration file *config* has the following two commands of interest:

Field   Meaning

passwdfile *file* . . .

> Sets the location of the password file. If not specified, the default is taken from the compile-time settings. Multiple password files can be specified.

unknown *sys_file_commands*

> Enables communications with systems not listed in the *sys* file (foreign or unknown systems). The argument is any valid command that can appear in the *sys* file, which will be put in effect when an unknown system calls. For example:

```
unknown pubdir /usr/spool/uucppublic/foreigners
unknown myname freesys
unknown called-login nuucp
```

> This entry sets the public directory, the local system name to be used, and requires a particular login ID for all calls that come in from an unknown system.

If the **unknown** command is absent, any unknown systems that manage to log in will be rejected when they try to handshake with **uucico**.

---

* As well as under the original names, with Taylor's BNU compatibility mode.

sys file

The Taylor *sys* file allows you to specify the access controls along with the rest of the system entry. These commands can also appear with the **unknown** command in the *config* master configuration file.

Note that Taylor UUCP accepts the keywords **true**, **false**, **yes**, and **no** as Boolean values; you may use whichever you feel is more appropriate.

Field   **Meaning**

callback *boolean*

> If true, hangs up and calls back the system that has just logged in. The default is false.

called-login *login_id* . . .

> Requires that incoming calls for this system use the specified login ID (or IDs). The keyword ANY can be used to specify that all login IDs are allowed. For good security, every system that calls in should have a login ID associated with it. Passive neighbors that never call you should have a nonexistent login ID listed. The default value is ANY.

called-chat *chat_script*
called-chat-timeout *seconds*
called-chat-fail *expect_string*
called-chat-seven-bit *boolean*
called-chat-program *command args*

> Runs a chat script upon receiving a call from this system. These commands work the same way as their counterparts (without the **called-** prefix) described in Chapter 10, *Setting Up a UUCP Link*. Although the Taylor documentation suggests using this feature to set special modem parameters for particular systems, you could also use it to retrieve authentication information about the incoming call.

> For example, on a TCP/IP network, you could run a program that verifies a caller's source address (similar to TCP wrappers). If your telephone connection supplies the caller's telephone number (such as an ISDN, 800 ANI, or the residence telephone "Caller ID"), it may be possible to retrieve the calling number for validation purposes.

> If the chat script fails, or the chat program returns a non-zero exit status, the incoming call is aborted.

send-request *boolean*
receive-request *boolean*
request *boolean*

> Allows or denies remote file transfer requests. **send-request** controls whether the remote system may attempt to send files to the local system; **receive-request** controls whether the remote system may attempt to retrieve files from the local system; and, **request** controls both at the same time. The default is **true**, which allows file requests.

call-transfer *boolean*
called-transfer *boolean*
transfer *boolean*

> Controls whether file transfers queued up for the remote system will be processed. **call-transfer** allows file transfers to take place when the local system originated the call; **called-transfer** allows file transfers when the remote system originated the call; and, **transfer** controls both directions. The default is true (allow transfers in both directions).

call-local-size *size time*
called-local-size *size time*

> Prevents files larger than *size* bytes from being sent out during the period of time specified by *time* (a time string). **call-local-size** controls files sent when the local system originated the call; **called-local-size** controls files sent when the remote system originated the call. The default is no size restrictions.

call-remote-size *size time*
called-remote-size *size time*

> Prevents the remote system from sending files larger than *size* bytes during the time periods specified by the time string *time*. This command is honored only if the remote side is also running Taylor UUCP.

local-send *directories*

> Restricts what files may be sent by local request (**uucp** or **uux**) to the remote system. *directories* is a list of directories, separated by spaces. You may use the ~ (tilde) as an abbreviation for the public directory, or prefix a directory with a ! (exclamation point) to exclude it from the list. The default is /, meaning a local user can send any file via UUCP to the remote system.

remote-send *directories*

> Limits the directories on the local system from which users on the remote system can fetch files. The default is the public directory.

local-receive *directories*

> Limits the directories on the local system that may be used for receiving files copied from the remote system at the request of a local user. The default is the public directory.

remote-receive *directories*

> Limits the directories that may be used to receive files copied from the remote system at the request of a remote user. The default is the public directory.

forward-to *systems*
forward-from *systems*
forward *systems*

> Lists the systems to, or from, which files may be forwarded. The **forward** command controls forwarding permission in both directions. The default is not to permit forwarding. For forwarding to work, the system doing the forwarding must either be a Taylor system that permits the forwarding operation, or a BNU system that allows this system to execute the **uucp** command. Taylor forwarding works by allowing remote systems to execute **uucp** in a special restricted mode (**uucp −u**), which only supports forwarding requests (assuming they are permitted via the UUCP configuration files).

sequence *boolean*

> Requires sequence numbers for conversations with the remote system. The default is false. Sequence numbers are stored in a file named after the appropriate system, in the *.Sequence* subdirectory of the spool directory. They must be readable and writable only by the *uucp* user; otherwise, **uucico** will refuse to talk to the remote system.[*] If both sides have Taylor UUCP, they will automatically start using conversation sequence numbers as needed. If the other side is not running Taylor, you must initialize its sequence number file with the same number that the other side has stored

---

[*] As of version 1.06.1, conversation sequence numbers do not work properly when Taylor UUCP is used with a BNU-style spool directory.

for that system. Taylor conversation sequence number files
are quite simple, consisting of the ASCII sequence number
on the first line.

command-path *directories*

Lists the directories (separated by spaces) that will be
searched when locating a command to execute on behalf of
a remote system. The default is compiled in from the *pol-
icy.h* header file.

commands *command_list*

Lists the commands (separated by spaces) that the remote
system is permitted to execute via **uux** requests. The default
is "**rnews rmail**." The keyword **ALL** allows all commands.

free-space *minbytes*

Rejects an incoming file if there are fewer than *minbytes*
bytes of free space after the file is received. This feature
works at the initial file request stage if both sides are using
Taylor UUCP, but during the file transfer **uucico** will check
periodically and abort the transfer if space is running low.
The default is compiled in from *policy.h*. Since checking
disk space is a system dependent feature, on some implementations this may not work properly.

pubdir *directory*

Sets the public directory to which the ˜ (tilde) shorthand
will be expanded. The default is compiled in from *policy.h*,
but is usually */var/spool/uucppublic*.

myname *sysname*

Sets the name the local system uses whenever speaking to
the remote system.

The call File

Taylor UUCP lets you place the login and password information for your
UUCP neighbors in a separate file. This lets you keep most of your UUCP
configuration files world-readable while hiding the logins and passwords in
a private file. To use the *call* file, your chat scripts must use the \L and \P
escapes to send the login and password.

This is the format of the *call* file:

```
system-name  login  password
```

Examples for using the *call* file are in Chapter 10, *Setting Up a UUCP Link*.

Running uuchk

The Taylor UUCP configuration checking command, **uuchk**, will read through your configuration files and print out a complete interpretation of every entry. It's particularly useful when using Taylor UUCP with BNU or Version 2 configurations, since it prints out the settings in a consistent format regardless from which configuration file they were read.

uuchk is much more flexible than its BNU counterpart: you can ask it to check the configuration for a single system with the −s option, rather than dump out your entire configuration. For example:

```
# uuchk -s fatcat
System: fatcat
 When called using any login name
 Call out using port TCP
 The possible ports are:
  Port name TCP
   Port type tcp
   TCP service uucp
   Characteristics: eight-bit-clean reliable end-to-end fullduplex
 Phone number 127.0.0.1
 Chat script ogin: \L word: \P
 Chat script timeout 10
 Chat script incoming bytes stripped to seven bits
 Login name Utabby
 Password scratchme
 At any time may call if any work
 May retry the call up to 26 times
 Sequence numbers are used
 May make local requests when calling
 May make local requests when called
 May send by local request: /
 May send by remote request: ~
 May accept by local request: ~
 May receive by remote request: ~
 May execute rmail pwd df
 Execution path /bin /usr/bin /usr/local/bin
 Will leave 50000 bytes available
 Public directory is /var/spool/uucppublic
 Will use any known protocol
```

It's easy to get lost in the deluge of different configuration options supplied in Taylor UUCP. To verify your changes, we recommend you always run **uuchk** after editing configuration files.[*]

Version 2 Security

Version 2 has the weakest security features of all the UUCP versions. Although basic control of file access and command execution are available, in most implementations you have no defense against UUCP spoofing by your local users or UUCP neighbors. To make matters worse, the primary configuration file for controlling file access, */usr/lib/uucp/USERFILE*, is easy to misconfigure. Since there is no Version 2 equivalent of the BNU **uucheck** to report on your permission settings, any errors you make are silently ignored, leaving your system more open than you intended.

CAUTION   If you need good security and access control on a system with
             Version 2, we strongly recommend you upgrade to Taylor UUCP
             instead of struggling with Version 2's limitations.

All Version 2 configuration files live in */usr/lib/uucp*. Here are the security related files:

USERFILE   Grants access to files and directories.

L.cmds   Lists commands that can be executed locally by remote sites.

SQFILE   Keeps conversation counts between machines.

Remote File Access: USERFILE

The text file */usr/lib/uucp/USERFILE* controls local access of files by both remote systems and local users. You should create one entry for each site or local user with a login entry in the */etc/passwd* file.

USERFILE entries specify these constraints on file transfer:

- Which files can be accessed by remote systems

- Whether a remote system must be called back by the local system to confirm its identity before communication can take place

---

[*] Since **uuchk** may reveal UUCP logins and passwords, make sure it is not executable by non-root users, and does not have any setuid permissions.

- Which files can be accessed by a local user—a local file is subject to both *USERFILE* and UNIX file permissions

You can choose to implement one or all of these constraints in the *USERFILE* entry for the remote system.

The entries are written in the following form:

   user,system [c] pathname(s)

An entry in *USERFILE* that uses all four fields might look like this:

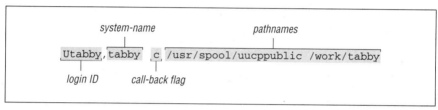

Figure 12–3: USERFILE

Field	Function in *USERFILE*
user	Specifies either the login name of a local user, or the login name that will be used by a remote system. A separate entry must exist in the *passwd* file for this UUCP login name. Each *USERFILE* should include at least one line with a blank *user* field. Even if the *user* is blank, you must have the comma in the entry.
system	Specifies the nodename (system name) of a remote system. Each *USERFILE* should include at least one line with a blank *system* field.
c	An optional *call-back* flag. If you put a "c" in this field, conversation between the two machines stops when the initial login by the remote system is made. **uucico** must call back the remote system in order to establish its identity before the next conversation can occur.
pathname	Consists of a list of absolute pathname prefixes separated by blanks. The remote system can access only those files beginning with these pathnames. A blank field indicates open access to any file in the local system.

Each Version 2 implements slightly different methods for parsing *USERFILE*.
As always, consult your system's documentation for the precise details. Here
are the key rules that apply to UUCP's parsing of *USERFILE*:

- When **uucp** and **uux** are run by users and when **uucico** runs in Master
  role, only the username part is used for checking access. The system
  name is ignored.

- When **uucico** runs in Slave role, only the system name part is used. The
  username is ignored.

- Within the course of one conversation, **uucico** can switch between Master and Slave roles an indefinite number of times. This dynamically
  affects the interpretation of *USERFILE*.

- In any given *USERFILE*, there must be one line that has an empty system
  name and one line that has an empty username. (In BSD 4.2 and up,
  they can be the same line. All other Version 2s require two separate
  lines.) It does not matter where they are in the file relative to lines that
  have a complete system name and username.

  The line that has no system name is used by **uucico** in Slave role, after it
  has already searched the entire *USERFILE* and cannot find a matching
  system name. The line that has no username is used by **uucp**, **uux**, and
  uucico in Master role only when it cannot find a matching username. In
  addition, the line without a system name is used by the **uuxqt** daemon.

If you have more than one line with the system name or username missing,
uucico will use the *first* occurrence of an empty system and/or username,
and silently ignore the rest.[*]

In all but a few outdated versions (SVR2 and Ultrix), the concept of login
validation is missing; there is no way to associate a system with a particular
login name. Your only hope for verifying a remote system's identity is to use
callback.

The following sections describe the types of entries you should have in your
USERFILE.

---

[*] Unless you're running the original 1979 Version 2 UUCP, which picked the last occurrence.

Username not specified

To allow users on your system to request outbound transfer of any file on your system, you must have an entry with the username not specified. For example:

```
,pyramid  /
```

If you don't have an entry with a blank username like this, you'll need to have a separate username line for each of the local users that need to use UUCP commands. The latter may be a better strategy in any case.

System name not specified

In order to allow file transfer from any other system while your system's **uucico** is in Slave role and to allow file access by **uuxqt** (even when started from your system), you must have one entry with the system name not specified. For example:

```
nuucp,      /usr/spool/uucppublic
```

Intuitively, you might expect that this line means any system logging in with the name *nuucp* should have access to */usr/spool/uucppublic*. Unfortunately, that intuitive view does not tell the true story. The fact that *nuucp* appears on this line is completely irrelevant to a system calling in. The userid field is ignored when the local **uucico** is in Slave role, which is how **uucico** starts up an incoming call.

Special permissions

To allow special directory permissions for individual systems, you should make sure systems calling in use a system-specific UUCP login and specify both that login name and the system's nodename (hostname) in *USERFILE*. For example:

```
Utabby,tabby /usr/spool/uucppublic /usr/spool/news /u2/csg
```

This entry allows systems who log in with any login ID but claim to be *tabby*, or any system that has logged in as *Utabby*, to access the directories */usr/spool/uucppublic*, */usr/spool/news*, and */u2/csg*.

As you may already have observed, giving out "public access" UUCP logins on a Version 2 system is a bad idea. Any special privileges you give to one system are available to anyone else who logs in and is willing to lie about their system name.

Requiring callback

Version 2 will use callback when a *c* is the first entry in the path list. This gives you a greater degree of certainty that you are talking to the right system. But remember that callback is not bulletproof, especially if you use the same modem for both outgoing and incoming calls.

Recommended configuration

Since Version 2 is so easily spoofed, it's a good idea to limit UUCP activity to the public directory. You can do this with a *USERFILE* that looks like this:

```
,        /usr/spool/uucppublic
# Next line not needed in BSD 4.2 or later
nuucp,   /usr/spool/uucppublic
```

In BSD 4.2 and up, the first line defines both the missing username and the missing system name case. In other implementations, however, two separate lines are required. In either case, file transfers are allowed only from the public directory.

If you or your users will be making use of **uucp** file requests, you may want to add a few entries to let users send files from their home directories (or any file on the system that they have read permission for). For example:

```
dave,    /home/dave
helen,   /
```

Remote Command Execution: L.cmds

The list of commands that may be executed by remote systems is stored in */usr/lib/uucp/L.cmds*. *L.cmds* should contain the program **rmail** if you want to receive mail via UUCP. On a BSD system, *L.cmds* should contain **uusend** if you want to use BSD's method of file forwarding.

A typical *L.cmds* file might contain the following list of commands:[*]

```
PATH=/bin: /usr/bin:
rmail
rnews
lp
```

BSD 4.2 and 4.3 systems include the **uusend** command in *L.cmds*, which allows file forwarding. This command is a security hole, since a remote

---

[*] Some implementations of Version 2 seem to ignore the PATH line as in the above example. If you do not seem able to set the path, run **strings** on the **/usr/lib/uucp/uuxqt** daemon to see if it sets an explicit path.

system could ask your system to send otherwise protected files like *L.sys*. (Since this file is owned by *uucp*, it would be available to **uusend** running set-user-id *uucp*.)

If the *L.cmds* file exists but is empty, remote commands cannot be executed on your system

Conversation Count Checks: SQFILE

As an added identity check for the remote system, you can create the file *SQFILE* in the directory */usr/lib/uucp*. This is an optional file that UUCP uses to keep a record of the conversation count and date/time of the last conversation for particular systems. *SQFILE* must have mode 400 and must be owned by the *uucp* user, and the */usr/lib/uucp* directory must be owned by and writable by *uucp* so that **uucico** can update *SQFILE* during each call.

SQFILE contains an entry for each system with which you agree to perform conversation count checks. The remote system must also have an entry for your system in its *SQFILE*, so you should ask the remote system administrator to create an entry for your system there.

Let's say you want to keep a count of your conversation with all of the remote systems to which you are linked. The initial entries in *SQFILE* should contain only the remote system name, one on each line. For example:

```
$ cat SQFILE
tomcat
tabby
$
```

The first conversation between the two systems adds the count and date/time to the entry. The UUCP program **uucico** updates the fields for each subsequent conversation that succeeds. For example, an entry in the *SQFILE* might look like this:

```
tomcat 9 10/11-10:54
```

There have been nine conversations so far between the local system and *tomcat*. The last conversation took place on October 11 at 10:54 a.m.

When one system calls another, it supplies its sequence number as part of the UUCP connection setup. If the receiving system has a different sequence number than the caller, it hangs up. This helps protect against UUCP spoofing, but it is by no means fool proof. The sequence number can be discovered by an intruder through the same means that they use to obtain a login

ID and password, and if you detect the spoofing at all, it will only be after the fact when the real system calls with an old sequence number.

When the sequence numbers get out of step, the system administrators on both sides have to get in touch and reset the *SQFILE* manually.

You will need to weigh whether the limited protection provided by conversation sequence numbers is worth the exposure of using less secure permissions on the */usr/lib/uucp* directory.

Forwarding

In BSD 4.2 and 4.3 systems, there is a special command called **uusend** that users can use instead of **uucp** if they want to forward files to a system that does not have a direct link to their own. **uusend** makes use of **uux** rather than **uucp** to do forwarding and requires that **uusend** exist, and be allowed in *L.cmds*, on each system in the forwarding chain. Since **uusend** can be a security exposure, we don't recommend using it.

System V-derived implementations of Version 2 UUCP support forwarding, but in a manner incompatible with all other types of UUCP. On these systems, UUCP neighbors that may forward files through your system are listed in a file named *ORIGFILE*, and their permissible forwarding destinations are listed in *FWDFILE* (all destinations are allowed if *FWDFILE* does not exist).

BSD/OS UUCP Security

Although BSD/OS UUCP appears at first to be Version 2-compatible, it has many extra features that can be accessed from the master configuration file */etc/uucp/CONFIG*. These features give you most of the BNU and Taylor security controls described previously in this chapter, although in slightly different forms. You should turn on UUCP login ID validation (the **LOGIN_MUST_MATCH** parameter), restrict anonymous UUCP logins (the **ANON_USERS** and **NOSTRANGERS** parameters), and use the **VERIFY_TCP_ADDRESS** parameter if applicable.

To see the complete list of parameters available, run this command:

```
$ man 5 uuparams
```

You can also use the **uuparams** command to list out configuration parameters and check for inconsistencies.

UUCP Security Checklist

Here is a summary of things to check for when evaluating the security of your UUCP installation.

UNIX Environment Security

This checklist applies to your overall UNIX environment:

- All UUCP configuration directories should be owned by *root*, and not writable by anyone else.* All UUCP configuration files should be owned by *root* or *uucp*, and not writable by anyone else. To keep the logins and passwords of your UUCP neighbors private, the systems database files (*Systems*, *L.sys* or *sys*) should be owned by UUCP and have permissions set to mode 0400.

- All UUCP crontab scripts should be owned by *root* (and readable to the world, or perhaps just the *uucp* group if your system supports it) and writable to no one.

- The UUCP spool directory and its subdirectories should be owned by UUCP and have extremely limited, if not completely limited, write and delete ability by other users. Debug output files or Taylor UUCP conversation sequence number files must be owned by UUCP, and unreadable by other users.

- Make sure the *uucp* administrative login has a password, or lock the account and do all UUCP administration as *root*.

- If you have many UUCP users, especially in a networked environment, consider switching to Taylor UUCP—with its application-specific password file—so that you do not need to create hordes of UUCP login users and their attendant risks.

- When you create UUCP login users, make sure all UUCP users have separate usernames with unique numeric UIDs—none of which correspond to the *uucp* user—and a common, nonwritable home directory. You may want to pre-install unreadable *.rhosts*, *.forward*, *.profile*, etc. files (or directories) owned by *root* to obstruct anyone else's attempts to create these files. If you create these files (or directories), set their permission to mode 0 (no access at all).

---

* Unless you want to use conversation sequence numbers in BNU or Version 2, in which case, the UUCP configuration directory must be owned by and writable by *uucp*.

- If you have UUCP login IDs and a TCP/IP networked environment, you must evaluate every network service on your machine to see how it behaves when someone tries to use it with a UUCP login and password. In particular, **ftpd**, **xdm**, and **dtlogin** must be secured against use by UUCP logins.

- If your system is connected to the Internet (even if only intermittently, via dialup SLIP or PPP), install TCP Wrappers or a similar package that restricts the sites on the Internet that can access your system's network services. If you accept incoming UUCP calls over TCP/IP, use the wrappers to restrict the hosts allowed to reach the UUCP login prompt.

- If you use **sendmail**, make sure that email to the *uucp* user is forwarded in */etc/aliases*, that the **sendmail** version is 8.7.1 or later, and that the **sendmail** security wrapper **smrsh** is in use. If you use any other mailer that reads files from a user's home directory, make sure UUCP users cannot create any files that could control email delivery.

UUCP Application Security

This checklist applies to the UUCP configuration files:

- Limit read and write access to your local filesystem as much as possible. If possible, deny file requests completely, or limit them to the public directory.

- Restrict commands available to remote systems as much as possible. In most cases, the only two commands needed are **rmail** and **rnews**.

- Use login name validation (VALIDATE= in BNU, called-login in Taylor) to prevent spoofing of your UUCP links.

- If you have many UUCP neighbors doing file transfers, consider giving them (or groups of them) separate public directories to reduce potential conflicts.

- If you support anonymous UUCP on your system, try to separate them from your regular UUCP links as much as possible: use a different public directory, a different writable file area (if they must have write access), and as few commands allowed as possible.

- With BNU and Taylor, run **uucheck** (or **uuchk**) to test your configuration files after making changes.

- On a BNU or Version 2 system, discourage use of **cu** unless your vendor has provided a fix for the `>:`*filename* problem.

- If you are using Version 2 UUCP, and are uncomfortable with any of the security limitations described here, upgrade to Taylor UUCP.

13

UUCP Administration

In order for UUCP to run smoothly, the following things must happen on a regular basis:

- **uucico** must be invoked regularly to retry failed calls.

- Any passive systems in your network must be polled regularly to see if they have traffic waiting for you.

- Jobs that have been queued unsuccessfully for a long time must be deleted, so that **uucico** does not keep trying forever.

- Execution requests that have been pending for a long time must also be deleted so that **uuxqt** does not keep trying forever.

- Files left in the UUCP public directory need to be deleted after they are no longer needed.

- The log files created by **uucico** cannot be allowed to grow larger forever. They must be compressed or truncated according to some reasonable scheme.

On most systems, these tasks are performed automatically by shell scripts that are invoked by **cron**, the system administrator's reliable assistant.

Most of these administration tasks revolve around the work files that UUCP keeps in its spool directory. To get a better understanding of what UUCP's maintenance needs are, we'll pay a quick visit to the spool directory.

Contents of the Spool Directory

The contents of the spool directory are constantly changing. In addition to log files, which are added to each time a transfer occurs, there are a large number of working files that are dynamically created (and just as dynamically deleted) in the course of communication between systems.

For the nitty-gritty details of spool directory files, see Appendix B, *The Spool Directory/Working Files*. The discussion in this chapter will concentrate on the purpose of spool directory files, and why the administrator must be concerned about them.

How a Job is Stored

As we discussed in Chapter 8, *How UUCP Works*, when a user issues a **uucp** or **uux** command, various files are created in the spool directory that are later read back by **uucico** as commands to perform the user's requests. There are three kinds of these "command" files: *command files,*[*] *data files*, and *execute files*.

Older Version 2 UUCP systems kept all of these files in the top level of the spool directory. On these systems, a large number of pending UUCP requests would slow UUCP down considerably, because of the inefficiencies associated with scanning a directory that has many, many files in it. All modern UUCP versions keep work files in subdirectories named after each system, greatly lessening the directory scanning problem.

Command files

The command file contains the instructions for **uucico**, such as the name of the file to be copied, its owner and permissions, its destination, and so on. Command files have names like "C.tabbyA1001," which are formed by the prefix "C.," the system name, a grade character, and a job sequence number. The job sequence number is incremented for every new job. BNU and Taylor UUCP maintain separate job sequence numbers for each UUCP neighbor.

Data files

Many UUCP jobs require temporary data files. One case is when local users use **uucp** with the **−C** option, which tells **uucp** to copy all data files to the spool directory before transferring them to the remote system. Another case

---

* BSD UUCP documentation uses the term "control files."

is any **uux** request—all mail and news transfers done by **uux** will have associated data files to feed into programs such as **rmail** or **rnews** on the remote system. For example, when a user sends email via UUCP, two data files are created: one with the text of the email message, the other containing the instructions for the execution of **rmail** on the remote system.

Data files are prefixed with "D." and have names similar to work files.

Execute files

When a remote system calls in with a request for command execution, an *execute* file with the prefix "X." is created. This file contains instructions for **uuxqt**. It is named similarly to work and data files, however, inasmuch as it is created by the **uucico** from the other system, its job number will not match up with any work file on your system. When someone on your system makes an execute request, a data file (D.*xxxx*) is created. It contains the text of what will become the execute file on the remote system.

Temporary Storage

As UUCP goes about its business, it often creates temporary files that are needed to support specific operations, such as receiving a file transfer or performing a command execution. Files used to hold data while a file is being received from another system have names beginning with "TM." When the transfer is finished, **uucico** moves the file to its final destination (which may be another work file if the file is part of a remote **uux** request). The **uuxqt** daemon keeps a directory to provide a temporary working area for the commands it executes on behalf of remote users. Data files that will be fed to the program under execution are placed here, and the directory is wiped clean after execution is finished.

Lockfiles

Since multiple copies of **uucico** can run at the same time, a way to keep each other from trying to use the same resources simultaneously is needed. This is accomplished through the use of *lockfiles*. Lockfiles begin with the "LCK." prefix, and are suffixed with the name of the resource that is in use, such as the name of a remote system or of a local serial port.

Older UUCP implementations keep lockfiles in the spool directory; newer ones keep them in a system-wide lockfile directory, such as */etc/locks* or */var/spool/locks*. This lets other programs share use of the serial ports used by UUCP, as long as they all use the same locking scheme.

Sometimes a lockfile persists even after a program has finished with the resource. A smart UUCP system will detect such a "stale" lockfile and remove it when the resource is next needed. Some not-so-smart systems will stop in their tracks until the system administrator comes around and manually removes the lockfile. You can tell if a lockfile is stale by examining the contents: a lockfile contains the process ID (PID) of the process that created it. If that process is no longer running, you can safely remove the lockfile.

Status Files

As discussed previously, status files contain the last known disposition of a remote site. They are read by the **uustat** command when a user wants to learn the status of a remote system, and **uucico** will check them before placing any calls. UUCP administrators usually have their first encounter with a status file when one needs to be removed to let **uucico** place a call. Status files are kept in the *.Status* subdirectory in a BNU or Taylor system, or prefixed with "STST." on a Version 2 system.

Corrupt Storage

No, UUCP is not in the bribe-taking business, but if an execution request cannot be processed for some reason, some versions of UUCP will save the job's files in the *.Corrupt* subdirectory (*CORRUPT* in BSD) in case you want to look through them afterwards. This can be an albatross around the spool directory's neck if many jobs suddenly start to fail (such as on a broken newsfeed); however, it can be a blessing if the failed jobs contain important data that is otherwise unrecoverable (such as incoming email).

Log, Error, and Statistics Files

Notice of every major UUCP operation is written to a logfile in the spool directory. These files are invaluable when setting up a new link or solving communications problems, but they are less interesting on a working link. Taylor and Version 2 UUCP keep one logfile for all UUCP activity, while BNU fragments logfiles into multiple directories, sorted by type of activity (*uucico, uucp, uux,* and *uuxqt*) and separated by system name.

In BNU and Version 2, major errors that occur during UUCP operation (such as missing spool files or inaccessible directories) are written to a separate error file (*/usr/spool/uucp/.Admin/errors* in BNU, */usr/spool/uucp/ERRLOG* in Version 2). This file should be checked from time to time, since any messages within usually mean a serious UUCP problem has occurred.

All versions of UUCP keep statistics on file transfers and the overall through-put of UUCP's communications links. The statistics file is a useful indicator of the overall health of your UUCP network, and should be checked every now and then to make sure that UUCP's transfer rates are in line with the speed of your UUCP links.

Spool Maintenance

If a UUCP request goes through cleanly, all temporary files are created and removed in due process. Logfiles will keep on growing until pruned, how-ever, and occasional job failures will create corrupt or orphaned workfiles that hog disk space. To prevent normal activity from overflowing, most sys-tems run scripts via the UNIX **cron** facility to trim logfiles and discard old workfiles.

A more pressing problem occurs when a neighboring system that normally receives a large volume of traffic suddenly shuts down. The job requests and data files on your side will start to fill up your spool directory. Many system administrators try to keep a few megabytes of extra space in the spool direc-tory filesystem to provide a buffer in case of such an outage.

But if the crisis hits and the spool directory overflows, all UUCP activity will grind to a halt.* When this happens, you may need to move some spool requests off to another filesystem (or delete some of them, especially for a Usenet feed) in order to create space for the rest of UUCP's traffic to get processed.

Automatic Maintenance

Most of the work for keeping a UUCP site running smoothly can be done by running maintenance scripts and programs at regular intervals. These scripts and programs are called via the **cron** daemon, UNIX's batch facility, which allows you to run commands according to a specific time schedule, with the privileges of any desired user. The commands for **cron** are stored in a *crontab* file. On most modern UNIX systems there is a separate *crontab* file for each user, stored in */var/spool/cron/crontabs/***user**.

Each *crontab* entry consists of six fields separated by spaces or tabs. The first five fields specify the minute (*0-59*), the hour (*0-23*), the day of the month (*1-31*), the month of the year (*1-12*), and the day of the week (*0-6*,

---

* And since the spool directory is usually in the */var* filesystem, electronic mail, print jobs, and other services will also be affected.

with Sunday=0). A star (*) indicates all permissible values for that field. The last field contains the shell command line to be executed at that time. For example:

```
56 * * * * /usr/lib/uucp/uudemon.hr
```

This line means that the script **uudemon.hr** will be executed on the 56th minute of every hour, day in and day out. And, this entry

```
0 4 * * * /usr/lib/uucp/uudemon.day
```

means **uudemon.day** will be executed daily at 4 a.m.; this line:

```
30 5 * * 0 /usr/lib/uucp/uudemon.wk
```

means **uudemon.wk** will be executed at 5:30 a.m. every Sunday.

BNU Maintenance Scripts

BNU UUCP comes with several maintenance commands, along with several scripts designed to be run via **cron**. BNU systems usually pre-install a sample **cron** table for the *uucp* user in the file */var/spool/cron/crontabs/uucp,*[*] with all the commands commented out. The first task in setting up automatic maintenance in BNU UUCP is to uncomment those entries. For example:

```
20 * * * * /bin/sh -c "/usr/lib/uucp/uudemon.poll > /dev/null"
25 * * * * /bin/sh -c "/usr/lib/uucp/uudemon.hour > /dev/null"
48 16 * * * /bin/sh -c "/usr/lib/uucp/uudemon.admin > /dev/null"
45 23 * * * /bin/sh -c "/usr/lib/uucp/uudemon.cleanup > /dev/null"
```

Our entries reflect a less aggressive maintenance strategy than the entries supplied with BNU, which call the **uudemon.hour** and **uudemon.poll** scripts twice an hour, and the **uudemon.admin** script three times a day. You should adjust the frequency of these scripts as needed by your site.

uudemon.poll

The **uudemon.poll** script reads in a table of passive systems that should be polled on a regular basis. The table is stored in the file */usr/lib/uucp/Poll* or

---

[*] Two exceptions are SunOS 4.0 and Solaris, which provide a sample **cron** table in */usr/lib/uucp/uudemon.crontab.*

/etc/uucp/Poll. Each line contains the system name and a list of hours during which the system should get called. For example:

```
# Syntax: "system <TAB> hour1 hour2 hour3 ..."
#
tomcat      7  12  18  23
faraway     3
#
```

On some systems, the syntax of this file is rather fragile: there must be a tab character after the system name, and the hours for polling must not have any leading zeroes. Whenever **uudemon.poll** is run, it checks to see if the current hour matches any of the hours listed in */usr/lib/uucp/Poll*. If it does, a dummy workfile is created in the spool directory for the system in question, and the next time **uudemon.hour** is run, a call is made to that system.

uudemon.hour

The **uudemon.hour** script is BNU UUCP's behind-the-scenes taskmaster. It runs **uusched**, the BNU scheduling program. The **uusched** command sees to it that **uucico** is invoked to call up any system that has jobs waiting for it. To balance out the workload, **uusched** randomizes the order in which the systems are called.

uudemon.hour also calls **uuxqt** to handle any unprocessed execution requests from remote systems that were not handled when they arrived.

uudemon.admin

The **uudemon.admin** script does a few perfunctory status checks and emails the results to the *uucp* administrator. It then scans the BNU logfiles to see if anyone is trying to manipulate the */etc/passwd* file, and fires off more email to the *uucp* administrator if it detects anything. This script has several bugs that, if triggered, cause it to send even more email, none of it particularly interesting.

We recommend you edit this script to cut down its email output and tailor it more towards your needs.

uudemon.cleanup

We've already met the taskmaster, now meet the janitor. The **uudemon.cleanup**[*] script is the man with the broom, walking behind the UUCP elephant and cleaning up the mess. You can run this script daily if

---

[*] Some UUCP implementations call this file **uudemon.cleanu**, in loving memory of the old UNIX filesystem's 14 character limit on filenames.

you have a high-traffic site, weekly—or even monthly—otherwise. **uude-mon.cleanup** takes care of the following chores:

- It moves all log files to a *.Old* subdirectory of the spool directory. The error log, statistics file, and other administrative logs are also moved there. Previously archived logfiles are renamed a few times before being permanently removed. This leaves you with several generations to scan through if you want to research a problem. The separate logfiles (named after your UUCP neighbors) are concatenated into one logfile before archiving.

- It runs the **uucleanup** command, which goes through the spool directory looking for workfiles that have not been processed. If a job has been stuck in the queue for more than a day (configurable on the **uucleanup** command line), **uucleanup** sends a warning message to the requester. After a few more days, **uucleanup** deletes the job, and sends a notice to the requester explaining what happened. **uucleanup** also looks for stray files and orphaned workfiles that have been hanging around for too long, and deletes them.

- It removes any old directories, core files, status files, and other unwanted UUCP detritus from the spool directory.

- It removes inactive files (older than one month) and empty directories from the public directory tree.

- It sends email to the UUCP administrator about any problems that happened during cleanup. **uudemon.cleanup** also sends mail about everything else under the sun, such as any messages found in the error log, a list of all UUCP requests since the last time **uudemon.cleanup** was run, a list of all UUCP requests denied, another copy of the UUCP queue status in case you didn't get the one that **uudemon.admin** sent you, a list of any unknown systems that were turned away, and finally, another email message announcing that the script has ended, with a summary of the spool directory disk consumption for good measure.

The chief drawback of this faithful janitor is that it insists on sending every piece of information in a separate email message, rather than producing a single report. You should modify the script to reduce its email output.

Taylor Maintenance

Taylor UUCP does not come with a fully-formed maintenance scheme like BNU. But among the Taylor UUCP source distribution, you will find a *contrib* subdirectory containing various tools you can use to build your automated maintenance scripts. For example:

- A **uuclean** script that uses Taylor-specific options in **uustat** to delete old jobs and send email to the users who originated them.

- A script to save and rotate logfiles (**savelog.sh**).

- Several polling scripts and programs that provide polling of passive systems and restarting of **uucico** for systems that have pending jobs waiting in the local spool directory.

- A few analysis programs that print UUCP traffic statistics.

Since these scripts and files are unsupported, they may or may not work without modification on your system. In general, you need to "roll your own" UUCP maintenance on a Taylor system.

Fortunately, the Taylor UUCP utilities come with a few extra options that do some of the work for you. You should also browse through the BNU and Version 2 UUCP sections in this chapter, since the overall maintenance strategy is the same for all versions of UUCP.

Restarting failed jobs

If Taylor **uucico** is invoked without any system specified, it will attempt to call all remote systems that have jobs waiting for them. A simple **cron** entry like this:

```
15 * * * * /usr/lib/uucp/uucico -r1
```

will cause **uucico** to wake up once an hour and try to call any systems that have local requests waiting for them.

Polling passive systems

You can poll a passive system by explicitly naming the remote system in a **crontab** entry like this:

```
25 * * * * /usr/lib/uucp/uucico -r1 -s system
```

Although this does not necessarily call the named system once an hour (if, for example, there is no modem available when **uucico** is invoked), it will do for most circumstances. To guarantee that the remote system will be called the next time **uucico** has an opportunity, you need to create a dummy control file in the spool directory.

Cleaning directories

An unsupported shell script version of **uuclean** is supplied with Taylor UUCP. It may need some modification to work properly on your system, but it will do a respectable job of sweeping out your spool directory. Here's an excerpt from a slightly modified version:

```
#!/bin/sh

bindir=/usr/bin

# Warn about all mail over two days old
${bindir}/uustat -c rmail -o 48 -N -Q \
    -W"Unable to deliver; will try up to one week"

# Return all mail over a week old
${bindir}/uustat -c rmail -o 168 -K -M -N -Q \
    -W"Could not be delivered for over one week"

# Throw away other requests over a week old
${bindir}/uustat -o 168 -K -M -N -Q -W"Over one week old"

# Warn about any executions, other than mail, over three days old
${bindir}/uustat -c rmail -o 72 -M -N -Q -W"Unable to execute for three days"
```

As you can see, most of the work is done by calling **uustat** with the right options. The −o *nn* option specifies how many hours must have gone by before a stale request is acted upon.

The **uuclean** script also deletes files that have been languishing in the spool directory longer than desired. Here is another excerpt:

```
spooldir=/usr/spool/uucp

# Now delete any old spool files
find ${spooldir} -type f -ctime +8 \
    -name '[CDX].*' -print -exec rm -f {} ";"

# Delete any old temporary files
find ${spooldir} -type f -atime +1 -ctime +1 \
    -name 'TM.*' -print -exec rm -f {} ";"

# Delete any old preserved files
find ${spooldir}/.Preserve -type f -atime +14 -ctime +14 \
    -print -exec rm -f {} ";"

# Delete any old failed execution files
```

```
find ${spooldir}/.Failed -type f -atime +14 -ctime +14 \
    -print -exec rm -f {} ";"
```

The final task is to purge the stale files and directories in the public directory tree like this:

```
pubdir=/usr/spool/uucppublic
find ${pubdir} -xdev -type f -atime +14 -ctime +14 -print -exec rm -f {} ";"
find ${pubdir} -xdev -type d -mtime +14 -exec rmdir {} ";" 2>/dev/null
```

Rotating log files

The **savelog.sh**[*] command supplied with Taylor UUCP supports migrating logfiles (from any source, including UUCP) to an archive directory, compressing them to save space, and removing them altogether when they get old enough. You can set this script up to suit your needs, or write your own based on the Version 2 script samples below.

Traffic statistics

The **uutraf**[†] Perl script supplied with Taylor UUCP provides a handy summary of your UUCP traffic. It reads in the statistics file and spits out a complete array of usage statistics. For example:

```
$ uutraf -taylor /usr/spool/uucp/Stats
  UUCP traffic on node tabby from 9/2-00:16:24 to 10/6-02:43:22
```

Remote	-----------	-K-Bytes-	----------	----Hours----		--Avg CPS--		--Files--	
Host	Recv	Sent	Total	Recv	Sent	Recv	Sent	Recv	Sent
fatcat	2910.4	1411.0	4321.4	0.6	0.3	1340	1332	77	70
uunet	277.8	146.2	424.0	0.0	0.0	33879	15040	19	39
princecat	145.4	277.7	423.1	0.0	0.0	18495	51426	27	14
panix	758.1	431.2	1189.3	0.1	0.1	2359	1665	54	17
Total	4091.7	2266.1	6357.8	0.7	0.4	1640	1717	177	140

You need to have the Perl interpreter on your system in order to run **uutraf**. If you are using Linux, it should be a part of your distribution. The Perl package can be obtained from FTP archives on the Internet (see Appendix L, *Other Resources*), or even in your local bookstore in *UNIX Power Tools*, also published by O'Reilly & Associates.

---

[*] **savelog.sh** is copyright 1987, 1988 by Ronald S. Karr and Landon Curt Noll.

[†] **uutraf** was written by Johan Vromans.

Version 2 Maintenance

If you're using Version 2 UUCP, your system is likely to have a version of **cron** that has only one master *crontab* file, with a user name in the sixth field of each entry. We will use this format for *crontab* examples in this section, instead of the more popular System V-style **cron** used in the rest of this chapter.[*]

A typical Version 2 system should have entries like this in its *crontab* (stored either in */etc* or */usr/lib*, depending upon the vintage of the system):

```
56 * * * *    uucp   /usr/lib/uucp/uudemon.hr
10 4 * * *    uucp   /usr/lib/uucp/uudemon.day
30 5 * * 0    uucp   /usr/lib/uucp/uudemon.wk
```

If these lines are commented out with hash marks (#) at the beginning of each line, remove the hash marks to enable automatic UUCP maintenance.

uudemon.hr

uudemon.hr attempts completion of UUCP jobs waiting on the local system. **uudemon.hr** usually contains at least the following commands:

```
cd /usr/lib/uucp
uucico -r1
```

It is normally executed by **cron** once an hour.

uudemon.day

uudemon.day cleans the spool directories and merges daily logfiles with the weekly logfiles. It is normally run at a fixed time, such as 4 a.m. each day.

Here is a sample **uudemon.day** script:

```
cd /usr/lib/uucp
uuclean -p -m -n168 >/dev/null 2>&1
uuclean -d.XQTDIR -p -n72 >/dev/null 2>&1
cd /usr/spool/uucp
mv LOGFILE temp
uniq -c temp >> Log-WEEK
rm temp
find /usr/spool/uucppublic -type f -mtime +30 -exec rm -f {} \;
```

---

[*] Older versions of BSD (and other UNIX platforms) use a *crontab* format that does not support the "user" field—all commands run as *root*. On those systems, use "su uucp -c *command*" to run UUCP maintenance jobs.

Here's what some of these commands mean:

- **uuclean** is called to delete old UUCP job requests. **uuclean** has four options:

  −n[*hours*] Specifies how old files can be (in hours) before they can be deleted.

  −p[*prefix*] Specifies the prefix (C., D., X., TM., STST., etc.) for the files to be deleted. If the *prefix* is not given, all types of working files will be deleted.

  −m   Sends email to the owner of the file when it is deleted.

  −d*dir*   Specifies a subdirectory (e.g., *.XQTDIR*) of the spool directory that is to be scanned instead of the spool directory itself.

  The first **uuclean** command kills all UUCP jobs that have been waiting on the local system for at least 168 hours (the −*n168* option), or seven days. The second **uuclean** kills **uuxqt** execution requests that have been trying to execute for at least 72 hours (the −*n72* option), or three days.

- The **mv** command moves the contents of today's log records (the file *LOGFILE*) to the end of the weekly log (*Log-WEEK*).

- The **uniq −c** command attempts to make the logfile more readable by combining any duplicate logfile messages into a single line.

- The **find** command removes all ordinary files from the public directory that are more than 30 days old.

If you find that your spool directory is overflowing, you may need to remove old files and directories from */usr/spool/uucppublic* and */usr/spool/uucp*. You can do this manually using the **rm** command, or you can shorten the time period parameters for the **uuclean** and **find** commands in the *uudemon.day* file. For example, if these commands are currently set as follows:

```
uuclean -p -m -n168 >/dev/null 2>/dev/null
find /usr/spool/uucp -type f -mtime +30 -exec rm -f {} \;
```

you can reset them so that jobs that have been waiting for at least 48 hours (instead of 168), and files in the public directory that have been there for at

least 15 days (instead of 30) would be deleted. The modified commands
would look like this:

```
uuclean -p -m -n48 >/dev/null 2>/dev/null
find /usr/spool/uucp -type f -mtime +15 -exec rm -f {} \;
```

You might also want to trim the logfiles.

uudemon.wk

uudemon.wk maintains the weekly logfiles and gets rid of those more than
two weeks old. It is usually executed at a fixed time, such as 5:30 a.m. every
Sunday, and may contain something like the following commands:

```
cd /usr/spool/uucp
rm -f o.Log-WEEK* o.SYSLOG*
mv Log-WEEK o.Log-WEEK
(date; echo ==================) >> o.Log-WEEK
mv SYSLOG o.SYSLOG
>> SYSLOG
pack o.Log-WEEK o.SYSLOG
```

Logfiles have backup files called *Log-WEEK* and *o.Log-WEEK*. *Log-WEEK*
contains log entries for the week to date, while *o.Log-WEEK* contains entries
for the previous week. *SYSLOG* is used by the UUCP programs to record the
amount of data sent and received by each system within a week. *o.SYSLOG*
is a backup file that holds the previous week's *SYSLOG* file.

Polling and Dummy Workfiles

The simple way to set up polling (see the discussion above on Taylor
UUCP) is to create a **cron** entry for each system you need to contact. But on
a system with a limited number of modems, this does not guarantee that a
call will actually be placed; if all devices are busy when the **cron** entry is
run, the system will not get polled. This is acceptable under some circumstances, but for expensive long-distance links that must be used during off-
peak hours, it is not enough.

The time-honored way to queue a poll to a remote system is to create a
dummy workfile. This is a null file in the spool directory that looks like a
UUCP job waiting for a particular system. It will trick **uucico** into thinking
there is work for the remote system, and it will place a call. When connected, **uucico** opens the dummy workfile and discovers the ruse, but
before finishing up it will ask the remote system to send any work that it
has waiting for the local system.

The dummy workfiles can be created either by a separate script that is scheduled to run a few minutes before **uudemon.hr**, or as part of **uudemon.hr** itself.

For example, adding the following lines would cause the local system to poll the passive systems named *fatcat*, *ruby*, and *jade*:

```
for i in fatcat ruby jade
do
        touch /usr/spool/uucp/C.${i}nPOLL
done
```

Be sure to check the format of workfile names on your system and match it exactly. While most systems have workfile names consisting of C.*node* followed by a single letter for the grade, and a four-character sequence number—this is not universal.

This scheme also works for Taylor and BNU UUCP. The BNU UUCP **uudemon.poll** script uses this method to force polls to passive systems. In Taylor UUCP 1.06.1, you can use this command to generate a dummy workfile:

```
$ uux -r system!
```

See Appendix B, *The Spool Directory/Working Files*, for more information on workfile naming conventions.

Keeping Track of UUCP Activity

Although UUCP is designed to run without needing human intervention, occasionally the administrator must step in to fix a problem. It's also a good idea to keep track of the performance, and disk usage of UUCP on your system to make sure it doesn't start consuming more than its share of system resources.

Reading uucp's Mail

Several daemons and programs will send email to the *uucp* user on a regular basis. For example:

- The **cron** daemon will send via email any error messages from the automatic maintenance scripts. On most systems, with a separate **cron** table for each user, this email will go directly to the *uucp* user. On systems with only a single *crontab* file (i.e., BSD), this email goes to *root*.

- The maintenance scripts themselves may send email, either when they detect problems or just to send the administrator the current status.

- Some of the commands called by the maintenance scripts, especially **uuclean**, send email to *uucp* to note canceled jobs or deleted files.

Most of the email is pretty uninteresting. But you can't ignore all of it: some of those messages, especially errors from **cron**, may indicate serious problems. If you don't like the email generated by your system's UUCP scripts, edit them to squelch those reports that you don't want to see.

On systems that use the **sendmail** mailer, you should redirect email to the *uucp* user via the */etc/aliases* file (*/usr/lib/aliases* on some older systems, */etc/mail/aliases* on Solaris). Don't forget to run the **newaliases** command (or **sendmail −bi**) after changing the alias table, so that **sendmail** will recognize your changes. For other mail delivery agents, consult your mailer's documentation for how to set up aliases.

Looking for Trouble

Sometimes your neighbor's troubles can become your own, especially when it's your UUCP neighbor who gets the blues. If large volumes of work continue to be queued up on your system for a neighboring machine that no longer answers the phone, your local disk may soon run out of space. If the downed UUCP feed is also your mail or news feed, you will no doubt want to solve the problem as soon as possible.

At minimum, you should make sure you see the output of a **uustat −q** command at least once a day. This is one of the many things about which BNU maintenance scripts send email, but if you're managing another variety of UUCP, it may be worth your while to add this command yourself.

If you want better real-time notification of UUCP problems, you could try a shell script like this:

```
#!/bin/sh

STATPREFIX=/var/spool/uucp/.Status/  # BNU status files
#STATPREFIX=/usr/spool/uucp/STST.    # Version 2 status files
ERRLIMIT=5

MYNAME=uuwatch.${LOGNAME:-}
WATCHDIR=/tmp

for system in 'uuname'
do
    STATFILE=$STATPREFIX/$system
    if [ -f $STATFILE ]
    then
        set 'cat $STATFILE'
```

```
            if [ ${2:?"bad status file"} -gt $ERRLIMIT ]
            then
                if [ ! -f $WATCHDIR/$MYNAME.$system ]
                then
                    touch $WATCHDIR/$MYNAME.$system
                    echo "UUCP trouble: $system: $*"
                fi
            else
                rm -f $WATCHDIR/$MYNAME.$system
            fi
        fi
    done
```

The above script tests for the presence of a status file for all UUCP neighbors, and complains if the number of retries has exceeded ERRLIMIT (five, in this example). It tries to keep track of whether it has printed a warning on a previous run by creating a file in the */tmp* directory. If run out of a user's **cron** entry, the user will receive email whenever a UUCP neighbor becomes hard to reach. (Unless explicitly redirected, the standard output and standard error of a **cron** command gets emailed to the user who invoked it.)

A script like this needs no particular privilege level to run: UUCP status files are readable to all. And since all versions of UUCP use the same status file format, you can use this script—or something like it—on any system.

Disk Space and Spool Congestion

If the amount of UUCP traffic through your system is relatively small, you needn't be concerned about disk usage. As long as your maintenance scripts are set up properly, UUCP will keep its usage within reasonable limits. But if you have a lot of traffic, or a lot of UUCP neighbors, a UUCP backlog might overflow the spool directory.

To see how much disk space is used by UUCP, use the **df** and **du** commands. **df** lists the amount of free disk blocks left on your disk(s); **du** shows where the space is being used. Obviously, you need to have a sense of both the amount of disk space on your system and the normal amount of traffic in order for these numbers to make sense. Writing a script to test for space usage in a filesystem is fairly straightforward. For example:*

```
UUCPSPOOL=/usr/spool/uucp
TOOHIGH=1400
if [ 'du -s $UUCPSPOOL' -gt $TOOHIGH ]
then
     echo "UUCP spool over $TOOHIGH blocks... Help!"
fi
```

If UUCP is critical to the operation of your system, you should move the spool directory to a separate filesystem. This will isolate it from other applications that use spooling, such as print queues and mail.

Tuning UUCP Performance

As wonderful and marvelous as UUCP is, most people have other tasks for their computer to work on. But on some occasions, UUCP traffic loads can rise to such a level that the system has trouble getting other work processed.

UUCP congestion is nearly as old as UUCP itself. In the early Version 2 implementations, all working files for all UUCP neighbors were kept in the spool directory. This worked fine for a while, but with many sites to call and many jobs to transfer, UUCP began to slow down as it spent more and more time reading in UNIX directories and less time actually moving data.

Another design limitation of Version 2 was that it would call **uuxqt** only after a call was over. So if a UUCP conversation transferred 100 execution requests, all the requests would have to wait until the conversation was over, causing a sudden burst of CPU activity when **uuxqt** was summoned to clear out its queue.

Both of these problems are more or less fixed in modern UUCP versions. Spool directories are subdivided to avoid UNIX's weaknesses with large directories. And **uucico** can summon **uuxqt** whenever a job is received, so execution requests no longer build up to a fever pitch at the end of a call.

---

* This shell script fragment uses the **du -s** command, which prints the total disk usage of a directory tree. On most systems, especially POSIX conformant ones, this number is in 512-byte blocks.

Too Many Processes

With the ability to fork off multiple **uuxqt** requests came a new problem: too many **uuxqt** daemons running at once can eat all the CPU, or swamp the swap space. Also, too many simultaneous copies of **uucico** can bog down the system. This usually isn't a problem because **uucico** needs a communications device in order to run, so you will usually run out of modems or serial ports before you run out of CPU cycles. But in a network environment, the only upper limit on **uucico** processes is the number of UUCP neighbors configured.

BNU UUCP has a mechanism for limiting the number of simultaneous **uucicos** and **uuxqts** that can be running. The limit is kept in the files *Maxuuscheds* and *Maxuuxqts*, respectively, in the configuration directory (except for Solaris, which uses the file */etc/uucp/Limits* to hold all three parameters). The default limit is set to a low number, such as one or two. This is rather conservative, so if you have a lot of UUCP traffic, edit these files to allow a higher limit.* Taylor UUCP lets you control **uuxqt** invocations in the *config* master configuration file. Here are the relevant commands:

max-uuxqts *number*

> Limits the maximum number of simultaneous **uuxqt** tasks. The default *number* of tasks is zero, which means no limit.

run-uuxqt *how*

> Controls when **uuxqt** is run by **uucico**. *how* may be a number, in which case **uucico** will start **uuxqt** whenever that many execution requests have been queued by the remote system, or at the end of the call, if needed. *how* can also be a keyword: **once** (only run **uuxqt** when **uucico** is finished with all of its calls), **percall** (run **uuxqt** after each UUCP conversation), or **never** (don't invoke **uuxqt** at all. To process execute requests, **uuxqt** must be called by some other means, such as **cron**. This mode can also be requested with the **–q** option on the **uucico** command line.

---

* A few older BNU implementations, such as the one used in IBM's AIX 3, do not support these files.

Maximum Throughput

Modern modems are quite good at providing error-free, high-speed links when set up properly. On such a link, the best way to transfer data is for each side to send it in continuous bursts, with the other side requesting retransmission whenever an error occurs. But UUCP's default protocol, the g protocol, is designed for 300-bps modems and noisy telephone lines. In that environment, small packets are used, with frequent pauses to wait for the remote side to acknowledge that the data arrived safely.

When you run a protocol designed for a slow link over a fast link, it still works; but, you waste large amounts of bandwidth on packet overhead, and waiting for responses. For example, if it takes a mere tenth of a second to get a response from the remote site, then on a 300-bps link you've lost only 30 bit times (enough time to send three characters) waiting for an acknowledgment. On a 38400-bps link, however, that tenth of a second has suddenly swollen to 3840 bits, taking away an opportunity to send 384 or more characters. In other words, the faster your modem is, the more time you waste when running with the wrong UUCP protocol.

On top of that, the standard UUCP conversation is a one-way street. When one side is sending, the other side can only listen, patiently accepting data no matter how many files it has waiting to send. On an active UUCP connection with which both sides have equal amounts of data to send, as much as half of the communications channel bandwidth may be wasted.

To address these problems, Taylor UUCP contains support for a new UUCP protocol. The i protocol, which made its debut in Taylor UUCP version 1.04, supports long packets, large data "windows" (how much data one side sends before waiting for an acknowledgment from the other), and bidirectional transfer—both sides can send files at the same time. This creates dramatic improvements in the utilization of the communications link.

If you are running Taylor UUCP, the i protocol will automatically be used over a modem or serial link with another Taylor site.

Old Protocols, New Tricks

For some UUCP versions, you may be able to improve their performance by changing their default protocol selections, or tuning protocol parameters. For example, the g protocol—warts and all— will work better over a high-speed modem if you can force UUCP to use the maximum packet and window sizes supported by the software on both sides of the link. Another tactic is to buy modems that support the g protocol in their firmware, such as those manufactured by Telebit. These modems, when set up properly, fool **uucico** into sending data faster, by providing local acknowledgments for packets. However, you'll have to buy two of them, one for each side of the link. It's probably cheaper to upgrade to Taylor UUCP and use the faster *i* protocol.

For a more thorough discussion of UUCP protocols, see Appendix J, *UUCP Protocol Internals*. Modem configuration is discussed in Appendix I, *Setting Up a Modem*. If you start tweaking protocol parameters, be sure to keep an eye on the UUCP statistics file, so that you can measure the results of your changes. The **uutraf** script described earlier in this chapter is a good tool for summarizing UUCP statistics and it works in both the Taylor and BNU UUCP environments.

14

Troubleshooting UUCP

A UUCP link is a system composed of modems, cables, operating system software (to drive the serial ports or network interfaces), the UUCP software, and its configuration and spool directory files. Now multiply all that by two—for the two computers trying to talk to each other—and you'll get an idea of just how many different opportunities there are for something to go wrong.

The key to solving a problem with UUCP, and most other computer networking troubles, is identifying where in the system the problem is occurring. In the pages that follow, we will discuss troubleshooting strategies and the most common problems that plague UUCP connections.

NOTE   If you have a specific UUCP error message, check Appendix C, *Status and Error Messages*, for the interpretation.

Troubleshooting Tips

You'll have an easier time fixing difficult problems if you approach them methodically. Although convincing recalcitrant computer software to behave is as much an art as a science, it doesn't hurt to be organized, proceed carefully, and remain calm.

Record Keeping

When you begin the troubleshooting process, pull out a notebook or a piece of paper and start taking notes. Write down what seems to be wrong, and everything you do to try and fix it. Writing down the steps you are taking to solve the problem will help you focus and if you need to ask anyone for help later on, your notes will help explain the problem and show others what you've tried so far to solve it.

If you are making changes to UUCP files or system configuration files, be sure to save old versions of the files. Using a source code control system, such as SCCS or RCS, is especially helpful because you can keep a history of each file change and log comments on the changes as you go. With the obtuse and error-prone syntax of many UNIX and UUCP configuration files, it's easy for mistakes to crawl in during one of your edits that will cause you even more grief later on. When a file is under source code control, you can always review past changes if there is any question whether your fixes did more harm than good.

Don't Trust Anything

Wrong assumptions about software or hardware behavior are among the biggest causes of computer communications problems. Too often, we assume that a component is working, and bypass it while searching for the source of a problem. It's almost like wearing blinders: an unspoken assumption about what "couldn't possibly be the problem" keeps you from realizing where the trouble is.

So be sure to doublecheck everything. If you're swapping serial cables, don't assume that a cable you've just pulled from the shelf is good—test it first. If you can't reach a UUCP neighbor via the network, first check the hostname and IP address to make sure you're talking to the right host. And if you see an unexplained message in the UUCP log, don't assume it isn't important—look it up in this book or in your system documentation.

A healthy skepticism about your UUCP software may also be needed; sometimes programs may not work as documented, or there may even be (gasp) bugs in the code. BNU UUCP, however, having been around for a long time, is reasonably bug-free. Software products of this age often tend to get most of their problems fixed, or the trouble spots are documented and called "limitations."

Taylor UUCP, on the other hand, is relatively new and is still undergoing development. This is a good thing, because some of these new features, like the *i* protocol, radically improve the performance and usability of UUCP; however, it also means that the occasional bug slips through.

Some users have reported that switching to Taylor UUCP has uncovered bugs in the serial port drivers on their system, probably due to increased utilization of the serial port.

Remain Calm

Don't change too many things at once when troubleshooting—you might make things worse. If a change doesn't seem to fix the problem, put it back; you should test only one thing at a time. If you come to an impasse, take a coffee break, or try again later. Getting frantic over a problem rarely makes it easier to fix.

Troubleshooting the Physical Connection

Problems at the physical layer of a connection—the path by which data flows from one computer to another—usually show up when trying to set up the connection with a remote system. But flow control or data transparency problems—when data is changed or lost on a communications link—can cause problems long after the connection is made, even when many bytes of data have already been transferred.

Other physical layer problems are more insidious; UUCP over a noisy serial line may still connect and transfer data, but it's going to be at a much lower rate than normal.

Serial Connection Problems

The most common problem when hooking up serial devices together is using the wrong cable. See Chapter 9, *The Physical Connection*, for a review of cabling and RS-232 basics.

Nothing happens

If the two devices you're trying to hook up can't detect so much as a single byte of data from each other, the cable between them is the first suspect. Make sure you know if the devices are wired DTE or DCE, and whether your cable is a straight-through or a null modem. For the latter, test the cable to see if it is wired correctly and to learn what will happen to the hardware handshaking signals.

A breakout box (or line analyzer, if you have that luxury) will help you see whether either side is able to send data. By faking the DCD and DSR signals, and looping TD to RD, you should be able to run **cu**, connect to the port, and see whatever you type echoed back to you. Put the breakout box on the other side of the cable, and check that the handshaking signals and the data are arriving at the right pins. If you have a working serial link nearby, use the breakout box to monitor activity on it, so that you get a feel for what a normal wire looks like.

Finally, make sure you have the cable plugged into the right port! The labels on the back of your computer may use one naming scheme ("Port 1," "Port 2"), while your computer's serial drivers use another (*/dev/tty0*, */dev/tty1*). On systems with multiple names for serial ports—based on whether you are receiving a call or making an outgoing call—using the wrong name (i.e., */dev/cua0* instead of */dev/ttyS0*) may doom your connection attempts.

Noisy lines

Long runs of RS-232 serial cables are prone to line noise, especially if they are run near power lines, fluorescent lights, or other sources of electrical noise. On a long cable run, with low-quality cable, you may see spurious data on the line when one end of the cable is not plugged in. Try relocating your cables away from noise sources, or switch to low-capacitance cable.

If you are having noise problems with a long RS-232 cable—over 200 feet—try lowering the baud rate. Consider connecting via a different method, such as dial-up links, over a network, or by inserting short-haul modems (also known as *line drivers*) on both sides of the link.

tty problems

The serial port drivers in your UNIX system are another possible trouble spot. Although **uucico** knows how to set most of the driver settings, some of them may need to be tweaked at boot time or by external programs. The usual offender is RTS/CTS flow control, which each UNIX system tends to support in different ways.

Modem Problems

Modern modems can be as sophisticated as the computer to which you connect them. More features, such as fax, voice mail, and ever-higher speeds, mean more chances for things to go wrong. Appendix I, *Setting Up a*

Modem, tells you how to configure your modem to minimize the chances of having problems.

Can't dial

Is the phone line properly connected to the modem? Most modems have two line jacks: one (usually labeled "LINE," "WALL," or "JACK") is for the connection to the phone line, and the other for an optional telephone that gets switched off when the modem is using the line. If you've mixed up the two jacks, your modem won't find the dial tone, or might dial but not connect properly. Other problems might be trying to use tone dialing on a pulse-only line, or failing to send a carriage return after the dialing commands in the chat script.

Can't connect

Make sure you've got the right number. If you hear the modems screeching their initial handshake, but they never connect, your modem (or the remote site's modem) may be misconfigured.

Your modem's configuration may have been changed by someone dialing out. To prevent this, you should program your modem to reset automatically when DTR is toggled, or at least have your UUCP dialing script reset the modem to a known state (such as with the **AT&F** or **ATZ** commands, described in Appendix I, *Setting Up a Modem*).

Sometimes, your modem may be trying to use features that confuse the remote modem. Try turning off your modem's various bells and whistles, or use a lower baud rate and dial in again. If you get stuck, grab the modem manual and go over all of the modem's configuration settings to see if any of them might be interfering with your connection.

Some brands of modems are finicky and won't always talk to other brands. If available, try a different modem and see if it works any better. If the remote side has more than one incoming modem, try them all and see if there's any difference.

When receiving calls, if your modem sends its responses (such as RING or CONNECT 38400) to the **getty** running on your computer, then the command echo from **getty** might trigger the modem into aborting the incoming call. This will manifest itself as a hangup just when the modems seem to be properly connecting. Appendix I, *Setting Up a Modem*, explains how to avoid this deadlock by turning off modem responses. You can also try using a more "modem-aware" terminal handler such as **mgetty**.

Carrier lost

Random hangups during the middle of a conversation are among the most frustrating problems to solve. First, look for any error messages from the UUCP programs on either side: when one side willfully disconnects, it logs the problem with an explanatory message.

Read through your modem's manual to see what diagnostics it supports. Many modems can be asked to print out the reason for the last failed call or show error statistics. You can also play with the modem's retrain, fallback, line quality monitoring, and similar features. Again, try lowering the modem's connection speed to see if it improves reliability. Be sure to try a voice call on the line: if you hear noise or static, then the phone line itself may be at fault.

Network Problems

If you're having trouble using UUCP over a network link, first make sure that other network services are working properly, especially between your machine and the UUCP neighbor to which you're trying to connect. Unless blocked by a network firewall, you should be able to both **ping** and **telnet** to the remote system. You can also use **telnet** to test the UUCP service on the remote system. For example:

```
$ telnet fatcat uucp
Trying 10.207.105.33...
Connected to fatcat.feelines.com
Escape character is '^]'.
login:
```

telnet should produce the remote system's UUCP login prompt; it's usually just "login:".

Check the IP address and hostname of the system to which you are connecting and make sure they're right. Don't try to run UUCP over the standard **telnet** service (port 23), because the daemon on the other side sends special protocol messages that **uucico** doesn't understand. If you are using **rlogin** as a relay program, make sure you're using the options that turn off escape character processing and allow full eight-bit transparency (**rlogin −8 −E** on Linux and BSD 4.4). If there are any terminal servers on the network between you and your UUCP peer, make sure they too are eight-bit clean.

If a remote system has trouble reaching your site over a network link, try setting up UUCP locally on your own network or set up a dummy link to yourself via the loopback interface (IP address 127.0.0.1). This should turn up any errors within your local configuration.

Troubleshooting the UUCP Session

Most of the problems that occur during a UUCP conversation are marked with an error message in the UUCP logfiles. Appendix C, *Status and Error Messages*, lists these messages in detail, along with explanations.

Some of the more common UUCP session problems, and their remedies, are described in the following sections.

Can UUCP Access its Devices?

A common problem when first setting up a UUCP link is the "cannot open" or "cannot access" error message that may appear when trying to run **cu** or **uucico**. It's usually caused by an ownership or permission problem for the special file in */dev* for your modem or serial link. In order for **cu** or **uucico** to use a serial device, the device special file must be owned by *uucp* and have both read and write permissions for the owner. This will often happen the first time you use a modem or serial line, simply because the default ownership of devices is the *root* user.

If you encounter this problem on a bidirectional line, you could have a conflict with the program that handles incoming calls on the port. Make sure you are running **uugetty** or a similar UUCP-aware terminal handling program. The ownership of the device special file is supposed to change to the user ID of whomever has dialed in to use it, and then back to *uucp* when the line is idle.

Is UUCP Ignoring You?

BNU UUCP is famous for silently ignoring errors in its configuration files. Watch out for case sensitive keywords in the *Permissions* file (SEND-FILES=YES is a syntax error, it should be SENDFILES=yes), or mixing up **Direct** and **direct** in *Devices* or *Dialers*. BNU also ignores lines that begin with a space or tab character.

Chat Script Woes

An error in your chat script can lead to an unreliable login process, or you may never connect at all. Running **uucico** with debug options should help you see where you're going astray. Here are some common errors:

- Forgetting about the "default" carriage return at the end of every send string, unless you suffix the send string with \c

- Trying to send, or expect, space characters—it won't work unless you use the \s escape in the chat script

- For complicated chat scripts, accidently skipping one of the expect or send strings, which confuses UUCP's parsing of the rest of the script

- Adding an extra character at the end of a send string may cause trouble in later sections of the chat script—always review an entire chat script when debugging it, not just the individual parts

- Experiencing parity mismatch: if the calling system is using one kind of parity during the login phase, and the answering system is using another, the chat script may fail—on BSD, SunOS, and Solaris systems, try adding the P_ZERO pseudo-send string into the chat script

Conversation Failures

When a UUCP conversation hangs up with a log message of "alarm" or "timeout waiting for data," it indicates that something is amiss with the data communications path. The usual causes follow:

- Serial port overruns: enable hardware flow control or lower the baud rate. On IBM PC compatibles, switch to a high-speed (NS 16550A or equivalent) serial port; older serial ports do not work well at high speeds. On SunOS or Solaris, hardware flow control may not work in both directions without the right operating system patch.

- Stolen characters: the modem or other communications device you are talking through is using XON/XOFF flow control—also known as software flow control—and is removing the flow control characters (character values 17 and 19) from the data.

If you can send small files with the *g* protocol, but not large ones, or if an *i* protocol conversation chokes after only a few packets are exchanged, you almost certainly have a flow control problem. Check your modem and serial port configuration: make sure hardware flow control is enabled, and that XON/XOFF flow control is disabled. If all else fails, lower the baud rate, or enable XON/XOFF flow control and use a protocol that can communicate through it (like the Taylor *j* protocol).

Another cause of problems in the communications path are intermediaries like terminal servers or port switches that do not provide an eight-bit clean connection, drop into a command mode upon receipt of an escape character, or have their own flow control issues. If you are using Taylor UUCP over a **pipe** link (i.e, running a program like **rlogin** to handle communications), you may have similar problems with the external program.

Mail and News Problems

UUCP has only a supporting role in transferring mail and news. The application programs on either side (i.e., **sendmail** or the newsfeed commands in C-News or INN) invoke **uux** to run their particular transfer program, such as **rmail** or **rnews**, on the remote machine.

If you can successfully invoke **rmail** or **rnews** via a **uux** request, in both directions, the problem is most likely with the mail or news configuration, not the UUCP setup.

See Appendix E, *Sendmail and UUCP*, and Appendix F, *News and UUCP*, for a quick overview on how those applications use UUCP to transfer data.

Finding Help

When you've reached the limits of your knowledge, or of your patience, it's time to ask for help. Seasoned advice on just about any computer topic is readily available via Usenet newsgroups, the World Wide Web, and perhaps even the company that sold you your system.

Read the Fine Manual

> *When all else fails, read the instructions.*
> *—A proverb of modern civilization*

It should be obvious, but don't forget to read the manual. A commercial UNIX system should have a few setup or system administration manuals, or at the very least a CD-ROM with all the documentation online and easily searchable. The trouble you're having may well have been addressed by your vendor's technical writers, even if it's buried amid things like "This page intentionally left blank" and "See document 6GY7X43 for information on UUCP protocol selection using RFC 1149 compliant communications links."

Although we've tried to make this book as complete as possible, some issues can only be addressed by vendor documentation, particularly system specifics like TTY drivers or subtle variations in UUCP features that are supported on different UNIX machines. Vendors often publish help files and instructive "cookbooks" on how to set up different features on their systems, including modems and UUCP. Some vendors also provide "faxback" services that let you receive brief documents via a fax machine.

FAQs, Newsgroups and Mailing Lists

The first place to look for answers is the *FAQ*, an acronym for Frequently Asked Questions.[*] An FAQ file for a particular topic will contain the collected wisdom of hundreds if not thousands of users. They are usually maintained by volunteers who clip the "answers" from Usenet posts or other sources.

To search for FAQ files, point your newsreader at the *comp.answers* newsgroup, and scan through the subject titles. First, check for an FAQ specific to your hardware or operating system and see if UUCP (or whatever subject you're having trouble with) is mentioned within. There is also a UUCP-related FAQ file that is regularly distributed on this newsgroup. Although it focuses on UUCP protocol internals rather than on general setup questions, it may still be of assistance.

When you've read the FAQ, and not yet found an answer, consider asking for help. In most cases, you will be better off directing your question to a UUCP oriented newsgroup such as *comp.mail.uucp*, rather than a newsgroup oriented towards your particular hardware.

Another resource for assistance is the mailing list for Taylor UUCP users. To join the mailing list, send a note to the mail robot at *taylor-uucp-request@cirr.com*.

When you've written your question, before sending it off, read through it carefully, as if you were someone else trying to help. Did you specify the kind of computer and operating system is at both sides of the link, and the version of UUCP you are using? Did you mention what you've tried so far? If you took notes while working on the problem, go over them and see if anything relevant should be included in the post.

---

[*] Most FAQ files also contain answers for those frequently asked questions. Otherwise, they would be far less useful.

Don't expect a response right away; news and mail sometimes can take a week or two to propagate throughout the Net. You may find that you get just as many wrong answers as right ones or you may get no reply at all.

Vendor Support

Every serious UNIX vendor provides support to their customers. All of the UNIX vendors mentioned in this book have Web servers online to advertise their products and provide support information to their customer base.

If the problem you are experiencing on your machine has been previously encountered by another user, the chances are good that you'll find a problem report on your vendor's Web server, along with the solution. A good vendor Web site will also include help files, instructional "cookbooks," or a Frequently Asked Questions file about their systems. Table 14–1 provides a sample list of vendor Web sites.

Table 14–1: UNIX Vendors on the World Wide Web

URL	Company	Operating Systems
http://www.bsdi.com/	Berkeley Software Development, Inc.	BSD/OS
http://www.digital.com/	DEC	Digital UNIX (OSF/1)
http://www.hp.com/	Hewlett Packard	HP-UX
http://www.ibm.com/	IBM	AIX
http://www.sco.com/	SCO	Open Server/Open Desktop
http://www.sgi.com/	Silicon Graphics, Inc.	IRIX
http://www.sun.com/	Sun Microsystems, Inc.	SunOS, Solaris

If you think your problem is due to software bugs or poor documentation from your UNIX vendor, try contacting their customer support. Vendor support policies vary depending on whether you've paid for a support contract, but you should at least be able to send them a problem report via email.

If you are using a "free" operating system such as Linux, FreeBSD, or NetBSD, you can find many Web sites with support information. Table 14–2 lists the home pages of the "free UNIX" operating systems.

Table 14–2: Web Pages for 'Free UNIX' Systems

URL	Operating System
http://www.freebsd.org	FreeBSD
http://www.linux.org	Linux
http://www.netbsd.org	NetBSD

You can also take a look at the *comp.os.linux.answers* newsgroup, or browse the *comp.unix.bsd* hierarchy.

The Heavy Artillery

When normal troubleshooting methods fail, it's time to roll out the big guns. The tools described in this section are not for the faint of heart. To use them, you must be comfortable with the intricacies of communications protocols, the "C" programming language, or poring through the blizzard of output generated by a UNIX tracing command.

Sniffers and Line Analyzers

External tracing tools such as line analyzers or network sniffers let you monitor the communications traffic between two systems, or between your system and the modem. This helps you pin down which side of the link is the source of a problem.

A line analyzer is a device that is wired in parallel with a serial cable and displays the data transferred over the wire. If you like to do things yourself, an inexpensive analyzer can be built with a personal computer, two serial ports, a custom cable, and the right software. A high-end analyzer can cost thousands of dollars, and monitor anything from your modem to a wide-area network link such as ISDN or T1.

A network sniffer can also be a PC running low-cost or free software, or a specialized portable computer that costs a small fortune. A sniffer can display or "sniff" any data on the local network segment. It can also focus on a single conversation between two computers, capturing the data as it passes over the LAN and letting you review the traffic afterwards.

A sniffer or line analyzer is called for when you want to see exactly what is transpiring over a communications link. Sometimes a trace of the line activity is the only way to ascertain what is going wrong with a conversation, and can save many hours of "finger-pointing" by identifying which system is the source of the trouble.

If you work at an organization with a large network, ask your network technicians if they have a sniffer or line analyzer available.

Most UNIX systems on an Ethernet network can act as a sniffer, with the help of commands like **tcpdump**, **etherfind**, **snoop**, or **netsnoop**. These commands monitor all traffic on the network and can print out the traffic you're interested in, or save it in a trace file for later analysis. **tcpdump** is a publicly available tool, although not all systems can support it.

Check your system documentation, and the helpfiles posted on the appropriate newsgroup for your system, to find out what network tracing tools are available.

System Trace Tools

Most UNIX systems have a trace facility that lets you display the system calls a program is making. You can see which files a UUCP command is reading or writing, and on some systems, dump out the data being transferred over the line. The name and capabilities of the trace commands vary widely on different UNIX systems; we list the ones we know about in Table 14–3.

Table 14–3: UNIX Tracing Commands

Operating System	Command
AIX	smit trace
BSD 4.4	ktrace
IRIX	par
Linux	strace
SunOS	trace
Solaris	truss

We'll show you some sample output from one of the friendlier trace facilities: the Linux **strace** command. A typical source of confusion in the Slackware distribution of Linux is the location of the UUCP configuration files. These locations are not documented in the online manual pages: you must find the source distribution directory and browse through *Makefile* or *policy.h*. But if you're handy with **strace**, you can run one of the Taylor UUCP commands and see which files the command accesses when trying to fulfill your requests. After reading the online manual pages for the **strace** command, you'll discover that the option **–eopen** limits trace output to file open calls. For example:

```
tabby:~$ strace -eopen uuname
open("/var/lib/uucp/taylor_config/config", O_RDONLY) = -1 ENOENT (No such file
  or directory)
open("/var/lib/uucp/hdb_config/Sysfiles", O_RDONLY) = -1 ENOENT (No such file
  or directory)
open("/etc/passwd", O_RDONLY)           = 3.
open("/var/lib/uucp/taylor_config/sys", O_RDONLY) = 3
open("/var/lib/uucp/hdb_config/Systems", O_RDONLY) = -1 ENOENT (No such file
  or directory)
fatcat
princecat
ihnp4
```

In this case, we see that the **uuname** command looks for configuration files in */var/lib/uucp/taylor_config* and */var/lib/uucp/hdb_config*. We also see that **uuname** tries to read both the Taylor and the BNU master configuration files (*config* and *Sysfiles*, respectively). Note the error returns for the files that do not exist, and the successes when reading the */etc/passwd* file and the Taylor *sys* file. When the last file has been read, in this case */var/lib/uucp/ hdb_config/Systems*, **uuname** prints out the list of neighboring systems.

Reading the Source Code

For particularly vexing problems, especially a hard-to-understand error message, the answer may be found within the source code of the program you are running. This is easy with Taylor UUCP, because the source code is publicly available (or you already have it if you installed Taylor UUCP on a commercial UNIX system).

Unfortunately, the BNU or Version 2 UUCP on a commercial version of UNIX does not come with source code. However, you can still deduce a few pieces of information by using the **strings** command, which looks for ASCII (i.e., human-readable) data in a program binary, and prints it out. Although you won't learn much about a program's behavior this way, you can learn the filenames that are hard-coded in the executable and the environment variables that are recognized by the code.

Since the **strings** command produces copious output, you usually filter it with **grep** to pick out only the information in which you are interested. For example, let's say that you want to know whether your version of UUCP supports sequence numbers. Since sequence numbers are stored in a file named *SQFILE*, you could try looking for the string "SQ" and see if there are any matches. For example:

```
# strings /usr/lib/uucp/uucico | grep SQ
/etc/locks/LCK.SQ
/etc/locks/LCK.SQ.
/usr/lib/uucp/SQFILE
/usr/lib/uucp/SQTMP
```

And in this case, we see that SQFILE and a few related files are indeed referenced in this version of UUCP.

In this appendix:
- *pubcheck*
- *uuget*
- *btoa/atob/tarmail*
- *tarmailchunky*

Useful Shell Scripts and Programs

This appendix contains a number of shell scripts and programs that we've used to make life with UUCP easier.

pubcheck

Here's a short but useful script that helps you keep track of what's in the UUCP public directory on your system:

```
#!/bin/sh

PUBDIR=/usr/spool/uucppublic
if [ "$#" != "0" ]; then
    find $PUBDIR -type f -print | grep $1
else
    find $PUBDIR -type f -print
fi
```

It lists all files that have been received and are waiting in the directory */usr/spool/uucppublic*.

pubcheck *pattern*

pubcheck is a useful aid for listing the files currently in the public directory. This command by default lists all the files; however, if you supply an argument, it will try to match that *pattern* to the pathnames. For example:

```
$ pubcheck
/usr/spool/uucppublic/receive/dale/eg1
/usr/spool/uucppublic/adrian/attlist
/usr/spool/uucppublic/laurel/macstuff
/usr/spool/uucppublic/mary/plans.john
```

```
/usr/spool/uucppublic/mary/report
```

$ **pubcheck mary**
```
/usr/spool/uucppublic/mary/plans.john
/usr/spool/uucppublic/mary/report
```

uuget

This script is a substitute for **uupick** if **uupick** is not available on your system.

```
#!/bin/sh

FILES=""
if [ "$1" ]; then
    SOURCE=$1
    PUBDIR=/usr/spool/uucppublic/$SOURCE
else
    PUBDIR=/usr/spool/uucppublic/receive/$LOGNAME
fi
if [ "$2" ]; then
    DESTINATION=$2
elif [ -d "$SOURCE" ]; then
    DESTINATION=$SOURCE
    PUBDIR=/usr/spool/uucppublic/$LOGNAME
else
    DESTINATION="."
fi
if [ -d "$PUBDIR" ]; then
    echo $PUBDIR":"
    ls -Fx $PUBDIR
    echo
    echo "To move All files, Select files or do Nothing,"
    echo "Enter [A/S/N]\c:"
    read input
    case $input in
        A*|a*) for q in 'ls -F $PUBDIR | grep -v "/"';
        do
        FILES="$FILES $PUBDIR/$q";
        done;;
        S*|s*) echo "Confirm files you want moved: [Y/N/Q]";
            for x in 'ls -F $PUBDIR | grep -v "/"';
        do
        echo "$x :\c";
        read answer;
        case $answer in
            Y*|y*) FILES="$FILES $PUBDIR/$x";;
            Q*|q*) exit;;
            N*|n*|*) continue;;
        esac
        done;;
```

```
            N*|n*|*)  exit;;
      esac
elif [ -f "$PUBDIR" ]; then
   FILES=$PUBDIR
else
      echo $PUBDIR "does not exist"; exit
fi
if [ "$FILES" ]; then
.  mv $FILES $DESTINATION
else
      echo "uuget: No Source File"
fi
```

This script moves files from the public directory to current directory or other location on filesystem.

> **uuget** [*source*[*destination*]]

source is the name of a subdirectory or file in the public directory; *destination* is the pathname of a directory to which the files will be moved.

If *source* is not supplied, the program looks for a subdirectory of the public directory that matches your login user ID (LOGNAME). If *source* is a subdirectory, the program lists that directory and asks you whether you want to move all or some of the files. (The program does not attempt to move subdirectories of this directory.)

If you want to select files, you will be prompted to answer Yes or No for each file.

```
To move All files, Select files or do Nothing,
Enter [A/S/N]
```

If *source* is a file in the public directory, it will be moved to the destination without prompting.

If the destination directory is not supplied, the source files are moved to the current working directory. Absolute or relative pathnames can be used.

As shown in the example below, the destination can be supplied as a single argument to the **uuget** command. The only stipulation is that this argument cannot also be a subdirectory off the public directory. (The default *source* directory is used.) Absolute pathnames help to make sure this argument is interpreted as a destination. Relative pathnames will work; however, the program checks to see if it can be the pathname of a subdirectory or file off the public directory. Thus, if there is a subdirectory of the public directory named *vmark*, you could not refer to a subdirectory off your current directory named *vmark*. You could do it using an absolute pathname, however, as shown here:

```
% uuget /work/vmark
```

Without arguments, **uuget** lists the files in the appropriate subdirectory of the public directory and asks you to take an action. You can move all or some files to the current working directory or do nothing. Assume the user's LOGNAME in the examples below is "dale."

```
% uuget
/usr/spool/uucppublic/dale:
status       takeme       takeme.too

To move All files, Select files or do Nothing,
Enter [A/S/N]s
Confirm files you want moved: [Y/N/Q]
status :n
takeme :y
takeme.too :n
```

The result is that the file */usr/spool/uucppublic/dale/takeme* is copied into the current working directory.

The next example supplies an argument that is interpreted as a subdirectory of the public directory. The file(s) in that directory is listed and again you are prompted to act. Answering "A" or "a" moves all the files in that directory to the current directory.

```
% uuget laurel
/usr/spool/uucppublic/laurel:
macstuff

To move All files, Select files or do Nothing,
Enter [A/S/N]a
```

The file */usr/spool/uucppublic/laurel/macstuff* is moved into the current working directory.

The next example shows two arguments. The first is the source directory off the public directory and the second is the absolute or relative pathname of the destination directory.

```
% uuget adrian /work/dale
/usr/spool/uucppublic/adrian:
attlist

To move All files, Select files or do Nothing,
Enter [A/S/N]a
```

The result is that the file */usr/spool/uucppublic/adrian/attlist* is copied into the directory */work/dale*.

You can supply a single argument and have it interpreted as the destination directory instead of the source directory. This example shows how the first argument, if interpreted as an existing directory, can be taken as the destination for the copy. The first argument is not interpreted as a subdirectory of the public directory and the default, the user's LOGNAME, is used.

```
% uuget /work/dale
/usr/spool/uucppublic/dale:
status       takeme        takeme.too

To move All files, Select files or do Nothing,
Enter [A/S/N]a
```

This command moves three files from the public directory into the directory */work/dale*.

btoa/atob/tarmail

btoa and **atob** convert binary files to ASCII and ASCII files back into binary, respectively. They are used for sending binary files within electronic mail messages when more modern protocols such as MIME-compatible mail clients are not available. **tarmail** is packaged with **btoa** and **atob**, and works with them to send UNIX archives produced by the **tar** command via email messages.

The entire package is available from many anonymous FTP and Web sites; a Web or Archie search on "tarmail" should turn up one close to you. It is usually found in volume 33 of the Usenet *comp.sources.misc* archives. *ftp://ftp.uu.net/usenet/comp.sources.misc/volume33/tarmail-2.3* is one possible location.

tarmailchunky

tarmailchunky lets you send large binary files over a mail link that only allows small messages. It requires the **btoa** command described in the preceding section.

```
#!/bin/sh
# "tarmailchunky" takes a file or list of files and creates a "tar file" it
# then compresses this data (using compress) and converts it to an ascii
# form (using btoa). If it is "too large" to fit into typical mail
# transport systems (some uucp sites break at 64K bytes), it will split
# the image into multiple parts and send them using the standard "mail"
```

```
# command.
if test $# -lt 3; then
   echo "Usage:  tarmailchunky mailpath 'subject-string' directory-or-file(s)"
   echo
   echo "tarmailchunky is a shell script that uses tar, compress, btoa, and"
   echo "split to send arbitrary hierarchies by mail.  It sends things as one or"
   echo "more < 64K pieces.  (see shell script to change this size)."
   exit
else
   mailpath=$1
   echo "mailpath = $mailpath"
   shift
   subject="$1"
   echo "subject-string = $subject"
   shift
   echo files = $*
   tar cvf - $* | compress | btoa | split -750 - /tmp/tm$$
   n=1
   set /tmp/tm$$*
   for f do
     {
         echo '---start beef'
         cat $f
         echo '---end beef'
     } | Mail -s "$subject - part $n of $#" $mailpath
     echo "part $n of $# sent (" 'wc -c < $f' "bytes)"
     n='expr $n + 1'
   done
   rm /tmp/tm$$*
fi
```

To decode a file sent by **tarmailchunky**, use the **untarmailchunky** script, which requires **atob** to operate properly:

```
#!/bin/sh
# "untarmailchunky" takes a an ordered list of mail messages (if they were in
# multiple parts, the must be fed to untarmail in order) and recreates
# the data stored by the original "tarmail" reversing each step along
# the way.
if test $# -ge 1; then
    sed '/^---end beef/,/^---start beef/d' $* | atob | uncompress | tar xvpf -
    echo remember to remove the tarmail files: $*
else
    sed '/^---end beef/,/^---start beef/d' | atob | uncompress | tar xvpf -
fi
```

B

The Spool Directory/ Working Files

When a UUCP job is submitted, files are created in the spool directory for processing by UUCP background programs (i.e., daemons). The most important files in the spool directory are the *workfiles*, which describe the UUCP job, the data to be transferred, and the commands to be executed. Other files in the spool directory are *logfiles*, in which messages about UUCP's activities, and a number of temporary files that are dynamically created in the course of communication between systems, are continually stored.

The pathname of the spool directory is usually */var/spool/uucp* or */usr/spool/uucp*. This appendix first shows you the structure of the spool directory in the different versions of UUCP, then describes the files that you'll find within it.

BNU Spool Directory

The BNU spool directory is really a directory tree. Separate subdirectories are created with the name of each remote system for which jobs are pending, with the workfiles, data files, and execute files stored within. Other files are stored in hidden subdirectories such as *.Status* for status files and *.Log* for logfiles.

Table B-1 shows the directory structure for a typical BNU system.[*]

---

[*] The underlying structure of the spool directory will vary on some systems; for example, on Solaris, the *.Log*, *.Old*, *.Status*, and *.Admin* subdirectories are actually links to */var/uucp*.

Table B–1: BNU Directory Structure

Directory	Contents
/var/spool/uucp/	
.Admin	Administrative files
.Corrupt	Corrupt workfiles and execute files that could not be processed
.Log/	Logfiles (see below)
.Log/uucico/	uucico execution logs, by system name
.Log/uucp/	uucp request logs, by system name
.Log/uux/	uux request logs, by system name
.Log/uuxqt/	uuxqt request logs (remote command executions on the local system), by system name
.Old/	Archive of old logfiles and administrative files
.Sequence/	Job sequence numbers for each system
.Status/	Status files for each system
.Workspace/	UUCP temporary workspace area
.Xqtdir/	Workspace for remote executions
system1/ system2/ system3/	Workfile directories for the specific systems

Within subdirectories, filenames are usually just the name of the specific system to which they refer. For example, in the *.Status* subdirectory, the files *fatcat*, *tabby*, and *hubcap* would be status files for the UUCP neighbors with those names. The exceptions are system directories, which contain workfiles with names like *C.fatcat3ab4*, and the *.Admin* and *.Old* subdirectories.

The *.Admin* subdirectory contains information about the operations of the UUCP system as a whole. Files in this directory are truncated (after being copied to the *.Old* subdirectory) whenever **uudemon.cleanup** is run. The *.Old* directory is also the repository for old UUCP logfiles from previous weeks. Table B–2 shows the contents of the *.Admin* subdirectory.

Table B–2: Contents of the .Admin Subdirectory

Directory	Contents
Foreign	Log of unknown systems calling in
audit	Log for incoming calls who turn on debugging
errors	Important error messages (i.e., ASSERT errors)[a]
uucleanup	Log from the **uucleanup** command
xferstats	File transfer statistics

a. ASSERT errors are described in Appendix C, *Status and Error Messages*.

Taylor Spool Directory

The Taylor UUCP spool directory closely follows the structure of the BNU directory. The two main differences are that it keeps a single logfile in the main spool directory, rather than atomized logs based on program and system name; and, the work directories for UUCP neighbors contain extra subdirectories to segregate the different kinds of workfiles. Table B–3 shows the contents of the Taylor UUCP spool directory.

Table B–3: The Taylor Spool Directory

Directory	Contents
.Received/	Lists of temporary files received from each system
.Sequence/	Conversation sequence numbers for each system
.Status/	Status files for each system
.Temp/	Temporary workspace
.Xqtdir/	Workspace for remote executions
Debug	All debug messages written here
Log	Logfile for all UUCP messages
Stats	Transfer statistics logfile
system1/	Workfiles for the named system
system1/*C./*	Control files
system1/*D./*	Data files
system1/*D.X/*	Data files destined to be execution files on a remote system
system1/*SEQF*	Job sequence number for this system
system1/*X./*	Exection files
system2/	Workfiles for another system
system3/	

A complete rundown of the Taylor UUCP spool directory and its contents is provided in the Taylor documentation. Remember, Taylor UUCP can also be configured to use the BNU spool directory format—this is the default in Slackware Linux systems.

Version 2/BSD Spool Directory

Version 2 UUCP keeps nearly everything in the main spool directory */usr/spool/uucp*. This causes performance problems on systems with heavy traffic due to UNIX directory lookup inefficiencies, but is not an issue on a lightly used system. BSD 4.3 has a similar, but tidier, spool directory with the different types of files organized by subdirectory, similar to BNU.

Files that refer to UUCP jobs or status have prefixes to indicate the type of file. (See Table B–4.)

Table B–4: Version 2/BSD 4.3 Spool Files

File/Directory	Function
AUDIT	Debug log for incoming calls that turn debugging on
C.	Prefix for control files
CORRUPT/	Directory for corrupted C. and D. files (BSD)
D.	Prefix for data files
ERRLOG	UUCP error log (ASSERT errors)
LOGFILE	General UUCP logfile
LCK..	Prefix for lockfiles
STST.	Prefix for status files
SYSLOG	File transfer statistics
TM	Temporary files
X.	Prefix for execution files

In BSD 4.3, each prefix is used to name a subdirectory that contains the files of that type. Data files are further segregated into the subdirectories *D./* for incoming data files, *D.system/* for outgoing data files, and *D.systemX/* for outgoing data files that will become execution files on the remote system. There is a separate *D.system/* and *D.systemX/* directory for each active UUCP neighbor.

File Formats

Here are the formats of the various files that UUCP uses in the spool directory to keep track of jobs and execution requests. This information should
be useful if you are monitoring UUCP activity, or trying to determine the
cause of a UUCP problem.

Workfiles

Workfiles contain instructions for **uucico** on which remote system to contact,
the type of transfer request, and where the file will be sent. They are created
by **uucp** and **uux**.

Except in Taylor UUCP, a workfile for a file transfer between the local system and system *tabby* would be named as shown in Figure B-1.

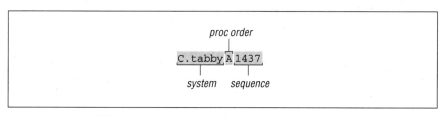

Figure B-1: Workfile naming

Field	Function in Workfile Name
system	Name of remote system for which work is queued; trun-cated to the first seven (or, in some implementations, six) characters.
proc order	Workfile processing order, or *grade*. **uucico** processes files in order from *A* to *Z* and then *a* to *z*. Default is *A* for files created by **uux** and *n* for files created by **uucp**. You can select whatever grade you want with the **−g** option to **uucp** and **uux**.
sequence #	Job sequence number for the workfile assigned by **uucico**. Used to ensure a unique filename.

Taylor UUCP uses a different scheme for naming workfiles. Since the workfile name is never seen by the remote system, this does not cause any
incompatibility with other UUCP versions. The workfile names begin with
C., then the grade of the job, then an 11-character string formed from the

current time and process ID. This scheme avoids having to lock the job sequence number file.

Each workfile can have up to 20 entries, with one entry for each request. Each entry has seven fields and an optional eighth field. An entry in a workfile may look like Figure B-2.

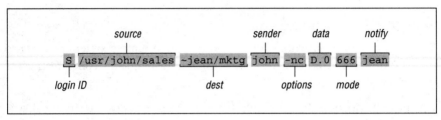

Figure B-2: Inside a workfile

Field	Function in Workfile
type	Type of request, which can be one of the following:
	S Sends a file from the local system to a remote system.
	R Copies a file from the remote system to the local system.
	X Sends an execution request to the remote system.
source	Source file pathname.
dest	Destination file pathname.
sender	Login name of the user that requested the work.
options	List of command options the user specified for the **uucp** or **uux** commands.
data	Name of data file for **uucico** to copy. It is "D.0" with the default −c option to copy the source file directly to the data file at the time of transfer. The data filename is given if the −C option (to copy the source file to the spool directory) is used. This field is used only with the S request.
mode	UNIX permissions of the source file in octal format. This field is only used with the S request.
notify	Login name of the user who should be notified upon completion of the job request. It is used only with the S request, and only when the −n or −m option of **uucp** and **uux** is given.

> *E* (Taylor UUCP only) Makes an execution request without requiring a separate *X.* file. Used when the command to be executed requires a single input file that is passed to it as standard input. Options are similar to the *S* command. The *E* command was introduced in Taylor UUCP version 1.04.

Our example tells **uucico** to send the file */usr/john/sales* to the file *mktg* in the login directory of *jean* and to send mail to *jean* (the −n option) when the transfer is complete. The request is made by user *john* on the local system. The file *sales* has read/write (666) UNIX permissions.

Data Files

Data files contain data to be transferred to the remote system. They are named similarly to workfiles, except that their names begin with the prefix *D.*, and the system name is followed only with job sequence numbers. Data files are created when the **uucp** is invoked with the −C option, or when **uux** is used to queue a command for execution on a remote system. In the case of **uux**, the data file contains the instructions for the remote **uuxqt**. It will be copied to an *X.* file (see below) on the remote system. In most cases, at least two data files are created for a remote command execution: one containing the execution information and command-line arguments, the other containing the input to the remote command (such as the text of an email message or a batch of news articles).

When both sides use Taylor UUCP, execution requests that only require a single file passed in on standard input will use the *E* command in the workfile. The *E* command runs the execution request without a separate *X.* file. Most, if not all, news and mail transfers can be transferred slightly faster when the *E* command is used.

Figure B–3 displays a data filename.

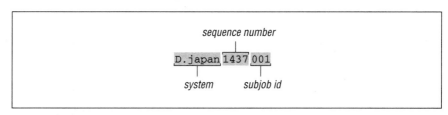

Figure B–3: Data file naming

Field	Function in Data Filename
system	Name of local system for files waiting to be transferred to another system; name of remote system for files received from another system. Truncated to the first seven characters (six in some implementations).
sequence #	A four-digit sequence number for the workfile assigned by **uucico**. This should be the same as the corresponding field in the workfile.
subjob id #	A three-digit number identifying additional data files associated with the same workfile. (This number is not used in all implementations.)

Execute Files

Execute files are work orders created by **uux** in the spool directory. They contain the command for execution, information about standard input and output, and files needed for executing the command.

Figure B–4 shows how an execute file would be named.

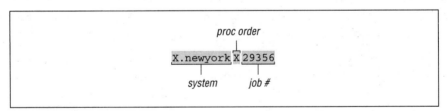

Figure B–4: An execute filename

An execute file is always prefixed with an *X..* The above example is the execute filename for the remote system *newyork*; its execute file job number is "29356." The processing order number for any execute file is always "X."

An execute file may contain lines with the following prefixes:

Prefix	Function
U	User line—identifies the requestor's login name and system.
F	Required file line—identifies the filename for transmission.

I   Standard input line—specifies the standard input.

O   Standard output line—specifies the standard output.

N   Status return line—if present, inhibits mailing of acknowledgment message of **uuxqt** command completion. Generated by **−n** option to **uux**.

Z   Error status return line—indicates that acknowledgment should be mailed only if command failed. Generated by **−z** option to **uux**. (This option not available in all versions of UUCP.)

R   Requestor line—identifies complete return address of requestor. Generated by **−a** option of **uux** to override the mail return address derived from the user line. Used by mailers that know how to forward mail more than one hop.

C   Command line—identifies the UNIX command for **uuxqt** to execute.

Each execute file contains at least one *U* line and one *C* line. The *F*, *I*, and *O* lines are present only if files are needed for command execution. An execute file can have multiple *F* lines.

The following is an example of an execute file:

```
U nadim newyork
F D.tabbyB0024
I D.tabbyB0024
C rmail lee_nicholson@ersatz.ora.com
```

Temporary Receive Files

uucico creates temporary files in the receiving system's spool directory to hold data during file transfers. These files are moved to a destination file if the transfer is successful. If the transfer fails, temporary files remain in the spool directory but do not prevent future transfer attempts. The **uuclean** program automatically removes leftover temporary files.

A temporary filename may look Figure B-5.

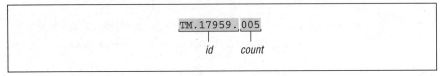

Figure B-5: Temporary filename

Field	Function in Temporary Filename
ID	Job sequence number assigned by **uucico**.
count	A sequential three-digit number starting at zero. It shows the number of files received.

Lockfiles

Lockfiles are created by **uucico** for each device, each system, and each file in use. These files are supposed to prevent multiple attempts to use the same device, duplicate conversations, and overwriting of files. All UUCP programs, and any other programs that share UUCP resources,[*] must respect each other's lockfiles for this to work properly. Version 2 UUCP keeps lockfiles in the spool directory; BNU uses a system-wide lockfile such as */var/spool/locks* (Solaris) or */etc/locks* (AIX). Taylor uses whatever you set the LOCKDIR definition to in the source file *policy.h*.

Lockfile names have the following format:

Name	Function
LCK..sys	File where *sys* is a system name (for example, *LCK..japan*).
LCK..dev	File where *dev* is a device name (for example, *LCK..cua0*).
LCK.file	File where *file* is an abbreviation for the following filenames: *LOG* for *LOGFILE*, *SQ* for *SQFILE*, and *SEQ* for *SEQF* file. For example, a locked *SQFILE* would be named as *LCK.SQ*.

Lockfiles usually contain the process ID of the process requesting the lock. In BSD 4.3, the process ID is stored in binary. You can print out the process ID with the **od** (octal dump) command. In other versions of UUCP, process IDs are stored in ASCII form, so you can use **cat**. For example:

---

[*] Such as programs that handle serial ports: **cu**, **uugetty**, **kermit**, and so on.

```
$ cat /var/spool/locks/LCK..tty08
3686
```

You can then use **ps** to find out who is running that process. If there is no process with that number running on the system, the lock is stale (i.e., no longer valid) and can be safely removed. Most versions of UUCP can detect a stale lockfile, and automatically remove it before they try to use that resource. Occasionally you may need to write your own script to remove stale lockfiles. Here's a sample Bourne shell script:

```
#!/bin/sh

LOCKDIR=/var/spool/locks
for lockfile in $LOCKDIR/*
do
    if [ -f $lockfile ] && kill -0 'cat $lockfile'
    then
        echo "Active lockfile: $lockfile"
    else
        echo "Removing stale lockfile: $lockfile"
        rm -f $LOCKDIR/$lockfile
    fi
done
```

System Status Files

In BNU and Taylor, status files have the name: *.Status/system*. Version 2 status files are named *STST.system*. An entry in the status file consists of six fields separated by blanks, as shown in Figure B–6.

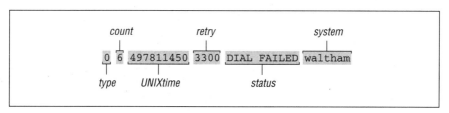

Figure B–6: Inside a status file

Field	Function in Status Files
type	Code from zero to five indicating the status of the job. The code is also explained in the *status* field.
count	Number of call attempts made by the local system; it is incremented each time **uucico** tries to call a remote system.

After the number of retries reaches an upper limit (26 is the default), **uucico** will give up.

UNIXtime   Time of the last connection attempt expressed in UNIX internal time format. (The number of seconds since January 1, 1970, GMT.)

retry   Number of seconds that **uucico** must wait before it tries calling the remote system again.

status   Status of the conversation.

system   Remote system name.

You may need to remove the status file when debugging a faulty link to a remote system. Otherwise, it will cause **uucico** to refuse future connection attempts with a "RETRY TIME NOT REACHED" message. Status file messages and their interpretations are listed in Appendix C, *Status and Error Messages*.

Logfiles

Logfiles are created by UUCP programs in the spool directory. They contain records of calls to remote systems, requests queued, execution of **uux** commands, file transfer results, and system errors. Logfiles messages are always appended to the end of the file, so the files need regular trimming to keep from growing too large.

UUCP logfile

The everyday comings and goings of UUCP work are logged in its regular logfile. In BNU, this is actually a small explosion of files. As shown in Table B-1, there is a separate logfile directory for each UUCP program—**uucico**, **uucp**, **uux**, and **uuxqt**—and within those directories, separate logfiles for each remote system. Taylor UUCP and Version 2 use a single file for these messages, named *Log* and *LOGFILE* respectively; they are stored in the spool directory.

A portion of the logfile is displayed when you use the command **uulog**. An entry in a BNU or Version 2 logfile may look like Figure B–7.

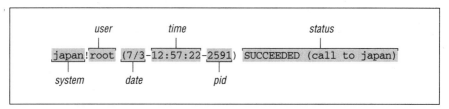

Figure B–7: A logfile entry

Field   Function in *Logfile*

user   Login name of the user who made the request.

system   Name of the system where the request originated.

date   When the request was made.

time   What time the request was made.

pid   Process ID of the program writing to the logfile.

status   Message describing the status of the call and the type of request. The status messages are listed in Chapter 6.

In BNU, the *pid* field is followed by a sequence number identifying successive log entries pertaining to the same UUCP job. There also may be a final field that lists the actual UUCP command being performed. Taylor UUCP uses a slightly different logfile format, but conveys the same information.

In BNU, the individual system logfiles are archived by combining them into a single logfile, typically once a day. This file is stored under the name *.Old/Old_Log_1*. (The previous combined logfile is moved to *Old_Log_2*. If you want to keep more than two combined logfiles, you can modify the section in **uudemon.cleanup** that saves them.)

In Version 2, logfiles have backup files called *Log-WEEK* and *o.Log-WEEK*. *Log-WEEK* contains log entries for the week to date, and *o.Log-WEEK* contains *LOGFILE* entries for the previous week. *LOGFILE* is automatically moved to the end of *Log-WEEK*, and *Log-WEEK* to the end of *o.Log-WEEK*.

LTMP

The UUCP programs write directly to the *LOGFILE* unless it is locked by *LCK.LOG*. When a lockfile exists, other programs create and write to temporary logfiles called *LTMP*. The **uulog** program automatically moves *LTMP* files to the end of *LOGFILE*.

The name of a temporary logfile consists of the prefix *LTMP.* and a process ID. An example of a temporary logfile name is *LTMP.6987*. Temporary logfiles have been done away with in many implementations of UUCP.

.Admin/xferstats and SYSLOG

In BNU, the file *.Admin/xferstats* contains log messages recording the amount of data sent and received by each system. In Version 2, this file is called *SYSLOG*.

An entry in *SYSLOG* appears in Figure B-8.

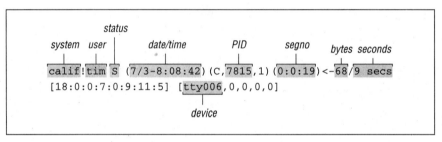

Figure B-8: An xferstats/SYSLOG entry

Field	Function in *xferstats/SYSLOG*
sys	Remote system name.
user	Name of sender.
status	*S* for "sent data," *R* for "received data," and *M* for "sent mail."
date-time	When the request was made.
pid	The process ID of the **uucico** that made the transfer.
seqno	Sequence number of successive parts of the same UUCP job.
bytes	Number of bytes sent or received.

secs   Processing time, in seconds, that the transfer used.

device   Device over which the connection was made.

Note that you can calculate the effective data transfer rate by dividing the number of bytes transferred by the time.

If you consistently get a much lower data rate than you expect from the nominal speed of the line, there are probably a lot of errors (and, hence, retried packets) on the line. It might also mean that your modem is connecting at a lower speed than you expect.

The Taylor UUCP version of this file is called *Stat*, and it lives in the main spool directory. The format is somewhat different than BNU, but the information presented is essentially the same.

.Admin/errors and ERRLOG

In BNU, the file *.Admin/errors* contains records of **uucico** system errors. The entries contain ASSERT messages generated by local UUCP programs that indicate the cause of a file transfer failure. The ASSERT errors do not go to the *ERRLOG* file if you invoke the debugging option (–x*n*) of the **uucico** program. In Version 2, this file is called *ERRLOG*.

ASSERT messages reflect conditions that do not fix themselves; the system manager must correct the condition. Figure B–9 displays an entry in the error file.

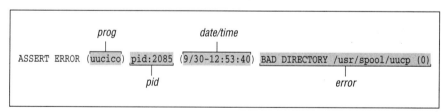

Figure B–9: An ASSERT message

Field	Function in *errors/ERRLOG*
prog	Name of the program that generated the error.
pid	The program's process ID.
date-time	When the error was made.
error	Message giving the nature of the error. This field contains a numeric code in parentheses that gives more information

about the message. A zero indicates the code is not relevant to the message.

In BNU, an entry in *.Admin/errors* also includes a final field giving the SCCS ID of the program that caused the error, the name of the source file, and the line in that file.

The entry above shows that the **uucico** program failed on September 30 at 12:53 p.m. because **uucico** cannot open the directory */usr/spool/uucp*. ASSERT messages are described in more detail in Appendix C, *Status and Error Messages*.

Job Sequence Files

Every job needs a unique job ID. Job IDs are usually formed from a *job sequence* number and the system name; they must not only be unique on the local system, they also should not duplicate the ID of any recently completed job. By keeping the job sequence number in a file, and constantly incrementing it, UUCP is guaranteed that it will not reuse a sequence number, and thus keep job IDs unique as well.

BNU keeps a separate job sequence number for each system, to further prevent the sequence number from wrapping. The job sequence number files are named *.Sequence*/system for each remote system. Taylor UUCP keeps job sequence files in the work directory for each system, under the name *SEQF*. Version 2 maintains a single job sequence file in the spool directory called *SEQF*.

All job sequence files contain a sequence number in four ASCII decimal or hexadecimal digits.

Conversation Sequence Files

Conversation sequence numbers, if enabled, are exchanged as a security measure whenever two UUCP sites begin a conversation. BNU and Version 2, when implemented, keep all conversation sequence numbers in the *SQFILE* in the configuration directory (*/usr/lib/uucp* or */etc/uucp*). Taylor UUCP keeps conversation sequence numbers in the *.Sequence* subdirectory of the spool directory, with a separate file for each remote system. It's easy to confuse this scheme with BNU job sequence numbers, and it is slated to get changed in future versions.

For the format of *SQFILE*, see Chapter 12, *Access and Security Considerations*. Taylor conversation sequence files use the same format as job sequence files: four ASCII digits.

Audit/Debug File

The audit file contains debug messages that have no other place to go. In BNU and Version 2, the most likely need for this file is when an incoming call turns on debugging in the UUCP initial handshake. Taylor UUCP logs all debugging messages to the audit file, regardless of whether debugging is invoked on an outgoing or incoming call.

In BNU, the audit file is in *.Admin/audit*. In Taylor, it is called *Debug*, and lives in the spool directory. If you compile Taylor UUCP to use a BNU-style spool directory, the default file location is *.Admin/audit.local*. Version 2 uses the name *AUDIT*.

If you are using Taylor UUCP, you will probably need to clear the audit file from time to time, since it will otherwise grow unchecked. BNU and Version 2 UUCP trim the audit file via **cron** scripts.

Status and Error Messages

BNU/Version 2 Messages

These messages may appear in the status file (*.Status/sysname* or *STST.sysname*) or one of the UUCP logfiles. A complete list should appear in your UUCP documentation.

If, after looking at the status message, you want **uucico** to try again, you must remove the status file (or use **Uutry −r** in BNU).

ALARM *n*

> **uucico** has waited too long for data from the remote side, and has hung up the connection. This is usually caused by a data transparency problem, such as the erroneous use of software flow in the modem or some other intermediate device on the connection. It could also be caused by serial port overrun due to lack of hardware (RTS/CTS) flow control, or running a port at too high a speed.

ASSERT ERROR

> An ASSERT error occurred. A more detailed message is written to the error file (*.Admin/errors* in BNU or *ERRLOG* in Version 2). The individual messages from the error file, such as BAD READ or STAT FAILED, are listed below.

AUTODIAL (*dev: Interrupted system call*)

> Modem is in use. (Version 2)

BAD LOGIN/MACHINE COMBINATION

> The nodename and/or login name used by the calling machine are not permitted in the *Permissions* file. Either you forgot to add a "LOGNAME=" entry for a new system, or someone is trying to spoof as one of your UUCP neighbors. The remote side will report an "RLOGIN" or "REMOTE REJECT AFTER LOGIN" error. (BNU)

BAD LOGIN/PASSWORD

> We called the remote system, but the login failed. It could be a wrong login/password, wrong number, a very slow machine, or failure in getting through the chat script. (Version 2)

BAD READ

> **uucico** could not read/write to a device. May also be caused by improper use of XON/XOFF flow control in the modem. If this is the case, the other side will get an ALARM or similar message. (Version 2)

BAD SEQUENCE CHECK

> Sequence number checking is in use (see Chapter 12, *Access and Security Considerations*), and the sequence numbers did not match. Either the two sides have fallen out of sequence (perhaps one of them had a system crash and was restored from an older backup), or a third party is attempting to spoof you. If the interloper had the right sequence number, then you will get this error message when the real system calls. Some versions of BNU will prohibit further calls from this system until the retry time in the status file expires (or until you remove the status file).

CALLBACK REQUIRED

> The remote system requires callback.

CALLER SCRIPT FAILED

> An error occurred executing the chat script in the *Systems* file. (BNU)

CAN NOT CALL (SYSTEM STATUS)

> An unexpired system status file keeps **uucico** from trying again. Check the status file for the reason.

CAN'T ACCESS DEVICE

For a new system, you specified a nonexistent or the wrong device in the systems file. If the device exists, the permissions on the device special file may be wrong. Otherwise, some other problem is happening with the device, such as wrong permissions or ownership after a **getty** or other outgoing caller used it. (BNU)

CONVERSATION FAILED

Something went wrong after a successful startup. Either the system on the other side went down, or the line was lost. Any partially completed jobs remain in the queue and will be tried again later. (BNU)

CONVERSATION SUCCEEDED

Communications with the remote system were successful and all files were transferred.

DEVICE FAILED

The *open* (2) of the device failed. (BNU)

DEVICE LOCKED

The requested device is being used by another process. (BNU)

DIAL FAILED
DIALER SCRIPT FAILED

UUCP could not dial the remote system. The remote side might be busy, not answering, or you have a bad dialing script or the wrong telephone number.

Enough already

Too many characters were received while waiting for a chat script expect string. Usually caused by calling a system with a long login message before the login prompt.

FAILED (call to *system*)

uucico was unable to negotiate either the chat script in *L.sys* or the conversation with the modem. (Version 2) BNU replaced this catch-all message with a number of more specific messages.

FAILED (conversation complete)

The conversation failed after successful startup. This usually means one side went down, the program aborted, or the line just hung up.

FAILED (DIRECT LINE OPEN *tty#*)

> Opening of the device failed. (Version 2)

HANDSHAKE FAILED (LCK)

> Lockfile exists for the system or device. Check to see if another **uucico** is already running, or if someone is using **cu** or other dialout programs. (Version 2)

LOGIN FAILED

> The login for the given machine failed. It could be a wrong login/password, a wrong number, a very slow machine, or a failure in getting through the chat script. (BNU)

NO CALL (MAX RECALLS)

> The maximum number of failed call attempts that can be made has been reached. Remove the status file to allow further calls. (Version 2)

NO CALL (RETRY TIME NOT REACHED)

> A recent attempt to call this system failed and **uucico** wants to wait until the retry time period elapses before making another call. To try again sooner, remove the status file.

NO DEVICES AVAILABLE

> Either all devices for outgoing calls are busy, or there is no valid device for calling the system. Check that the device named in *Systems* corresponds to an entry in *Devices*. (BNU)

OK

> The last conversation with this system ended successfully.

REMOTE DOES NOT KNOW ME (RYou are unknown to me)

> The remote system does not have the name of your system in its *Systems* file, and it does not allow unknown systems to log in. (BNU)

REMOTE HAS A LCK FILE FOR ME (RLCK)

> The remote system may be trying to call you at the same time you are calling it, or it may have a lock file left over from a previous attempt. (BNU)

REMOTE REJECT AFTER LOGIN (RLOGIN)

> Your system logged in with a valid login/password, but the remote system does not think that your login is allowed to use UUCP. Most likely, the remote forgot to put you into their *Permissions* file or the equivalent. (BNU)

REMOTE REJECT, UNKNOWN MESSAGE

> The remote system rejected your call with a nonstandard message. The remote may be running a hacked or buggy UUCP implementation. (BNU)

STARTUP FAILED

> Login succeeded, but the initial "shere" handshake failed. This may be because the two sides could not agree on a common UUCP protocol to use. (BNU)

SUCCEEDED (call to *system*)

> Successfully connected to the named system.

SYSTEM NOT IN Systems

> One of your users made a request for a system not in your *Systems* file. (BNU)

TALKING

> A conversation with the remote system is currently in progress.

TIMEOUT (*system*)

> The other system did not answer within a set period of time. Depending on the chat script, **uucico** may keep trying and still get through. (Version 2)

WRONG MACHINE NAME

> The machine you just called is using a different name than the one you expected it to use. (BNU)

WRONG TIME TO CALL

> The *L.sys* or *Systems* file does not allow a call at this time.

ASSERT Messages

ASSERT messages reflect conditions that do not fix themselves; the system manager must find the problem and fix it. These messages appear in the error file (*.Admin/errors* in BNU or *ERRLOG* in Version 2). They are usually caused by filesystem problems, such as bad permissions or ownerships, missing directories, or the disk is full.

Any of the UUCP commands or daemons may generate an ASSERT error; the name of the program that encountered the error should be logged in the error message. If the error has an error return code associated with it, such as a file open error, the number will be in parentheses as part of the error message.

If you experience an ASSERT error not listed here, contact your UNIX vendor for assistance.

ARG COUNT (*num*)
> One of the system files has too few fields. The actual number of fields is *num*.

BAD DEVICE ENTRY
BAD LINE ·
BAD SPEED
> An entry in *L-devices* or *Devices* is incorrect.

BAD DIRECTORY
> **uucico** cannot open a directory.

BAD UID
BAD LOGIN_UID
> The user ID is not defined in */etc/passwd*. The filesystem is in trouble, or the */etc/passwd* file is inconsistent. If you are using NIS, check the *networks* database.

BAD WRITE
> **uucico** cannot write to a remote line or device.

CAN NOT GET SEQLOCK
> **uucico** cannot create *LCK.SEQF*.

CAN'T ALLOCATE
> A dynamic allocation failed.

CAN'T CHDIR
CAN'T CREATE
CAN'T CLOSE
CAN'T LINK
CAN'T OPEN
CAN'T READ
CAN'T STAT
CAN'T UNLINK
CAN'T WRITE

A system call on the file named in the error message failed. Check permissions, ownerships, whether the appropriate directories exist, and disk space. If the named file is a device special file, check it for the correct major and minor numbers.

CAN NOT FIND UID

Same as "BAD UID" (see above).

CAN'T FORK

An attempt to fork a new process failed. This may happen when a system is heavily burdened, and cannot create new processes.

CAN'T LOCK

An attempt to create a lockfile (LCK) failed. Check the locks directory (see your system documentation for the specific name).

CAN'T MOVE TO CORRUPTDIR

A problem has occurred moving files to the *.Corrupt* subdirectory of the spool directory. Make sure the directory exists and check the permissions and ownership.

FILE EXISTS

A control file or data file could not be created because it already exists. There may be a problem with the job sequence numbers in the *.Sequence* subdirectory of the spool directory or there may be an internal error. The file in question may have been left behind by a previous UUCP process.

FSTAT FAILED IN EWRDATA

There is something wrong with the Ethernet media.

LINK ERROR

uuxqt cannot link an execute file to */usr/spool/uucp/.XQTDIR*

No uucp server
> Make sure the **uucp** service is properly defined in */etc/services* or the NIS maps.

PCGET READ
PKXSTART
> The remote machine hung up, or aborted the conversation.

PERMISSIONS file: BAD OPTION
> There is a syntax problem in the *Permissions* file.

RETURN FROM IOCTL
> An ioctl() call failed that should not have failed. This is probably due to a system driver problem. Make sure the device special file in question has the correct major and minor numbers.

STAT FAILED
> **uucico** could not access the named file. There may be a permission problem or an I/O error with the filesystem, or a problem with the *stty* modes on a serial port.

SYSLST OVERFLOW
> Too many jobs are queued for a single system.

SYSTAT OPEN FAIL
> **uucico** cannot open an *STST* file. The modes may be wrong, or there is a file with bad modes in the directory.

TOO FEW LOG FIELDS
> *L.sys* has too few fields.

TOO MANY LOCKS
> **uucico** cannot create another lockfile; there is probably an internal error or a system resource problem.

TOO MANY SAVED C FILES
> See "SYSLST OVERFLOW" above.

ULIMIT TOO SMALL
> The current process has a file size limit that is too small. Since file transfers may fail, they will not be attempted.

WRONG ROLE

> An internal logic problem occurred. Contact your vendor.

XMV ERROR

> **uuxqt** could not move an execute file into the *.Xqtdir* subdirectory of the spool directory. Check the permissions and ownership of *.Xqtdir*.

Taylor UUCP Messages

When compiled in BNU compatibility mode, Taylor UUCP uses some of the same messages in the status file as BNU. It otherwise issues somewhat different—and usually more understandable—error messages. We do not list all possible messages here: some are similar to the ASSERT messages in BNU in that they indicate serious system problems with the local environment (or with the way you compiled your particular version of Taylor UUCP). If you are stymied by an error message not listed here, try looking it up in your Taylor UUCP source distribution.

device_name: Port already locked

> **uucico** could not obtain a lock for the named device.

All matching ports in use

> There were no ports available to make a call; they were in use or there is a problem with the device file. Look for an error message just above this one, detailing why the device file could not be opened.

Bad introduction string
Bad protocol handshake (*xxx*)
Bad protocol response string
Bad response to handshake string (*xxx*)
Bad startup string (expected 'Shere' got '%s')

> These errors may happen during the UUCP handshake; the remote side did not send the expected response. Either you are talking with a buggy implementation of UUCP or the messages are somehow getting damaged in transit.

Bad login

> The remote system called in with a login/password combination that was not in the Taylor UUCP password file.

Call failed
> The last attempt to contact the remote system failed.

Call from unknown system *system-name*
> The named system is not in the local systems file.

Called wrong system (*system-name*)
> The system called answered with a different system name than expected.

Conversation complete
> The last conversation with the remote site was successful. All files were successfully transferred.

Dial failed
> Could not dial the remote system; the dialing script did not complete properly.

Error in *xxx* protocol parameters
> You specified invalid protocol parameters for one of the UUCP protocols. Check your configuration files.

Handshake failed (*reason*)
> Login was successful, but the subsequent UUCP handshake failed, with the indicated reason code. See Table 11-1 in Chapter 11, *Setting Up a UUCP Link*, to interpret the codes. Typical reason codes here are "RLOGIN" (machine failed login ID validation) or "RYou are unknown to me" (machine not in systems file).[*]

Login failed
> The last call to the remote system failed during the chat script phase. Make sure you have the login, password, and chat script.

No matching ports
> No port that matched the requirements for calls to the system could be found. You may have forgotten to define your modem, or defined your modem or system improperly (i.e., with the wrong baud rate).

---

[*] Yes, UUCP really spells the error message that way, with the mixed case and embedded spaces.

No mutually supported protocols

> The two sides logged in successfully, but could not agree on a protocol. Check the configuration files on both sides; perhaps one is trying to force the other to use an unsupported protocol.

No sequence number (call rejected)

> Conversation sequence numbers are in use for the remote system, but it did not supply a sequence number during the UUCP handshake. Make sure the remote side is also configured to use sequence numbers. For an existing link, either the remote side accidently lost the sequence number information or someone is trying to spoof you.

No supported protocol

> The remote side sent back a "Use this protocol" message without listing a protocol to use for the conversation. The two sides will not be able to communicate until they agree on a protocol.

Out of sequence call rejected

> The remote side did not have the right conversation sequence number. Someone may be spoofing as the remote system, or may have successfully spoofed as the remote system in the past so the genuine system is now out of sequence. A more innocuous possibility is that one side restored an old sequence number file from a system backup after a crash.

Port unavailable

> The last connection attempt failed and no port was available to make the call.

sigact (*nnn*): *xxx*
sigvec (*nnn*): *xxx*

> **uucico** received an unexpected signal. It may be due to a programming error or a compilation problem with the local version.

System *xxx* used wrong login name *yyy*

> System *xxx* used a login name different from the one specified by the **call-login** keyword in the configuration entry for that system.

System already locked

> A call is already in progress with this remote system: only one call at a time is allowed. You may also see the message "RLCK."

Talking

A conversation with the remote system is in progress.

Timeout

No valid data received from the remote system. This is usually caused by a flow control, buffer overrun, or other data transparency problem. The remote side could have also stopped transmitting (perhaps due to a crash) or the line may have been lost.

Too many retries

The maximum number of failed call attempts has occurred—no more retries are allowed. Remove the status file if you want **uucico** to try again in spite of this.

Wrong time to call

The time field in the systems entry for this system does not permit a call at this moment.

UUCP for Non-UNIX Platforms

You don't need UNIX to run UUCP. Commercial products, shareware, and freeware programs exist to provide UUCP connectivity for just about every common personal computer configuration, and even a few uncommon—or impersonal—ones. The products include programs that mimic their UNIX counterparts, dedicated personal mail and news readers, and extensions to commercial office mail systems (such as Microsoft Mail or cc:Mail) that let them receive and forward mail over a UUCP link. A number of bulletin board systems (BBSs) for personal computers also support connectivity via UUCP.

Connecting these packages to a UUCP link is similar to the configuration process for the UNIX-based UUCP software. You will need a system name, phone numbers, chat script, and the like in order to connect to a remote site. If you are an email junkie who absolutely has to stay in touch, you can install one of these packages on your laptop (assuming it isn't already running a UNIX variant) and set up a UUCP connection to your home system.

Some of these packages also support network connections, or connect with existing local-area network mail programs.

This list is by no means exhaustive: new products appear from time to time, and UUCP functionality is occasionally added to existing products. We have also focused on listing a wide range of products rather than every product in a single category. Consult an online source such as the newsgroups *comp.mail.uucp* or *comp.os.msdos.news-mail* for up-to-date listings.

Personal Connectivity

These packages provide UUCP functionality for a personal computer. They allow both incoming and outgoing UUCP calls, and include mail and news reading software.

AmigaUUCP

AmigaUUCP is a set of utilities and documentation that implement mail and news functionality on an Amiga computer. The package includes a mail reader, news reader, and batch scheduler. AmigaUUCP is publicly available software; see the newsgroup *comp.sys.amiga.uucp* for more information.

MKS Toolkit (PC)

The well-regarded MKS Toolkit from Mortice Kern Systems provides UNIX utilities for MS-DOS, Windows, Windows 95, Windows NT, and OS/2 environments, thus giving the PC user all the familiar UNIX commands (**sort**, **awk**, **sed**, and so on). It also includes a Korn shell that can replace the standard DOS or OS/2 command interpreter. MKS Toolkit includes UUCP connectivity and a menu-driven UUCP configuration program. It also comes with a version of the UNIX **mailx** utility, and a C News package. MKS Toolkit is a commercial product. For more information, contact Mortice Kern Systems at *toolkit@mks.com* or (800) 265 2797.

UUPC/Extended (PC)

UUPC/Extended is a UUCP package for DOS, Windows, OS/2, Windows NT, or Windows 95. It is published by Kendra Electronic Wonderworks, (617) 279-9812. UUPC/Extended can be downloaded from several anonymous FTP sites, such as *ftp://ftp.clarkson.edu/pub/msdos/uupc*. It includes a mail reader, but not a news reader; however, there are several mail and news readers available that will work with UUPC/Extended. UUPC supports a good number of UUCP protocols, and all but the DOS versions support UUCP over a TCP/IP network.

UUPLAN and THURN (PC)

UUPLAN and THURN are packages that include UUPC/Extended and alternate news/mail readers. You can fetch them from *ftp://risc.ua.edu:/pub/network/pegasus/misc* and *ftp://ftp.wcape.school.za:/pub/msdos/uucp*.

The Pegasus Mail reader, available separately or with UUPLAN, is free software and can also deliver mail on Netware or via SMTP/POP3.

Waffle (PC)

Waffle, by Tom Dell, is not only a BBS, but also a Usenet news and UUCP mail system. It allows an MS-DOS PC to be a Usenet node. Waffle is shareware; that is, trial versions can be downloaded by anonymous FTP from numerous sites, such as *ftp://oak.oakland.edu/SimTel/msdos/waffle* or *ftp://wuarchive.wustl.edu/mirrors/msdos/waffle*.

UUCP for Windows (PC)

UUCP for Windows, by Don Read (*dread@i-link.net*) is a collection of programs that manage an unattended gateway and mail router for Windows 3.1x machines. It includes a dial-only UUCP host, a full SMTP client and server implementation, an MSMail (simple MAPI) interface, and a POP3 Mail retriever.

UUCP for Windows is commercial software. A time-limited version of the package can be downloaded from *ftp://ftp.i-link.net/pub/pc/wuu20.exe*.

UUPC 3.0 (Mac)

UUPC 3.0 is a freeware implementation of UUCP. It includes support for high-speed modems and is known to work with the Eudora mail reader. You should be able to find UUPC 3.0 on a Mac software archive FTP site, such as *ftp://sumex-aim.stanford.edu* or *mac.archive.umich.edu*.

UUCP/Connect (Mac)

Formerly known as "uAccess," this is a commercial product. It provides a point-and-click user interface for setting up the UUCP connection, rather than editing files directly. It also can be used with Eudora. For more information, contact *sales@intercon.com*.

Office Mail Products

These companies sell add-ons for commercial mail products to connect them to UUCP.

TenFour

TenFour Sweden sells a product called TFS Gateway, which provides UUCP and SMTP gateways for Microsoft Mail, Lotus cc:Mail, Lotus Notes, Novell Groupwise, and others. Information about TenFour products is available at http://www.tenfour.com or *http://www.tenfour.se*.

Mimelink

Another Swedish company (Advox) sells a UUCP gateway for Microsoft Mail or Lotus cc:Mail called Mimelink. For more information, you could take a look at *http://www.advox.se*, or send email to *info@advox.se*.

UUCP for VMS

DECUS UUCP is an implementation of UUCP for a DEC Vax system. We mention it here for historical purposes only, since there has been no new development since 1992 and the software does not run on OpenVMS. The package is available at ftp://ftp.uu.net/systems/vms/uucp, and runs under VMS 5.4-x or VMS 5.5.

E

Sendmail and UUCP

Mail and UUCP Overview

Electronic mail is generally handled by two categories of programs:

- *Mail User Agents* (MUAs) are the programs run by users that let them compose outbound email or view incoming email. They are also known as mail client programs. Typical MUAs on a UNIX system are **mail**, **mailx**, **pine**, **elm**, or the suite of commands included with the MH (Mail Handler) package. Some Web browsers also include MUA functionality.

- *Mail Transfer Agents* (MTAs) are the programs that send email from one computer system to another. They do not interact with regular users, except perhaps a system administrator testing or debugging email delivery. They are called by the MUAs to handle the delivery of email created by local users, and run as daemons in the background to process email arriving from another system. The most (in)famous MTA for UNIX is **sendmail**; other MTAs include **smail**[*] and MMDF.[†]

UUCP programs don't fit into these categories. As we explain in the *Preface*, UUCP is only a *transport*: a way that computer data is dragged from one place to another. For electronic mail to travel from one computer to another via UUCP, the MTA on one system must know how to use UUCP to get the data across, and the MTA on the receiving system must get properly invoked in order to read the data and turn it into electronic mail.

---

[*] The *Linux Network Administrator's Guide* (also published by O'Reilly & Associates) has a chapter on setting up **smail**.

[†] The UNIX Email Software Survey FAQ (by Chris Lewis) is posted regularly on *comp.answers* and has an extensive list of electronic mail software available for UNIX systems.

Getting from Here to There

To illustrate how an MTA such as **sendmail** and UUCP work together to transfer email, we'll follow the life of an email message from one UNIX system to another.

An email message begins as a few thoughts in a user's head. The user runs a mail client program, such as **elm**, **pine**, or even the UNIX stalwart **mail**. This program lets the user compose the message and specify the email's destination, subject, and other delivery information. For example:

```
helen@jade: mail joe@feelines.com
Subject: Whatchya know, Joe?
Dear Joe:
    This is a test mail message.  If you don't receive this,
please let me know as soon as possible.
    -- Helen
CONTROL-D
```

When the user finishes the message, the mail client program calls **sendmail**,[*] and feeds the email message to **sendmail** via standard input. Here's a sample invocation:

```
Command line created by mail client:
/usr/lib/sendmail -bm joe@feelines.com

Standard input fed to sendmail:
From: Helen Waite (helen@jade.ora.com)
To: joe@feelines.com
Subject: Whatchya know, Joe?

Dear Joe:
    This is a test message...
```

sendmail receives the message, checks the destination and return addresses, and adds whatever required headers were not supplied by the mail client program (such as the "Date" header with the current date and time, and the "Message-ID" header with a unique string used for tracking the message). Then, it runs the destination of the message through the "rules" in the *sendmail.cf* configuration file, and chooses a "delivery agent" (yet another external program) to send the message on its way. This is when most **sendmail** configuration problems occur: you must tell **sendmail** to select the right delivery agent to route your email correctly.

---

[*] Mail client programs can do nothing with an email message except hand it off to the local mail transfer agent. The commands to do this are usually compiled into the mail client programs.

Once **sendmail** decides to route a message via UUCP, the delivery agent uses the **uux** command, which calls **rmail** on the remote system. The email message is fed to **uux** via standard input, to be used as standard input to **rmail** when executed on the remote system. For example:

```
Command line created by sendmail:
/usr/bin/uux - -r -ahelen@jade.ora.com -gC princecat!rmail (joe@feelines.com)

Standard input fed to uux:
From helen@jade.ora.com Tue Oct  3 01:35:16 1995
Return-Path: helen@jade.ora.com
Received: (from helen@localhost) by jade.ora.com (8.7.8/8.7.8) id BAA00995
        for joe@feelines.com; Tue, 3 Oct 1995 01:35:15 -0400
Date: Tue, 3 Oct 1995 01:35:15 -0400
From: Helen Waite (helen@jade.ora.com)
Message-Id: <199510030535.BAA00995@jade.ora.com>
To: joe@feelines.com
Subject: Whatchya know, Joe?

Dear Joe:
     This is a test message...
```

uux creates a work file and associated data file to execute **rmail** on the remote system (*princecat* in this case); since **sendmail** uses the **uux −r** option by default, the remote system is not called yet. The email will sit in the UUCP spool directory until **uucico** is invoked, presumably from an hourly **cron** table entry. Note that **uux** is invoked with other options to set the grade (priority) of the email, and to specify the user who will receive error notifications if any errors happen further down the line.

When **uucico** runs, it calls the remote system, and transfers the job files. When **uuxqt** is run on the remote system (usually right after the job is transferred), it opens the job files, and runs the **rmail** program with the email message copied from the source system as standard input.

```
Command line created by uux and executed by uuxqt on the remote system:
rmail joe@feelines.com

Standard input fed to rmail:
From helen@jade.ora.com Tue Oct  3 01:35:16 1995
Return-Path: helen@jade.ora.com
Received: (from helen@localhost) by jade.ora.com (8.7.8/8.7.8) id BAA00995
        for joe@feelines.com; Tue, 3 Oct 1995 01:35:15 -0400
Date: Tue, 3 Oct 1995 01:35:15 -0400
From: Helen Waite (helen@jade.ora.com)
Message-Id: <199510030535.BAA00995@jade.ora.com>
To: joe@feelines.com
Subject: Whatchya know, Joe?
```

```
Dear Joe:
      This is a test message...
```

Now the message is in the hands of **rmail**. **rmail** is another one of those programs that doesn't know how to deliver email. It performs a few transformations on the message, such as converting multiple UUCP-style email headers into a single header line to simplify **sendmail** processing, and then calls **sendmail** to deliver the message (the same way **mail** or another mail client invoked **sendmail** in the example above). If **rmail** encounters a problem, it will exit with an error, which should provoke **uuxqt** to send a notification back to the user named in the −a option of the **uux** invocation on the system that sent the email (*jade.ora.com*, in this case).

Finally, when **sendmail** receives the message from **rmail**, it examines the destination, and either delivers it locally (if it is for a local user) or sends it on its merry way (if it is destined for yet another system). Each time a message passes through a system this way, it is called a *hop*. A message can take many hops, over many different kinds of networks and using different kinds of network transports, before it reaches its final destination.

Note that for systems that use MTAs other than **sendmail**, the overall flow of mail and execution of programs is still the same. For example, in a system with **smail** installed as the MTA, both **sendmail** and **rmail** are links to **smail**.

Setting Up sendmail for UUCP Links

The **sendmail** mail transfer agent gets its configuration information from the */etc/sendmail.cf* file. This file has a bad reputation as difficult to edit, because it is written in a uniquely incomprehensible format that is designed for easy parsing by a computer rather than easy understanding by a human. All the ins and outs of a **sendmail** configuration file cannot be explained in this appendix; instead, we'll assume you have some other source of documentation for your version of **sendmail** on hand and we'll focus on the configuration parameters that affect mail transport via UUCP.[*]

To tune a vendor version of **sendmail**, you will need to edit the configuration file directly. The following sections explain what parts of a *sendmail.cf* file need to be altered for UUCP, and your vendor's documentation should fill in any gaps.

---

[*] There are at least two excellent books that explain **sendmail** from top to bottom: one is *sendmail* by Bryan Costales (published by O'Reilly & Associates), another is *Sendmail: Theory and Practice* by Avolio and Vixie, published by Digital Press.

Using Version 8 Template Files

The publicly available version of **sendmail** allows the system administrator to build the *sendmail.cf* file from template files that are compiled into complete configuration files by the **m4** macro processor. In version 8 of **sendmail**, these template files are suffixed with *.mc* (for macro configuration files), and can be found in the *cf* subdirectory of the **sendmail** source distribution. Here's an example of a template file for a UUCP-only site that relays all email to another system via UUCP:

```
include('../m4/cf.m4')
OSTYPE(operating_system_name)
Cwlocalhost local_system_name1 local_system_name2
FEATURE(nodns)
FEATURE(always_add_domain)
MAILER(local)
MAILER(uucp)
MAILER(smtp)
define('SMART_HOST', uucp-dom:my_uucp_relay)
```

The critical portion of this template file is the *SMART_HOST* macro, which expands to instructions telling **sendmail** to relay all email to the host *my_uucp_relay* (here you would put the hostname of the UUCP neighbor who relays your email), using the *uucp-dom* mailer definition. The *uucp-dom* mailer definition tells **sendmail** how to pass email to another system using **uux**.

These templates (usually named with a *.mc* extension, for *m*acro *c*onfiguration) are expanded into **sendmail** configuration files with the **m4** command like this:

```
# m4 mysystem.mc > mysystem.cf
```

And the output of the **m4** run can be copied to */etc/sendmail.cf*.

Editing sendmail.cf

If you need to edit *sendmail.cf* directly, be sure to keep it under source code control or to otherwise save old versions. Try to minimize the changes. For a simple configuration, make sure you change these things:

- Whether all non-local email will be sent out via UUCP, or only for a few particular destinations

- The name of the UUCP neighbor that will relay email

- The command line needed to invoke **uux** to deliver email to the UUCP relay host

Be careful when editing *sendmail.cf*: an erroneous entry can wildly change the behavior of **sendmail**.

Mail routing

For a vendor version of **sendmail**, check the vendor documentation for the preferred way of directing email via UUCP. Most vendors heavily comment the pre-installed */etc/sendmail.cf* file to help you navigate your way through the maze of mail configuration.

If you wish to deliver some email via UUCP and some via another route, such as SMTP over a local network, things get more complicated. You'll need to tell **sendmail** which email addresses go where. This can be done with the database features of **sendmail**, with class macros, or with vendor-specific tricks. For example, some versions of **sendmail** can run the **uuname** command at configuration time to embed the list of UUCP neighbors into the configuration file.

We recommend you use Internet style, or domain-name, addressing whenever possible, so that you can continue to use the same email addresses if you later change your mail delivery configuration or get a direct Internet connection.

Version 8 and IDA **sendmail**—two of the publicly available versions—support a powerful *mailertable* feature, which lets you route email based on the domain name. This would be used if, for example, most of your email went via the Internet, but email to the *feelines.com* domain needed to be redirected to a UUCP link.

UUCP relay host

If all your outbound email is going via UUCP, you can generally change one or two lines in *sendmail.cf* to name the desired relay host. You will also need to specify how to send email to that relay host. In **sendmail** version 8, these are done like this:

```
# Smart host to relay all non-local mail
DSuucp-dom:nexus
```

The UUCP neighbor *nexus* is defined as the "smart host" that knows how to deliver email destined for remote places.

UUCP Mailer Definition

The **sendmail** configuration file */etc/sendmail.cf* contains various mailer definitions that tell **sendmail** how to invoke an external program to route email. We'll analyze a typical mailer definition found in **sendmail** version 8:

```
# domain-ized UUCP mailer
Muucp-dom,        P=/usr/bin/uux, F=mDFMhu, S=52/31, R=21, M=200000,
                  A=uux - -r -a$f -gC $h!rmail ($u)
```

This alphabet soup tells **sendmail** how to build a **uux** command line to send email. The *$* symbol indicates a macro, which gets expanded in the command line similarly to the way a command shell or **make** expands variables. These are the **sendmail** macros used here:

```
$f   "from" or sender of email
$u   "to" or destination of email
$h   "host" chosen to relay the email
```

sendmail parses the sender and recipient of the letter, and from the recipient's address, calculates which mailer (and mail relay host, or UUCP relay host in this case) to use. The resulting invocation of **uux** might look like this:

```
/usr/bin/uux - -r -asender@here.com -gC relay_host!rmail (receiver@there.com)
```

Note that parentheses are used around the destination address to prevent **uux** from interpreting the destination argument as a remote filename. This could happen when sending to bang-path addresses like *raspi!gnobmon*.

You can customize this definition if desired; for example, if you want UUCP to try and deliver the email immediately, rather than queue up email for later delivery, you can remove the *–r* option in the *A=* definition.

Inbound Email

The big catch with configuring inbound email via UUCP is that you don't have much control over it; it's in the hands (metaphorically speaking) of the "well-connected" computer that acts as your mail relay. The best way is to get an official Internet domain name registered, with an MX record (mail forwarding entry in the world-wide Domain Name Service) pointing at your mail relay host for your local site. If you are dealing with an Internet Service Provider (ISP), this is usually part of their service. The ISP will also configure their MTA to route email for your domain name over your UUCP link, and your MTA must be configured to recognize that this email is to be delivered at your local site. The latter feature is controlled by the *Cw* line in */etc/sendmail.cf* like this:

```
Cwlocalhost tabby tabby.feelines.com feelines.com
```

This entry lists the names used by your local system. You should list all possible variations of your local hostname, including your UUCP nodename, your fully qualified domain name, and any domain names under which you receive email (like *feelines.com* in the preceding example).

Sendmail Tips and Troubleshooting

Here are a few tips for setting up and diagnosing problems with your **sendmail** configuration:

- The default maximum message size for email sent out on a UUCP link is a bit on the low side: a mere 100,000 bytes. This is easily updated by changing the *M=* field in the desired UUCP mailer definition.

- Use domain-name (*user@domain*) addressing whenever possible; the old-style "bang-path" (*system!user*) is more difficult to set up and will make it harder for people to send email to you.

- If you get this error:

  ```
  NOQUEUE: SYSERR(root): My host name (xxxx) does not seem to exist!
  ```

  you have a name services problem. Your **sendmail** configuration wants to look up your local host name, but it is not defined anywhere. If you are on a TCP/IP network, you need to fix whatever's wrong with your */etc/resolv.conf* or */etc/hosts* files. But, if you are not on a TCP/IP network, or use TCP/IP only for dynamic dial-up connections, one easy fix is to add a dummy entry in */etc/hosts* like this:

  ```
  # dummy entry to keep sendmail happy
  10.10.10.10    your_hostname_here
  ```

- To tell how **sendmail** will try to deliver a message without actually sending one, try this:

  ```
  $ sendmail -bv user@destination
  ```

And to test out changes on a new *.cf* file without updating */etc/sendmail.cf*, try this:

```
# sendmail -Ctestfile.cf -oQ/tmp -bv user@destination
```

- When investigating **sendmail** problems, make sure the *syslog* messages sent by **sendmail** are being sent somewhere. Check the file */etc/syslog.conf* to see where messages are going, and run **tail −f** in another window—or in the background—on the log file so that you'll see new messages appear when they are sent.

- After changing */etc/sendmail.cf*, if **sendmail** is running as a background daemon, you must stop and restart it before it will notice the changes. In addition, older versions of **sendmail** use static, pre-compiled configuration files that must be recreated with **sendmail −bz**.

News and UUCP

Once the only game in town for transferring Usenet news, UUCP is still used for newsfeeds via dial-up links and sometimes even over TCP/IP networks. This appendix provides a general overview of how news software works with UUCP, and touches upon the UUCP-specific portions of C news and INN, two common news packages for UNIX systems.

How UUCP Feeds Work

Newsfeeds over UUCP are made possible by the **rnews** command, which receives articles from a remote site and feeds them into the local news spool. The standard input to **rnews** is a *compressed batch* file,[*] which contains one or more articles run through the **compress** command to save space during the file transfer.

Articles travel from one Usenet node to another via the following steps:

- The news system keeps a running list of articles that will be sent to the neighboring system.

- At regular intervals, usually via a **cron** entry), a batching program runs. This batching program takes the list of articles and uses it to create a compressed batch file.

---

[*] Actually, compression is optional, but almost always preferable. One possible exception is when using older modems with the MNP5 compression algorithm; sending compressed files over those links could reduce throughput. This is not a problem with more recent modems that use the V.42/LAPM compression scheme, which does not waste extra time trying to compress already-compressed data.

- The batching program invokes **uux**, which requests that **rnews** be run on the remote system with the compressed batch file as standard input. **uux** is usually invoked with the **−r** option, which means that the jobs will wait until **uucico** is started.

- **uucico** transfers the UUCP jobs to the remote system, where **rnews** is executed. **rnews** receives the compressed batch file on its standard input, separates and uncompresses the articles, and inserts the articles into the local news spool (perhaps with the help of another command, such as **inews** or **relaynews**).

UUCP Newsfeeds Over TCP/IP

In some situations, it may be preferable to use UUCP for newsfeeds on a TCP/IP network. The standard method for feeding news over TCP/IP—known as Network News Transfer Protocol (NNTP)—was designed for interactive links and can be extremely inefficient on a connection with long turnaround times, such as a satellite link. Since UUCP is always willing to wait until the dial-up network connection is available, UUCP newsfeeds also perform well with systems that use dial-up PPP or SLIP to connect to the Internet.

To use UUCP over TCP/IP with a news package, first make sure that you've got TCP/IP properly set up, then test your UUCP links. If they work as expected, follow the news package's instructions for setting up UUCP feeds. Your news software does not know or care that your UUCP transfers are happening over a network link.

Setting Up C News

The C news package keeps most of its configuration files in the */usr/lib/news* directory. For example:

- */usr/lib/news/sys* contains the list of newsfeeds. The *flags* field in the newsfeed entry is usually **f** for a compressed batch feed. The *cmds* field can be left blank, since invoking **uux** is the default.

- */usr/lib/news/bin/batch/sendbatches* is the C news batching program. It must be run from **cron** at regular intervals to create the batch files and to run **uux**.

- */usr/lib/news/batchparms* controls the maximum size of the batches and other parameters, such as the maximum number of outstanding batches permitted. The latter is detected via the **queuelen** script, which may have to be changed for a Taylor UUCP spool directory.

- Batching errors are written to */usr/lib/news/batchlog*. You may want to check this file if you are experiencing feed problems.

Setting Up INN

INN supplies a sample **send-uucp** script that calls the **batcher** program to create UUCP news batches. If desired, C News-style batching can be added with a package written by Christophe Wolfhugel, available at *ftp://ftp.univ-lyon1.fr/pub/unix/news/inn/contrib*.

Newsfeed Tips

- On a newsfeed with heavy traffic in both directions, you will benefit greatly from using the bidirectional Taylor *i* protocol. This feature has made Taylor UUCP very popular with ISPs.

- The site you are feeding must allow your system to run the **rnews** command to insert your articles into its spool. Likewise, your site must permit **rnews** to be run by any site that provides you with a newsfeed.

- The worst thing that can go wrong with a UUCP newsfeed is that a remote site cannot be contacted, and your UUCP spool directory fills up with articles queued for that site. If your news spool and UUCP spool are on the same partition, all news processing will grind to a halt. Most news packages have mechanisms to test for full spool directories, but you will have to test them to make sure they work with your particular system.

- The *Linux Network Administrator's Guide* by Olaf Kirch, published by O'Reilly & Associates, has a chapter on setting up C News. An electronic version is also available from the Linux Documentation Project.

G

The UUCP Mapping Project

This appendix was contributed by Stan Barber, the manager of the UUCP Mapping Project. He can be reached at *uucpmap@academ.com*, or *academ!uucpmap*. The UUCP Mapping Project started in the early 1980s as a means to facilitate the exchange of electronic mail among sites using UNIX. With the evolution of the Internet into mainstream use in various parts of the world, the use of UUCP for this purpose has diminished; however, in developing areas, UUCP still remains an inexpensive way for machines and their users to communicate with each other.

How Does It Work?

Each site that actively participates in the Mapping Project must submit a map containing connectivity information about that site. Details on creating the map are in the next section. These maps are compiled by volunteers in various regions of the world. These volunteers, called regional coordinators, devote time to settling UUCP host name conflicts, providing pointers to relevant mapping information, and maintaining map files—all in the hopes of producing as accurate a database of mapping information as time permits. The coordinators forward these maps to a central site, which maintains the master database. The entire contents of this database are then posted on a monthly basis to the Usenet newsgroup *comp.mail.maps* as well as archived at various locations around the world.

Sites that want to make use of the database extract the database files from the postings in *comp.mail.maps* or acquire the files from archive sites around the world. The files are then fed to a program—like **pathalias**—that builds a custom list of pathways from the site using the database to all other sites in the database. This pathways information is then used by mail transport programs—like **sendmail** or **smail**—to determine how to get mail from the site using the database to the mail recipient's site using successive UUCP transfers through all sites in the path.

How to Build the Map

The map is a plain text file with a specific format. It consists of two parts: the first part is for general information about the site, and the second part contains the connectivity information.

The first part contains information about the site being registered. There are a number of fields. Each field is one line. No continuation lines are permitted. This is generic form of these fields:

```
#<field id letter><tab><field data>
```

#N System Name — REQUIRED

The first field of each map begins with "#N" and is called the name field. In this field, the UUCP name of the computer is recorded. This is typically the output from executing the command **uuname –l**. Alternate names for this machine may be appended to this field as well. Each of these alternate names (like an Internet domain name) must follow the UUCP name and multiple entries must be separated by commas. All names must be lower case. All names must only contain ASCII letters and numbers. Dashes may also be used as long as the first letter in the name is not a dash. Periods may be used as long as the resulting name is a legitimate Internet hostname. The first entry in the name field must not exceed fourteen characters.

#F Internet Forwarder — OPTIONAL

The next field is optional. It is called the forwarder field and is used to designate what site on the Internet services this UUCP host as an MX forwarder. This field begins with "#F" and all data for this field must be fully qualified Internet domain names. Multiple entries may be entered and must be separated by commas.

#S System Hardware; System Software — OPTIONAL

The next field defines the hardware and software run at this site. This field begins with "#S." Any descriptive text for the hardware and software is acceptable. The description of the hardware is separated from the description of the software by a semi-colon. This field is optional.

#O Organization Name — REQUIRED

The organization name is the next field and it begins with "#O." This field is required. If the machine is personal, the phrase "Personal System" should be put here.

#C Contact(s) — REQUIRED

The character sequence "#C" begins the contact name field. This required field contains the name of the person(s) who should be contacted about questions concerning this map entry. Multiple persons may be listed and each name must be separated by commas.

#E Contact(s) Email address(es) — REQUIRED

The electronic mail address(es) for reaching the contact person(s) is the next field. Each address should either be specified in Internet RFC-822 style, or by using the UUCP mail format of "system-name!userid." When using this UUCP mail format, only one system name should be specified. Multiple addresses may be specified, and must be separated by commas. This field begins with "#E" and is required. Please note that generic addresses are suggested where appropriate.

#T Contact(s) Telephone Number(s) — OPTIONAL

The next field is the voice telephone number(s) for reaching the contact person(s). The field begins with "#T"; this is the format for the phone numbers:

```
+<country code><space><area code><space><prefix><space><number>
```

Multiple numbers may be listed and each number must be separated by commas. This field is optional, but use is strongly encouraged.

#P Postal Address — REQUIRED

The next field is required. It begins with "#P," and contains the postal address at which the organization receives postal mail. The address should be put on one line with the various components separated by commas. This address in combination with the organization name and the contact name(s) should make it possible to get postal mail to the contact(s).

#L Location — OPTIONAL

The Latitude and Longitude denoting the location of the system is specified in the next optional field. This field begins with a "#L" and the format of the rest of the line is: MM [SS] "N"|"S" / DDD MM [SS] "E"|"W" ["city"]. There are two fields, with optional third. The first number is Latitude in degrees (NN), minutes (MM), and seconds (SS), and a N or S to indicate North or South of the Equator. Then, there is a slash that serves as a separator. The second number is Longitude in degrees (DDD), minutes (MM), and seconds (SS), and a E or W to indicate East or West of the Prime Meridian in Greenwich, England. Note that seconds are optional, but the more accurate it is, the more accurate the maps can be of the network (including blow-ups of various high density areas, like New Jersey, or the San Francisco Bay Area).

#R Remarks — OPTIONAL

The next field is for remarks. It starts with "#R" and is optional. This field may be repeated multiple times if required.

#U Usenet Peers — OPTIONAL

Another optional field beginning with "#U" follows. In this line, other sites that exchange Usenet news via—UUCP or NNTP—with this site are listed. Where possible, the UUCP name should be used, or else the Internet domain name. Each name should be separated by a comma.

#W Last modified — REQUIRED

The final field starts with "#W" and is required. This field indicates who last modified this map file and when this modification was last performed. This field should contain an email address, a name in parentheses, followed by a semi-colon, and the output of the UNIX "date" program. The rules for creating the email address are the same as those discussed in the section on the "#E" field.

Connectivity Information — REQUIRED

Connectivity information is listed next. The format consists of the system name (the first entry from the #N field), followed by a tab character, followed by one or more peering system names with associated information on polling intervals. This is the format of this peering information:

```
system-name(polling-interval)
```

When more than one entry is made, a comma must separate each entry. The peering system-name may be enclosed by angle brackets to indicate that it does not forward email via UUCP. The polling-interval may consist of any of the following values:

```
Symbolic Name    Value    Comment
    LOCAL          25      local area network
    DEDICATED      95      high speed dedicated
    DIRECT        200      local call
    DEMAND        300      normal call (long distance, anytime)
    HOURLY        500      hourly poll
    EVENING      1800      time restricted call
    DAILY        5000      daily poll
    WEEKLY      30000      irregular poll
```

To obtain the name of the peering systems, output from executing the command "uuname," or the first field from the L.sys or Systems file may be used. Typically these peering systems would have a value of "DIRECT" if they can be called without incurring long distance charges, and "DEMAND" otherwise. Systems accessed via UUCP over the Internet should have a value of "DEDICATED."

Continuation lines that begin with a tab character may be used. The end of the previous line must be a comma. Numeric values should not be used for the polling-interval information.

Where to Send the Map

Once the map is built, it should be sent to the UUCP Mapping Project. The easiest way to do this is to send email to *uucpmap@academ.com* on the Internet. It will be forwarded to the appropriate regional coordinator.

When to Change the Map

The map should be updated anytime any information changes. Basically, this outline should be followed to regenerate the map with the new information and the new map should be emailed to the "Project."

How to Delete a Map Entry

If a site no longer wants to participate in the project, it is important to insure that the peers have been informed of this. Those peers should update their maps to remove reference to the site leaving the project. An email message to the "Project" requesting that a map be deleted should be sent by one of the map contacts to finish this process.

Copyright Statement

This Appendix is Copyright 1996, by Stan Barber. All Rights Reserved. Reproduction with Attribution granted, as long as the preceding copyright statement is reproduced in full.

In this appendix:
- *The comp.sources*
  Archives

UUCP Management Tools

The comp.sources Archives

There are a number of potentially interesting sources available in the *comp.sources.unix* and *comp.sources.misc* archives. We haven't tested them, but thought we should at least list them so you can explore on your own. These files are fairly old; most new work on UUCP is centered around Taylor UUCP, such as the management scripts included with the Taylor source package.

These files can be retrieved via anonymous FTP from numerous sites, such as *ftp.uu.net*, *plaza.aarnet.edu.au*, *ftp.cs.umn.edu*, and many others.

The descriptions given in Tables H–1 and H–2 are brief and often uninformative, but they are all that is provided in the summary listings of the archive. If you are interested in more information, however, simply retrieve the file in question.

To obtain any of these sources, use anonymous **ftp** to *ftp.uu.net* or a similar site that archives *comp.sources.misc*. The full pathname will usually begin with either *usenet/comp.sources.unix* or *usenet/comp.sources.misc*. The volume number shown in the table will be the second element of the pathname, and the filename itself the final element (unless the final component is itself a directory name). For example, you would find *uuencode* in the file *usenet/comp.sources.unix/volume7/uuencode*.

Table H–1: UUCP-Related Programs in comp.sources.unix

Volume	Program	Description
volume1	uucpanz.s5 uucpanz.v7 uuquei	uucpanz for System V. Another UUCP status program: uucpanz. A uuwizard's utility for UUCP queue snooping.
volume2	uuhosts	uuhosts (updated).
volume3	times.awk uuhosts2 uuhosts3 uuhosts4 uumail uumail2 uumail2.fix	UUCP info from LOGFILE (awk script). Newer uuhosts (too many changes for diff listings). uuhosts uuhosts 1.69 An opath/pathalias based UUCP mailer. uumail release 2. Fix to uumail release 2.
volume4	uumail3/part[1-2].	uumail 3.0
volume5	getmaps	Automated UUCP maps.
volume6	s3uuque	uuque for System III/V in C.
volume7	paths.mk uucp+nuz.tulz uuencode	Makefile to build UUCP paths. Erik Fair's UUCP & Usenet toolbox. Uuencode and uudecode.
volume8	uucp.x25pad uumail4/part[01-04] uutty/part[01-02]	UUCP X.25 f protocol and PAD dialer. Uumail release 4.2. Bidirectional getty/login for System V.
volume9	uumail.pch	Uumail 4.X patch.
volume15	ultrix-modem uumailclean	UUCP/CU access on one modem. Clean-up backlogged UUCP mail.

Table H–2: UUCP-Related programs in comp.sources.misc

Volume, Period	Program	Description
volume3 (1 January 88 - 20 April 88)	uuxqt-hack	A quick uuxqt fix for compressed news.
volume3 (24 April 88 - 19 July 88)	pcmail/part[01-08] pcmail/patch1	UUCP mail for PC's. UUCP mail for PC's: minor patch.
volume5 (22 October 88 - 29 December 88)	xenix-poll	Script to poll other UUCP sites.
volume6 (18 January 89 - 22 May 89)	findpath.sh uupoll	UUCP Pathfinder v1.1 Uupoll.
volume9 (4 November 89 - 6 January 90)	umdb/part[01-02] uustatus	UUCP Map Database. curses-oriented uustat (sort of).
volume15 (October 90- 18 December 90)	getty_ps/part[01-05]	Enhanced SYSV Getty/Uugetty, Ver 2.0.
volume26	uutraf/part0[1-4]	UUCP Traffic Analysis & Reporting (August 1992)

I

Setting Up a Modem

Modems have changed radically over the years since the first UUCP software was written. Originally "dumb" boxes that could not even dial the phone without assistance, now they can accept commands via their serial ports, perform data compression, error correction, baud rate conversion, or handle fax and even voice mail. This appendix takes a brief look at how to set up a modem so that it works with UUCP instead of against it.

Modem Innards

At first glance, all modems seem to be alike—just about every modern modem uses a command interface patterned after the Hayes Smartmodem.[*] But no two modems from different manufacturers are exactly alike; although they accept the same commands for the basic operations of a modem such as dialing and answering the phone, they often diverge in other functions like data compression, flow control, and their fax and voice capabilities.

The "standard" modem has two modes: *command* mode and *data* mode. When first turned on, a modem is in command mode, and it waits for either commands on its serial port or an incoming call. All commands begin with the letters **AT** (for "ATtention!") and end with a carriage return (character value 13). When the modem connects to a remote modem, it switches into data mode. At this point, the modem's serial port becomes a conduit for data to and from the remote modem and the computer attached to the remote modem.

---

[*] Smartmodem is a trademark of Hayes Microcomputer Products, Inc.

The modem's software environment is composed of settings, either in *registers*—locations in the modem's memory with pre-defined meanings for the values placed in them—or in modes toggled by different commands. The contents of registers can be listed out with the ATS*nnn?* command; *nnn* is a number from zero to whatever the modem manufacturer decides is the highest register number. Registers usually contain numbers that directly affect the modem's behavior. For example, register S0 is the number of rings before the modem automatically answers a call (if set to zero, the modem never answers); register S7 contains the number of seconds the modem will wait to hear the remote carrier after dialing a phone number (the default is usually 45 seconds).

The modem can save a subset of its registers and command settings into nonvolatile memory, so that it will be in a known state upon the next power-up. The usual command for saving the modem's current state is **AT&W**.

Even when the modem is in data mode, you can still send it commands: the *escape sequence* **+++** (three plus signs) will toggle the modem back into command mode. You can then issue commands to dump out registers, change a few settings, hang up, or return to data mode. To prevent the escape sequence from being triggered accidentally, most modems will recognize the escape sequence only when there is a short pause before and after it. The escape character can be changed or turned off entirely, by setting register S2 to a value above 127.

In addition to their software settings, some modems have toggle switches for controlling the power-up state, and a few have external switches that let you change the modem's configuration whenever you feel like pushing a button.

Talking to the Modem

Once you've connected a modem to your computer (as described in Chapter 9, *The Physical Connection*), you need to go over its configuration and set it up for UUCP calls. The factory default settings are almost always wrong for UUCP use, since the modem manufacturers aim their sales at personal computer owners, the IBM PC-compatible, or Apple software market.

High-Speed and Higher Speed

No matter how fast your high-speed modem is, your computer should be faster. High-speed modems get some of their speed via data compression: the remote modem compresses a block of data before sending it over the phone line, and the local modem uncompresses it before sending it over the serial port to your computer.[*] In order to gain any advantage from this scheme, your computer must be talking to the modem at a higher baud rate than the maximum modem-to-modem transmission rate. Since the modem can reduce the size of data in transit by as much as 50 percent, your computer should communicate with the modem at a baud rate at least twice the modem's transmission rate. This means setting your serial port baud rate to 4800 for a 2400-bps compressing modem, 19200 for a 9600-bps compressing modem,[†] 38400 for a 14400-bps modem, 57600 (or 115200, if possible) for a 28800-bps modem, and so on. Note that above 9600 bps, the modem data rates no longer match serial port rates.

Unfortunately, some versions of UNIX—or the hardware they run on—are not capable of the higher baud rates. In this case, use the fastest baud rate your system is capable of (or upgrade it!). Sometimes, the system is fine, but the application software is unable to use the higher baud rates because the developer did not know the system supported them, or the program was written for an older system. In Linux, the **setserial** command, by meddling with the serial port driver, can trick these programs into running at unsupported speeds like 57600 or 115200 bps.

Once you've chosen the baud rate with which you will talk to the modem, you generally don't have to bother configuring your system to support lower rates. All high-speed modems can convert the baud rate of an incoming call to whatever rate you've set the serial port (as long as the serial port speed is the same or faster than the modem connect speed).

You must have some form of flow control enabled to use high-speed modems this way. We recommend using hardware flow control, but if that is not possible, you may be able to use XON/XOFF flow control with the right UUCP protocol (as described in Appendix J, *UUCP Protocol Internals*).

---

[*] Your modem has data compression if it supports V.42bis and/or MNP Class 5.

[†] Some 2400-bps modems and most, but not all, 9600-bps modems support data compression. Modems 14400 bps and up almost always support data compression, but beware of "software compression" on some low-end modems that requires the host computer to run special software in order to use compression. These schemes do not work on UNIX systems.

Configuring the Modem

To configure a modem, you need to start a communications session with a program like **cu**, **tip**, **kermit**, **seyon**, or any other communications package. It may be difficult on some systems to connect with **cu** or **tip** because they may demand that carrier (the DCD signal) be present before connecting. This is usually fixable with the right command-line options; if not, use another communications package or bring the modem to a friendly personal computer for configuration (the ubiquitous Microsoft Windows contains a terminal program that works fine for configuring modems).

Modem configuration is less of an issue if you only make outgoing calls, because you can place any needed configuration commands in the modem dialing database file (BNU *Dialers* or Taylor UUCP *dial*). But for incoming or bidirectional lines, the modem's behavior should be planned in advance, and saved in the modem's nonvolatile memory so that it always powers up in the right state.

By default, modems will send responses whenever something happens (i.e., "RING" when the phone rings or "CONNECT" when a call is successfully answered). These messages play havoc with the standard UNIX **getty** command that handles incoming calls on serial ports; they think the modem's messages are those of a user calling in, and they'll echo the data back to the modem. The modem thinks the echoed data is a command to abort the incoming call, so it hangs up the line. As a result, no one can ever call in.

To work around this problem, you can set the modem to turn responses off by using the **ATQ1** command, for "quiet mode". But when the modem is used for an outgoing call, you want responses turned on so that you can see the results of your dialing commands. This will sabotage any future incoming calls, unless the user or program remembers to restore the modem to its original state.[*]

One solution to this dilemma is to use the modem's ability to reset itself between calls. This feature is usually turned on with the **AT&D3** command. When enabled, the modem hangs up and resets itself to its power-up state whenever DTR is dropped by the computer. On a properly set up computer, with the correct cable to the modem, DTR will be de-asserted whenever a program finishes using a serial port.

---

[*] The **complete-chat** and **abort-chat** commands in Taylor UUCP (see Chapter 10, *Setting Up a UUCP Link*) can do just that for you; these work well, unless one of the UUCP programs crashes while using the modem.

Another solution is to use a modem-aware version of **getty**, in particular **mgetty**. **mgetty** understands modem responses like "RING" or "CONNECT," and detects whether the incoming call is for a regular login, fax, or UUCP. We like the idea of software that understands modern modems, rather than forcing them to act like the outdated modems expected by the UNIX **getty** program. To obtain **mgetty**, see Appendix L, *Other Resources*.

Modem Power-up Settings

Here are the most common parameters you need to set on a modem that will be used for UUCP calls:

- Flow control—if your computer supports RTS/CTS flow control, set the modem to use it as well (usually **AT&K3**). Otherwise, set the modem to use no flow control; you must always use a serial port rate equal to the modem connection rate. RTS/CTS flow control is usually the default setting for high-speed modems.

- DCD—assert DCD only when connected to a remote modem (**AT&C1**). The default setting is usually **AT&C0**, which means that the modem will "lie" about carrier and always give the DCD signal to the computer.

- DTR—hang up any active connection—and preferably, reset the entire modem—when DTR is de-asserted (**AT&D3**).

- Responses—do not send responses to commands and do not send the "RING" message when the line is ringing (**ATQ1**).

- Baud rate—if you have RTS/CTS flow control, have the modem always use its highest possible speed on the serial port regardless of the speed the modem-to-modem session is using.

- Auto answer—for a modem that will be accepting incoming calls, you need to enable auto answer mode (**ATS0=1**).

- Escape sequence—Switching back to command mode while online is a convenience for people, but it will immediately sink a UUCP session if this feature is accidentally triggered. You can disable the escape sequence with **ATS2=255**.

- Echo—when in command mode, do not echo commands (**ATE0**). The modem's command echo, meant for human beings, sometimes confuses computer programs.

- Incoming baud rate—some modems have a register setting for the default baud rate they use to communicate with the host computer on an incoming call, others use the same baud rate last used by the computer on an outgoing connection. Usually, this is not a problem, but on some systems you may need to send modem commands at boot time, or regular intervals thereafter, to remind the modem of the baud rate it should use. This can be done with the **kermit** or **chat** commands, among others. (See Appendix H, *UUCP Management Tools*.)

After you have set up the modem to your satisfaction, review the configuration with the modem's status reporting command (usually **AT&V**). Then, save the configuration (with **AT&W**).

Dialing Out

Since the desired modem settings for outgoing calls aren't quite the same as those needed for incoming calls, you should set the modem's parameters as part of the chat script that dials the modem. A typical chat script supplied with BNU UUCP for dialing a Hayes-compatible modem looks like this:

```
""   \dA\pTE1V1X1Q0S2=255S12=255\r\c OK\r \EATDT\T\r\c CONNECT
```

Before dialing, the chat script tries to wake up the modem and change its configuration with one long burst of modem commands. Here are some of those commands:

A\pT   Inserts a short pause between the **A** and the **T**, probably to support a few slow or buggy modems that might otherwise miss the attention sequence. The pause is superfluous with modern modems, but it doesn't hurt. The start of all Hayes-compatible modem commands must begin with **AT**.

E1   Turns on command echo. This dialing script will use echo checking when sending the phone number (the \E chat escape).

V1   Turns on word responses. The responses are in English words, since that's what this chat script expects the modem to send. This is done in case the modem is set for numeric response codes (**V0**).

X1   Limits the set of status messages the modem will use. Unfortunately, this turns off some useful response messages like "BUSY" or "NO DIALTONE," but it keeps out messages that might confuse the chat script—in particular, the "RINGING" message that some modems send when they "hear" the tone signal that represents a phone ringing on the other side. You may prefer to use **X4** if you want your modem to report some of the extra responses.

QO   Turns off "quiet mode" so that the modem will respond to
          UUCP's dialing commands.

S2=255

S12=255 Turns off the modem escape sequences. S2 is the register that
          stores the escape character; setting it to anything above 127 dis-
          ables escaping back to command mode. For good measure, the
          script also sets S12: the number of 1/50th-second increments the
          modem should wait after receiving the escape sequence before
          going into command mode. Any data received in the interim
          aborts the escape. Setting S12 to the maximum should also dis-
          able the escape sequence.[*]

Modems with UUCP Support

A few modem manufacturers, notably Telebit Corporation, offer modems
with built-in support for the UUCP protocol. These modems "spoof" the host
computers to which they are attached. The modems acknowledge *g* protocol
packets locally, and use a different modem-to-modem protocol to ship the
data across the link. This saves on packet turnaround times, and can substantially speed up the throughput of a UUCP session. In the days before
simple Internet access, Telebit modems were quite popular with UUCP
users, especially for Usenet feeds.

To use a spoofing modem, you will need to turn on the UUCP protocol support when you dial out. On a Telebit Trailblazer Plus, for example, this is
done by sending the command **ATS111=30** (set register S111 to 30). If you
are answering calls with a Trailblazer Plus, set register S111 to 255; this lets
the originating modem decide in the protocol to use. You must have UUCP-
spoofing modems on both sides of the link for this feature to work.

Although UUCP-aware modems were a good idea when they came out, they
have been superseded by recent improvements to UUCP software. The Taylor *i* protocol or the SVR4 *G* protocol, for example, make much more efficient use of a high-speed modem link.

---

[*] Some modems do not support S12, since they must pay a license fee to Hayes, who has
patented the escape character guard time feature.

Fine-Tuning the Modem

Special conditions may require close attention to some of your modem's more obscure configuration parameters. For example:

• When calling hosts that take a long time to answer, you may need to have the modem wait longer for a response. You can do this by using register S7, or just put extra commas after the phone number. In extreme cases, you may need to convince UUCP to wait longer as well—use the appropriate escapes in the chat script, such as the Taylor \W escape, or with extra \d send strings after the phone number.

• On noisy or low-quality phone lines, it may be helpful to tune the modem configuration to use shorter packets in its internal protocols (AT\A0 for modems that use MNP Class 5). Check your modem's documentation to see what protocol tuning commands it supports.

• If you spend lots of money on international phone calls, check your modem's documentation to see if it supports an inactivity timeout. When supported, this feature will hang up the phone line if neither side sends data for more than a preset interval (5 minutes should be more than enough). This will prevent an expensive phone bill if the host computer somehow forgets to hang up the connection.

• Another way to keep the phone bill down on large file transfers is to avoid connecting at a slow baud rate. Most modems will valiantly attempt to communicate at the highest speed possible, even if it is only 2400 bps. To keep from getting caught with a slow link, you can configure the modem to hang up if it cannot connect at a minimum speed. The AT+MS command on many high-speed modems lets you configure the minimum and maximum connection rates the modem will use. Other modems also support this feature, although the exact command may vary.

• If you find you are setting a lot of modem parameters at dial-out, it may be simpler to use the AT&F command to load a "factory" configuration that is close to your desired settings. Some modems support multiple factory defaults, selectable via AT&F1, AT&F2, etc. Many modems have multiple profile support also. This allows you to save the power-up modem settings in profile 0 (AT&W0), the dial-out settings in profile 1 (AT&W1), and load in profile 1 when dialing out via the chat script (with ATZ1).

- You can speed up a modem's dialing by changing the S11 register, which controls the duration of the dialing tones for each digit. Modern telephone exchanges will happily accept 50 millisecond tones (ATS11=50), although older equipment will balk at this speed.

- If you use the same phone line for incoming and outgoing calls, set ATS0=0 as part of your dial-out commands. This will prevent the modem from answering the line if a call should come in while a program is attempting to use the modem for an outgoing call.

- Some modems issue the "CONNECT" message before they are really ready; if they receive data within the first second or two after issuing the "CONNECT" message, they get confused and hang up. If this happens to you, put an extra \d delay at the end of the chat script for that modem.

- If your modem does not support automatic initialization when DTR is dropped (AT&D3), there is a workaround: use either the Taylor UUCP **complete-chat** and **abort-chat** commands to reset the modem whenever **cu** or **uucico** finish using them, or have a **cron** entry that sends a reset (ATZ) command to the modem. This batch job would need to run every few minutes, and to exit gracefully if the modem is in use. You should be able to do it with either **kermit** or the specialized **chat** command described in Appendix H, *UUCP Management Tools*.

- A few enlightened modem manufacturers include a setting for systems that have difficulty using a serial port without Carrier Detect. This setting, when available, keeps Carrier Detect asserted except when an active connection hangs up. Then, the modem de-asserts Carrier for a few seconds before raising it back up again. This allows you to use modem control on systems that would otherwise refuse to dial the modem without first seeing Carrier Detect.

Internal versus External

Internal modems are a popular option for IBM PC-compatible computers, mostly due to their lower price. However, they have their disadvantages that may not be worth the initial cost savings.

Internal modems have the following attributes:

- They are generally less expensive than external modems.
- They cannot get knocked off the desk by your cat.

- They have no serial cables or power cord to worry about since the modem cord connects directly to the PC's ISA bus.

- High-speed internal modems come with a built-in NS 16550A (or compatible) serial port. This is a big cost saver, and a convenience on older PC's that have less capable 8250 ports. To use an external modem on these machines, you'd also have to buy a high-speed serial I/O card.

External modems have these qualities:

- They have status lights: you can see the states of modem control signals when data is being transferred. This helps when debugging a link.

- They can be used on any computer, not just IBM PC-compatibles with ISA slots.

- They can be replaced or upgraded without opening up your computer.

- They have a power switch: the modem can be turned on and off without affecting the host system. And, you can save electricity on those rare occasions when you use your computer without going online.

We recommend using external modems when running UNIX on an IBM PC-compatible computer. But, there's nothing wrong with buying an internal modem when it's appropriate. If a PC that has the old, slow serial ports or if your desk has no more space for computer accessories it may be a good idea to purchase an internal modem.

J

UUCP Protocol Internals

The first versions of UUCP, designed for use over noisy, low-speed phone lines, used UUCP's native *g* protocol. Although the *g* protocol specification allows for flexible packet sizes and transmit windows, most implementations supported only small 64-byte packets and a three-packet window size. On high-speed or reliable links, these limitations waste much of a communication line's bandwidth.

Over the years, newer protocols have been defined and added to the different versions of UUCP. These protocols were often created for specific communications technologies that would not work effectively with the *g* protocol, such as X.25 PAD links or TCP/IP network connections. Taylor UUCP introduced the *i* protocol, which is specifically designed to address the problems of older UUCP protocols; as a result, it out-performs all of its predecessors.

Selecting a Protocol

The first step in choosing a protocol is finding out which ones are supported by the UUCP software at the two sites that will be communicating. Then, evaluate the characteristics of the link between them:

• *Is the link reliable?* A reliable link has built-in error recovery. Local area network links, including dial-up SLIP or PPP connections, are reliable because the network transport software makes sure all data is delivered without errors. Links between modern modems that use LAPM (V.42) or

MNP error correction are "mostly reliable," as are X.25 network connections.[*]

- *Is it transparent?* A nontransparent link will "eat" or block the passage of certain characters. The most common example is a link that cannot turn off software (XON/XOFF) flow control; the two flow control characters, decimal 17 and 19, are interpreted as commands to hold or resume transmission, rather than being sent as data. Some links, like X.25 PADs or other front-end processors, may clear the high bit of the data bytes, making it impossible to use any character above decimal value 127. And links using the **telnet** or **rlogin** commands may need to screen out the "escape character," if this feature cannot be disabled via command line options.

- *How fast is it?* A high-speed link can afford to use large packet sizes, since it can resend packets quickly. On a low-speed link, unless reliable, you will want to stick to shorter packets, since retransmissions are much more "costly" in terms of communications time.

- *What about the turnaround time?* Turnaround time is the time needed to receive an acknowledgment of a message. Links with a high turnaround time, such as satellite links, will benefit from *sliding window* protocols that send large blocks of data in advance without waiting for acknowledgments.

- *Can the two sides tell when the other is ready to receive data?* If one side sends packets when the other is unable to handle them, they must be discarded, wasting valuable bandwidth. This is essentially another form of flow control, but we'll call it *pacing* in this section to avoid confusing it with XON/XOFF or CTS/RTS flow control. Pacing should be provided by the UUCP communications protocol, unless it knows that there is an underlying layer somewhere that is already performing this service (like the TCP/IP network layer, or an X.25 network).

When setting up a link, you can specify a list of protocols in the preferred order for a particular link. The first available protocol in the list supported by the remote side will be used. For example, in Taylor UUCP the command **protocol itefg** in the *port* or *sys* files asks UUCP to use the *i* protocol if possible, with *t* as a second choice, *e* as a third choice, and so on. In BNU UUCP,

---

[*] Even reliable modem links may see errors on occasion, since they might be introduced via interference on the serial cables between the modems and the computers. Also, a link through an X.25 PAD, although reliable, can suffer a "reset" condition at any time, losing any data in transit.

a comma and a protocol list can be appended to a device type in either the
Devices or *Systems* files. Here's an example in *Devices*:

```
TCP,et - - Any TCP -
```

This example (from a SunOS system) will use the *e* protocol if available,
otherwise the *t* protocol.

You need to specify a protocol list only if you are trying to solve a communications problem that appears to be protocol-related, or if you want to
maximize the utilization of your UUCP links.

UUCP Protocol List

Only a handful of UUCP protocols are needed to support the vast majority
of communications links:[*]

The g Protocol

UUCP's native protocol, the *g* protocol, is a packet based, pacing, error cor-
recting protocol. It requires an eight-bit clean (i.e., completely transparent)
connection. Although branded as inefficient, it is not the protocol that is
wasteful so much as many implementations of it, which support only small
64-byte packet sizes and three-packet window sizes. Unless both sides of
the link are willing to negotiate larger packet and window sizes, the *g* protocol will waste large amounts of bandwidth when used on a high-speed link.
The *g* protocol specification contains a few features not used by UUCP, such
as the ability to renegotiate packet and window sizes during the communications session.

Appendix K, *The UUCP g Protocol*, describes the *g* protocol in detail.

The G (Big G) Protocol

UNIX System V Release 4 uses this protocol, which is essentially the regular
g protocol, but, it has larger packet and window sizes enabled. The choice
of a new protocol letter allows system administrators to easily identify sites
that support the full *g* protocol specification.

---

[*] Much of this section is based on the UUCP protocol descriptions in the Taylor UUCP documentation and the "UUCP Internals Frequently Asked Questions" file distributed on Usenet,
both written by Ian Lance Taylor.

The t Protocol

The *t* protocol is intended for reliable links that guarantee end-to-end data delivery, such as TCP/IP network connections. It requires a completely transparent connection. It does no error checking or pacing, since these functions are presumed to be part of the link connection.

The e Protocol

The *e* protocol is also intended for use over reliable network links, such as TCP/IP. Again, it does no error checking or pacing. (The *e* and *t* protocols originated in the AT&T BNU and BSD branches of UUCP, respectively, hence the overlap. Some newer UUCP versions support both protocols.)

The i Protocol

The *i* protocol was written by Ian Lance Taylor and introduced in Taylor UUCP version 1.04. It requires a completely transparent connection, and performs error checking and pacing. It has sliding windows, allows files to be sent in both directions simultaneously. It is ideal for high-speed links, since it uses large window sizes and permits data to be exchanged in both directions simultaneously; this essentially doubles throughput on a UUCP link with heavy traffic in both directions.

The j Protocol

The *j* protocol is a variant of the *i* protocol, also written by Ian Lance Taylor and introduced in Taylor UUCP version 1.04. It is designed for use on communications links that intercept a few characters, and are thus not fully transparent. It is not meant to be used on links that intercept many characters, such as seven-bit links. The two sides initialize the *j* protocol by exchanging the list of characters to be avoided, and subsequently communicate using the *i* protocol encapsulated in *j* protocol packets. The only function of the *j* protocol is to avoid the "dangerous" characters that cannot be passed through the link; all other protocol functions, such as error correction and pacing, are performed by the encapsulated *i* protocol. The *j* protocol is useful for a link that has XON/XOFF flow control, since the protocol can be told to avoid those two characters.

Following are several other UUCP protocols that are specific to particular hardware or software systems.

The v Protocol

The *v* protocol is used by UUCP/Extended, a popular UUCP package for personal computers. It is a version of the *g* protocol that supports packets of any size, as well as dynamically changing the packet size during the session.

The x Protocol

The *x* protocol is used with machines that have built-in X.25 network support, and can send transparent data over an X.25 circuit without interference from the X.28/X.29 PAD layers that might occur when using external X.25 multiplexors or PADs. The protocol uses 512-byte packets, and relies on being able to sense a zero-length packet sent from the other side.

The y Protocol

The *y* protocol was developed by Jorge Cwik for FX UUCICO, a PC UUCP communications program. It is meant for use over a "mostly reliable" link that performs error correction and pacing. The *y* protocol does perform error detection, but its only corrective action when an error is detected is to drop the line.

The a protocol

The *a* protocol resembles the high-speed ZMODEM protocol. It was contributed to the Taylor UUCP distribution by Doug Evans. It requires an eight-bit, but not necessarily fully transparent connection; it also can be told to avoid transmitting all control characters (character values 0 through 31), which lets it work in an environment with software flow control (XON / XOFF) turned on.

The d Protocol

The *d* protocol is used with DataKit, an AT&T proprietary networking technology used in telephone central offices.

The f Protocol

The *f* protocol is for seven-bit links, in particular X.25 PAD links that are "mostly reliable" but occasionally lose a packet or two. It limits the characters used on the link to the printable ASCII character set from decimal 32 (the space character) to decimal 126 (the tilde character). There is no pacing in the protocol, because it is meant for links that have XON/XOFF flow

control enabled. It uses 256-byte packets, and calculates checksums on a
per-file basis rather than on individual packets. If a file is received with an
error, the entire file is resent. The checksum is not considered reliable when
used with large files, so using it over a serial connection requires
XON/XOFF flow control and error-correcting modems. Some people do not
consider it trustworthy even under those circumstances.

Tuning a Protocol

Some versions of UUCP, in particular Taylor UUCP, allow their protocol
parameters—packet sizes, window sizes, and timeouts—to be adjusted by
the system administrator.

The Taylor UUCP documentation gives a complete description of the protocol parameters that are available for tuning via the **protocol-parameter** command. In most cases tuning is not necessary, but if you are trying to squeeze
the maximum performance out of a line, you might want to force the largest
possible packet size to speed up throughput or shorten error timeouts to
minimize idle time. Be sure to examine your throughput statistics before and
after tuning protocol parameters to make sure your changes are having the
desired effect.

SVR4 implementations of UUCP that support the *G* protocol accept tuning
parameters in the *Devices* file. For example:

```
ACU,G(7,512)g cua/b - 9600 hayes \D
```

This entry specifies a window size of seven and a packet size of 512 on outbound calls over this device. If the *G* protocol is not available on the
answering system, *g* protocol will be used instead.

In Solaris, you can also set the default protocol ordering and protocol
parameters in the */etc/uucp/Config* file. See the comments in that file for
more information.

Consult your vendor documentation for other versions of UUCP that may
support tuning.

K

The UUCP g Protocol

The following description of the UUCP *g* Protocol was written by Jamie Hanrahan of Kernel Mode Systems, San Diego, after he implemented a version of UUCP for VMS. This description of the *g* Protocol was presented as a paper at the Fall 1990 DECUS Symposium in Las Vegas. It has been edited and updated somewhat for publication, including removal of a section on workfile contents (covered previously in Appendix B, *The Spool Directory/Working Files*).

Initial Handshake (Shere Exchange)

- It occurs after call placement and login.

- It's initiated by answering system.

- All messages begin with \020 (CTRL–P, also known as DLE) and end with \000 (NUL). A few systems use \012 (LF) to terminate messages instead of \000.

- It's sent and received in "raw mode," which mean it has no carriage returns, no line feeds, etc.

```
Caller                                          Answerer
------>                                          <--------

(places call, gets carrier,
gets login prompt, logs in)
                                    (uucico program starts)
                                      \020Shere=hostname\000
\020Shostname\000

                                           \020ROK\000
```

- Hostnames are the respective systems' UUCP hostnames.

- Caller's Shostname message may include any or all of the following optional elements:[*]

      Shostname -Qseq -xdbg -pgrade -vgrade=grade

  - *seq* = call sequence number (or 0).

  - *dbg* is a digit, answerer sets its debug level accordingly.

  - *grade* indicates what class of files are being transferred (e.g., mail, news, arbitrary files). Taken from systems file entry; not sent or supported by all systems. Some implementations support −p, some support −v, some both, and some neither.

- Old answerers may send just Shere instead of Shere=*hostname*.

- The "ROK" message states that the answerer has accepted the call. The answerer may reject the call with any of the following messages:

  - RLCK—answerer thinks it's already talking to that caller.

  - RCB—answerer wants to call the caller back (to avoid imposter callers).

  - RBADSEQ—call sequence number is wrong (caller is an imposter, or more likely, sequence numbers weren't updated properly at one end or the other).

---

[*] Since this paper was written, several other optional elements have been added: −R indicates knowledge of how to restart failed UUCP transmissions; −U is used to report the maximum file size that the caller can create; and −N is a Taylor UUCP extension for size negotiations and for sending a capabilities mask. For more information, see the Taylor UUCP documentation or Ian Lance Taylor's UUCP Internals FAQ on *comp.mail.uucp*.

- RLOGIN—caller's login name (username) isn't known to answerer's UUCP (USERFILE or Permissions file).

- RYou are unknown to me—caller's hostname isn't known to answerer (as determined by *L.sys* or *Systems* file).

If caller receives any of these, it simply hangs up. (The answerer hangs up after sending the reject message, possibly waiting a few seconds so that the modem disconnect won't prevent the message from reaching the caller.)

If answerer "accepts the call":

```
Caller                              Answerer
------>                             <--------

                                   Pprotlist
Uprot
```

where:

- *protlist* is a list of the protocols, each identified by a single letter (e.g., *g)* supported by the answerer.

- *prot* is a single protocol from *protlist* selected by the answerer.

• Caller can send UN (and then hang up) if it supports no protocols in common with answerer.

At this point the two machines have agreed on a protocol. We'll assume that it's the *g* protocol, so that the last two messages may have been something like this:

```
Caller                              Answerer
------>                             <--------

                                   Pfgt
Ug
```

At this point both systems call the *gturnon()* function, which causes the *g* data-link protocol to start up.

g Protocol Packet Formats

All subsequent communication (until after the *g* protocol shutdown) is in "packet mode."

- Each packet has a six-byte header.
- Control packets have only a header.
- Data packets have a header and a data segment.

Packet Header Format

```
+-------+-------+-------+-------+-------+-------+
|  DLE  |   K   |  cklo |  ckhi |  ctl  |  XOR  |
+-------+-------+-------+-------+-------+-------+
```

The first byte is always DLE (octal 020, hex 10). The second byte is the "K-byte." For a control packet it is always nine (i.e., a tab character). For data packets it indicates the transmitted (physical) length of the following data segment, as shown here:

K-byte Value	Data Segment Length (bytes)
1	32
2	64
3	128
4	256
5	512
6	1024
7	2048
8	4096
9	control packet

The third and fourth bytes are the low and high bytes, respectively, of a checksum computed on the data segment (if any), plus the control byte. (The checksum computation is described later.)

The fifth byte is a bitmapped command byte, described in the next section. The last byte is a simple XOR of the middle four bytes. The first and last bytes perform a framing and validation function for headers.

The Control Byte

The "control" byte is bit-mapped as follows:

```
  7   6   5   4   3   2   1   0
+-------+-----------+-----------+
| T   T | X   X   X | Y   Y   Y |
+-------+-----------+-----------+
```

The T field denotes the type of packet. For example:

```
T Value    Packet Type
-------    ----------------------------------------
0          control packet
1          alternate channel data packet (unused in UUCP)
2          long data block
3          short data block (to be described later)
```

The interpretations of the X and Y fields vary with the packet type (control versus data). For control packets the X field is the type of control packet and the Y field is a parameter, as shown here:

X Value	Name	Y Field Interpretation
1	CLOSE	No significance
2	NAK	Last correctly received packet number
3	SRJ	Packet number to retransmit
4	ACK	Last correctly received packet number
5	INITC	Maximum window size to use
6	INITB	Maximum data segment size to use
7	INITA	Maximum window size to use

The "data segment size" on the INITB packet is encoded like the KBYTE but with numbers one lower; for example, an INITB packet with a Y field of one indicates a data segment size of 64 bytes.

Most descriptions of UUCP refer to types two and four as "RJ" (reject) and "RR" (receiver ready), respectively.

SRJ ("selective reject") is not used in known implementations.

Data Packets

For data packets, the X field is the sequence number of the packet, and the Y field is the "ACK number," which is the sequence number of the last packet correctly received by the system sending the data packet. (See the section on data transfer and acknowledgment.)

A data packet header is always followed by a data segment of size indicated by the Kbyte.

Long Data Packets

If the packet type is "long data," all "n" bytes of the data segment (where "n" is denoted by the Kbyte) contain data.

Short Data Packets

If the packet type is "short data," the data segment is still sent in its entirety, but the first one or two bytes indicate the difference between its physical (transmitted) length and the number of bytes to be passed to the presentation level (its "logical length"). For example:

```
 7   6   5   4   3   2   1   0
+---+---------------------------+
| 0 | length difference (1-127) |
+---+---------------------------+
```

If the difference is too large to fit in seven bits, the data segment would look like this:

```
 7   6   5   4   3   2   1   0   7   6   5   4   3   2   1   0
+---+-------------------------+-----------------------------+
| 1 | length difference(lo bits)| length difference (high bits) |
+---+-------------------------  +   ---------------------------+
        first byte of data segment     second byte of data segment
```

For example, a data packet with a physical segment size of 64 (Kbyte=2), but an effective (logical) length of zero, would be sent by sending a "short data" packet where the data segment consisted of a byte with the numeric value 64. For example:

```
 7   6   5   4   3   2   1   0
+---+-------------------------+
| 0 | 1   0   0   0   0   0   0 |
+---+-------------------------+
```

This would be followed by 63 additional bytes (whose contents would be ignored by the receiver).

g Protocol (Data Link Layer) Initialization

The *g* protocol is initialized via an exchange of the INITA, INITB, and INITC packets. Here's a simple approach:

- Each system starts sending INITAs to the other.

- Upon receiving an INITA, send an INITB.

- Upon receiving an INITB, send an INITC.

- When both have sent and received an INITC, initialization is complete.

When the INITx packets are received, each system sets its UUCP parameters (data segment size and maximum transmit window size) to the smaller of what it can handle and what it gets from the packet.

g Protocol Data Transfer and Acknowledgment

After initialization, data packets are exchanged. Thus, all subsequent traffic consists of Shortdata, Longdata, ACK, and NAK packets (until the end of the session, when CLOSE packets are exchanged). Here's how it works:

- Each data packet must be acknowledged by the receiver.

- Data packets can be acknowledged only in sequence.

- If a data packet arrives corrupted (as determined via checksum), the receiver sends a NAK (requesting retransmission) or simply does not send an ACK, which allows the sender to time out awaiting an ACK (this has the same effect).

- The first packet sent by each transmitter has sequence number one. Packet sequence numbers are modulo eight (i.e., 1, 2, ..., 7, 0, 1, ...).

- UUCP, in most implementations, uses a transmit window size of more than one (typically three, maximum seven due to the three-bit packet sequence numbers).

  - After sending one data packet, the sender need not wait for an ACK before sending the next data packet, until window size unACK'd packets have been sent.

  - Colloquially this is known as a "windowed" protocol. (As opposed to stop-and-wait, like most Kermit implementations.)

-   After the transmit window is full (i.e., window size unACK'd packets have been sent), transmitter must wait for an ACK of at least the first packet in the transmit window before sending another packet.

-   g protocol's receive window size is one; at any given time there is only one packet which is valid to be received.

•   An ACK provides the number of the last correctly-received packet, and implies that all earlier packet numbers have also been correctly received. Thus, a single ACK may acknowledge multiple packets.

•   The "ACK number"—the number of the most recent correctly-received message—also appears in the Y field of the headers of data packets. If a system is about to acknowledge a packet, but happens to have a data packet to send, it need not send an explicit ACK; putting the number of the packet to be ACK'd in the Y field of the data packet is sufficient. This doesn't happen often, because UUCP's "upper layers" don't use the link in both directions at once.

•   A NAK provides the same number as an ACK, but requests retransmission of all outstanding packets with higher (modulo eight) numbers.

•   Both ACKs and NAKs provide acknowledgment for not only the indicated packet, but also all previous packets in the transmit window ("stacked ACKs"). This is known as a "go back n" protocol. It is relatively easy to implement but performance suffers when errors occur. More complex protocols allow a receive window size of greater than one with "selective reject," and this was in fact the intent of the SRJ control packet. An SRJ says "retransmit this one packet, I didn't get it right." This avoids having to resend an entire transmit window to correct an error in just one packet.

A Simple Data Exchange

Here's a simple data exchange:

```
Sender                                    Receiver
------>                                    <--------

Data 1
                                  (receives Data 1 OK)
                                             Ack 1
Data 2
                                  (receives Data 2 OK)
                                             Ack 2
```

```
(receives Ack 1)
Data 3
                                    (receives Data 3 OK)
                                               Ack 3
(receives Ack 2)
Data 4
                              (receives Data 4 in error)
                                               NAK 3
(receives Ack 3)
Data 5
                        (receives Data 5 OK but out of seq.)
(receives NAK 3)
(resends everything in window)
Data 4
Data 5
                                    (receives Data 4 OK)
                                               Ack 4
Data 6
                                    (receives Data 5 OK)
                                               Ack 5
(receives Ack 4)
Data 7
                          etc...
```

Data Link Layer: Tales from the Front

Corrupted Packet Headers

When looking for a packet, the receiver should scan for a DLE, then read the next five bytes following and check the XOR. The receiver should also note the following:

- If the XOR check fails, the "packet header" cannot be trusted. Scanning for the next DLE begins at the next byte following the current DLE (not six bytes after it).

- If the XOR check succeeds, but something's wrong with the header (illegal Kbyte value, for example), the receiver should treat this like an XOR failure. (XOR checks aren't all that robust.)

Corrupted Data Segments

If the header on a data packet is good (XOR is okay), but the checksum indicates that the data segment is corrupt, follow these steps:

- Send a NAK to indicate receipt of a corrupted data packet.

- Rescan the input looking for the next control packet, starting with the first byte of the data segment.

We don't skip over the data segment because the data checksum failed, we can't trust the header either. Perhaps it's just some "lucky" line noise that seemed to be a header, and the real packet header is hiding in what we thought was the data segment.

Missing Packets (Out-Of-Sequence Packets)

The UUCP g protocol employs a receive window size of one; that is, there is only one packet that may be received at any time (the next one that follows the previous correctly-received packet).

If an out-of-sequence packet is received, the correct response is to send a NAK (with the Y field, as always, being the number of the last good packet).

Too Many NAKs

It is not good to send a NAK for every error condition. To do so would cause extra retransmissions and slow down the transfer. Let's revisit the simple data exchange diagrammed previously, but instead, we'll show one side sending a NAK for every error:

```
Sender                                          Receiver
------>                                         <--------

Data 3
                                receives Data 3 OK)
                                        Ack 3
(receives Ack 2)
Data 4
        (data 4 is corrupted on the link)
                                (receives Data 4 w/error)
                                        NAK 3 (#1)
(receives Ack 3)
Data 5
                        (receives Data 5 out of seq.)
                                        NAK 3 (#2)

Data 6
                        (receives Data 6 out of seq.)
                                        NAK 3 (#3)
(receives NAK 3 #1)
Data 4
Data 5
Data 6
```

```
                                          (receives Data 4 OK)
                                                         Ack 4
(receives NAK 3 #2)
Data 4
Data 5
Data 6
(receives Ack 4)
                              (receives Data 4 out of seq.)
                                                        NAK 4
                    etc...
```

UNIX UUCPs address this by being very "shy" about sending NAKs, mostly just letting the sender time out. This works but hurts throughput.

DECUS UUCP keeps track of the number of received error packets and sends the NAK only if the number modulo and window size equal one. Thus, we send the first NAK right away, but no more until at least a window-size worth of packets has been received.

Duplicate Packets

If a packet is received with a number that's already been received and ACK'd, it's one of the following:

- A duplicate of one we got earlier; our ACKs got lost, so the sender timed out and is resending its window.

- A future packet, and the intervening seven packets were bad (but this can't happen, since maximum window-size is seven, not eight).

Since packets must always be ACKd in sequence, the only correct thing is to send a NAK indicating the last good (in sequence) received packet.

Control Packet Priority

The control packet types denote the priority of the packets. That is, if several control packets are to be sent, the lower-numbered ones are sent first. (CLOSE before anything else, for example.) Control packets in turn have priority over data packets.

Varying Physical Packet Lengths

Although the protocol allows for data packets with different K values (physical lengths) to be sent in a session, in most implementations, both ends always use the value negotiated at the start of the session.[*]

Interpacket Noise

The DLE that begins a packet should follow right on the heels of the previous packet. Berkeley 4.3 UUCP has a bug that causes it to send two null bytes between packets. A robust implementation will not report errors when it encounters two null bytes while looking for a DLE.

Common Parameters

Almost all implementations seem to use a window size of three and a data packet physical length of 64 bytes (Kbyte = 2). Some implementations will agree to use a larger window size or packet length, but do not do so correctly.

Checksum Details

The checksum that is placed in the packet header for data packets has this value:

```
MAGIC - (chksum(buf,len) ^ (0xFF & cbyte))
```

For control packets, the checksum value is simply:

```
MAGIC - (0xFF & cbyte)
```

where:

> "buf" is the data segment
> "len" is its (physical) length
> "chksum()" is shown below
> "cbyte" is the value of the control byte
> "MAGIC" is 0125252 (octal) (i.e., alternating bits set)

If a data packet is resent, the checksum must be recalculated, as the checksum includes the control byte, and the Y field (last good received packet

---

[*] Some implementations of UUCP will send shorter data packets when possible to save bandwidth. In Taylor UUCP, this behavior can be disabled with the **short-packets false** configuration command.

number) of the control byte might change between transmissions of the same data packet.

```
/*
 * the checksum routine, copied from G. L. Chesson's article,
 * modified by John Gilmore to reflect actual behavior
 * (see References)
 */

int
chksum(s,n)
register unsigned char *s;
register n;
{
        register short sum;
        register unsigned short t;
        register short x;

        sum = -1;
        x = 0;
        do {
                if (sum < 0) {
                        sum <<= 1;
                        sum++;
                }
                else
                        sum <<= 1;
                t = sum;
                sum += *s++ & 0377;
                x += sum ^ n;
                if ((unsigned short)sum <= t)
                        sum ^= x;
        } while (--n > 0);

        return(sum);
}
```

File Transfer Messages (Application Layer)

The data packets and acknowledgments form a reliable data link that the two **uucico** programs use to exchange messages and files.

At the start of a UUCP session the caller is in master mode and the answerer is in Slave. The caller searches its UUCP spool directory for work (queued requests to send or receive files). Each such "work request" results in an "S" (request to send), "R" (request to receive), or "X" (remote request for UUCP) message being sent to the Slave:[*]

     S   sourcefile_on_master targetfile_on_slave ...

     R   sourcefile_on_slave targetfile_on_master ...

     X   sourcefile uucphost!targetfile ... (not covered here)

The Slave will respond with one of the following:

(for send requests)

SY	OK
SN2	Not permitted
SN4	Can't create temporary file

(for receive requests)

RY<mode>	OK (gives protection mode of file)
RN2	Not permitted

If the master receives any of the reject messages it simply looks for its next queued work request. If the master receives an "OK," the master (for file send requests) or the Slave (for file receive requests) sends the file to the other side. The receiver of the file then sends one of the following messages to the sender:

CN5	Couldn't move temp file into place
CY	File received OK

Role Exchange

When the master has no more queued work requests it asks the Slave if it wants to hang up. The Slave then looks for work and, if any is found, the two systems exchange master and Slave roles.

---

[*] Taylor UUCP supports an additional "E" request/response for command executions without transferring an extra data file as is done with the "X" request. See the Taylor UUCP documentation or the UUCP Internals FAQ for more information.

For example, Slave has no work, hangup is agreed upon:

```
Master                                        Slave
------>                                        <-----

H
                                                  HY
HY
          (at this point both systems invoke
          the g protocol shutdown routine)
```

For example, Slave has work, roles are exchanged:

```
Master                                        Slave
------>                                        <-----

H
                                                  HN

          (at this point roles are exchanged)
Slave                                         Master
----->                                         <------

                              S file1 file2 ...
```

When the new master runs out of work it will again ask the former master if it wants to hang up (as more work may have been queued on that side during its tenure as Slave). The process repeats until neither system finds any work for the other.

Sending Messages and Files (Presentation Layer)

Sending Messages

- Messages (S, SY, SNn, R, RY, RNn, CY, CNn, H, HY, HN) are sent in longdata packets.

- Some UUCPs send the last (or only) part of a message in a shortdata packet.

- As many packets as necessary for the message are used.

- The message is terminated by a null byte.

- Only one message is sent at a time.

- Some UUCPs seem to expect the rest of the packet to be padded with nulls.

Sending Files

- Since UNIX, and therefore UUCP, has no concept of "file attributes," the file is simply copied, byte for byte, into packets and transmitted. (The file protection mode is sent either as a parameter on the S message or with the RY message.)

- Transmission of a shortdata packet with logical length of zero indicates end of file (that is, the previous packet contains the last bytes in the file).

These details are specific to the g protocol; thus, g protocol includes both the data link and presentation layers.

g Protocol Shutdown

When both systems have agreed (via H, HY, HY message exchange) to hang up, they each call the *gturnoff()* function, causing CLOSE control messages to be exchanged. For example:

```
(either)                                        (either)
-------->                                        <--------

                                                   CLOSE
CLOSE
```

Over and Out

After the data-link layer has exchanged CLOSE messages, one more set of "over and out" messages is exchanged like this:

```
Caller                                              Answerer
------>                                           <--------

OOOOOO   (six "O"'s)
                             (seven "O"'s)   OOOOOOO
```

Note that since the *g* protocol has already been turned off, these message
are not preceded by six-byte headers. They are, however, preceded by DLE
and terminated by NUL, as were the Shere, Shostname, Pprots, etc., messages at the beginning of the session.

A Complete Session

The caller sends one file and receives one, after which the answerer sends
one file. (ACKs, NAKs, and retransmits for the *g* protocol are not shown.)
For example:

```
Caller                                              Answerer
------>                                           <--------

(places call, logs in, etc.)
                             (uucico program starts)

   (subsequent transmissions are framed by DLE .... NUL)

                                       Shere=hostname
Shostname

                                              ROK
                                              Pfgt
Ug

   (subsequent packets have "g" protocol headers)

Control(INITA)                           Control(INITA)
Control(INITB)                           Control(INITB)
Control(INITC)                           Control(INITC)
Longdata(S fromfile1 tofile1 ...)
                                         Longdata(SY)
Longdata(file contents)
Longdata(file contents)
        ...
Shortdata(last few bytes of file)
Shortdata(logical length 0)
                                         Longdata(CY)
Longdata(R fromfile1 tofile1 ...)
```

```
                                        Longdata(RY)
                              Longdata(file contents)
                              Longdata(file contents)
                                          ...
                         Shortdata(last few bytes of file)
                            Shortdata(logical length 0)
Longdata(CY)
Longdata(H)
                                        Longdata(HN)
                         Longdata(S fromfile1 tofile1 ...)
Longdata(SY)
                                 Longdata(file contents)
                                 Longdata(file contents)
                                          ...
                         Shortdata(last few bytes of file)
                            Shortdata(logical length 0)
Longdata(CY)
                                        Longdata(H)
Longdata(HY)
                                        Longdata(HY)


Control(CLOSE)                          Control(CLOSE)

    (subsequent transmissions are framed only by DLE .... NUL)

OOOOOO
                                        OOOOOOO
```

References and Acknowledgments

This section contains references and acknowledgments for this appendix.

UUCP Protocols

(The following two papers were instrumental both in preparing this article and in implementing UUCP *g* for VMS. I believe that all of the material in these two papers is incorporated in this article.)

Chuck Wegrzyn posted a Usenet article (date unknown) that described the Shere exchange, over-and-out exchange, and the application layer.

"Packet Driver Protocol" by G. L. Chesson of Bell Laboratories (October 5, 1988), distributed via Usenet and Internet, is the standard reference on the *g* protocol data-link layer.

The UUCP System

UUCP Implementation Description, by D. A. Nowitz, part of most complete UNIX documentation sets (check the Supplementary Documents volumes, if present) provides a general description of each program in the UUCP suite.

"HoneyDanBer UUCP—Bringing UNIX Systems into the Information Age" by Bill Rieken and Jim Webb, ;login: (journal of the Usenix Association), Volume 11, Numbers 3 and 4 (May/June and July/August, 1986). Describes "external" features of one of the newest UNIX UUCP implementations, including new filename conventions, logging, and error handling.

General

A widely-recognized work on the subject of data communications protocols is *Computer Networks* by Andrew S. Tanenbaum (Prentice-Hall). Algorithms are included for several different types of windowed data-link protocols.

Kermit, A File Transfer Protocol, by Frank da Cruz (Digital Press), provides a very lucid description of the sliding-window extension to Kermit. Although windowed Kermit differs in several important ways from UUCP *g*, this material was of tremendous assistance in designing the windowed *g* implementation for DECUS UUCP, and in understanding the subtle nuances of windowed protocols.

Critiques and Proofreading

The following people graciously reviewed and sent comments on early versions of this paper:

- Christopher J. Ambler
- Jordan Brown
- Eric Johansson
- Nick Pemberton
- Mark Pizzolato

Other Resources

UUCP and UUCP-Related Software

Taylor UUCP

Taylor UUCP sources are available from any FTP site that mirrors the GNU archives. The current version as of this writing is at *ftp://prep.ai.mit.edu/pub/gnu/uucp-1.06.1.tar.gz*, but the version numbers will no doubt change as new releases appear.

The primary task of configuring Taylor UUCP is to set up the *policy.h* file with settings desired for your site. See the *README* file in the source distribution for instructions on compiling and installing the software.

uucpd

The **uucpd** daemon, described in Chapter 10, *Setting Up a UUCP Link*, enables incoming UUCP calls on a TCP/IP socket. It can be used on a Linux system with Taylor UUCP if you want to receive TCP/IP calls, and use the regular */etc/passwd* password file instead of the Taylor UUCP password file. The 4.4 BSD source of **uucpd** is available from *ftp.cdrom.com*, in the directory */pub/bsdsources/4.4BSD-Lite/usr/src/libexec/uucpd/uucpd.c*, as well as other sites with 4.4 BSD or FreeBSD source. It can also be found on CD-ROM archives that include BSD source, such as the O'Reilly & Associates *4.4BSD-Lite CD-ROM Companion*.

To get the BSD **uucpd** working on a Linux system, make the following changes to *uucpd.c*:

```
203,205c203,205
< #ifdef BSD4_2
<         execl(UUCICO, "uucico", (char *)0);
< #endif BSD4_2
---
> /* #ifdef BSD4_2 */
>         execl(_PATH_UUCICO, "uucico", (char *)0);
> /* #endif BSD4_2 */
```

And compile it with this command:

```
cc -DBSDINETD uucpd.c -o uucpd
```

The chat Command

Linux, FreeBSD, and NetBSD systems come with the **chat** command, which is a standalone implementation of the chat scripts used by UUCP. You may find **chat** useful if you need to run dialing scripts to reset a balky modem, or you have other specialized modem-setting requirements.

To obtain **chat**, download the **pppd** package, which includes **chat**. It is available on many FTP archives, including Linux and FreeBSD archive sites. One source is *ftp://sunsite.unc.edu/pub/Linux/system/Network/serial/ppp*.

mgetty+sendfax

mgetty is a modem-aware line handling program like **getty** or **uugetty**. **mgetty** can use a modem's responses to tell whether an incoming call is a data or fax call, and invoke the appropriate program for it. It can detect a UUCP login, and run a different program to process UUCP logins. **mgetty** also supports "Caller ID" identification of the calling party, assuming that your modem and telephone service supply it; it also can accept or refuse calls based on the phone number of the caller.

The current version of **mgetty** can be found at *ftp://sunsite.unc.edu/pub/Linux/system/Serial/*, and many other Linux archive sites.

Other Software

TCP Wrappers

If you don't already have them, and your system accepts incoming TCP/IP connections from sites on the Internet, we strongly recommend you obtain the TCP Wrappers software (*ftp://ftp.cert.org/pub/tools/tcp_wrappers/*) that allows you to pick and choose the sites that can access your system.

sendmail

Although all UNIX vendors supply a version of **sendmail**, many sites that do not need vendor-specific features prefer to use the Berkeley version because it is usually more up-to-date. If you are running Linux, and using the **sendmail** that was packaged with your Linux distribution, you should get the current version anyway to make sure you have the latest security fixes.

The official site for Berkeley **sendmail** is *ftp://ftp.cs.berkeley.edu/pub/sendmail*.

smail

The **smail** mail transfer agent is usually included as in installation option in a Linux distribution. It is generally more straightforward to set up with UUCP than **sendmail**, and has many of the same features. The primary archive site for **smail** is *ftp://ftp.uu.net/networking/mail/smail*.

Kermit

Kermit is both a file transfer and terminal emulation program. We refer to it several times in this book because it's so darn useful: it can be used instead of **cu** or **telnet** to contact a remote system, has a scripting language that lets you reset modems and automate many communications tasks, and can transfer files when you let it talk to another program that supports the Kermit protocol on a remote host.

The implementation of Kermit for UNIX systems is called C-Kermit, and is available at *ftp://kermit.columbia.edu*. Versions of Kermit for many other platforms are also available. For further information, contact the Office of Kermit Development and Distribution, Columbia University, 612 West 115th Street, New York, NY 10025 USA; phone +1 212 854-3703, fax +1 212 663-8202, email *kermit@columbia.edu*.

Additional Reading

Protocols

If you are interested in file transfer protocols, the book *Kermit: A File Transfer Protocol*, by Frank da Cruz, published by Columbia University (ISBN 0-932376-88-6), has a good discussion of sliding window protocols similar to those used by UUCP.

You can download several published papers about UUCP protocols from *ftp://ftp.clarkson.edu/pub/msdos/uupc/protocol*, including the paper on which Appendix K, *The UUCP g Protocol*, is based.

The *UUCP Internals FAQ*, by Ian Lance Taylor, is posted regularly to the newsgroup *comp.mail.uucp*. It describes various UUCP internal formats and protocols. We have used it as a reference for a few sections in this book. It should be available at any FAQ archive, such as *ftp://rtfm.mit.edu*

Linux and UUCP

Linux Network Administrator's Guide, published by O'Reilly & Associates (and available via the Internet from the Linux Documentation Project), has chapters on setting up serial ports and using UUCP. We highly recommend it to anyone using Linux with UUCP (or any other form of networking).

The *Linux UUCP HOWTO* file is posted regularly to the newsgroup *comp.os.linux.answers*. It contains basic instructions for setting up Taylor UUCP on a Linux system. It should also be on your Linux distribution CD or at any Linux archive.

Articles About UUCP

Here is a short list of published articles about UUCP, which in spite of their age, may still be interesting:

- Bob Toxen, "Linking Up with the Outside World: An Introduction to UUCP," *UNIX Review*, 2(6):39-41, Review Publications Company, September 1984.

- Bill Rieken and Jim Webb, "HoneyDanBer UUCP—Bringing UNIX Systems in the Information Age, Part 1: Performance, Security, and Networking Facilities," 11(3):27-36, *;login* (Usenix), May/June 1986.

- Bill Rieken and Jim Webb, "HoneyDanBer UUCP—Bringing UNIX Systems in the Information Age, Part 2: Error Handling, Administrative Aids, and User Enhancements," 11(4):10-35, *;login* (Usenix), July/August 1986.

The *4.4BSD System Manager's Manual*, published by O'Reilly & Associates, has two chapters on UUCP:

- *Installation and Operation of UUCP*, by D. A. Nowitz and Carl S. Gutekunst (Chapter 14). This paper describes the BSD 4.3 version of UUCP. It was last revised in August, 1986.

- *A Dial-Up Network of UNIX Systems* by D. A. Nowitz and M. E. Lesk (Chapter 15). This circa-1979 article describes the original implementation of UUCP.

These papers have appeared in many other places, such as vendor documentation or technical journals.

SunOS and Solaris

Stokely Consulting publishes two useful tutorials for connecting modems to a SunOS or Solaris system; they are available at *http://www.batnet.com/ stokely/index.html*.

UNIX and UUCP History

For a historical perspective on UNIX, UUCP, the Internet, and the culture surrounding their development, we recommend two books by Peter Salus: *Casting the Net* (ISBN 0-201-87674-4) and *A Quarter Century of UNIX* (ISBN 0-201-54777-5); both are published by Addison-Wesley Publishing Company.

Index

@ (at sign), 62
! (bang), 5, 62
$ (dollar sign), 74
= (equal sign), 42
(hash mark), 74, 128
– (hyphen), 128, 152
% (percent sign), 62
~ (tilde), 9
    escape sequences, 44-56
~~ (tilde-tilde), 45

a UUCP protocol, 363
access, 15
    to configuration files, 212
    control, 78
    to debugging information, 184
    directory and file permissions, 15,
        204
    problems, 179, 275
    security and (see security)
    special Version 2 permissions, 239
acoustic coupler, 84
activity, tracking, 261-264
ACU (Automatic Call Unit), 84
acucap file, 78
address, email, 62
.Admin directory, 292, 304-306
administration, 69-74, 247-267
    login, 129
    record keeping, 270

spool maintenance, 251
uucp account, 88, 207, 211
AIX
    configuring serial ports, 111
    uucpadm command, 130
aliases, 172, 211, 224
AmigaUUCP utilities, 322
anonymous UUCP, 82
answering a call, 136
ASCII characters, from binary, 64, 289
ASSERT messages, 309, 314-317
asynchronous communications, 94
at batch facility, 58
at sign (@), 62
atob program, 67, 289
audit file, 307
automatic
    Call Unit (ACU), 84
    configuration checking, 130
    error notification, 14
    login, 80-82
    maintenance, 251-261
    speed conversion, 121

bang (!), 5, 62
batch processing, 1
baud rate, 41, 116, 178, 351
    character transmission delays and,
        198

About the Authors

Ed Ravin has been helping computers talk to each other for over 14 years. Currently, he works as a systems administrator at a research institute in New York City. His past achievements include connecting a major online service to the Internet and coauthoring a bulletin board system for the Commodore 64. When not slaving away at a computer screen, he can be found leading bicycle trips in the New York City region or sparring with City Hall over clean air, open space, and urban transportation issues.

Tim O'Reilly is founder and president of O'Reilly & Associates, publisher of the X Window System series and the popular Nutshell Handbooks® on UNIX. Tim has had a hand in writing or editing many of the books published by O'Reilly & Associates. He is also the author of a book about science-fiction writer Frank Herbert. Tim's long-term vision for the company is to create a vehicle where creative people can support themselves by exploring interesting ideas. Technical book publishing is just the first step. Tim graduated cum laude from Harvard in 1975 with a B.A. in classics.

Dale Dougherty is president and CEO of Songline Studios, an affiliate of O'Reilly & Associates specializing in the development of online content. The founding editor of the Nutshell series, Dale has written *sed & awk*, *DOS Meets UNIX* (with Tim O'Reilly), *Using uucp and Usenet* (with Grace Todino), and *Guide to the Pick System*.

Grace Todino is currently residing in Gabon. While working as a technical writer at O'Reilly & Associates, Inc., Grace was one of the original authors of the Nutshell Handbooks® *Managing uucp and Usenet* and *Using uucp and Usenet*, precursors to this volume.

Colophon

Our look is the result of reader comments, our own experimentation, and feedback from distribution channels. Distinctive covers complement our distinctive approach to technical topics, breathing personality and life into potentially dry subjects. UNIX and its attendant programs can be unruly beasts. Nutshell Handbooks help you tame them.

The animal featured on the cover of *Using and Managing uucp* is a grizzly bear. The grizzly is a very large brown bear about six to eight feet long and weighing between 400 and 500 pounds. The grizzly lives in the forests of western North America.

Edie Freedman designed the cover of this book, using a 19th-century engraving from the Dover Pictorial Archive. The cover layout was produced with Quark XPress 3.3 using the ITC Garamond font.

The inside layout was designed by Edie Freedman and Nancy Priest and implemented in gtroff by Lenny Muellner. The text and heading fonts are ITC Garamond Light and Garamond Book. The illustrations that appear in the book were created in Macromedia Freehand 5.0 and Adobe Photoshop by Chris Reilley.

More Titles from O'REILLY™

Network Administration

Getting Connected: The Internet at 56K and Up

By Kevin Dowd
1st Edition June 1996
424 pages, ISBN 1-56592-154-2

A complete guide for businesses, schools, and other organizations who want to connect their computers to the Internet. This book covers everything you need to know to make informed decisions, from helping you figure out which services you really need to providing down-to-earth explanations of telecommunication options, such as frame relay, ISDN, and leased lines. Once you're online, it shows you how to set up basic Internet services, such as a World Wide Web server. This book tackles issues for the PC, Macintosh, and UNIX platforms.

DNS and BIND

By Paul Albitz & Cricket Liu
1st Edition October 1992
412 pages, ISBN 1-56592-010-4

DNS and BIND contains all you need to know about the Internet's Domain Name System (DNS) and the Berkeley Internet Name Domain (BIND), its UNIX implementation. The Domain Name System is the Internet's "phone book"; it's a database that tracks important information (in particular, names and addresses) for every computer on the Internet. If you're a system administrator, this book will show you how to set up and maintain the DNS software on your network.

TCP/IP Network Administration

By Craig Hunt
1st Edition August 1992
496 pages, ISBN 0-937175-82-X

A complete guide to setting up and running a TCP/IP network for practicing system administrators. *TCP/IP Network Administration* covers setting up your network, configuring important network applications including sendmail, and issues in troubleshooting and security. It covers both BSD and System V TCP/IP implementations.

Networking Personal Computers with TCP/IP

By Craig Hunt
1st Edition July 1995
408 pages, ISBN 1-56592-123-2

This book offers practical information as well as detailed instructions for attaching PCs to a TCP/IP network and its UNIX servers. It discusses the challenges you'll face and offers general advice on how to deal with them, provides basic TCP/IP configuration information for some of the popular PC operating systems, covers advanced configuration topics and configuration of specific applications such as email, and includes a chapter on NetWare, the most popular PC LAN system software.

sendmail

By Bryan Costales, with Eric Allman & Neil Rickert
1st Edition November 1993
880 pages, ISBN 1-56592-056-2

Although sendmail is used on almost every UNIX system, it's one of the last great uncharted territories—and most difficult utilities to learn—in UNIX system administration. This book provides a complete sendmail tutorial, plus extensive reference material. It covers the BSD, UIUC, IDA, and V8 versions of sendmail.

Using & Managing UUCP

By Ed Ravin, Tim O'Reilly, Dale Dougherty, & Grace Todino
1st Edition September 1996
424 pages, ISBN 1-56592-153-4

Using & Managing UUCP describes, in one volume, this popular communications and file transfer program. UUCP is very attractive to computer users with limited resources, a small machine, and a dial-up connection. This book covers Taylor UUCP, the latest versions of HoneyDanBer UUCP, and the specific implementation details of UUCP versions shipped by major UNIX vendors.

BSD 4.4

4.4BSD System Manager's Manual

By Computer Systems Research Group, UC Berkeley
1st Edition June 1994
804 pages, ISBN 1-56592-080-5

Original UNIX papers—terse, but incredibly precise—remain the definitive work for many UNIX topics. This volume includes man pages for system administration commands (section eight of the online reference manual), plus papers on many system administration utilities and tasks—all of interest to serious UNIX administrators.

4.4BSD Programmer's Supplementary Documents

By Computer Systems Research Group, UC Berkeley
1st Edition July 1994
596 pages, ISBN 1-56592-079-1

Supplementary Documents remain the single, authoritative source for many UNIX programs, particularly within programming. This volume contains the original Bell and BSD research papers, providing in-depth documentation of the UNIX programming environment, plus up-to-date papers on new features of 4.4BSD. This book also includes a two-part tutorial on interprocess communication (IPC) under 4.4BSD UNIX.

4.4BSD Programmer's Reference Manual

By Computer Systems Research Group, UC Berkeley
1st Edition June 1994
886 pages, ISBN 1-56592-078-3

For all their faults, UNIX "man pages" are among the most useful and widely used documentation for any system. Nothing beats the ease of use of an alphabetical listing . . . a brilliant strategy. This reference volume collects man pages for system calls, libraries, and file formats, covering sections two through five of the online man page collection. Also useful for related UNIX implementations, including SunOS, BSDI, and Linux.

4.4BSD User's Supplementary Documents

By Computer Systems Research Group, UC Berkeley
1st Edition July 1994
712 pages, ISBN 1-56592-076-7

UNIX's power came from hundreds of brilliant programmers who created and documented tools to solve day-to-day problems. They'd typically write a reference document (a "man page"), and if the tool was significant, a technical paper (or "supplementary document") describing its use. This volume collects papers relating to miscellaneous "user" tools, principally text editors and document processors, and provides in-depth documentation of complex programs such as the shell, editors, and word processing utilities.

4.4BSD User's Reference Manual

By Computer Systems Research Group, UC Berkeley
1st Edition June 1994
905 pages, ISBN 1-56592-075-9

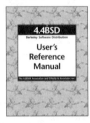

UNIX has always been known for its obscure online "man pages," those invaluable reference pages that offer precise documentation of hundreds of powerful—and sometimes confusing—utilities. While these "nuggets of wisdom" make no effort to provide any tutorial help, nothing beats the ease of use of an alphabetical listing for each program.

This volume collects the man pages for the more than 275 user programs that make up the user portion of the 4.4BSD UNIX release—plus additional pages for games and miscellaneous information—and is helpful even if you don't use the BSD version of UNIX. Many of the commands are identical to those in other UNIX versions, as are many of the freeware programs. You may find yourself turning first to this book to look up options for programs like Perl, GNU Emacs, compress, patch, g++, or kerberos. This volume is also useful for many related UNIX implementations, including SunOS, BSDI, and Linux.

Stay in touch with O'REILLY™

Visit Our Award-Winning World Wide Web Site

http://www.ora.com/

VOTED

"Top 100 Sites on the Web" —*PC Magazine*
"Top 5% Websites" —*Point Communications*
"3-Star site" —*The McKinley Group*

Our Web site contains a library of comprehensive product information (including book excerpts and tables of contents), downloadable software, background articles, interviews with technology leaders, links to relevant sites, book cover art, and more. File us in your Bookmarks or Hotlist!

Join Our Two Email Mailing Lists

LIST #1   NEW PRODUCT RELEASES: To receive automatic email with brief descriptions of all new O'Reilly products as they are released, send email to: **listproc@online.ora.com** and put the following information in the first line of your message (NOT in the Subject: field, which is ignored): **subscribe ora-news "Your Name"of "Your Organization"** (for example: **subscribe ora-news Kris Webber of Fine Enterprises**)

List #2   O'REILLY EVENTS: If you'd also like us to send information about trade show events, special promotions, and other O'Reilly events, send email to: **listproc@online.ora.com** and put the following information in the first line of your message (NOT in the Subject: field, which is ignored): **subscribe ora-events "Your Name" of "Your Organization"**

Visit Our Gopher Site

- Connect your Gopher to **gopher.ora.com**, or
- Point your Web browser to **gopher://gopher.ora.com/**, or
- telnet to **gopher.ora.com** (login: **gopher**)

Get Example Files from Our Books Via FTP

There are two ways to access an archive of example files from our books:

REGULAR FTP — ftp to: **ftp.ora.com** (login: **anonymous**—use your email address as the password) or point your Web browser to: **ftp://ftp.ora.com/**

FTPMAIL — Send an email message to: **ftpmail@online.ora.com** (write "help" in the message body)

Contact Us Via Email

order@ora.com — To place a book or software order online. Good for North American and international customers.

subscriptions@ora.com — To place an order for any of our newsletters or periodicals.

software@ora.com — For general questions and product information about our software.
- Check out O'Reilly Software Online at **http://software.ora.com/** for software and technical support information.
- Registered O'Reilly software users send your questions to **website-support@ora.com**

books@ora.com — General questions about any of our books.

cs@ora.com — For answers to problems regarding your order or our products.

booktech@ora.com — For book content technical questions or corrections.

proposals@ora.com — To submit new book or software proposals to our editors and product managers.

international@ora.com — For information about our international distributors or translation queries.
- For a list of our distributors outside of North America check out: **http://www.ora.com/www/order/country.html**

O'REILLY™

101 Morris Street, Sebastopol, CA 95472 USA
TEL 707-829-0515 or 800-998-9938 (6 A.M. to 5 P.M. PST)
FAX 707-829-0104

TO ORDER: **800-889-8969** (CREDIT CARD ORDERS ONLY); **order@ora.com**; **http://www.ora.com**
OUR PRODUCTS ARE AVAILABLE AT A BOOKSTORE OR SOFTWARE STORE NEAR YOU.

Listing of Titles from O'REILLY™

INTERNET PROGRAMMING

CGI Programming on the
World Wide Web
Designing for the Web
Exploring Java
HTML: The Definitive Guide
Web Client Programming with Perl
Learning Perl
Programming Perl, 2nd. Edition
(Fall '96 est.)
JavaScript: The Definitive Guide,
Beta Edition (Summer '96)
Webmaster in a Nutshell
The World Wide Web Journal

USING THE INTERNET

Smileys
The Whole Internet User's Guide
and Catalog
The Whole Internet for Windows 95
What You Need to Know:
Using Email Effectively
Marketing on the Internet Fall 96)
What You Need to Know: Bandits on
the Information Superhighway

JAVA SERIES

Exploring Java
Java in a Nutshell
Java Language Reference
(Summer '96 est.)
Java Virtual Machine

WINDOWS

Inside the Windows '95 Registry

SOFTWARE

WebSite™ 1.1
WebSite Professional™
WebBoard™
PolyForm™

SONGLINE GUIDES

NetLearning
NetSuccess for Realtors (Summer '96)
NetActivism (Fall '96)

SYSTEM ADMINISTRATION

Building Internet Firewalls
Computer Crime:
A Crimefighter's Handbook
Computer Security Basics
DNS and BIND
Essential System Administration,
2nd ed.
Getting Connected:
The Internet at 56K and Up
Linux Network Administrator's
Guide
Managing Internet Information
Services
Managing Usenet (Fall '96)
Managing NFS and NIS
Networking Personal Computers
with TCP/IP
Practical UNIX & Internet Security
PGP: Pretty Good Privacy
sendmail
System Performance Tuning
TCP/IP Network Administration
termcap & terminfo
Using & Managing UUCP (Fall '96)
Volume 8: X Window System
Administrator's Guide

UNIX

Exploring Expect
Learning GNU Emacs, 2nd Edition
(Summer '96)
Learning the bash Shell
Learning the Korn Shell
Learning the UNIX Operating
System
Learning the vi Editor
Linux in a Nutshell (Summer '96)
Making TeX Work
Linux Multimedia Guide(Fall '96)
Running Linux, 2nd Edition
Running Linux Companion
CD-ROM, 2nd Edition
SCO UNIX in a Nutshell
sed & awk
Unix in a Nutshell: System V Edition
UNIX Power Tools
UNIX Systems Programming
Using csh and tsch
What You Need to Know:
When You Can't Find Your
UNIX System Administrator

PROGRAMMING

Applying RCS and SCCS
C++: The Core Language
Checking C Programs with lint
DCE Security Programming
Distributing Applications Across
DCE and Windows NT
Encyclopedia of Graphics File
Formats, 2nd ed.
Guide to Writing DCE Applications
lex & yacc
Managing Projects with make
ORACLE Performance Tuning
ORACLE PL/SQL Programming
Porting UNIX Software
POSIX Programmer's Guide
POSIX.4: Programming for
the Real World
Power Programming with RPC
Practical C Programming
Practical C++ Programming
Programming Python (Fall '96)
Programming with curses
Programming with GNU Software
(Summer '96)
Programming with Pthreads
(Fall '96 est.)
Software Portability with imake
Understanding DCE
Understanding Japanese
Information
Processing
UNIX Systems Programming for
SVR4

BERKELEY 4.4 SOFTWARE DISTRIBUTION

4.4BSD System Manager's Manual
4.4BSD User's Reference Manual
4.4BSD User's Supplementary Docs.
4.4BSD Programmer's Reference Man.
4.4BSD Programmer's Supp. Docs.

X PROGRAMMING

THE X WINDOW SYSTEM

Volume 0: X Protocol Reference Man.
Volume 1: Xlib Programming Man.
Volume 2: Xlib Reference Manual
Volume. 3M: X Window System
User's Guide, Motif Ed.
Volume. 4: X Toolkit Intrinsics
Programming Manual
Volume 4M: X Toolkit Intrinsics
Programming Manual, Motif Ed.
Volume 5: X Toolkit Intrinsics
Reference Manual
Volume 6A: Motif Programming Man.
Volume 6B: Motif Reference Manual
Volume 6C: Motif Tools
Volume 8 : X Window System
Administrator's Guide
Programmer's Supplement
for Release 6
X User Tools (with CD-ROM)
The X Window System in a Nutshell

HEALTH, CAREER, & BUSINESS

Building a Successful Software
Business
The Computer User's Survival Guide

Dictionary of Computer Terms
The Future Does Not Compute
Love Your Job!
Publishing with CD-ROM

TRAVEL

Travelers' Tales: Brazil (Summer '96)
Travelers' Tales: Food (Summer '96)
Travelers' Tales: France
Travelers' Tales: Hong Kong
Travelers' Tales: India
Travelers' Tales: Mexico
Travelers' Tales: San Francisco
Travelers' Tales: Spain
Travelers' Tales: Thailand
Travelers' Tales: A Woman's World

International Distributors

Customers outside North America can now order O'Reilly & Associates books through the following distributors. They offer our international customers faster order processing, more bookstores, increased representation at tradeshows worldwide, and the high-quality, responsive service our customers have come to expect.

EUROPE, MIDDLE EAST AND NORTHERN AFRICA (except Germany, Switzerland, and Austria)

INQUIRIES
International Thomson Publishing Europe
Berkshire House
168-173 High Holborn
London WC1V 7AA, United Kingdom
Telephone: 44-171-497-1422
Fax: 44-171-497-1426
Email: **itpint@itps.co.uk**

ORDERS
International Thomson Publishing Services, Ltd.
Cheriton House, North Way
Andover, Hampshire SP10 5BE,
United Kingdom
Telephone: 44-264-342-832 (UK orders)
Telephone: 44-264-342-806 (outside UK)
Fax: 44-264-364418 (UK orders)
Fax: 44-264-342761 (outside UK)
UK & Eire orders: **itpuk@itps.co.uk**
International orders: **itpint@itps.co.uk**

GERMANY, SWITZERLAND, AND AUSTRIA

International Thomson Publishing GmbH
O'Reilly International Thomson Verlag
Königswinterer Straße 418
53227 Bonn, Germany
Telephone: 49-228-97024 0
Fax: 49-228-441342
Email: **anfragen@arade.ora.de**

AUSTRALIA

WoodsLane Pty. Ltd.
7/5 Vuko Place, Warriewood NSW 2102
P.O. Box 935, Mona Vale NSW 2103
Australia
Telephone: 61-2-9970-5111
Fax: 61-2-9970-5002
Email: **info@woodslane.com.au**

NEW ZEALAND

WoodsLane New Zealand Ltd.
21 Cooks Street (P.O. Box 575)
Wanganui, New Zealand
Telephone: 64-6-347-6543
Fax: 64-6-345-4840
Email: **info@woodslane.com.au**

ASIA (except Japan & India)

INQUIRIES
International Thomson Publishing Asia
60 Albert Street #15-01
Albert Complex
Singapore 189969
Telephone: 65-336-6411
Fax: 65-336-7411

ORDERS
Telephone: 65-336-6411
Fax: 65-334-1617

JAPAN

O'Reilly Japan, Inc.
Kiyoshige Building 2F
12-Banchi, Sanei-cho
Shinjuku-ku
Tokyo 160 Japan
Telephone: 81-3-3356-5227
Fax: 81-3-3356-5261
Email: **kenji@ora.com**

INDIA

Computer Bookshop (India) PVT. LTD.
190 Dr. D.N. Road, Fort
Bombay 400 001
India
Telephone: 91-22-207-0989
Fax: 91-22-262-3551
Email: **cbsbom@giasbm01.vsnl.net.in**

THE AMERICAS

O'Reilly & Associates, Inc.
101 Morris Street
Sebastopol, CA 95472 U.S.A.
Telephone: 707-829-0515
Telephone: 800-998-9938 (U.S. & Canada)
Fax: 707-829-0104
Email: **order@ora.com**

SOUTHERN AFRICA

International Thomson Publishing Southern Africa
Building 18, Constantia Park
240 Old Pretoria Road
P.O. Box 2459
Halfway House, 1685 South Africa
Telephone: 27-11-805-4819
Fax: 27-11-805-3648

O'REILLY™